CRISIS INTERVENTION
IN
CRIMINAL JUSTICE/SOCIAL SERVICE

Fourth Edition

CRISIS INTERVENTION IN CRIMINAL JUSTICE/SOCIAL SERVICE

Edited by

JAMES E. HENDRICKS, Ph.D.

Criminal Justice and Criminology
Ball State University
Muncie, Indiana

and

BRYAN D. BYERS, Ph.D.

Criminal Justice and Criminology
Ball State University
Muncie, Indiana

CHARLES C THOMAS • PUBLISHER, LTD.
Springfield • Illinois • U.S.A.

Published and Distributed Throughout the World by

CHARLES C THOMAS • PUBLISHER, LTD.
2600 South First Street
Springfield, Illinois 62704

© 2006 by CHARLES C THOMAS • PUBLISHER, LTD.

ISBN 0-398-07638-3 (paper)
ISBN 0-398-07639-1   (hard)

Library of Congress Catalog Card Number: 2005054853

With THOMAS BOOKS *careful attention is given to all details of manufacturing
and design. It is the Publisher's desire to present books that are satisfactory as to their
physical qualities and artistic possibilities and appropriate for their particular use.*
THOMAS BOOKS *will be true to those laws of quality that assure a good name
and good will.*

Printed in the United States of America
MM-R-3

Library of Congress Cataloging-in-Publication Data

Crisis intervention in crimial justice/social service / edited by James E.
  Hendricks and Bryan D. Byers.–4th ed.
      p. cm.
  Includes bibliographical references and indexes.
  ISBN 0-398-07638-3 – ISBN 0-398-07639-1 (pbk.)
  1. Police social work–United States. 2. Crisis intervention (Mental
health services)–United States. 3. Assistance in emergencies–United States.
4. Victims of crimes–Counseling of–United States. I. Hendricks, James E.
(James Earnest). II. Byers, Bryan.

HV8079.2.C75 2006
361'.06–dc22
                                                         2005054853

To Cindy
And to all of those who fought and died in Vietnam
5th Marines, Class of 1969

J.E.H.

To Leah and Adam
And my mother and father, Clarisse and Dean Byers
B.D.B.

CONTRIBUTORS

Jennifer R. Arnold, M.P.A., chapter co-author, is a graduate of Ball State University in Muncie, Indiana. She has over four years experience working with court-ordered juveniles in an independent living treatment facility. Ms. Arnold has also served as a Court Appointed Special Advocate (CASA), as well as having worked with the Chief Probation Officer of the Delaware County Office of Adult Probation. She is currently assisting in the evaluation of a central Indiana drug court program.

Daniel E. Ashment, M.P.A., chapter co-author, received his Bachelor Degrees in Psychology and Sociology from Utah State University. He also holds a Masters Degree in Public Administration with a Criminal Justice Concentration from Ball State University. He has had extensive security and managerial experience throughout his career.

Bernard E. Blakely, Ph.D., is professor emeritus of sociology at Ball State University and has been director of a number of social service oriented grants. His field experience includes gerontology and consultation. His areas of expertise are applied research in elder abuse and teaching research methodology.

Michael G. Breci, Ph.D., is a professor in the School of Law Enforcement at Metropolitan State University and was formerly a professor of criminal justice at St. Cloud State University, St. Cloud, Minnesota. Dr. Breci has ten years of field experience as a probation and police officer. His publication record, as well as his consulting work, is varied and extensive. In particular, Dr. Breci is well known in the area of police responses to domestic violence.

Michael P. Brown, Ph.D., is a professor of criminal justice and criminology at Ball State University. He holds a doctorate from Western Michigan University in Sociology and has also taught at Utica College of Syracuse University. Dr. Brown's interest in criminal justice and criminal justice education has led to involvement as a program evaluator and in academic program assessment. In addition to criminal justice education and program assessment, he also has research interests in community-based corrections and intermediate sanctions. Dr. Brown has conducted extensive research in, and has presented on, the topic of ethics and ethical decision making in criminal justice.

Bryan D. Byers, Ph.D., chapter author and volume co-editor, is professor of criminal justice and criminology at Ball State University. His previous teaching experience includes faculty positions at Valparaiso University and the University of Notre Dame. Dr. Byers has published five books in the areas of social psychology, elder abuse, and criminal justice and is the author of over twenty journal articles and thirty national presentations. He also has served as a deputy coroner, an adult protective services investigator, youth leader, and prosecuting attorney field investigator. Dr. Byers' expertise in crisis intervention and death notification includes years of research, in-service training, and experience.

Barbara A. Carson, Ph.D., is a professor of sociology and corrections at Mankato State University. Prior to her service there she was a criminal justice faculty member at Ball State University. During her employment at the University of New Hampshire, as a doctoral fellow under the auspices of the National Institute of Mental Health, and while working at Boy's Town (NB), she conducted research on child abuse and neglect. Dr. Carson continues to conduct research in these areas as they relate to the criminal justice system.

Richard D. Clark, Ph.D., is a professor at John Carroll University near Cleveland, Ohio. His previous teaching experience includes a position on the criminal justice faculty at Bowling Green State University. Previously, he was employed as a project director with a four-year longitudinal project assessing reactions to violent (homicide, suicide and accidents) and natural death. Dr. Clark has extensive experience in the areas of juvenile delinquency and victimization. He has served as a juvenile justice staff member as well as a research analyst. Dr. Clark has published extensively.

Diane M. Daane, J.D., is a professor of criminal justice and criminology at the University of South Carolina at Spartanburg. Prior to her service at Spartanburg she was a criminal justice faculty member at Ball State University and also served as a faculty member at Kearney State College in Kearney, Nebraska. She has worked as a staff defense attorney and provided legal assistance to the U.S.

Department of Justice as well as having served as a halfway house supervisor and correctional caseworker. She has published and presented a number of papers on the subjects of rape reform and the legal aspects of rape.

Dr. Blakely's co-author, **Ronald Dolon, Ed.D.,** is also employed at Ball State University as a professor of social work. In addition to his teaching and research experience, Dr. Dolon has served as an adult protective services investigator, a caseworker for the Department of Public Welfare, and as a school social worker. Currently, he serves as a consultant to various agencies dealing with elder abuse and victim advocacy.

Cindy S. Hendricks, Ph.D., is a professor of education and Interim Associate Dean at Bowling Green State University. A scholar of national reputation in the areas of reading and addressing the affective domain of children's learning, Dr. Hendricks has published numerous journal articles and a book entitled *Sensitive Issues: An Annotated Guide to Children's Literature K-6* (Oryx). Dr. Hendricks is a former Chair of the Board of Directors of the American Reading Forum and is a member of the International Reading and College Reading Associations. She has also presented nationally and has engaged in various consulting capacities. Prior to her service in Bowling Green State University's College of Education, she was a faculty member in education at Ball State University and served for several years in middle and secondary education.

James E. Hendricks, Ph.D., contributor and volume co-editor, is professor and chairperson of criminal justice and criminology at Ball State University. Previously, he was a member of the University of Tennessee and the Southern Illinois University faculties. His field experience includes the positions of police officer, chief deputy sheriff, deputy coroner, director of a victim advocate program, correctional counselor, and mental health worker. In addition, Dr. Hendricks served as a combat marine corpsman in the Vietnam War. His research interests include crisis intervention, law enforcement, and victim advocacy. He has published five books and is the author of fifty journal articles. Dr. Hendricks is a diplomat and certified crisis intervener of the American Board of Examiners in Crisis Intervention. He is also a member of the Education and Training Committee of the International Association of Chiefs of Police.

Dr. Carson's co-author, **Bruce K. MacMurray, Ph.D.,** is a professor of sociology and criminal justice at Anderson University in

Anderson, Indiana. Dr. MacMurray also has worked as a sociology professor at Northeastern University (Boston, MA), the University of Nebraska, the University of Iowa, and Coe College in Cedar Rapids, Iowa. Research, grant writing, and consulting work on the topics of ethics, plea bargaining in child abuse cases, and family violence make up his areas of expertise.

Janet E. Mickish, Ph.D., is Executive Director of the Colorado Coalition on Domestic Violence. Her twenty years of field experience includes work in domestic violence and rape/sexual assault crisis intervention. Prior to her service on the coalition she was employed as a criminal justice faculty member at Ball State University. As a result of her teaching, research, and consulting work, Dr. Mickish has enjoyed national recognition.

Veronica L. St. Cyr, M.P.A., chapter co-author is a graduate of Ball State University with degrees in criminal justice and public administration. She is currently working in the security field, is a licensed private investigator, and has worked in adult probation. She has achieved the rank of black belt in tae kwon do and is a 2004 PKC Indiana State and National Champion as well as a 2005 USKA National Champion.

INTRODUCTION

This collection of original works is intended for pre-service and in-service criminal justice and social service crisis interveners. Interveners are those persons who come into contact with victims of domestic violence/spouse abuse, child abuse and neglect, elder abuse and neglect, rape and sexual assault, loss of a loved one or any other type of crisis. Interveners come in many forms–they are firefighters, police officers, social workers, childcare caseworkers, correctional personnel, probation/parole officers, clergy, emergency medical personnel, victim advocates, shelter care personnel, psychological counselors, and professionals from many other criminal justice and social service areas.

The purpose of this book is to provide theoretical, analytical, and practical knowledge for first responders. Face-to-face interaction with the client/victim is part of the comprehensive approach advocated by this book, which requires interveners to assess the nature of a crisis, and the condition of the victim, in order to determine the appropriate course of action.

For the victim, a crisis can be a crossroads of danger and opportunity. Interveners must recognize and respond to that opportunity, providing the necessary support to the victim, who is often in a heightened state of anxiety. Effective communication skills, along with adequate training and preparation for intervention, are keys to quality interaction between the intervener and the client/victim.

Each chapter in this book offers a theoretical overview of a particular facet of intervention, as well as models and methods for applying crisis theory to crisis situations faced by interveners. Although crisis situations are composed of similar elements, each crisis is unique within the personal domain due to individual diversity. The comprehensive balance of theory and practice presented in this volume should enable the intervener in coupling his/her general knowledge of human psychology and emotional crisis with the specific and novel characteristics of various crisis situations.

This volume represents the Fourth Edition of *Crisis Intervention in Criminal Justice/Social Service.* This volume retains important information, in a revised format, from the third edition while adding important and timely topical information. It is our hope that the reader will find the information valuable in the delivery of crisis intervention within the domains of criminal justice and social services.

JAMES E. HENDRICKS
BRYAN D. BYERS

ACKNOWLEDGMENTS

We would like to acknowledge and thank all of the contributors in this volume for their professional work and timely contributions. A special acknowledgment for editorial assistance goes to Jennifer Arnold, Daniel Ashment and Veronica St. Cyr for their outstanding work and assistance.

J.E.H.
B.D.B.

CONTENTS

CRISIS INTERVENTION
IN
CRIMINAL JUSTICE/SOCIAL SERVICE

Chapter 1

HISTORICAL AND THEORETICAL OVERVIEW

JAMES E. HENDRICKS and BRYAN D. BYERS

INTRODUCTION

The fields of crisis theory and intervention have received considerable research attention during the latter half of the twentieth century (Lindemann, 1944), but the field has not been stagnant given recent crisis intervention scholarship (Gilliland, 1997; Roberts, 2000; Wainrib and Bloch, 1998). The field of crisis intervention has realized a renewed popularity. Many have realized the utility of crisis intervention theory and techniques in responding to crisis events that have adversely impacted individuals within the contexts of disastrous events in our schools and communities. School shootings, acts of domestic terrorism, and natural disasters have all helped us to realize the applicability of crisis intervention skills for those in crisis.

All individuals experience crises in life in response to personal and societal events, and these crises often call for the attention of concerned others. Until recently, our society was composed largely of tightly-knit extended and nuclear families, and assistance was provided by these entities when crises arose. The greater mobility of subsequent generations, however, caused the ties that held families together to unravel. Thus, family members were denied immediate and, many times, long-term contact with supportive persons they had depended on in the past. Therefore, crisis intervention expanded beyond the domain of the family unit becoming professional in nature.

Professionals responded accordingly to the growing demand of crisis-related issues in society and individual responses. The already-established fields of psychiatry, psychology and medicine supplied the earliest forms of assistance (Lindemann, 1944). Later, social service and criminal justice agencies

3

assumed the bulk of assistance given in this country (Caplan, 1964). Today, criminal justice agencies are important conduits to crisis intervention (Hendricks and McKean, 1995; Romano, 1990).

While the focus of this book is on the relationship between crisis intervention and the substantive fields of criminal justice and social service, it is important to develop a theoretical foundation of crisis theory. Therefore, this chapter begins with a definition of a crisis. The chapter then turns to a discussion of the origins and foundations of crisis theory. We then address the anatomy of individual crisis situations. That discussion is followed by the topic of crisis and community. We follow with important interpersonal communication skills that facilitate crisis intervention. Crisis assessment is then addressed and this is followed by a discussion of the crisis intervention process. The final three topics in the chapter deal with crisis intervention in criminal justice/social services, crisis intervention and cultural diversity, and the government's role in promoting crisis intervention. First, we begin with the definition of a crisis.

DEFINING "CRISIS"

Since crisis intervention has been shown to be effective in countering many types of dangerous emotional and mental reactions, professionals require a sound definition of what a "crisis" is in order to determine when, and where, assistance is needed. It is important to note, however, that a crisis is a response to an event or set of events that occur in a person's life. Crisis producing events are referred to in the literature as "precipitating events" or "hazardous events" (Byers, 1987; Hendricks and McKean, 2001).

The *Encarta World English Dictionary (2001)* defines a crisis as "a situation or period in which things are very uncertain, difficult, or painful, especially a time when action must be taken to avoid complete disaster or breakdown" and "a time when something very important for the future happens or is decided." Past research seems to support this definition. Both Caplan (1964) and Quierdo (1968) observed the instability of persons in times of crisis. Also, Aguilera, Messick, and Farrell (1970) defined a person in crisis as one who has reached a turning point in his or her life. Repeatedly, these definitions surface, in one form or another, throughout the literature. Drawing on these classical views, Byers (1987) defines a crisis as:

> The unpleasant psychological and social feelings/sensations, which result from the onset of a perceived insurmountable stressful life event, disrupting stability, and accompanied by an inability to adjust or cope. (p. 105)

Since a crisis disrupts stability, change is a natural consequence. Rapoport (1962) and Lindemann (1944) each noted that a crisis usually involves change. Likewise, Erickson (1959) recognized that crisis entails the unexpected, but he extended this definition to include changes that take place naturally during the human growth and aging cycle. Noting the common elements in these definitions, Hendricks (1985) and Hendricks and McKean (1995) derived the following elements that may precede, accompany, or follow a crisis:

- Anxiety and stress produce a hazardous event (crisis).
- The event occurs suddenly and unexpectedly.
- The event may be one single event or a number of events.
- Stress mounts, as the person is unable to effectively cope or solve the problem.
- As a result of overwhelming stress and failure to adequately cope with stress, maladaptive behavior ensues.
- The crisis gains momentum and personality fragmentation occurs.
- As this crisis is occurring, there is increased likelihood that another crisis will occur (a common crisis-producing event is the feeling that "I have failed to cope adequately").
- The crisis victim/survivor moves toward specific types of maladaptive behavior, including criminal behavior.
- If effective intervention does not occur, the crisis victim/survivor reaches a physical and psychological breaking point and permanent damage is likely.

These authors also list the characteristics of those who may be particularly prone to a crisis as a result of unexpected external events or amplified reactions to developmental changes found in life. The reader might bear in mind that these are potential, common social and individual characteristics of those who may experience a crisis, are not necessarily exhaustive, and may be present in those who do not experience crises or hazardous events. The following traits may be referred to as *crisis risk factors:*

- Unemployment, underemployment, or dissatisfaction with one's present occupation or position.
- Drug abuse (including alcohol).
- Difficulty coping with minor problems, i.e., problems encountered by the general population on a daily basis.
- Low self-esteem, persistent feelings of insecurity.
- History of unresolved crises or emotional disorders.
- Underutilization of support systems and minimal access to support systems

(personal, family, social).
- Few permanent relationships (lack of social integration with others).
- Feelings of alienation from others (family, friends, society).
- Demonstrates impulsiveness and an uncaring attitude.
- History of frequent personal injuries and/or frequent involvement in property damage incidents. (Hendricks & McKean, 1995, p. 9)

While the aforementioned characteristics or traits of a person prone to crisis span the individual, his/her relationships, and his/her place within society and in social groups there have been additional efforts to determine the individual characteristics of those experiencing a crisis event. Therefore, and related to these characteristics, others have found that those experiencing crisis have certain commonalties. For instance, Brockopp (1973, p. 93) identified what he termed "personality characteristics" of those in crisis and are as follows:

- A lowered span of attention, focusing on the foreground images with a restricting of the background or setting within which the problem occurs.
- A ruminative, introspective stance. He [she] looks inside himself [herself] for possible reasons for the occurrence of the crisis situation or explanations as to how he [she] can resolve it. At the same time he [she] shows a great deal of anguish, fear, and both internal and external distress.
- An emotional reaching out for help and support and a seeming inability to control his [her] emotional responses.
- A great deal of testing behavior, much of which is impulsive and unproductive.
- A change in his [her] relationship to people.
- Reduction in orienting attitudes and a lack of perspective about himself [herself] as a person in time, space and in community.
- A great deal of searching behavior in an attempt to solve his [her] problem by looking for usable features of his [her] environment which may help in the resolution.
- Having a large fund of information available to him [her] relative to the problem with which he [she] is confronted, but this is usually in a very disorganized state and therefore not useful to him [her].

Others have also identified various crisis event elements. Romano (1990) lists dimensions or characteristics common to crisis events that further aid one in defining the traits of crisis situations. As she notes, crises may involve:

(a) *Need for action:* It [the crisis] is a situation in which the requirements for actions are high among participants, yet the ability to cope with the event is lowered.

(b) *Goals and objectives:* It [the crisis] usually threatens the goals and objectives of those involved and is followed by an outcome whose consequences shape the future of the participants.

(c) *Loss of control:* Once caught in crisis, reduced control over the events and the effects of these events as well as heightened urgency often produce stress.

(d) *Time element:* The crisis is acute rather than chronic, although it's [the crisis] length is usually unspecified and limited.

(e) *Perception of crisis:* There may be some difficulty in identifying and defining a crisis because what is a crisis event to one person may not be experienced as such to another.

(f) *Coping ability:* Overall, a crisis is any event that reduces an individual's ability to cope with a given situation.

(g) *Opportunity:* Crisis may also consist of a convergence of events that result in a new set of circumstances presenting an opportunity for change and growth. (Romano, 1990, p. 13)

These characteristics, and the work of others in the field, enable us to come closer to a definition of "crisis." First, it is clear that a crisis may be the result of an anticipated (or what most would expect such as the onset of major life changes) or an unanticipated event. The onset of the original event, in turn, produces a hazardous event when the original event is defined as unpleasant, disruptive, and traumatizing and coupled with inappropriate or inadequate coping mechanisms. Second, it seems rather clear that a crisis often involves others. This may be the case in the event of interpersonal conflict or the death of a loved one, just to name two possible instances where accidental crises may occur. The individual always operates within the context of others and social groups, whether it be responding to the onset of retirement or some other type of life change. The involvement of others in the formation of a crisis emphasizes their *interpersonal* dimension. Finally, one must recognize that individuals may experience potentially crisis-producing events differently. That is, the same event may produce a crisis for some, while not for others. Moreover, an event may produce varying degrees of crisis reaction for various individuals. Given the potentially unique feature of the crisis situation, one must emphasize the *interpersonal* nature of crisis situations. That is, individuals all have a unique ability to define and respond to events and situations in the social environment in different ways. Therefore, the *interpersonal* experience of the individual in response to the *event* which in some way involves others in the *interpersonal* environment is the foundation for understanding the dynamics of crisis formation.

ORIGINS AND FOUNDATIONS OF CRISIS THEORY

Though the term "crisis intervention" emerged in the late 1970s, studies in the area were conducted as early as the 1950s (Gilliland and James, 1997). The origins of crisis theory, however, date back to works cited in medical and psychology journals and records of the 1920s. This early research, conducted without the benefit of the umbrella term "crisis intervention," focused on such seemingly diverse and unrelated areas as "mental conflict," "hysteria," "time-limited mental health care," "short-term psychotherapy," and "acute grief." For example, a study conducted by Dershimer (1928) examined conflict between parents and children. Dershimer theorized that problems between parent and child originate from a power struggle. The resolution to these problems, according to Dershimer, lies in the use of an objective third party to mediate the conflict. Howard (1932), who studied conflict, suggested that psychologists should not merely diagnose a problem, but treat the patient as well. Accordingly, crises need to be addressed in a direct, personal manner and treated through conscious appeal. In essence, Howard (1932) recommends the use of empathy with treatment for successful conflict resolution.

One form of conflict, common today, is the domestic dispute. According to Hendricks (1985) and Hendricks and McKean (1995, 2001), domestic disputes are situations that police address daily. These earlier contributions are undeniably important to the development of steps and procedures in addressing crisis situations and to an understanding of the theoretical and conceptual nature of crisis events. Dershimer's (1928) work in domestic disputes is relevant even today because of the number of cases that arise every year, the considerable danger to professionals in defusing them, and the far-reaching damage these events inflict on family members and communities. His research suggests, in fact, the utility of mediation for both parties (Dershimer, 1928). This concept, new in his time, is the standard crisis intervention procedure used today. In addition, Howard's discovery of the role of empathy in successful conflict resolution is another cornerstone on which today's crisis intervention theory and application resides.

The study of crisis intervention, and its applied nature, gained momentum in the 1940s. Numerous studies conducted on the effects of disaster and accidents brought new light to crisis theory and practice. At the forefront are the efforts of Lindemann, Erickson, Caplan, and Quierdo. Lindemann (1944), one of the first physicians to study crisis intervention, focused on the causes and prevention of mental disturbance. In a well-known study of acute grief caused by crisis, he observed the survivors of the Boston Coconut Grove fire. From this, he discovered a series of reactions commonly experienced by those thrust into crisis situations. These reactions surrounding acute grief were termed ". . . somatic distress, preoccupation with images of the deceased, guilt, hostile reactions, and loss of patterns of conduct . . ." (p. 142). In addition, Lindemann (1944) noted the seriousness of grief postponement. He maintained that grief postponement is a type of crisis that occurs when a victim/survivor faces a tragedy and displays little or no reaction. Furthermore, Lindemann (1944) found that, without intervention, individuals experiencing denial and grief postponement were likely to develop personality disturbances such as psychotic-like behavior and morbid reactions. Thus, Lindemann's (1944) studies were valuable in that they established a sequence of probable reactions on the problems of the victim/survivor, and predicted how certain persons, depending on their reactions to grief, might proceed through a crisis.

In later studies, Lindemann (1979) made great strides when examining the effects of crisis-related stress on the human body. In one particular study, he examined ten different cases involving people who were diagnosed as having ulcerative colitis. In each case he determined that the physical disorder was developed after the onset of crisis due to the loss of close loved ones. His research on the effects of psychosomatic illness revealed that crises are detrimental to the physical as well as the person's mental well-being.

Others have also made great contributions to the theory and practice of crisis intervention. For instance, Erickson (1959, 1963) contributed much to the foundation of crisis intervention and concentrated on the typologies of crisis. The types of crisis to be noted have also been discussed elsewhere (Lester & Brockopp, 1973; Aguilera & Messick, 1974; Morrice, 1976; Romano, 1990). According to Erickson (1959, 1963), there are two varieties that might befall the individual. The first type, maturation–developmental, involves natural physical and social changes in a person as he or she ages, such as adolescence or retirement. This type of crisis has also been referred to as "internal" crisis (Romano, 1990). One might consider this variety in the context of the social identity of the individual given the assumption that developmentally-based crises occur as a result of the maturational process and emerge from one's own unique, personal interpretation of such events. The second variety, accidental-situational crisis, also sometimes referred to as "external crises" (Romano, 1990), usually involves unexpected loss and/or trauma due to some event which challenges, and taxes, the individual's normal coping mechanisms. According to Romano (1990), this type of crisis is characterized as being sudden and unexpected, unpredictable, and arbitrary. Victims of violent crime and physical abuse, as well as those who unexpectedly lose a loved one, can suffer from accidental-situational crises.

THE ANATOMY OF INDIVIDUAL CRISIS

Erickson's work, like that of Lindemann, furthered the field of crisis intervention and demonstrate that crises may come in more than one variety, may have many sources, and thrust the individual into psychological disequilibrium. Burgess and Baldwin (1981), building on the work of classical crisis intervention theory, outline *six classes of crisis*. The first class of crisis they describe is the *dispositional* crisis. This type is defined as involving ". . . distress resulting from a problematic situation . . ." (Burgess & Baldwin, 1981, p. 35). The second class is the crisis of *anticipated life transition.* As one may see, this variety resembles the maturational-developmental variety described above. This type of crisis is characterized by a normative life transition over which the person may not have complete control, such as a new job, promotion, parenting status change, which is coupled with an inability to cope effectively with the event. The third variety is the crisis resulting from *sudden traumatic stress.* While also typified by the cause resting outside the individual's locus of control, this crisis type is often the type of crisis one visualizes when hearing the term "crisis." These are characterized by the trauma which is produced and is often the type of crisis which accompanies criminal victimization and other, related crisis situations found in criminal justice and social services (crisis case management, domestic violence, protective service intervention, etc.). Burgess and Baldwin's (1981) fourth type is termed *Maturational/Developmental Crises.* This particular nomenclature is often used to describe the aforementioned crisis types within crisis theory parlance. However, Burgess and Baldwin use this designation to describe the Eriksonian-type developmental crises which people are believed to face through the life-course. As these authors write (p. 37), these crises result from

> . . . attempts to deal with interpersonal situations which reflect a struggle with a deeper, but usually circumscribed, developmental issue that has not been resolved adaptively in the past and that represents an attempt to attain emotional maturity. . . .

As one may readily observe, this type is reminiscent of the Erikson psychosocial crisis stages through which one may pass during the life-course.

The final two varieties, *crises resulting from psychopathology* (class 5) and *psychiatric emergencies* (class 6), like class three crises, may often be encountered in criminal justice and social service intervention. Class five crises are those where the crisis is the result of "preexisting psychopathology" or a psychopathology leading to maladaptive crisis resolution. Class five crises may be seen as being coupled with chronic psychiatric issues while class six crises are more acute such as drug or alcohol induced psychosis.

CRISIS AND COMMUNITY

Moving beyond the scope of the individual, Caplan (1964) emphasized the community's responsibility for facilitating the recovery of those facing crises. "Community" can have several different meanings such as the spiritual, physical, ethnic, racial, emotional and social. The various social groups' individuals circulate within serve to maintain individual stability and help in restoring equilibrium in the aftermath of crisis. Caplan (1964) believed that the community should be an environment conducive to healthy relationships, which utilize coping mechanisms and problem-solving skills. Thus, the prevention of mental disorders is dependent upon the consistency and wellness of inter-community relationships. Expanding on this idea, Caplan developed a conceptual model that illustrated how an individual maintains equilibrium in his or her community. This theory suggests that the individual continually strive to keep healthy relationships within the community environment. Therefore, an individual coping with a crisis struggles to restore his or her balance. If, however, the community is itself not a healthy one, the person is crisis may not experience restored equilibrium. This may cause deeper confusion, anxiety, and depression for the individual, thereby calling for crisis intervention. Caplan's work emphasizes the need for the community and its agencies to work together to assist individuals in need. Today, advocates trained in crisis intervention do this by training and networking community programs and by promoting general community welfare through preventive programs and response efforts. Recently, such efforts have come in the form of school safety programs (OJJDP, 1998), responding to domestic terrorism (OVC, 2000), addressing hate crime victimization (OVC, 2000) and general guidelines for "community crisis response" (OVC, 1999). These efforts have enabled crisis intervention to move away from a sole clinical focus to a public setting in which all citizens, in any given community, may assist in serving those in need. Therefore, crisis theory, and corresponding interventive steps, involved not only the dyadic relationship between intervener and client, but also the relationship between those in crisis, community, and the larger society.

Another researcher who believed in the role of community was Quierdo (1968), who conducted his studies during the 1930s in post-war Amsterdam. He developed a psychiatric first-aid service, which was originally used while screening patients for admittance to mental institutions. He discovered that intervention in a patient's own environment–before entry into the hospital–was therapeutic in itself. As he wrote:

It is almost impossible to exaggerate the impact of the experience when the patient is seen in his own surroundings on those–as we all were at the time–

who have been trained exclusively to deal with patients in a hospital setting. . . . In this first contact–often in the tense atmosphere of an acute crisis–a picture is unfolded where, I am convinced, never can be obtained in any other way. (p. 299)

Quierdo's method, termed "emergency first aid," was later used in the military and finally came to be synonymous with crisis intervention. According to Hendricks (1985) and Hendricks and McKean (1995, 2001), methods similar to Quierdo's were used during the Vietnam, Korean, and Second World wars. Instead of being away from the front, soldiers suffering from combat fatigue were sent to the rear of the combat zone to receive support. Research indicates that these soldiers were successful in regaining equilibrium within their immediate, albeit threatening, environment.

While it may be said that effective crisis intervention may take place in close proximity to the crisis producing environment, which is certainly applicable to many criminal justice and social service related crisis situations, it must also be said that the victim/survivor or person experiencing a crisis must feel safe. Without this measure of security, the crisis client will be unable to focus on the crisis through the guiding strategies of the intervener and efforts to confront and resolve the crisis would be rendered ineffective. One only needs to examine disaster settings, whether natural or humanly created, to see the important role of a community on all levels including the physical community, the social community, and the psychological community. In the aftermath of the recent Oklahoma City terrorist bombing, one has been able to observe the role of community in facilitating the healing process in response to individual and community level crises precipitated by the bombing. Classical crisis theorists, Caplan (1964) being one of the most important, have focused on the critical role which the community plays and has been a significant foundation for the disciplines of community psychology and community psychiatry (Slaikeu, 1990), which are close cousins to crisis intervention.

While much of the focus of these related areas has been on the prevention of community crisis situations with appropriate steps such as planning for societal changes (employment, economy) and promoting mental hygiene and community mental health programs, a treatment focus has still been retained and has been critical in the efforts of crisis intervention delivery agencies such as the American Red Cross in their efforts to facilitate effective crisis coping in response to large-scale community crisis situations. As Cohen (1990) has outlined, community-oriented crisis intervention has a significant place in response to crisis on the community and societal levels. In fact, the United States Department of Justice has disseminated a number of important resources on community-based crisis response (OVC, 1999). In the final analysis, all crises involve others, either directly or indirectly, and one must expect individual psychology and coping ability to be influenced by social and structural changes at the community level that call for a community-wide response.

CRISIS INTERVENTION INTERPERSONAL COMMUNICATION SKILLS

Although crisis intervention takes many forms and is used to resolve a variety of different emotional problems, there are certain elements common to all types. These core elements are essential to the success of each crisis resolution. This section will focus on these elements and how crisis intervention professionals may utilize them. Researchers and crisis personnel agree that the purpose of modern day crisis intervention is to return the crisis victim/survivor to the former, or pre-crisis, level of functioning (see Byers, 1987 for a review of these ideas). As opposed to many other types of therapy and counseling, crisis intervention addresses only the problem (crisis) at hand. Therefore, crisis intervention is *focused* on a particular event or issue and the individual's maladaptive response to the event or issue. In other words, the client may have numerous personal problems that contribute to the crisis, but the intervener's task is to deal directly with the maladaptive response to the crisis-producing event, which has thrust the individual into disequilibrium and ineffective psychological functioning. Once the crisis has passed or has been resolved, however, the intervener may refer the client to another therapist to resolve any other problems. For this reason, crisis intervention is considered a variety of short-term therapy.

This unique type of therapy requires equally unique, specialized techniques. Lindsay (1975), for example, observed that the skills necessary for successful intervention must be more responsive and focused than those needed for conventional therapies. Golan (1978) also emphasized the importance of focusing attention on the causes or sources of a client's crisis. Grando (1975) found that assuring clients that they would not undergo further trauma was an additional, important aspect of intervention. In other research, Baldwin (1980) found the most important ingredient in intervention is for the intervener to emphasize present victim/survivor stress. Kalafat (1983), in reviewing assistance strategies, discovered the importance of the intervener's knowledge of the crisis as well as his or her ability to predict the victim's/survivor's future behavior. Hoff and Miller (1987) listed communication skills as vital to interveners. In addition, Wells, Getman, and Blau (1988) stressed the value of attentive listening on the part of the intervener as necessary to successful therapy. From these efforts, a general framework of crisis intervention may be established. Most crisis intervention scholars seem to agree that sound crisis intervention is a combination of effective interpersonal communication, an ability to focus the client on the crisis and crisis producing event, and the intervener's skill in guiding the person experiencing the crisis through the process of recovery.

Most researchers agree that the main thrust of crisis intervention concentrates on the here and now, or what caused the crisis and how to assist the victim/survivor toward some resolution. Once this is recognized, many other skills necessary for resolution become apparent. One critical skill is the ability of the intervener to anticipate responses or reactions of the victim/survivor to intervention. For example, the use of *open-ended questions* helps minimize the victim's/survivor's use of abrupt one-word answers that hide feelings or emotions and have the potential to stifle interaction between client and intervener. This verbal technique has also been shown to have utility in hostage negotiation settings (Noesner and Webster, 1997). Such strategies help to break down barriers and open the communication process. As Noesner and Webster (1997) note, ". . . negotiators must by able to guide expressive subjects into clearly stating the nature of their dilemmas and articulating their demands so that law enforcement can address them" (p. 2).

Another valuable tool is the use of *empathy*. Empathy creates a bond of trust between the intervener and the person in crisis. Through empathy the intervener may obtain a better understanding of what the client is experiencing. This further extends the trust, which is necessary in order for the individual to accept assistance. Empathy, in turn, involves other skills. For instance, *active listening,* which allows the intervener to accurately assess the overt and covert (emotional) content of the client's conversation, plays a lead role in the use of empathy. However, active listening, the highest level of communicated listening, is essential throughout the entire crisis intervention process. It involves an ability to discern both the meaning and the emotional content of the message. Some experts believe this is the single most important skill that a crisis intervener can possess, in that it enables the professional to "read" the victim's/survivor's emotional state—which sometimes may be homicidal or suicidal. *Nonverbal cues,* such as excessive nervousness, crying, long pauses in conversation and deep sighs, also must be recognizable to the effective intervener. These actions may be very effective indicators to the intervener of the client's emotional state.

Finally, because of the stressful nature of crisis intervention, interveners also must be aware of their own strengths, weaknesses and limitations. To best serve those coming for assistance, interveners must be certain of their own emotional and mental health. Knowing one's limitations is important in order to recognize when other professionals might better serve the client and when it may be appropriate to refer. Not recognizing such situations could result in increased levels of anxiety for both counselor and client and is destructive to the client's emotional recovery. Often, this recognition is emphasized during training, in order for crisis professionals to improve on, and to recognize, their skills and abilities.

With these important skills and abilities in place, the crisis intervener must take note of two important dimensions of crisis intervention. These are the crisis interview and the crisis intervention process. The crisis interview is subsumed within the crisis intervention process. A crisis interview is a very complex setting in which crisis intervention takes place and within which the intervener may guide the process of intervention. According to Gordon (1988), there are six key features to the effective crisis interview. These are:

1. Establishing rapport with the patient (client).
2. Rapidly understanding the patient's (client's) perspective.
3. Obtaining a history (that is, a history of how the crisis was produced).
4. Constructing a formulation about the patient (client) and about the meaning of the stressful event to him or her.
5. Actively negotiating with the patient (client) about the problem.
6. Actively negotiating with the patient (client) over solutions to the problem (p. 36).

With these principles in mind, the trained intervener may begin the process of assisting the client to the plateau of pre-crisis functioning. This facilitation is normally conducted within the context of phases or stages of crisis intervention. Such stages or phases in the intervention process enable the encounter to have two, equally important, characteristics. First, following a phase/stage approach enables the intervener to interject structure and stability into the life of an individual who is psychologically disorganized. And second, the use of stages or phases affords the intervener an important reference point from which to further facilitate the crisis intervention process and to gauge progress within the encounter. For information on such phase/stage models, too lengthy to discuss here and not within the historical and theoretical purview of this chapter, one may wish to consult the works of Hendricks (1985), Hendricks and McKean (1995), Roberts (1990), Slaikeu (1990), Foxman (1990), France (1990), and Burgess and Baldwin (1981).

CRISIS ASSESSMENT

Historically, within the field of crisis intervention, it has been assumed that assessment is an element of crisis intervention practice. Given the historical foundations of crisis theory and intervention come from the medical model, there has been a focus on "diagnosis" followed with "treatment." However, assessment of a crisis situation is multifaceted and complex spanning the physical, emotional, and social being.

The crisis assessment process is an evaluative one. It is a process whereby the intervener is able to examine the situation, the client, available resources and promote a healing environment for the person in crisis. Assessment can be defined as:

> . . . the process of subjecting the client to a formal evaluation and analysis of his or her deficiencies and needs, as well as the risks he or she poses to the community, so that realistic counseling plans and strategies can be worked out. (Walsh, 1988; p. 2)

A focus on the "here and now" is vital to effective crisis assessment. Oftentimes, the intervener does not have the luxury of knowing much in the way of client background or history. Therefore, the intervener is faced with perhaps one of the greatest challenges in a therapeutic setting: providing efficient and effective treatment without the benefit of a full client mental health history. Typically, the focus is on the current situation and what the person in crisis is experiencing. This point emphasizes the "here and now" nature of crisis intervention.

The overarching goal of crisis assessment is for the intervener to gain as much insight and understanding of the crisis situation as possible and to bring some stability to the crisis setting. This involves keeping an open mind and being aware of multiple problems, possibilities, and opportunities. Crisis assessment in many ways is a collaborative process between client and intervener. In order to engage in crisis intervention with a client, the intervener must have a receptive client. When engaged in crisis assessment, one must always be focused on client needs. That is, given the intervener's understanding of the situation and the crisis, what is the person's best interests and how can the intervener work with the client to achieve them? A successful assessment will help provide structure to an unstructured situation.

Providing structure often involves a focus on the "precipitating" or "hazardous" event–the event or experience that produced the crisis. During the assessment encounter it is important to focus on the client's interpretation or perception of events. That is, by exploring the meaning given to crisis producing events, the intervener can better understand and empathize with the client. During the assessment process, the intervener must provide guidance and support. While there are many "assessment models" (Hendricks and McKean, 1995), an approach developed by Gilliland and James (1997) allows the intervener to boil down the problem and work toward crisis resolution. Their assessment considerations include (1) defining the problem; (2) ensuring client safety; (3) providing support; (4) examining alternatives; (5)

making plans; and (6) obtaining commitment. These are presented here as issues for the intervener to keep in mind while working through the intervention process.

Defining the problem involves understanding the crisis or problem as perceived by the client. This consideration involves "walking in the client's shoes," so to speak, and engaging in empathy, genuineness, and attentive listening. It is critical that one understand the problem or crisis as does the client. Since the intervener is attempting to understand the client's perceptions, this step involves interpreting the problem or crisis based on the client's "definition of the situation" (Byers, 1987). When attempting to understand the client's definition of the situation, the intervener must be empathic and understanding.

The second consideration described by Gilliland and James (1997) is "ensuring client safety" (p. 30). Other crisis intervention assessment models also place this consideration at the forefront (Hendricks and McKean, 1995). When ensuring client safety, the intervener must ward off potential dangers to the client such as physical or psychological harm. However, it seems reasonable to extend this consideration to the intervener and anyone else who might be a part of the intervention or an innocent bystander. Thus, ensuring safety might be viewed as a strategy whereby the intervener exercises "control" over the situation in such a way that if danger were to rear it's head the intervener could respond appropriately. This consideration could mean taking the client to a safer environment, searching persons (including the client) for weapons that might be used to harm the self or others, and asking certain people to leave the intervention setting.

Another important consideration is "providing support" to the client (Gilliland and James, 1997). This consideration is filled with verbal and non-verbal considerations. In other words, and according to the authors, one can *articulate* support for a client and also *show* support for a client. Demonstrating support, either verbally or non-verbally, affords the client a sense of security. Support allows the client to feel secure, protected, and safe—emotionally and physically. Support can be demonstrated through the use of empathy, active listening, demeanor, body posture, and eye contact. Thus, one must demonstrate support before it can be perceived as being "provided."

The fourth consideration is "examining alternatives" (Gilliland and James, 1997). Since a crisis often makes the client immobile, unable to process information, and impacts decision-making ability, the intervener needs to provide insight into alternatives available to the client. Whatever alternatives are explored, and possibly selected, must be in the client's best interest. Options in the best interest of the client are those which do not prolong client pain and provide the best option, at the time, for re-establishing client emotional equilibrium. Clients need to be guided into positive and productive alternatives through the intervener's understanding of the "definition of the situation" and available options. While the intervener may be aware of the plethora of options, one must be cautious in offering too many options since clients in crisis can easily be overwhelmed when given too much information (Gilliland and James, 1997).

Another important assessment consideration is "making plans" (Gilliland and James, 1997). As a critical issue in any crisis intervention encounter, the intervener can serve as an important conduit as the client strives for emotional equilibrium. Making plans involves looking to the future and toward a commitment to a stronger self, able to recover from the current crisis and to learn from the crisis-producing event. To assist the client in making plans one must assess his or her ability to tap interpersonal as well as intrapersonal resources. Interpersonally, the client must be willing to explore his or her social support network of friends and family. Intrapersonally, the client must be amenable to tapping into inner strength and all it has to offer. When exploring options and making plans with the client it is critical to remain cognizant of issues of self-determination. In a word, the client needs to always be a part of the process or be enfranchised. It is easy for a crisis intervener to want to "do everything" for the client. However, the client must be a stakeholder in the process in order for crisis intervention to fully assist the client.

The final consideration during the crisis intervention process is "obtaining commitment" (Gilliland and James, 1997). As noted by Gilliland and James (1997), this consideration logically flows from "making plans." This consideration requires that the intervener assess the client's ability to understand the suggestions and guidance offered during the crisis intervention process and put these principles into action when future crises arise. Sometimes, obtaining commitment simply requires that the client know when to ask for help.

A CRISIS INTERVENTION PROCESS

As was the case with crisis assessment, space limits the ability to fully discuss the complexities of the crisis intervention process–the stages or phases involved in providing intervention to those in needs. The authors provide this process because it has proven effective in theory and practice. It is not, however, the only process or procedure one might follow in rendering crisis intervention services. There are five stages or phases to this process. They include Information Gathering, Control, Direction, Progress Assessment, and Referral (Hendricks, 1984; Hendricks and Byers, 1986). It is important for the intervener, when conducting these steps, to remain cognizant of the assessment issues addressed above.

Information Gathering

While the assessment of the crisis and client functioning follow the entire crisis intervention process, the first step, Information Gathering, emphasizes understanding the nature of the crisis, the precipitating event, and other important initial considerations. The intervener will note that the immediacy of the situation necessitates that client and intervener safety is paramount. Therefore, the intervener, especially a first responder, should scan and study the environment to ascertain possible dangers to the client and/or the intervener. This step draws on the assessment concern of "ensuring client safety." It likely seems obvious that the police crisis intervener would need to be aware of potential dangers. However, other criminal justice and social service interveners need to be aware of this concern as well. For instance, child protection workers, elder abuse investigators (adult protective services workers), probation officers, and parole officers all need to be aware of possible environmental dangers. Once potential danger is ruled out, and intervention can proceed, it is essential to learn about the client and to work on defining the nature of the problem. The assessment consideration here, then, is "defining the problem." By engaging in active listening skills, the intervener is able to explore the identity of the client (who is the client?), the nature of the crisis (what is the crisis?), the circumstances of the crisis (when and where did the crisis take place?).

Control

"Control" in crisis intervention sounds, at the outset, like an attempt to manipulate the encounter and the control is in the hands of the intervener. However, nothing could be further from the truth. The goal of this step is restore the client's "self-control." Self-control is the ability to make decisions, control one's own behavior, to resist temptations, and to not act on impulse. When a person is in crisis, s/he is not thinking clearly. Therefore, not only is one's life out of control but the client will have difficulty controlling his/her own actions and exercising sound reasoning and judgment. It is vital that the intervener provide "support" (Gilliland and James, 1997) during this phase. Providing support involves demonstrating strength. The client in crisis is able to then draw from this strength. Ultimately, the intervener desires the client to exercise his/her own levels of control and not depend on him/her for such strength and support. Therefore, encouraging client self-determination and autonomy during this process is important given the intervener will not always be available. A simple rule of thumb is appropriate at this juncture:

the least amount of control the better. However, the intervener must judge for him/herself the level needed depending on the lethality of the situation and the client's propensity for danger to self and/or others.

During this phase, the client and intervener build on the information gathering stage by continuing to work collaboratively on refining the definition of the crisis and how the client was thrust into his/her crisis state. There are important strategies during the control stage, which can serve to de-escalate the emotion and trauma of the situation. For instance, the intervener will wish be calm, clear, concise, and genuine. However, the formality one uses during this phase will be a function of the participants and the setting. For instance, the intervener may see a need to use a more serious and distant tone and therefore may use formal titles (e.g., Mr., Mrs., Ms., and Miss). In other instances, the intervener may find it more useful to use the person's first name. Either approach can best be determined in face-to-face interaction.

Whenever one engages in face to face social interaction with a crisis client, it is important to use interpersonal space wisely. One should gauge the appropriate distance from the client based on his/her nonverbal behavior. It is evident, nonverbally, when an intervener has invaded the personal space of the client and this should be avoided. Such social psychological invasion will do nothing but serve to deteriorate the encounter and create client discomfort.

One way to allow the client to be comfortable is to encourage him/her to express feelings. Feelings of anger, frustration, sadness, and disbelief are common to a person in crisis. When the client is expressing his/her feelings the intervener may demonstrate active listening by reflecting content or feeling back to the client. For instance, a client may say, "I just don't understand why he would do this to me." In response, the intervener might say, "You don't understand why he would treat you this way." This is a reflection of content, because the intervener is reflecting back to the client the basic nature and "content" of the communication. Suppose, however, if the client were to say, "I just can't take this anymore, it is just too much!" The intervener in this instance might say, "You feel overwhelmed." This is a reflection of "feeling" because the intervener is extracting the client's feelings from the statement. There are many types of reflection that interveners can use to assist the client and to encourage more verbal expression. For a substantive list and techniques one should see Alfred Benjamin's book *The Helping Interview* (1987). Through the use of various supportive verbal techniques, the intervener may calm the situation, the client, and move toward constructive decisionmaking.

Direction

Direction affords the client to exercise his or her autonomy and express desired outcomes to the crisis situation. It is wholly appropriate to ask the client what she/he wishes as an outcome. Clearly articulating this question to the client conveys that the intervener is a concerned "problem solver" and interested in crisis resolution on behalf of the client. In providing direction, one helps the client in examining possible solutions to the crisis. For the most part these "solutions" are focused on short-term client functioning. This is, in part, due to the fact that crisis intervention is intended to be a "brief" encounter with the client. Much of what one will do in direction is related to the assessment considerations described above which include examining alternatives and making plans.

When examining alternatives with the client, one may also offer suggestions to the client. Suggestions allow more client autonomy than advice. Advice indicates to the client that s/he might be expected to engage in a particular behavior; advice is more direct. While there may be a place for advice during the crisis intervention encounter, one might try suggestions first in order to enfranchise the client and help him/her toward autonomy. Recall our earlier discussion of how clients might define the situation. Direction affords the intervener the opportunity to help the client "reframe" the situation. "Reframing" is a common therapeutic technique which provides the client with an alternative way of thinking about his/her plight. In order to be successful with re-framing, one must explore possible reasons for the crisis. This necessarily involves an exploration of precipitating events. Through a psychohistorical coexamination of the hazardous event(s) and the nature of the crisis, the client and intervener can, together, move toward direction whereby the client is able to feel and demonstrate more self-direction and independence.

Referral

The final stage we will discuss is referral. The purpose of referral is to help the client in making future plans and to establish client commitment to positive intra and interpersonal change. It is imperative that the intervener explore services that might be needed by the client. These could include follow-up counseling, psychiatric assessment, referral to an advocacy group–just to name a few. Ultimately, the intervener wishes for the encounter to proceed toward closure whereby the client is able to function without the intervener's presence and assistance.

CRISIS INTERVENTION IN CRIMINAL JUSTICE AND SOCIAL SERVICES

The importance of crisis intervention training in the criminal justice system and within the social service community is indisputable. Further, knowledge of crisis intervention steps provides the intervener with some guidance and structure when addressing a crisis situation. Moreover, the role and importance of crisis intervention within criminal justice and its interface with social service is clear (Romano, 1990) given the many different crisis situations police and other criminal justice and social service personnel and agencies may be expected to respond to. Day after day, agencies which include police departments and other helping agencies, are generally the first to respond to crisis situations, which include suicides, accidental deaths, death notifications, domestic disputes, child and elder abuse, the special needs of the mentally ill and handicapped, the socially displaced, and all varieties of crime–violent and property alike.

In reference to crime, and according to the *Sourcebook of Criminal Justice Statistics* (1994), 6,621,140 crimes of violence were reported as part of the National Crime Victimization Survey (NCVS) during 1992–every one is a potential candidate for a crisis. Most of these cases, when reported, are addressed in part by the police. Breslen's (1978) research reveals that police receive at least one domestic violence call per day. The use of intervention is invaluable in restoring stability to these potentially explosive situations. Not only can crisis intervention help prevent further disruption at the scene of a crime or disturbance, it may also help victims/survivors to begin immediately to deal with their crises. Newfield and Reish (1975) noted that because most mental health agencies are not equipped with twenty-four hour social and crisis intervention services, police officers should be able to do more than make referrals to persons needing crisis intervention. Many times, because of time or location constraints, intervention agencies are not immediately accessible. Therefore, police should be trained to assist with crisis intervention in their role as first responders. These same researchers, Newfield and Reish (1975), also evaluated the Portsmouth–Chesapeake crisis intervention training program for police–an innovative prospect at the time, as most similar programs were not instituted until the early 1980s (Hendricks and Thomas, 1990). This 90-hour, volunteer-based program included nearly all officer ranks. The high enrollment/low dropout rate combined with the positive responses of individuals indicated the strong acceptance of the program by the group as a whole. Similar programs were instrumental in paving the way for victim/survivor advocate training programs in the law enforcement community. Not only did these early programs improve the visibility of crisis intervention, but they resulted in greater empathy for victims/survivors by police who received training, according to Arthur, Sisson and McClung (1977). After training, nearly 90 percent of assistance cases were handled by police in a more positive manner, with respect to the victim/survivor. Today, crisis intervention training for police is standard procedure in many departments and jurisdictions. Though police are not indifferent to the needs of the victim/survivor, such training is necessary for them to understand victims/survivors and to obtain victim/ survivor cooperation in a time of crisis. In this way, crisis intervention is a benefit to law enforcement officers, and is a valuable tool in defusing potentially dangerous crisis situations.

In a survey of the 50 largest police departments, Hendricks and Thomas (1990) assessed the benefit crisis intervention training has had on job performance and reducing disturbances. Benefits included fewer call-backs in domestic dispute cases, less stress for officers, improved police community relations, more accurate information from victims/survivors concerning victimization and more willingness on the part of victims/survivors to cooperate with prosecution and to testify. Also, the departments reported higher rates of prosecution and improved investigative response. Though police response can be an important component in successful intervention, it may be unavailable. In a study conducted by Finn and Lee (1985), benefits of police referral to crisis intervention centers (providing social and crisis services) were assessed. According to the researchers, these programs assist victims/survivors by locating witnesses, drawing better information concerning the event from the victim/survivor and providing relevant information to the police if necessary. Although the best method of assistance requires police involvement, much is to be gained from referrals to crisis centers. Though crisis intervention at the law enforcement level is critical, some victims/survivors require assistance throughout the entire criminal justice process and by other, related agencies once contact with the criminal justice system has ceased. For instance, Shapland and Cohen (1987) studied victim/survivor complaints while progressing through the system. Victims reported feelings of being lost, neglected, and helpless. Meese (1987) also addressed this issue on the federal level. Believing that victims/survivors need assistance in all parts of the criminal justice system, he recommended both short- and long-term training for every employee coming in contact with victims/survivors—from U.S. district attorneys to parole officers. Focusing on the role of the judiciary, Finn (1986) recognized the trauma to persons who must repeatedly recount experiences of victimization in the courtroom. He argues that court should be handled in such a way as to reduce this testifying traumatization, which can further add to a victim's/survivor's stress. Cullen and Gilbert (1982) studied the effect of crisis on victims/survivors in correctional facilities. Their study revealed that in the first six months of 1980, nearly 150 prisoners died of violent means in state and federal prisons. They argue that incarceration itself has crisis potential, and that prisoners can benefit from crisis intervention. Though most of the training received by criminal justice agencies is focused on law enforcement and crime control (Hendricks, 1982), the system as a whole is beginning to recognize the importance of crisis intervention training on all levels. As a result, new programs are being developed and implemented to that end throughout the country's criminal justice system.

While the role of crisis intervention in social service has been no less obvious than that of criminal justice. Social service agencies have provided critical crisis intervention services for decades. Such services may include 24-hour crisis and suicide lines intended to diffuse the hazardous crisis situation and to facilitate adequate referral. In addition, such agencies provide important services to the community in terms of education and training and support groups, which may serve to prevent certain types of crises.

Additionally, the direct services to clients/victims/survivors, much like their criminal justice counterparts are realized daily. Romano, in *Taking Charge: Crisis Intervention in Criminal Justice* (1990), advocates for an integrated approach to crisis intervention which not only takes into consideration the important role that criminal justice and social service agencies play, but also the role of the medical, psychological, counseling, social work, and psychiatric branches of the helping community. As she writes, the importance of an integrated model may serve our communities well:

> Evidence is accumulating to indicate that knowledge of a multidimensional model for crisis intervention is imperative for the criminal justice crisis intervener. Large numbers of persons present multiple human problems along with their presenting complaints when they are referred to criminal justice agencies. These problems do not easily lend themselves to simple explanations or resolutions. In this day of multiple human problems, the growing awareness of the interrelationship of human service systems, mental health workers, medical personnel, and criminal justice personnel has resulted in the need for collaboration. . . . (Romano, 1990, p. 2)

CRISIS INTERVENTION WITHIN A CULTURALLY DIVERSE SOCIETY

Crisis intervention, in its traditional sense, emerged like many other areas of scholarly and practical expertise from the works of those concerned and interested in the betterment of humanity and society. Crisis theory and intervention may be applied effectively to anyone experiencing a crisis or traumatic stress, but the profession of crisis intervention has long realized that American society is culturally diverse and crisis intervention skills and strategies are being practiced more and more in societies around the globe. For these reasons, it is important to be sensitive to the minority crime victim

(Ogawa, 1999) and others in crisis.

Aguilera, Messick, and Farrell (1970) may have been the first to address the issue of cultural diversity and crisis intervention. In the chapter titled "Sociocultural Factors Affecting Therapeutic Intervention" in *Crisis Intervention: Theory and Methodology,* these authors discuss the potential limitations of traditional, Eurocentric, middle-class psychotherapy techniques in addressing the crises of non middle-class groups. The interesting characteristic of this discussion, however, is the obvious focus on "social class" differences as these seem to be made synonymous with "sociocultural" differences. What may be a natural consequence of the time period in which the work was published, during a period in U.S. history when the Johnson Administration war of poverty programs were in full operation, may appear today as not being inclusive to other, equally important groups which may, or may not, also possess the social label of "underclass." Tidwell (1992) maintains that crisis intervention may serve the underclass and underrepresented groups quite effectively. In her client-centered approach to the topic of crisis intervention and the underclass, Tidwell (1992) states that crisis counseling may better serve the underclass than other types of psychotherapy. She maintains that many members of the underclass may simply not have the time or the cultural affinity (Tidwell, 1992; p. 245) to engage in other, more traditional forms of therapy. The author also states that crisis counseling may also serve to break social barriers for the underclass and may actually serve as a vehicle for social empowerment.

In a slightly different light, Romano (1990) discusses important cultural characteristics and describes these as barriers to communication. She warns against the use of stereotypes and prejudiced attitudes in attempting to respond to particular client groups. Moreover, according to Romano (1990) one must also be aware of possible cultural differences in traditions, customs, values, and beliefs that may present challenges for the intervener in the course of providing crisis intervention services. More recently, the field of social work has devoted energy through the *Journal of Multicultural Social Work* to help potential helpers in being cognizant of cultural nuances and realities. As Chau (1991) states:

> The key element in ethnic competent practice is, of course, the place of cultural values and norms in assessment and intervention. Thus effective programs and interventions for minority individuals demand that needs assessment must give sensitive consideration to the unique sociocultural conditions confronting them and the meaning these conditions have for problem-solving. (p. 33)

From these works, and others like them, one may begin to see and recognize the importance of cultural diversity in the crisis interview and intervention process. It is for this reason that the field might recognize some basic corollaries of crisis theory and intervention pertinent to these sociocultural realities. These are:

Corollary 1: Given different cultural, racial, ethnic, subcultural, and subgroup differences, crises may be experienced in diverse ways.

Corollary 2: Differing experiences, or reactions, to crisis producing events will evoke various coping mechanisms, which may be endemic to the group identity of the person experiencing the crisis.

Corollary 3: Crisis intervention approaches, while striving for optimal efficiency, may be the most effective if tailored to the sociocultural realities of the group to which the person experiencing the crisis belongs.

With these considerations in mind, and with a strong foundation of crisis theory and process, one may begin to best serve those in crisis in order to assist them in regaining their pre-crisis level of functioning.

THE ROLE OF GOVERNMENT AND THE STATES IN PROMOTING CRISIS INTERVENTION

While crisis theory was still in its embryonic stages, the federal government and the individual states initiated steps to develop and install intervention programs throughout the country. The National Mental Health Act of 1946 financed mental health research and professional training, thus facilitating the emergence of mental health programs in the 1950s and 1960s. In addition, the establishment of the Joint Commission of Mental Illness and Health led directly to the Community Mental Health Center Act of 1963, which provided more funding—to the states, in order to create and expand public mental health centers and services. As the field of crisis intervention expanded to involve social work and criminal justice agencies, so did government funding. The Victims of Crime Act of 1984, for example, financed programs such as victim/survivor/witness assistance training for law enforcement officers. The Victim Witness Assistance Act, enacted in 1982, also provided additional funds for crisis intervention training within the criminal justice system. On the state level, Anderson and Woodard (1985) reported that thirty-eight states, the District of Columbia, and the Virgin Islands had taken to steps to enact bills funding victim/survivor assistance programs. Today, we see most of these programs still providing important crisis and non-crisis services to the victim/survivor. Although crisis intervention training was not often the target of these key pieces of legislation, training programs in crisis intervention received funding indirectly as a result of these types of legislation.

While some government efforts have been indirect, others have provided more direct funds for crisis intervention services. For instance, the Illinois

Violent Crime Victim's Assistance Act is a more specific example of a state's direct contribution to crisis intervention. According to Bensinger (1986), this particular act provided for sensitivity training to professionals whose jobs involve contact with crime victim/survivors. The increasing financial involvement of all levels of government has allowed crisis intervention programs to flourish and to produce professionals better equipped to assist those in need of assistance. In this way, the field of crisis intervention gained a practical hold on society and communities to complement its ever-growing body of theory.

While we see a direct relationship between prior classical theory and contemporary efforts, much of what we refer to as crisis intervention has developed into specialized programmatic responses. Enabling federal legislation is just one example. Just as society has become more complex and specialized, so has the field of crisis intervention. As a result, what one sees today, is a more focused and specialized crisis intervention delivery system, which has matured with society and is targeted for particular crisis related problems and clientele. The following chapters in this volume are a testament to this specialized focus.

CRISIS INTERVENTION: STRESS AND BURNOUT

If one were to create a job that would promote stress and burnout, crisis intervention would serve as a good model. Crisis intervention staff are often overworked, unappreciated, and underpaid (at any price). In addition, there is the ever-constant vigilance required to do an adequate job, and the ever-present threat of violence. These are factors that can lead crisis intervention staff to suffer from job-related stress and burnout.

For the purpose of this chapter, crisis intervention is defined as professional endeavors aimed at the prevention or minimization of danger to the self, to others, or to property. Crisis intervention has implications at the sociopolitical, organizational, and individual levels.

A review of societal mandates provides a segue into a discussion of crisis intervention at the sociopolitical level. Cultural anthropologists contend that the primary mandate of a society is to protect itself from without. The primary task of a society is to protect its members from invasion and its sustenance (e.g., food stores, oil) from depiction by a foreign power. Examples are the maintenance of open shipping lanes in the Caribbean (e.g., the invasion of Grenada in 1983) and the flow of oil from the Persian Gulf (e.g., Desert Storm). The second mandate of a society is to protect itself from within. Threats from within include sedition, anarchy, disasters, and crime. To protect themselves from within, societies establish emergency response mechanisms, such as police and fire departments, and various rescue and disaster response services.

Crisis intervention in criminal justice and the social services is primarily concerned with the second mandate, implemented by the government through its authority to police and parent. Under criminal law, it is difficult to intervene until a law has been violated. Intervention prior to the commission of an offense is predicated on the willingness of the potential offender to cooperate with the counsel of others. An example is a man with a history of battering who is escalating the battering behavior and who agrees to spend the night at a friend's house on the advice of responding officers. The parental authority of the state, known as the doctrine of *parens patriae*, on the other hand, provides for intervention under certain circumstances even without the cooperation of the potential perpetrator. This type of intervention is typically noted when discussing crisis intervention in the human services. It allows the state to place an individual, who poses a threat to him/herself or others as the result of mental disease or defect, in protective custody or to involuntarily hospitalize. An example would be the involuntary hospitalization of a suicidal person (presumed to be depressed) who will not accept help voluntarily. Due process is protected in both criminal and parenting policing functions and by different mechanisms (a discussion beyond the scope of this chapter).

To intervene in crisis situations implies that we are aware of what the outcome of that situation will be. Therefore, crisis intervention is predicated on the ability of crisis interveners to predict human behavior. This poses a myriad of methodological (Monahan, 1981) and ethical (Grisso and Appelbaum, 1992) considerations. While the prediction of violence by mental health professionals is significantly better than chance (Mossman, 1994; Wynkoop, 1995) and is better than once believed (Monahan, 1981), it is still fraught with misclassifications, which pose unique difficulties in protecting the civil liberties of the individuals whose behavior is being predicted (American Bar Association, 1989). Conversely, there are the potential victims whose safety also requires consideration. The prediction of dangerousness, as tenuous as it may be, is nonetheless expected by society. Indeed, it is required by law (e.g., *Tarasoff v. Regents of the University of California*).

States typically define what is required to suspend certain civil rights of individuals who meet certification criteria for involuntary psychiatric hospitalization. These criteria provide good examples for the operationalization of a crisis situation. Michigan and Texas, for example, allow the involuntary hospitalization of individuals who, due to disease (e.g., mental illness) or defect (e.g., cognitive limitations), are in imminent danger of harming themselves or others, or who pose a risk to themselves by virtue of not being able to care adequately for themselves (e.g., aimlessly wandering in traffic, not eating). Federal law, in addition to dangerousness, also considers significant threat to property as a criteria worthy of intervention. Other forms of intervention against the will of persons involved would be removal of children or the aged from an abusive or neglectful home, or guardianship for persons who are no longer competent to manage their own affairs. Crisis intervention professionals should acquaint themselves with the statutes in their jurisdictions that impact their practice.

At the organizational level, policies and procedures often define what constitutes an emergency, and set protocol, or a plan of intervention, for workers to follow. While agency policies and procedures can help in the decision-making process, they can also be a source of frustration for the crisis intervention professional. For example, when the present author worked in emergency mental health services, his area (i.e., the area served) was the entire county. If a call was received from outside the county, the unit could not respond. This helped determine the client population; however, it sometimes led to frustrating remarks and actions from angry family members and law enforcement personnel. People seem to expect helpers to have no boundaries ("Aren't you supposed to help?," "You're not much of a helper!"), including areas and skills, and can become quite irate when counseled to contact the appropriate authority.

At the individual level, the boundaries of what constitutes crisis intervention can become blurred. Each of us will interpret what constitutes a crisis on the basis of our own personalities, experiences, and philosophies. It is not difficult for an agency to define an emergency, or how a particular emergency is to be managed. It is much more difficult for an individual professional to inform people that they will be placed in protective custody, that they are going to the state hospital against their will, that their child is to be removed from their home, or that a loved one has committed suicide. These, and other similar, experiences tend to shape our beliefs of what constitutes crises and crisis intervention, and also shape our perceptions of what aspects of crisis intervention are stressful to us.

CONCLUSION

Human nature requires us to help one another. This is the basis of crisis intervention, though its academic origins can be found as late as the early twentieth century. Original studies conducted by Quierdo, Lindemann, Erickson, and Caplan provide groundwork upon which modern crisis theory is based. The 1960s and 1970s were a time of application and growth. Government assistance enabled programs of all forms to spring up across the country. Only recently, however, has the criminal justice system been a focus of crisis intervention activity. This is a trend that is likely to expand and grow as criminal justice officers and administrators realize the effectiveness of intervention techniques in preventing further crime and/or crisis situations. Today, crisis intervention is a respected and effective therapy used by trained professionals who take a sincere interest in assisting those in need. While it is critical to examine the stress and stress-related reactions of crisis clients, we must also consider the potential stress helpers might experience as well.

ACKNOWLEDGMENTS

Mr. Michael W. Thomas contributed to an earlier version of this chapter. Dr. Timothy Wynkoop contributed information on stress and burnout for this chapter. We thank both of them for their contributions.

CHAPTER QUESTIONS

1. In what fields did crisis intervention begin? When was the shift and where can it be found today?
2. List at least five common elements present during most crises as well as at least five characteristics of people who are prone to them.
3. List some of the important skills necessary for proper intervention.
4. What is the primary goal of crisis intervention?
5. Provide a brief overview of the history of crisis intervention prior to 1970. In your answer include reference to the works of Lindemann, Erickson, Caplan, and Quierdo.
6. What are some facts that indicate there is a close relationship between crisis intervention and criminal justice?

CHAPTER EXERCISES

Exercise 1

As a victim advocate, you have been called to the emergency room of the hospital on a "rape call." What assessment information would you want to know right away (primary)? What assessment information can wait (secondary)?

Exercise 2

You are responding, as a member of a mobile crisis team, to a domestic violence case. How would you proceed in assessing the case?

Exercise 3

Crisis Intervention "Referral" Exercise–*Brainstorm* on all the possible referral and follow up services available to a victim of domestic violence. Examine the yellow pages of your local telephone directory to identify possible victim resources.

Exercise 4

To explore the meaning and significance of precipitating events, team up with a partner from class and engage in a brief assessment interview. One person will serve as the "client" and the other person will serve as the "crisis intervener." The person serving as the client may share a real crisis experienced at some point in his/her life or the client may construct one. In the former, the exercise will require some self-disclosure so both parties need to be comfortable. First, the "client" will share the nature of his/her "crisis." Second, the "intervener" will listen to the information and attempt to discover the nature of the precipitating event that prompted the crisis. It will be the job of the intervener to gain as much insight and information as possible about the precipitating event. While engaged in the exercise, the intervener needs to use the communication skills discussed in this chapter. At the close of the exercise the intervener and client will critique the encounter and discuss ways the intervener might have been more effective in assessing the nature and impact of the hazardous event.

Simulated Exercise 5

You are a police administrator in touch with the needs of line officers. You notice that stress seems to be mounting among the police department ranks in response to rising violent crime within the community, and the police mandate to respond to this problem. You propose to construct a plan to address the potential of stress-related problems within the department and the probable onset of burnout. What would be the key elements of your plan?

APPENDIX A

Additional Internet Resources

The following list provides information in regards to the historical and theoretical overview of crisis intervention. Furthermore, these websites present the reader with information specifically on crisis theory, individual crisis, types of crisis, and crisis intervention plans and management.

Business 2 Business Continuity:
  http://www.b2bcontinuity.com/
Nonprofit Risk Management Center
  http://www.nonprofitrisk.org
  http://www.nonprofitrisk.org/csb/csb_cris.htm
Crisis Theory & Crisis Intervention:
  http://hhd.csun.edu/shelia/433/433crisis.html
International Critical Stress Foundation, Inc.:
  http://www.icisf.org
Center for Grief:
  http://www.centerforgrief.com/
Crisis Intervention Services:
  http://www.cismc.org
Crisis Prevention Institute, Inc. (CPI):
  http://www.crisisprevention.com/
What is a Crisis? Lesson Outline:
  http://mil.ccc.cccd.edu/classes/humanservices102/lesson1.htm
New York City Alliance Against Sexual Assault, Crisis Intervention Fact Sheet:
  http://www.nycagainstrape.org/survivors_factsheet_21.html#7
2004 Minnesota State Statutes:
  http://www.revisor.leg.state.mn.us/stats/256B/0624.html
Criminal Justice Mental Health Consensus Project:
  http://www.consensusproject.org/topics/flowchart/ps03-on-scene-assessment
Office for Victims of Crimes, Pre-Crisis Planning for Local Communities:
  http://www.ojp.usdoj.gov/ovc/publications/infores/crt/chap14.htm
Crisis Intervention Network:
  http://www.crisisinterventionnetwork.com/index.html
Law Enforcement Wellness Association:
  http://www.cophealth.com/
Peer Support Training Institute:
  http://peersupport.com/

REFERENCES

Aguilera, D.C., Messick, J.M. & Farrell, M.S. (1970). *Crisis intervention: Theory and methodology.* St. Louis: C.V. Mosby.

American Bar Association. (1989). *ABA criminal justice mental health standards.* Washington, D.C.: Author.

Anderson, J.R. & Woodard, P.L. (1985). Victim and witness assistance: New state laws and the system's response. *Judicature, 68,* 6, 221–224.

Arthur, G.L., Sisson, P.J. & McClung, C.E. (1977). Domestic disturbances: A major police dilemma, and how one major city is handling the problem. *Journal of Police Science and Administration, 5,* 4, 421–429.

Baldwin, B.A. (1980). Styles of crisis intervention: Toward a convergent model. *Professional Psychology, 11,* 1, 113–120.

Baldwin, B.A. (1979). Training in crisis intervention for students in the mental health professions. *Professional Psychology, 10,* 2, 161–167.

Ballou, M. & Rebich, C. (1977). Crisis intervention: A call for involvement for the health professional. *The Journal of School Health, 47,* 10, 603–606.

Benjamin, A. (1987). *The helping interview.* Boston: Houghton Mifflin.

Bensinger, G.J. (1986). Victim assistance in Illinois: A case study. *International Journal of Comparative and Applied Criminal Justice, 10,* 2, 231–238.

Breslen, W. (1978). Police intervention in domestic confrontation. *Journal of Police Science and Administration, 6,* 3, 293–301.

Bunn, T.A. & Clarke, A.M. (1979). Crisis intervention: An experimental study of the effects of a brief period of counseling on the anxiety of relatives of seriously injured or ill hospital patients. *British Journal of Medical Psychology, 52,* 2, 191–195.

Burgess, A.W. & Baldwin, B.A. (1981). *Crisis intervention theory and practice: A clinical handbook.* Englewood Cliffs, NJ: Prentice-Hall, Inc.

Byers, B.D. (1987). Uses of clinical sociology in crisis intervention practice. *Clinical Sociology Review, 5,* 102–118.

Caplan, G. (1964). *Principles of preventive psychiatry.* New York: Basic Books.

Chau, K.L. (1991). Social work and ethnic minorities: Practice issues and potentials. *Journal of Multicultural Social Work, 1,* 1, 23–39.

Cohen, R.E. (1990). Post-disaster mobilization and crisis counseling: Guidelines and techniques for developing crisis-oriented services for disaster victims. In A.R. Roberts (Ed.), *Crisis intervention handbook: Assessment, treatment and research* (pp. 279–300). Belmont, CA: Wadsworth.

Cullen, F.T. & Gilbert, K.E. (1982). *Reaffirming rehabilitation.* Cincinnati, Ohio: Anderson.

Dershimer, F.W. (1928). A theory of the origin of all conflict and the mechanism of psychoanalysis. *Psychoanalytic Review, 15,* 2, 162–164.

Encarta World English Dictionary (2001). www.dictionary.msn.com.

Erickson, E.H. (1959). Identity and the life cycle. *Psychological issues monographs.* New York: International Universities Press.

Erickson, E.H. (1963). *Childhood and society* (2nd Edition). New York: W.W. Norton.

Finn, P. (1986). Collaboration between the judiciary and victim/witness assistance programs. *Judicature, 69,* 4, 192–198.

Finn, P. & Lee, B. (1985). Working with victim/witness assistance programs: Benefits for law enforcement. *The Police Chief, 52,* 6, 54–57.

Foxman, J. (1990). *A practical guide to emergency and protective crisis intervention.* Springfield, IL: Charles C Thomas, Publisher, Ltd.

France, K. (1990). *Crisis intervention: A handbook of immediate person-to-person help* (2nd Edition). Springfield, IL: Charles C Thomas, Publisher, Ltd.

Gilliland, B.E. (1997). *Crisis intervention strategies.* Pacific Grove, CA: Brooks/Cole.

Gilliland, B.E. & James, R.K. (1997). *Crisis intervention strategies* (3rd Edition). Pacific Grove, CA: Brooks/Cole.

Golan, N. (1978). *Treatment in crisis situations.* New York: Free Press.

Gordon, C. (1988). Crisis intervention: A general approach. In S.E. Hyman (Ed.), *Manual of psychiatric emergencies* (2nd Edition) (pp. 35–41). Boston: Little, Brown and Company.

Grando, R. (1975). An approach to family crisis intervention. *Family Therapy, 2,* 3, 201–214.

Grisso, T. & Appelbaum, P. S. (1992). Is it unethical to offer predictions of future violence? *Law and Human Behavior, 10,* 621–633.

Haywood, C.H. & Roy, R. (1975). Crisis intervention and community mental health systems. *Crisis Intervention, 6,* 1, 22–42.

Hendricks, J.E. (1982). A review of police training academy schedules. Unpublished manuscript.

Hendricks, J.E. & McKean, J.B. (2001). *Crisis intervention: Contemporary issues for on-site interveners* (3rd Edition). Springfield, IL: Charles C Thomas, Publisher, Ltd.

Hendricks, J.E. & McKean, J.B. (1995). *Crisis intervention: Contemporary issues for on-site interveners* (2nd Edition). Springfield, IL: Charles C Thomas, Publisher, Ltd.

Hendricks, J.E. (1985). *Crisis intervention: Contemporary issues for on-site interveners.* Springfield, IL: Charles C Thomas, Publisher, Ltd.

Hendricks, J.E. & Thomas, M.W. (1990, March). Police victim/survivor/witness training: A national study. Presented at the 1990 Meeting of the Academy of Criminal Justice Sciences.

Hoff, L.A. & Miller, N. (1987). *Programs for people in crisis.* Boston: Northeastern University Book Program.

Howard, F.M. (1932). A case study of mental conflict. *The Training School Bulletin, 28,* 175–178.

Kalafat, J. (1983). Training for crisis intervention. *Crisis Intervention, 1,* 55–69.

Lester, D. & Brockopp, G.W. (Eds) (1973). *Crisis intervention and counseling by telephone.* Springfield, IL: Charles C Thomas, Publisher, Ltd.

Lindemann, E. (1979). *Beyond grief. Studies in crisis intervention.* New York: Jason Aronson.

Lindemann, E. (1944). Symptomatology and management of acute grief. *American Journal of Psychiatry, 101,* 141–148.

Lindsay, R.S. (1975). *Crisis theory: A critical overview.* Nedlands, Western

Australia:Department of Social Work, University of Western Australia.

Lowman, J. (1979). Grief intervention and sudden infant death syndrome. *American Journal of Community Psychology, 7*, 6, 665–677.

Maguire, K. & Pastore, A.L. (1994). (Eds.) *Source book of criminal justice statistics 1993.* U.S. Department of Justice, Bureau of Justice Statistics, Washington, D.C.: USGPO.

Meese, E. II. (1987). Making victim/survivor assistance part of the criminal justice process. *The Police Chief, 54,* 12, 11.

Monahan, J. (1981). *Predicting violent behavior: An assessment of clinical techniques.* Beverly Hills: Sage.

Morrice, J.K.W. (1976). *Crisis intervention: Studies in community care.* Oxford: Pergamon.

Mossman, D. (1994). Assessing predictions of violence: Being accurate about accuracy. *Journal of Consulting and Clinical Psychology, 62,* 783–792.

Newfield, N.L. & Reish, J. (1975). Crisis intervention training for police: An innovative program. *Crisis Intervention, 6,* 4, 28–35.

Noesner, G.W. & Webster, M. (1997). Crisis Intervention: Using Active Listening Skills in Negotiations. *FBI Law Enforcement Bulletin, 66,* 8, p. 13.

Ogawa, B.K. (1999). *Color of justice: Culturally sensitive treatment of minority crime victims.* Boston: Allyn and Bacon.

Oppenheimer, J.R. (1967). Use of crisis intervention in casework with the cancer patient and his family. *Social Work, 12,* 2, 44–52.

OJJDP. (1998). *Combating fear and restoring safety in schools.* U.S. Department of Justice, Office of Juvenile Justice and Delinquency Prevention (OJJDP). Washington: U.S. Government Printing Office.

OVC. (2000). *Responding to terrorism victims: Oklahoma City and beyond.* U.S. Department of Justice, Office for Victims of Crime (OVC). Washington: U.S. Government Printing Office.

OVC. (1999). *Community crisis response.* U.S. Department of Justice, Office for Victims of Crime (OVC). Washington: U.S. Government Printing Office.

Parad, H.J. (1966). The use of time-limited crisis intervention in community mental health programming. *Social Service Review, 40,* 3, 275–282.

Quierdo, A. (1968). The shaping of community mental health care. *The British Journal of Psychiatry, 114,* 4, 293–302.

Rapoport, L. (1962). The state of crisis: Some theoretical considerations. *The Social Science Review, 36,* 211–217.

Roberts, A.R. (2000). *Crisis intervention handbook: Assessment, treatment, and research.* New York: Oxford University Press.

Roberts, A.R. (1990). *Crisis intervention handbook: Assessment, treatment, and research.* Belmont, CA: Wadsworth.

Romano, A.T. (1990). *Taking charge: Crisis intervention in criminal justice.* New York: Greenwood Press.

Shapland, J. & Cohen, D. (1987). Facilities for victim/survivors: The role of the police and the courts. *Criminal Law Review,* 28–38.

Slaikeu, K.A. (1990). *Crisis intervention: A handbook for practice and research* (2nd

Edition). Boston: Allyn and Bacon.

Tarasoff v. Regents of the University of California, 131 *California Reporter 14,* 551 P 2d 334 (1976).

Tidwell, R. (1992). Crisis counseling: A right and a necessity for members of the underclass. *Counseling Psychology Quarterly, 5,* 3, 245–249.

Wainrib, B.R. & Bloch, E.L. (1998). *Crisis intervention and trauma response.* New York: Springer Publishing.

Wells, C.B., Getman, R. & Blau, T.H. (1988). Critical incident procedures: Crisis management of traumatic incidents. *The Police Chief, 55,* 10, 70–76.

Wynkoop, T. F. (1995, June). Prediction of dangerousness. Symposium presentation, *Psychology and the Law,* The Johns Hopkins University School of Medicine, Baltimore.

Chapter 2

ETHICS IN CRISIS INTERVENTION PRACTICE

MICHAEL P. BROWN

INTRODUCTION

The roles and responsibilities of crisis interveners are as diverse as the people with whom they come into contact and the crises to which they respond. Crisis interveners include such diverse occupations as the clergy, physicians, nurses, teachers, law enforcement officers, prosecutors, judges, probation officers, victim advocates, social workers, and other mental health professionals. Together, these and other trained interveners compliment each other to provide a complete array of crisis services.

In spite of their occupational differences, crisis interveners tend to fall into two distinct groups. First-order crisis interveners help victims through the initial shock that follows crises. Second-order crisis interveners, on the other hand, provide services that help victims adapt, adjust, and grow from crises. Both first-order and second-order crisis interveners assist victims to become survivors.

Under "normal" circumstances, human social behavior is difficult to predict and control. It becomes even more complex when one considers the potential range of reactions that may follow crisis events that vary by type and severity, from natural disasters to criminal victimization. Similarly, not all interveners are equally skilled at responding to crisis events. For example, crisis interveners differ in terms of educational background, extent and type of training, and the competencies they possess. These differences exist not only between but also within occupational groups.

Professional differences are expected, especially when academic disciplines develop in the midst of competing philosophies and theories. However, a code of ethics defines a standard by which all professionals, within a particular occupation, are held. Regardless of the type of training one has received or the philosophy to which one subscribes, a professional code of ethics prescribes appropriate conduct and defines parameters within which professional decisions are made.

The purpose of this chapter is to analyze ethics in crime victim intervention practice. It does this by exploring the roles and responsibilities of law enforcement officers and social workers and examines how their respective professional codes of ethics characterize appropriate intervention strategies and provides for a continuum of support services for crime victims. The chapter concludes with an examination of ethical systems and how they relate to crisis intervention within the law enforcement and social work professions.

CRISIS INTERVENTION: PROCESS AND PRACTICE

The origin of crisis intervention has been traced to the nation's first suicide prevention center, established in 1906 in New York City (Roberts, 1991). This notable beginning epitomizes the nature and intent of crisis intervention, for to contemplate suicide suggests a reaction to a crisis event(s) that is beyond a person's adaptive capabilities. To effectively address an exigent problem it is essential that resources, external to the individual who is in crisis, are made available which assuage a crisis event.

According to Caplan (1961), an individual normally experiences homeostatic stability-a balance between the affective and the cognitive. When psychological, physiological, or social forces adversely affect this homeostatic state, an individual attempts to restore that preexisting balance through extant coping resources. An individual enters a state of crisis when a disturbance or an obstacle is not rectified by simply deploying their traditional repertoire of problem-solving activities (Caplan, 1961). It is at this juncture that intervention is necessary to achieve a relative state of cognitive and affective equilibrium. If intervention is unsuccessful, the result may be, at the very least, a "major disorganization of the personality . . ." (Blaufarb & Levine, 1972, p. 16).

At its most basic level, crisis intervention can be characterized as a process involving at least two individuals–a person in a state of crisis and a crisis intervener. To bring clarity to this complex process, researchers have attempted to identify factors that precipitate crisis events such as cognitive style (Cropley and Field, 1969), situational support systems (Fattah, 1979), and the nature of coping mechanisms (Canon, 1939; Bandura, 1977). Others have proposed clinical models, based upon psychological research and theory, to help effectuate the resolution of crises (see, for example, Dewey, 1910;

Caplan, 1964; Rapoport, 1967; Golan, 1978; Roberts and Schenkman-Roberts, 1990). Still others have argued that the personality characteristics of interveners, their motives, willingness to take risks in potentially volatile situations, and desire to help others are crucial determinants of effective crisis intervention (Foxman, 1990).

Understanding and appropriately responding to crises are complex endeavors. Crises take many forms. Crime victims range from victims of property crime to assault or rape and from homicide survivors to victims of stalking or harassment. Also, crime victims vary in the depth and breadth of coping resources from which they can draw. Hence, reactions may range from sublimation to hostility. Likewise, the ability of crisis interveners to respond to diverse situations and clientele vary by the depth and breadth of competencies and skills from which they can draw.

Although research has demonstrated that formal training improves the effectiveness of intervention (see for example, Arthur, Sisson, and McClung, 1977; Hendricks and Thomas, 1990) and that training in small groups which allows for active participation is most effective (Axelberd and Valle, 1979; Glauberman, 1976; Wright, 1977), there is no uniform standard—with regard to content and duration—for such training. While it is common for professional interveners to be trained in basic intervention techniques, some jurisdictions, due to the lack of commitment and/or resources, offer little or no formal training in specialized areas. Such specialized training includes how to intervene in crisis situations involving victims from diverse cultural backgrounds or how to effectively intervene in the crises of the elderly or very young.

Professional codes of ethics (discussed more fully later in this chapter) for persons working in human (or social) service occupations—e.g., criminal justice practitioners and human service workers—are intended to provide foundations upon which decisions are made when intervening in crises. Such codes accomplish this aim by delineating the roles and responsibilities of human service professionals, and they are based upon the notion that assistance is to be delivered without regard to beliefs, values, and prejudices (Reamer, 1982). Criminal justice professionals, for example, have a responsibility to intervene in matters involving the violation of criminal laws. Through its various components (i.e., police, courts, and corrections), the justice system attempts to protect members of society. Most often, however, the criminal justice response follows victimization. Hence, there are victims/survivors—of domestic assault, child abuse, and homicide survivors, for example. Criminal justice professionals are crisis interveners by virtue of their roles and responsibilities. As a consequence of their profession, criminal justice practitioners assist victims and survivors who are in crisis.

Similarly, the primary purpose of human service agencies is to help persons who are in need of assistance. According to Holland and Kilpatrick (1991, p. 138), "Social work exists because society is concerned about the vulnerable, the disenfranchised, the isolated, and the suffering." Human service agencies intervene in times of crisis and their clients include persons living in absolute poverty, the homeless, and those in need of psychological counseling. Human service agencies and their representatives may also attempt to provide relief to persons who receive assistance from the criminal justice system.

Therefore, professional codes of ethics provide the bases for making objective intervention decisions. Professional interveners must initially decide whether, in a given situation, intervention is appropriate. If such a determination is made, interveners must then ascertain when and how to intervene. Such decisions, fraught with ethical considerations and potentially influenced by a variety of factors (e.g., one's training and philosophical leanings), are rooted in the precepts of professional codes of ethics.

In recent years, ethics have increasingly come to the center of discussions concerning the decisions made by criminal justice professionals. For example, it has become customary to discuss the ethical conduct of law enforcement (Heffernan & Stroup, 1985) and correctional officers (Buckley, 1984). Moreover, concern over ethics extends beyond the behavior of practitioners to include those seeking careers in criminal justice and related fields. This matter was made poignantly clear when the Joint Commission on Criminology and Criminal Justice Education and Standards recommended ". . . required courses in the ethics of working in the criminal justice system" (Ward and Webb, 1984, p. 19).

Likewise, professional ethics have become a prevailing issue in other human service occupations, especially social work (Reamer, 1987). The impetus behind the concern over ethics, according to Reamer (1987), is an increase in complaints filed against human service professionals. Additionally, Reamer (1987, p. ix) contends that a ". . . greater understanding of the ethical context in which professionals' judgments often are made" has resulted in widespread debate regarding professional ethics. Consequently, practitioners and students preparing for careers in human service occupations should be exposed to ethical principles and how these relate to commonly encountered ethical dilemmas (Byers, Brown, and Jurkovac, 1995).

PRINCIPLES OF CRISIS INTERVENTION PRACTICE

Law enforcement officers and social workers are the foci of this chapter because, as crisis interveners, they represent a comprehensive intervention modality (see Table 2.1). First-order crisis intervention, according to Slaikeu (1990), is provided at the time and place crises occur. When crises are precipitated by criminal events, law enforcement officers are typically the first officials who come into contact with victims. As first-order interveners, law enforcement officers respond by providing psychological first aid.

Table 2.1. First- and Second-Order Crisis Intervention–A Comprehensive Model

	First-Order Intervention	*Second- Order Intervention*
Duration:	Minute/Hours	Weeks/Months
Profession:	Police	Social worker
Setting:	Community	Community/Clinical
Goals:	Provide support; reduce distress; refer to and/or establish linkages to helping resources.	Resolve crisis; integrate event into life; prepare for the future.
Intervention Strategy:	Psychological first aid	Multimodal crisis therapy

Source: Adapted from Slaikeu, K. (1990). *Crisis Intervention: A Handbook for Practice and Research* (2nd Edition), p. 102.

Psychological first aid involves creating a supportive and caring environment and ". . . referring the person in crisis to other helping resources" (Slaikeu, 1990, p. 102). The resolution of the crisis is not a goal pursued by first-order crisis interveners. Rather, this form of intervention should attempt to accomplish the following objectives:

1. *Make psychological contact*–It is important to enable the person in crisis to "Feel, heard, understood, accepted, and supported" (Slaikeu, 1990, p. 108). Attention should be paid to reducing the level of emotional distress experienced by the victim or survivor and to reactivating the victim's "problem-solving capabilities" (Slaikeu, 1990, p. 108).

2. *Explore dimensions of the problem*–After information has been gathered regarding the precipitating event, the victim's personal and social resources, lethality, and the decisions that must be made immediately and over the next several days and weeks, the crisis intervener should rank order the needs of the victim–"immediate needs" and needs to be addressed later (Slaikeu, 1990).

3. *Examine possible solutions*–"An attempt should be made to identify . . . solutions to [the victim's] immediate needs and later needs" (Slaikeu, 1990, p. 109). In order to accomplish this objective, the intervener

should determine what the victim has already attempted to solve the crisis and the options available to the victim (Slaikeu, 1990).

4. *Assist in taking concrete action*–Solutions to meet immediate problems should be set in motion. Such assistance may range ". . . from active listening to giving advice and . . . from actively mobilizing resources to controlling the situation (Slaikeu, 1990, p. 109).

5. *Follow-up*–Generally, two objectives are pursued. First, the intervener seeks to determine whether lethality is reduced, adequate support has been offered, and that resources have been established to meet the immediate needs of the victim or survivor (Slaikeu, 1990). Second, the intervener attempts to ensure that resources are available to meet the victim's/survivor's future needs (Slaikeu, 1990).

First-order crisis intervention is critical to law enforcement efforts and victims becoming survivors (Office for Victims of Crime, 2000). The initial contact will affect how victims adjust, not only to the immediate crisis but also how they adjust in the future. It will also determine the likelihood that a victim will later participate in the criminal investigation and prosecution (Office for Victims of Crime, 2000).

Where first-order crisis intervention ceases, second-order crisis intervention begins. Second-order crisis intervention is distinctly different from first-order intervention. It is a therapeutic endeavor in which social workers, for example, formally trained in short-term therapy, assist victims in resolving their crises (Slaikeu, 1990). Also referred to as multimodal crisis therapy, second-order crisis intervention accomplishes this aim by preparing individuals for the future. Therefore, a state of equilibrium is reestablished–one which reflects the totality of life experiences, including the crisis event (Slaikeu, 1990).

Multimodal crisis therapy is traditionally performed in a formal counseling setting. It is oriented toward addressing four dimensions of crises, each of which is viewed as being critical in reestablishing a sense of equilibrium following crisis events. According to Slaikeu (1990, p. 143), second-order interveners should attempt to help their clients to: "(a) physically survive the crisis experience, (b) identify and express feelings that accompany the crisis, (c) gain cognitive mastery over the crisis, and (d) make a range of behavioral and interpersonal adjustments necessitated by the crisis."

Although it is helpful to conceptualize crisis intervention as a process involving psychological first aid and multimodal crisis therapy, they are abstract concepts in need of further explanation. To gain insight into the principles of crisis intervention, and to the roles and responsibilities of crisis interveners, it is fruitful to review research that has explored crisis intervention for persons who come into contact with the criminal justice system.

THE LITERATURE

Crisis intervention research in criminal justice has traditionally studied offenders. For example, Beigel and Russell (1972) and Farberow (1980a & b) have, after extensive study, expounded upon the need to more adequately train jail personnel (correctional officers) on the dangers of suicide, especially among newly incarcerated inmates. These researchers have noted that there are a number of events—such as feelings of shame, the loss of social support systems, and the deleterious and dangerous environment existing in jails—that bring about crises for offenders.

Likewise, a number of crises have also been identified among newly released inmates who reenter society after having served many years of confinement. The extent to which such releases bring about crises depends upon the strength of the offender's social support system while imprisoned (Kantor and Caron, 1978). The transition from incarceration to free society is especially difficult for persons who lack the skills necessary to effectively compete in the job market. Speer (1974) recommends job placement and training services to mitigate these feelings of crisis for parolees. Contemporary correctional practices reflect Speer's (1974) recommendation, frequently requiring parolees to participate in job training and placement programs.

Crisis intervention for crime victims has also been extensively researched, with emphases primarily placed upon rape victims/survivors and victims/survivors of domestic violence. Sutherland and Scherl (1976) indicate that rape victims/survivors tend to react in a predictable pattern consisting of three stages:

1. Stage #1: The victim/survivor is in a state of shock over the occurrence of the rape.
2. Stage #2: The victim/survivor attempts to return to her normal routine and, in the attempt to do so, may suppress feelings of crises.
3. Stage #3: The victim/survivor may attempt to begin to resolve the crisis brought about by the rape by talking about the incident. Feelings about the rape may also be expressed through the victim's/ survivor's behavior.

During each stage the client is responsive to crisis intervention and, therefore, professional interveners should be aware of the behaviors (or reactions) concomitant with each stage. For example, during the first stage victims/survivors may need assistance in deciding whether or not to involve the justice system (Slaikeu, 1990). Victims/survivors may also need help in notifying friends or family members of the rape. As victims enter the second stage, they may refuse assistance. Interveners must stand at the ready when this stage is entered, as assistance may later be requested (Slaikeu, 1990). Depression characterizes the third stage; the need for counseling becomes acute (Slaikeu, 1990).

Knowledge of crisis stages is of vital importance to those who initially come into contact with rape victims, such as law enforcement officers (Slaikeu, 1990). Crisis intervention experts agree that intervention should be offered immediately following a crisis event. When this is accomplished, intervention efforts are most likely to be effective (Golan, 1978). Social workers or other professional human service interveners who come into contact with rape victims/ survivors must also be aware of the stages of crisis in order to accurately determine which support services are most needed by the victim (Slaikeu, 1990).

Research on victims/survivors of domestic violence, which includes child and spouse abuse, has been instructive as to how crisis interveners can reduce the risks of future victimization (see, for example, Borgman, Edmunds, and MacDicken, 1979; Helfer and Kempe, 1976; Romano, 1990; Steinmetz and Straus, 1974; Straus, 1976). These studies indicate that intervention should focus on (1) relieving the physical and psychological trauma associated with domestic violence and (2) establishing support services and developing coping resources for the abuser to lessen the likelihood of reabuse.

Crisis intervention research has also explored the trauma associated with being a victim of property crime. Crisis intervention for victims of property crime may be especially difficult for professional interveners (Romano, 1990). Whereas interveners may intuitively appreciate the anguish and distress which accompanies rape and domestic violence, Romano (1990) contends that interveners may minimize crises precipitated by property loss. According to the "Crime-Crisis Continuum" developed by Hendricks and Greenstone (1982), rape and assault offenses are among the most traumatic for victims/survivors; property crimes are the least traumatic. Additionally, the extent of the crisis is dependent on the victim's/survivor's individual perception of the precipitating event e.g., crime (Hendricks and Greenstone, 1982). Likewise, the seriousness of a crisis is contingent on the intervener's perception of the precipitating event (Hendricks and Greenstone, 1982).

To the intervener, property loss may simply be seen as the loss of monetary resources. However, to the victim, the value of the item consists of more than its monetary value and includes sentimental value and the inconvenience associated with the loss (Romano, 1990). These conflicting perspectives can heighten the feelings of crisis, and they are therefore counterproductive to the intervention process. It is for this reason that Romano (1990) asserts that the intervener must empathically view the circumstances surrounding the loss of property from the victim's perspective.

PROFESSIONAL ETHICS

Considering the vulnerability of crime victims, their need for assistance, and the fragile crisis intervention process, it is imperative that professional codes of ethics are thoroughly expounded upon and evaluated for their utility in crisis intervention practice. Earlier in this chapter, professional codes of ethics were described as providing a framework within which decisions are made in the performance of one's duties. Codes of ethics were also described as the basis from which objective intervention decisions are made. Although accurate, these characterizations provide only a glimpse of the intent and purpose of professional codes of ethics.

Codes of ethics have an external function. That is, they can be interpreted as promises or vows to meet specified minimum standards of conduct. Therefore, as a form of external regulation, professional codes of ethics encourage predictable and competent behaviors. While these codes are intended to guide behavior, their main purpose is to serve as a road map for ethical decision making and practice based on the discretion of each practitioner.

The public expects those who have vowed to affirm the precepts of professional codes of ethics to do so without fail. It feels betrayed by the unethical conduct of professionals, especially human service providers such as law enforcement officers and social workers, who have promised to conduct themselves with integrity. Consequently, to regain the publics' trust and as an additional measure of external control, citizens have been invited to assist in the evaluation of professional conduct.

Civilian review boards, for example, may be asked to investigate, adjudicate, and recommend courses of action against law enforcement officers who are found to have acted unprofessionally (Gaines, Sutherland, and Angel, 1991). The establishment of ethics committees is another course of action that has been taken to help assure that professional duties are performed ethically. However, contrary to civilian review boards, which respond to claims of ethical misconduct, ethics committees are proactive. Acting solely in an advisory fashion, ethics committees in social work deliberate ethical dilemmas which are encountered in the course of performing one's occupational duties (Reamer, 1987). The final decision, then, regarding the course of action to be taken, resides with the individual social worker.

Professional codes of ethics, even when taken in concert with the insights contained within the recommendations of civilian review boards or ethics committees, are not sufficient to resolve commonly encountered ethical dilemmas (Reamer, 1987). Ethical dilemmas are complex phenomena, which cannot be resolved by simply turning to formal behavioral prescriptions. For this reason, some scholars have proposed that more time and effort should be devoted to teaching ethics (Jones, Owens, and Smith, 1995).

According to Jones, Owens, and Smith (1995), the contemporary movement toward community policing exemplifies the need for teaching ethics to prospective and veteran police officers. Law enforcement officers have traditionally exercised vast discretion in the performance of their duties. "With the advent of community-based policing, traditional methods of control and accountability may be even less effective than before. Community policing decentralizes police authority [i.e., supervision] . . ." (Jones, Owens, and Smith, 1995, p. 23) and therefore requires police officers to exercise even greater discretion than before.

The potential for unethical conduct increases as the use of discretion increases. Therefore, from recruits participating in basic training to veteran law enforcement officers and administrators who receive advanced (in-service) training, a priority needs to be placed upon the ". . . core ethical values of policing, such as honesty, fidelity, and personal integrity . . ." (Jones, Owens, and Smith, 1995, p. 25). The assumption underlying such training is that police officers will internalize the values that are necessary to conduct themselves in an ethical manner.

The teaching of ethics to social workers has a similar goal–the internalization of what is fundamentally ethical given the situation at hand. The emphasis placed on ethics training for social workers acknowledges that codes of ethics are insufficient to arrive at an ethical conclusion to complex situations. The priority placed on ethics training also acknowledges that past training has been inadequate in preparing social workers to meet occupational demands.

Although professional codes of ethics have limited external utility, and need to be augmented through training and review boards, they are said to have numerous internal functions. In fact, ". . . it is becoming increasingly common for codes [of ethics] to be used as internal documents, setting out guidelines for individual providers and managers, and developing organizational or professional commitment or cohesion" (Kleinig and Zhang, 1993, p. 13). For example, codes of ethics might represent a minimum standard of commitment and/or behavior to which professionals aspire (Kleinig & Zhang, 1993). Codes of ethics may also improve occupational performance by advancing a ". . . shared culture or ethos . . .", which in turn may foster." . . . associational ties and organizational cohesion . . ." (Kleinig & Zhang, 1993, p. 14). Furthermore, ". . . codes of ethics . . . [frequently] function as the core of or framework for the ethical training of service providers" (Kleinig and Zhang, 1993, p. 15).

Ethical Systems

Whether considering professional codes of ethics, ethical recommendations proposed by ethics committees, or ethics as part of basic and advanced law enforcement training, ethical systems serve fundamental purposes. Ethical systems define behaviors as "right" and "wrong" (Pollock, 1994). They are characterized by Baelz (1977) as:

1. *Prescriptive.* Ethical systems define appropriate behavior and therefore impact upon how we live.
2. *Authoritative.* Ethical systems are not subject to debate; they are beyond question.
3. *Universal.* Ethical systems define what is wrong for all persons; relativity is logically incongruent with ethical systems.
4. *Not being self-serving.* Ethical systems are oriented toward what is in the best interests of others.

Five ethical systems are commonly discussed in the literature: religious ethics, ethical formalism, utilitarianism, egoism, and ethical relativism (Pollock, 1994). However, the application of Baelz's (1977) characterization of ethical systems includes only three: religious ethics, ethical formalism, and utilitarianism. Egoism is exempted from formal consideration as an ethical system because it promotes individual self-interests (Pollock, 1994). Ethical relativism is likewise excluded because it is contrary to the notion that ethical systems are authoritative. Instead, ". . . what is good changes depending on the values and life circumstances of the individual or group . . ." (Pollock, 1994, p. 29).

For these reasons, this chapter considers how religious ethics, ethical formalism, and utilitarianism contribute to professional codes of ethics. The following is not an attempt to thoroughly describe these ethical systems. Rather, general principles are introduced in order to provide the reader with a basic knowledge of what each system postulates.

Religious Ethics: As an ethical system, religious ethics assumes the existence of a perfect, rational, and willful God. Due to God's perfect character, his will is beyond question. ". . . [W]hat is right and good cannot be questioned as long as it comes from the authority of God" (Pollock, 1994, p. 14). Similarly, proponents of religious ethics ordinarily assume a legalistic perspective which is predicated on the notion that what is "wrong is always wrong" (Pollock, 1994).

Ethical Formalism: This ethical system rests on the belief that rules accompany social roles, and as long as everyone follows those rules there will be social order (Pollock, 1994). Kant (1949), the principal proponent of ethical formalism, asserts two ethical imperatives. Categorical imperatives place importance on the intent of one's actions, not on the result of actions.

This dictum, which stands at the center of ethical formalism, is deontological since ". . . the important determinant for judging an act to be moral or not is not its consequences but only the motive or intent of the actor" (Pollock, 1994, p. 19). Parenthetically, hypothetical imperatives are concerned with actions which facilitate certain ends–actions which would, for example, advance the greatest good for the greatest number. Teleological approaches, such as utilitarianism, epitomize hypothetical imperatives (Pollock, 1994).

Utilitarianism: This ethical system defines good actions by the consequences they bring (Pollock, 1994). As Pollock (1994) explains, actions are judged by the extent to which they contribute to the good of the majority. Utilitarianism takes two forms. Act utilitarianism is concerned with the act itself, and emphasizes the examination of the utility of the act for all persons it somehow touches (Pollock, 1994). Rule utilitarianism is similarly concerned with the utility of actions, but it also encourages the consideration of the precedent set by actions (Pollock, 1994). Therefore, rule utilitarianism is concerned with the long-term effects of actions.

PROFESSIONAL CODES OF ETHICS AND THE BASES OF ETHICAL SYSTEMS

The Law Enforcement Code of Ethics

An examination of the *Law Enforcement Code of Ethics,* by the International Association of Chiefs of Police (1992) (see Appendix A), reveals the central tenets of ethical formalism. For example, as a professional code of ethics, there is an emphasis on performing the role of law enforcement officer and living within the law, rebuffing the temptations that might lead one to accept bribes and gratuities. As its categorical imperative, the law enforcement code of ethics indicates that police officers are motivated to provide service to the community. Numerous examples exist of hypothetical imperatives. For instance, law enforcement officers are to relentlessly prosecute criminals and to cooperate with other law enforcement agencies in the pursuit of justice.

Examples of utilitarianism are also found within the law enforcement code of ethics. To act in such a way as to obtain the greatest good for the greatest number, law enforcement officers should strive to achieve the objectives and ideals the code espouses. Police officers are also to be mindful of others' welfare and, simultaneously, improve their knowledge and competence so as to better serve the public. Evidence of act utilitarianism is found within the law enforcement code of ethics (e.g., the taking of actions to safeguard the lives and property of citizens), as is rule utilitarianism (e.g., to respect the constitutional rights of all citizens). Conversely, although police officers dedicate themselves to law enforcement before God, the precepts of religious ethics do not inform the law enforcement code of ethics. Indeed, there is no presumption that the law enforcement code of ethics reflects God's will.

Social Work Code of Ethics

The *National Association of Social Workers Code of Ethics* (1999) (see Appendix B) is based upon ethical formalism. The specificity with which it defines the roles and responsibilities of social workers illustrates the centrality of this ethical system. The categorical imperative of the social workers code of ethics is found in the statement that indicates that the social worker's primary responsibility is to the client. Moreover, social workers should serve their clients with devotion, loyalty, determination, and the maximum application of professional skill and competence. An example of a hypothetical imperative is found in the code as part of the discussion of the present and future of social work. According to the social workers code of ethics, the social worker should uphold and advance the values, ethics, knowledge, and mission of the profession.

Utilitarian principles are also found in the social workers code of ethics. By way of example, the code indicates that social workers should help bring social service to the general public. Act utilitarianism is exemplified in the notion that for social workers to be most effective in performing their duties, they should base intervention upon recognized knowledge relevant to the issue(s) at hand. Rule utilitarianism is likewise represented in the social workers code of ethics, and can be found where it states, for example, that social workers should advocate changes in policy to improve social conditions and to promote social justice. Another example of rule utilitarianism is found in the statement: social workers should act in ways that expand choice and opportunity for all persons. There is no discernible influence of religious ethics on the social workers code of ethics.

PROFESSIONAL CODES OF ETHICS AND CRISIS INTERVENTION PRACTICE: EXPLICIT AND IMPLICIT DICTUMS

Although law enforcement officers have been characterized as first-order crisis interveners (Slaikeu, 1990) and the ethical systems (ethical formalism and utilitarianism) upon which they perform their duties are congruent with the role of intervener, the law enforcement code of ethics seems silent as to the police officer's role as intervener. However, one might argue that the law enforcement code of ethics implicitly suggests that police officers are crisis interveners. For example, service to the community, a fundamental duty of law enforcement officers, may logically include crisis intervention. Likewise, the axiom stipulating the duty of law enforcement officers to protect the innocent against deception, the weak against oppression or intimidation and the peaceful against violence and disorder could be characterized as intervention. Therefore, the law enforcement code of ethics embodies the nature, purpose, and duties of police work, of which crisis intervention is a component.

The National Association of Social Workers Code of Ethics is explicit in defining the role of the second-order crisis intervener. Whereas the code does not expressly describe intervention modality, it does specify the types of behaviors that impact upon the effectiveness of intervention. For example, the code places a priority on the professional social worker to strive to become and remain proficient in their professional duties. In addition, the social worker is encouraged to resist the pressures and influences that have the potential to interfere with the exercise of professional discretion and judgment. Furthermore, the social worker is warned to avoid relationships or commitments that conflict with the interests of clients.

ETHICS IN CRISIS INTERVENTION PRACTICE

To this point in the chapter, ethics have been dealt with in a theoretical or philosophical fashion. As indicated earlier, the purpose of this chapter was to examine the role of professional codes of ethics in crisis intervention practice for law enforcement officers and social workers. The following scenario attempts to demonstrate how the roles and responsibilities of law enforcement officers and social workers are influenced by their respective codes of ethics.

History and Precipitating Events

Mary and Robert have been married for three years. Mary has two sons, Jim and Ryan, from a previous marriage. Mary and Robert have a two-month-old infant son, Benjamin.

A neighbor, after having witnessed Robert chase Ryan out of their home, spank him, and carry him back into the house, called the police out of fear for Ryan's safety.

Crisis Intervention and the Police

Upon arriving at the home of Mary and Robert, Officer Smith heard a child crying from within the residence. Officer Smith was greeted at the front door by Robert who was visibly upset, with a flushed face and out of breath. Upon hearing why Officer Smith was called to his home, Robert became defensive and informed Officer Smith that nothing had happened and that whatever occurs within his home was his business and his alone.

Officer Smith asked to speak with Mary, who was visible from the front door holding a crying child. Mary invited Officer Smith into the house and explained that her child, Ryan, had fallen recently while playing outside; he had skinned his knees and bumped his head on a tree. Robert, still upset, indicated that Ryan and his brother, Jim, were accident-prone and were always hurting themselves. Robert also mentioned that he hoped that Benjamin would not be as clumsy when he grew up.

Based upon the neighbor's report and Robert's visible anger, Officer Smith informed Robert and Mary that he was concerned about the safety of the children. Upon hearing this, Robert shouted at Officer Smith–there was nothing he needed to be concerned about. Mary began to cry.

Upon inspection, Officer Smith determined that Ryan was not in need of medical treatment for his skinned knees and bump on his head. There were no definitive signs of abuse. When Mary was asked whether Ryan or the other children were being hit by Robert, Officer Smith received a stern "no." Deciding not to arrest Robert at that time, Officer Smith devoted his energies toward reducing the pervasive tension within the home.

After consoling Mary, Officer Smith asked if there was a friend or relative who would be willing to take the children for the night. Mary informed Officer Smith that her mother lives in town and frequently takes the children to "give her and Robert a break." The children were brought to Mary's mother's home. Before Officer Smith departed, he informed Mary that a social worker would contact her to further inquire into Robert's behavior toward Ryan and the other children.

Crisis Intervention and Social Work

The following afternoon, Rose, a social worker at the community mental health clinic, visited Mary at her home. In a much more calm and rational mood than the previous day, and in the absence of Robert, Mary admitted that her husband sometimes lost his temper with Ryan and Jim, occasionally resulting in the children being harmed. Furthermore, she stated that Robert had never lost his temper with Benjamin, their two-month-old son. Mary also admitted that she and Robert recognized that his behavior was a problem and that six months earlier they had enrolled in a parenting class. However, two weeks ago, Robert convinced Mary to leave the class because "it was not helpful."

Rose, inquiring about Jim and Ryan's father, learned that Mary and her first husband had recently agreed to a change in custody. In less than two months, Jim and Ryan's father would be the custodial parent and they would permanently move to their father's home. Upon hearing this, Rose suggested that the children move to their father's home earlier than planned and that Mary and Robert meet with her over the next several months to address Robert's expression of anger. Rose stressed that it was imperative that Robert learn to control his anger before Benjamin became the next target of his frustration. Mary agreed to allow Jim and Ryan to move to their father's home earlier than originally planned and set a time to meet with Rose when both she and Robert could attend.

Crisis Resolution

Although the immediate crisis was diffused by removing Ryan and Jim from their mother's home, the process of crisis intervention is not complete. Ryan and Jim, their mother, Mary, and their stepfather, Robert, will all need counseling. Indeed, Ryan and Jim's father may be in need of counseling once he learns of what has been happening to his children. In the interest of brevity, these issues are not discussed here. Rather, the fictitious events described above are used as an illustration for a brief discussion of ethics in crisis intervention.

Officer Smith, in accordance with the law enforcement code of ethics, used his discretion to safeguard the lives of citizens and to protect the weak and vulnerable from violence and disorder. Officer Smith demonstrated that he was mindful of the welfare of others. Officer Smith's performance was ethical and his decision to intervene in the interest of protecting Ryan and Jim appears to have been effective. Likewise, Rose's professional conduct conformed to the social workers code of ethics. Moreover, her primary interests rested with her clients—Ryan and Jim.

CONCLUSION

Crisis intervention practice is best understood as a process, one that necessitates a diversity of skills, skill levels, and the thoughtful exercise of discretion. Professional codes of ethics provide insight to the public and direction to professionals as to roles and responsibilities that must be fulfilled in the wake of crisis events. Some codes of ethics are explicit in their charge; others require interpretation.

Notwithstanding, professional codes of ethics are recognized as having limited utility. The public has called for deliberate attention to be paid to the apparent increase in breaches of professional ethical conduct. In response, professional and political initiatives have been set into motion to appease public outcry as well as to establish ethical standards and to effectively address ethical misconduct. With these goals in mind, perhaps educational endeavors hold the most promise in creating the ethical standards necessary to best serve those in crisis.

DISCUSSION QUESTIONS

1. Describe the nature and intent of professional codes of ethics.
2. Compare and contrast psychological first aid with multimodal crisis intervention.
3. Discuss the purposes of teaching ethics to law enforcement officers and social workers.
4. Compare and contrast religious ethics, ethical formalism, and utilitarianism.
5. Discuss how ethical systems contribute to professional codes of ethics.
6. Specify the categorical imperatives of the law enforcement code of ethics and social workers code of ethics.
7. Provide examples of hypothetical imperatives in the law enforcement and social work codes of ethics.

SIMULATED EXERCISES

Simulated Exercise 1

Develop a professional code of ethics for law enforcement officers and social workers based solely on religious ethics.
   a. Which religious belief system is most appropriately used when developing a code of ethics? Why?
   b. Are there contradictions within the religious belief system that has been chosen that make it difficult to construct a professional code of ethics? If so, what are they?

Simulated Exercise 2

Develop a training session in ethics for law enforcement officers and social workers.
   a. Describe its content matter.
   b. What would the training session emphasize?

Simulated Exercise 3

Critically examine the law enforcement code of ethics and the social workers code of ethics. What (if anything) needs to be added to promote ethical and more effective crisis intervention practice?

Simulated Exercise 4

In the section entitled "Ethics in Crisis Intervention Practice," what could Officer Smith have done differently given the situation, and still acted ethically? What could Rose, the social worker, have done differently, and still acted ethically?

Simulated Exercise 5

After careful review of the law enforcement code of ethics and the social workers code of ethics, list in order of importance the ethical principles they espouse.

APPENDIX A

Additional Internet Resources

The following links offer the reader with further information on the ethics in crisis intervention practice more specifically, principles and professional ethics which include various codes of ethics.

National Association of Social Workers:
    http://www.naswdc.org/pubs/code/default.asp
American Psychological Association:
    http://www.apa.org/ethics/homepage.html
The Institute for Criminal Justice Ethics:
    http://www.lib.jjay.cuny.edu/cje/html/forensicscience.html
Criminal Justice Program Code of Ethics:
    http://www.centralia.ctc.edu/Depts/CriminalJustice/ethics.shtml
National Association of Blacks in Criminal Justice:
    http://www.nabcj.org/about%5Fcode.html
Paul's Criminal Justice Page, Criminal Justice Ethics:
    http://www.paulsjusticepage.com/cjethics.htm
The International Association of Chiefs of Police:
    http://www.theiacp.org/profassist/ethics/focus_on_ethics.htm
Academy of Criminal Justice Sciences:
    http://www.acjs.org/pubs/167_671_2922.cfm
Northeastern Association of Criminal Justice Sciences:
    http://www.neacjs.org/
Association of Traumatic Stress Specialists:
    http://www.atss-hq.com/about_us/code.cfm
British Society of Criminology:
    http://www.britsoccrim.org/ethics.htm
Texas Department of Criminal Justice, Code of Ethics:
    http://www.tdcj.state.tx.us/ace/ethics/ethics-codeofethics.htm
Judges Association of Middle America:
    http://www.jamahome.org/web/judgeethics.htm
U.S. Courts.com, Code of Conduct:
    http://www.uscourts.gov/guide/vol2/ch1.html
Probation Officer's Association of Ontario, Inc.:
    http://www.poao.org/ethics.htm

American Probation and Parole Officer's Association:
  http://www.appa-net.org/about%20appa/codeof.htm
Indiana Victims Assistance Network:
  http://www.victimassistance.org/www/code.htm
Office of Victims of Crime:
  http://www.ojp.usdoj.gov/ovc/assist/nvaa/ch22meda.htm
American Counseling Association:
  http://www.counseling.org/resources/ethics.htm
Ontario Association of Social Workers:
  http://www.oasw.org/ENG/ETHICS.HTM

REFERENCES

Arthur, G., Sisson, P. & McClung, C. (1977). Domestic disturbances: A major police dilemma, and how one major city is handling the problem. *Journal of Police Science and Administration, 5,* 4, 42 1–429.

Axelberd, M. & Valle, J. (1979). Effects of family crisis intervention training on police behavior. *Journal of Crisis Intervention, 10,* 18–27.

Baelz, P. (1977). *Ethics and belief.* New York: Slabury Press.

Bandura, A. (1977). Cognitive processes mediating behavioral change. *Journal of Personality and Social Psychology, 35,* 3, 125–133.

Beigel, A. & Russell, H. (1972). Suicidal behavior in jail prognostic considerations. *Hospital and Community Psychiatry, 23,* 361–363.

Blaufarb, H. & Levine, J. (1972). Crisis intervention in an earthquake. *Social Work, 17,* 16–19.

Borgman, R., Edmunds, M. & MacDicken, R. (1979). *Crisis intervention: A manual for child protective workers.* Washington, D.C.: United States Department of Health, Education and Welfare, DHEW Publication.

Buckley, L. (1984). What does the future hold for criminology undergraduates in Canada: A look at past trends and future prospects. *Journal of Criminal Justice, 14,* 47–60.

Byers, B., Brown, M. & Jurkovac, T. (1995). Assessment of student learning and ethical dilemmas: Applications for criminal Justice education. Paper presented at the 1995 annual meeting of the Academy of Criminal Justice Sciences, Boston, MA.

Canon, W. (1939). *The wisdom of the body* (2nd Edition). New York: W.W. Norton & Co.

Caplan, G. (1961). *An approach to community mental health.* New York: Grune and Stratton.

Caplan, G. (1964). *Principles of preventive psychiatry.* New York: Basic Books.

Cropley, A. & Field, T. (1969). Achievement in science and intellectual style. *Journal of Applied Psychology, 53,* 132–148.

Delattre, E. (1989). *Character and cops: Ethics in policing.* Washington, D.C.: American Enterprise Institute for Public Policy Research.

Dewey, J. (1910). *How we think.* Boston: Heath Co.

Farberow, N. (1980a). Clinical developments in suicide prevention in the USA. *Crisis, 1,* 16–26.

Farberow, N. (1980b). *The many faces of suicide.* New York: McGraw-Hill.

Fattah, E. (1979). Some recent theoretical developments in victimology. *Victimology, 4,* 2, 198–213.

Foxman, J. (1990). *A practical guide to emergency and protective crisis intervention: Dealing with the violent and self-destructive person.* Springfield, IL: Charles C Thomas, Publisher, Ltd.

Gaines, L., Sutherland, M. & Angel, J. (1991). *Police administration.* New York: McGraw-Hill.

Golan, N. (1978). *Treatment in crisis situations.* New York: Free Press.

Glauberman, L. (1976). *Training the police in crisis intervention techniques.* Unpublished Doctoral Dissertation, Syracuse University.

Heffernan, W. & Stroup, T. (1985). *Police ethics: Hard choices in law enforcement.* New York: John Jay Press.

Helfer, R. & Kempe, C. (1976). *Child abuse and neglect: The family and the community.* Cambridge, MA: Ballinger Publishing Co.

Hendricks, J. & Greenstone, J. (1982). Crisis intervention in criminal justice. Paper presented at the 1982 annual meeting of the Academy of Criminal Justice Science, Louisville, KY.

Hendricks, J. & Thomas, M. (1990). Police victim/witness training. A national study. Paper presented at the 1990 annual meeting of the Academy of Criminal Justice Science, Denver, CO.

Holland, T. & Kilpatrick, A. (1991). Ethical issues in social work: Toward a grounded theory of professional ethics. *Social Work, 36,* 2, 138–144.

International Association of Chiefs of Police. (1992). The law enforcement code of ethics. *The Police Chief, LIX,* 1,15.

Jones, T., Owens, C. & Smith, M. (1995). Police ethics training: A three-tiered approach. *FBI Law Enforcement Bulletin,* June, 22–26.

Kant, I. (1949). *Critique of practical reason,* translated by L. Beck. Chicago, IL: University of Chicago Press.

Kantor, S. & Caron, H. (1978). Intensive crisis intervention with ex-cons: A controlled field experiment. Paper presented at the 1978 annual meetings of the American Psychological Association, Toronto, Canada.

Kleinig, J. & Zhang, Y. (1993). *Professional law enforcement codes: A documentary collection.* Westport, CT: Greenwood Press.

National Association of Social Workers. (1999). The National Association of Social Workers Code of Ethics (www.naswdc.org/code/ethics.htm).

Office for Victims of Crime. (2000). *First response to victims of crime.* Washington, D.C.: U.S. Department of Justice, Office of Justice Programs, Office for Victims of Crime.

Pollock, J. (1994). *Ethics in crime and justice. Dilemmas and decisions* (2nd Edition). Belmont, CA: Wadsworth.

Rapoport, L. (1967). Crisis-oriented short-term casework. *Social Service Review, 41,* 31–43.

Reamer, F. (1982). *Ethical dilemmas in social service*. New York: Columbia University Press.

Reamer, F. (1987). Ethics committees in social work. *Social Work*, May–June, 188–192.

Roberts, A. (1991). Conceptualizing crisis theory and the crisis intervention model. In A. Roberts (Ed.), *Contemporary perspectives on crisis intervention and prevention*. Englewood Cliffs, N.J.: Prentice-Hall, Inc.

Roberts, A. & Schenkman-Roberts, B. (1990). A comprehensive model for crisis intervention with battered women and their children. In A. Roberts (Ed.), *Helping crime victims and witnesses: Policy, practice, and research* (pp. 186–205). Newbury Park, CA: Sage.

Romano, A. (1990). *Taking charge: Crisis intervention in criminal justice*. Westport, CT: Greenwood Press.

Slaikeu, K. (1990). *Crisis intervention: Handbook for practice and research* (2nd Edition). Needham Heights, MA: Allyn and Bacon.

Speer, D. (1974). The role of the crisis intervention model in the rehabilitation of criminal offenders. *JS.A.S. Catalog of Selected Documents in Psychology, 4,* 133.

Steinmetz, S. & Straus, M. (1974). *Violence in the Family*. New York: Harper & Row.

Straus, M. (1976). Sexual inequality, cultural norms, and wife beating. In E. Viano (Ed.), *Victims and society*. Washington, D.C.: Visage Press.

Sutherland, S. & Scherl, D. (1976). Patterns of response among rape victims. In R. Moos (Ed.), *Human adaptation: Coping with the crisis*. Lexington, MA: D.C. Heath & Co.

Ward, R. & Webb, V. (1984). *Quest for quality*. New York: University Publications.

Wright, R. (1977). *Family crisis intervention training program internal evaluation report*. Washington, DC: Department of Justice LEAA, National Institute of Law Enforcement and Criminal Justice.

Chapter 3

DOMESTIC VIOLENCE

JANET E. MICKISH

The subject of spouse or partner abuse is a serious one in American society (Cardarelli, 1997; Harway and O'Neil, 1999) and for the criminal justice system. Spouse abuse, domestic violence, or partner abuse consists of an act of violence or psychological intimidation committed by a spouse, boyfriend, girlfriend, or cohabitating partner. The term "victim" is used to describe the person who has just been victimized or a person who has died as a result of the victimization. A survivor is a person who has been victimized and is working to gain a sense of control and autonomy. Survivor is the dominant term used in this chapter.

"Anyone who lives in a violent home experiences an essential loss. The one place on earth where they should feel safe and secure has become a place of danger . . . the shadow of domestic violence has fallen across their lives and they are forever changed" (U.S. Attorney General's Task Force Report on Family Violence, September 1984). Public and scholarly opinion about the appropriate role of the State as an arbiter of family disputes has undergone considerable revision in the past century, fueled in part by a growing awareness of the prevalence and magnitude of the domestic violence problem (NIJ/CDC, 2000; Family Violence: Interventions for the Justice System, October, 1993).

This chapter presents a discussion of our current knowledge about domestic violence. The chapter will help the intervener think about domestic violence in a comprehensive way. No two situations are ever the same. There are no formulas or simple answers to the "causes" or "elimination" of domestic violence. There is only the presentation of information that the intervener can apply to each new situation as it unfolds. While there are a variety of ways to define domestic violence–psychological, sociological, feminist–in

59

the context of this chapter, it will be defined in terms of applicable laws and criminal sanctions. Assault, battery, homicide, weapon use, kidnapping, rape, unlawful imprisonment, malicious mischief, harassment, reckless endangerment, tampering with a witness, restraining order violation, and trespassing are some of the most frequent crimes involved in domestic violence cases.

INTRODUCTION

Domestic violence has been a part of the American cultural landscape and an aspect of many marital relationships for millennia. An adult female today is more likely to be sexually assaulted, beaten, and killed in her own home at the hands of her male partner than anyplace else, or by anyone else in our society (Gelles and Straus, 1988; p. 18). In 1998, one-third of all female murder victims were killed by intimate partners (Meuer, Seymour, Wallace, 2000). According to the National Institute of Justice (Bachman, 1994), "On average each year, women experienced 572,032 violent victimizations at the hands of an intimate. . ." (p. 6). Moreover, it is estimated that "Between 1.8 and 4.0 million American women are abused in their homes each year" (Bureau of Justice Assistance, 1993; p. 1).

Criminal justice agencies and courts have dealt with hundreds of thousands of overt (assault, battery, reckless endangerment) and hidden (divorce, child custody) cases of domestic violence, while denying that it should be of concern to them or to the public. Within the past 15 years there has been a change in the political climate as domestic violence has been increasingly recognized as a social problem worthy of public attention and action. In fact, much research has been devoted to the changing response to spousal abuse (Buzawa and Buzawa, 1992, 1996). It is, however, still shrouded in mystery and myth. People ask, "What does it mean?" "How could he do it?" "Why does she stay?" "Why are our homes and relationships so dangerous?" and "What can we do to stop the violence?"

Domestic violence occurs in every race, class, ethnic group, and life style. However, and according to available data, there may be differences in reported abuse based on race and education levels (Bachman, 1994). We do not know as much about domestic violence in same sex relationships as we do about its occurrence in heterosexual relationships. There is increasing evidence that it does exist between some same sex couples and is as lethal there as in heterosexual relationships (BLPC, 1987; Island and Letellier, 1991; Lobel, 1986; Renzetti, 1988). Moreover, research has demonstrated that women who live with intimate female partners experience less violence than women living with male partners (NIJ/CDC, 2000). We also know that 98 percent of all currently documented domestic assaults are committed by men against women. According to the FBI (1989), and based on comparable National Crime Victimization Survey data, family related violence against men accounts for no more than 5 percent of the combined violent victimization against males (Bachman, 1994; p. 6). This is confirmed by the NIJ/CDC (2000) study. Therefore, the perpetrator will be referred to as "he" and the survivor as "she" even though some domestic violence cases will involve people of the same sex and perhaps acts of domestic violence by women perpetrated against men, albeit both are rarer.

The emergency and crisis intervention personnel likely to be called to the scene are the police, fire fighters (rescue squad), emergency medical technicians, and, increasingly, victim/witness assistants from a local criminal justice agency or domestic violence program. It is important to understand that family violence—child, spouse, and elder abuse—is the only category of crime in which the perpetrator voluntarily remains on the scene, expecting no negative consequences for his behavior and perceiving your intervention as a violation of his rights. Normally, by the time police are first called to the scene, physical violence has occurred many times before.

NATURE AND EXTENT

With 50 percent of all marriages experiencing at least one episode of domestic violence (Straus et al., 1981), the family is "perhaps as or more violent than any other single American institution or setting (with the exception of the military . . . in time of war)" (Straus, 1981; p. 4). In 25 percent of homes where domestic violence occurs, the abuser will use violence against his female partner five or more times per year (Straus et al., 1981). The time a batterer is most likely to first use physical violence is when his wife is pregnant: 25 percent of battered women are pregnant (Gelles, 1979; Walker, 1979). Typically, each time the abuser uses violence, he increases the severity and intensity of his violence (Walker, 1979). It is not surprising, therefore, that the U.S. Surgeon General found domestic violence the leading cause of injury for women.

In 2000, the National Institute of Justice–United States Department of Justice, in conduction with the Centers for Desease Control (CDC), released findings from the National Violence Against Women Survey (NIJ/CDC, 2000). The survey utilized telephone interviews with a random sample of 8,000 U.S. women and 8,000 U.S. men. The results of the study include:

- Twenty-five percent of the surveyed women and 7.6 % of the surveyed men reported being raped, and/or physically assaulted during their life-

time by an intimate partner.
- 1.5 million women and 834,732 men reported such violence in the last 12 months.
- Estimates showed that there were 4.8 million intimate partner rapes and physical assaults are reported by women annually.
- There are 2.9 million intimate partner victimizations committed against men every year.
- Five percent of surveyed women and nearly one percent of surveyed men reported having been stalked by a current or former partner.
- Female intimate partner violence victims also often experience psychological abuse.
- Males who live with male partners experience more intimate violence than men who live with female partners.
- Most intimate partner violence is not reported to criminal justice authorities.

These statistics are telling of the nature and extent of domestic violence and partner abuse.

Domestic violence is widespread, deadly, and complex. In fact, "28 percent of all female murder victims [in 1991] were killed by their husbands or boyfriends" (Bureau of Justice Assistance, 1993; p. 1). In yet another report, however, nearly 40 percent of all female homicide victims were found to have been killed by a spouse or intimate partner while the statistic for male victims was only 9 percent (Roth, 1994). Battering occurs among all education, income levels and ages and in all races and ethnic groups. Domestic violence destroys lives, families, and communities. Often beginning subtly with a demeaning remark, sharp criticism, a push or shove, the foundation of intimidation and coercion is laid. As the abuser escalates the frequency and severity of his violence, the costs and effects spread in concentric circles outward, affecting every facet of American life.

The cost of battering to the victim/survivor, the children, the perpetrator, and society is staggering. For the person being abused, the cost may be her life. If she lives, she has a much higher rate of drug/alcohol abuse, depression, suicide and suicide attempts, anxiety, psychiatric disorders, miscarriage, medical/health problems (U.S. Surgeon General, 1985) and disabilities (Hickman, 1990). Personal crimes of assault cost survivors nearly $650 million dollars per year (Klaus, 1994). Moreover, it has been estimated that the average victim cost per "domestic" is about $21,000.00 (Cohen, 2000).

The cost to children is immediate and cumulative. The vast majority of children living in a household where their mother is abused are aware of or witness the physical abuse (Sonkin et al., 1985). To compound the child's trauma, the adult male who is beating his female partner is, typically, also beating his children (Bowker et al., 1988; Bureau of Justice Assistance, 1993). Accordingly, the probability of a man who was beaten as a child to engage in subsequent violence against an intimate is tenfold (Bureau of Justice Assistance, 1993). The immediate cost is a loss of a sense of safety. Children's behavior may "regress." They may get poor grades because they are unable to concentrate in school or do their homework. They may act out violent behaviors toward objects, animals, siblings, and schoolmates. As adults, males from these homes are more likely to beat their female partners and children (Gelles and Cornell, 1990) than males who come from nonviolent homes.

Men pay a price for their violence. The cost to men is the opposite of what they believe their violence will bring them. Batterers might experience increased isolation from themselves and others, increased anxiety, loss of self-esteem, loss of a feeling of power and control. They feel guilt, shame, humiliation, confusion, and fear (Lindsey, 1990). Ultimately, they lose their female partner and children—emotionally and/or physically. They may also lose thousands of dollars (legal fees), their jobs, their freedom, and their lives. The cost to the community and society is monumental. Medical expenses from domestic violence total at least three to five billion dollars annually; businesses forfeit at least another $100 million in lost wages, sick leave, lost productivity, and absenteeism. Millions in tax dollars are consumed by criminal justice and social services for those involved in domestic violence (Cohen, 2000).

While the financial costs are astonishing, the emotional cost is even more alarming. Communities, like individuals, experience a collective loss of safety. They feel anxiety and strain. When this happens, many people become increasingly isolated, believing they will find safety in hiding. As domestic violence increases, families flee their homes, leaving jobs and unpaid mortgages. Businesses fold when a batterer or survivor cannot fulfill business obligations. The tax base shrinks. Community funds that could be spent on education, services, physical improvements, and cultural programs are diverted to criminal justice agencies, "special education" programs for underachieving or disruptive students, and medical expenses. Much like Alice in Wonderland, the community feels that it is running as fast as it can to stay in the same place—and it is losing ground fast.

The discussion of domestic violence includes information about the victim/survivor as well as the perpetrator. Historically, only information about victims and survivors has been studied and presented. The result was a tendency to view domestic violence as a "victim" or "female" issue. By focusing on the survivor and "why she was beaten" or "why she stays," to the exclusion of addressing the batterer's responsibility for his violent behavior, the survivor became transposed; violence against her became, if not her fault, her responsibility. When we perpetuate the notion that his violence has something to do with her, we normalize his violence; we make it invisible. Making him and his behavior invisible allows battering to continue unabated. Unlike other crime scenes, the batterer is likely to be present when the police arrive. Understanding the perception, attitude, and behavior of batterers enables interveners to work in a safer, more efficient manner. Focusing only on what we can do to, for, with, and about the survivor is like a group of people huddled tightly around a woman all shifting to and fro trying to figure out how to help her be safe. The batterer, standing outside the circle, leisurely tosses hand grenades over the heads of the "helpers," scoring direct hits every time. We must, therefore, provide resources for the survivor and constraints along with negative sanctions against the perpetrator.

This chapter lays the foundation for understanding domestic violence as a social, institutional, and personal problem. Only by viewing it as such can we begin to develop, implement and maintain safe, effective strategies to stop domestic violence through empathic psychological aid and criminal justice intervention.

DOMESTIC VIOLENCE AND CRIMINAL JUSTICE

If domestic violence is so widespread and damaging, what is the criminal justice system doing about it? Inquiry into violence toward women in family relationships reveals that social institutions have historically protected and perpetuated the right of a man to act violently toward his wife and other "property" (Breslin, 1983; Eisenberg and Micklow, 1976; Herskowitz, 1966; Jensen, 1978; Lerman et al., 1981; Martin, 1976; Walker, 1979). Not surprisingly, that right has been maintained and reinforced throughout the criminal justice system by the police (Bannon, 1975; Berk and Newton, 1985; Dobash and Dobash, 1979; Langley and Levy, 1978; Scott, 1981), prosecutors (Lerman, 1981, 1986; U.S. Civil Rights Commission, 1982a, 1982b; Fields, 1978; Martin, 1978; Dobash and Dobash, 1979) and the courts (Jacobson, 1977; Parnas, 1970). However, there have been recent, innovative efforts to assist local criminal justice authorities in responding effectively to domestic violence (Bureau of Justice Assistance, 1993). Moreover, recent federal initiatives such as the *Violence Against Women Act of 1994,* making the crossing of a state line for the purpose of assaulting a spouse or domestic partner a federal crime, have helped bolster the cause of domestic violence.

Because this is a book about on-scene crisis intervention, our focus will be the initial law enforcement and victim/witness assistant response. Over the past decade and a half, a series of forces came together, reflecting and precipitating a dramatic shift in public attitudes, orientations, and policies about

domestic violence:
1. Scientific studies and reports about the nature, extent and response of the criminal justice system (e.g., U.S. Commission on Civil Rights, 1978, 1982a, 1982b; U.S. Department of Justice, 1980, 1986; U.S. Surgeon General, 1985; U.S. Attorney General, 1984; NIJ/CDC, 2000).
2. Lawsuits concerning the failure of the criminal justice system to respond to battered women (see next section).
3. Social action by a national domestic violence movement (Russell, 1982; Schecter, 1982).
4. Increased realization of how dangerous the scene of a domestic violence incident is to police (U.S. Department of Justice, 1986).
5. Increased documentation that criminal justice sanctions toward perpetrators helps reduce the number of initial incidents of domestic violence and recidivism (Bae, 1981; Bard, 1971; Carmody et al., 1987; Elk and Johnson, 1989; Gilles and Mederer, 1985; Hamberger, 1990; National Institute of Justice, 1986; Potter, 1978; Sonkin, 1987).

The shift has been from support for, to rejection of, male violence. Increasingly the criminal justice response now focuses on control of the perpetrator and protection for the survivor.

Litigation Against the Police

On December 8, 1976, twelve married battered women filed a class action complaint in New York against various New York City Police Department officials and employees of the New York City Family Court to enforce the defendants' obligations to provide assistance (*Bruno v. Codd* 47 NY 2d 582, 1979). This was to be the first in a long series of cases brought against–and lost by–the police in domestic violence cases for
1. Failing to respond to requests for assistance.
2. Refusal to arrest alleged perpetrators when there was probable cause to believe they had committed a crime.
3. Refusal to enforce orders of protection.
4. Generally, refusing to treat domestic violence cases the same way they treat cases of crimes outside the family (see NCWFL, Item no. 24, 1989, for a complete list of cases).

Administratively, the impact of these cases throughout the country has been the recognition that:
- Domestic violence is a dangerous crime and should be treated like other dangerous crimes.
- The nature, seriousness, and pervasiveness of domestic violence establishes a "special relationship" and a resulting "duty to protect" the alleged victim.

- The department discriminates against victims and survivors of domestic violence when it (implicitly or explicitly) encourages its officers to "defuse" domestic violence cases, using arrest as a last resort.
- New "pro-arrest" arrest policies and procedures are necessary.
- Officers must be adequately trained.

As a result of these changes, most police officers evaluate the situation and arrest the alleged perpetrator. A large number of officers, however, are beginning to arrest both the perpetrator and the survivor, alleging that, because it is too difficult for them to decide who the "real" perpetrator is, they will leave it to a judge to decide. Currently, communities are working to remedy this abuse of authority and discretion as new lawsuits are in the formative stages.

Additionally, victim/witness units have sprung up in police departments, sheriff's offices, and prosecutor's offices totaling over 4,000 (National Institute of Justice, 1988). Some 2,000 organizations provide direct domestic violence services (Saathoff and Stoffel, 1999). These units are designed to provide support and referrals for victims of crime—the majority of whom are survivors of domestic violence. Each jurisdiction provides different services within different time frames. Services range from immediate on–scene support to a contact by phone days or weeks later. Frequently (especially in rural areas) the victim/witness assistant is employed by a local domestic violence program and works in concert with the criminal justice system.

THEORETICAL OVERVIEW AND CONSIDERATIONS

Definitions and Terminology

Definitions help to frame the discussion. "Academic" definitions are presented here to establish a technical outline of the issues and their resolution. Each of us also harbors "emotional" definitions and responses to domestic violence. Rarely do the two definitions match. Many people (intervener as well as survivor and perpetrator) have been injured or killed and lawsuits lost because the intervener acted out of unresolved emotion rather than knowledge.

There are many ways to define domestic violence. Within the criminal justice system, it is defined in terms of applicable laws and criminal sanctions. There are also a variety of terms used to refer to adult-to-adult domestic violence. The most common include: family violence, battering, domestic assault, marital violence, spouse abuse, and wife beating. In this chapter, these terms are used interchangeably. Because domestic violence centers around intimacy, it is important to note that we consider violence between boyfriends and girlfriends, ex-spouses, same sex couples, and others with an ongoing or prior intimate relationship in the same category as violence between married partners.

Domestic Violence

Although commonly thought of as hitting, shoving, kicking, stabbing, etc., domestic violence may also be sexual or psychological. It involves

> The infliction or threat of infliction of any bodily injury or harmful physical contact or the destruction of property or threat thereof as a method of coercion, control, revenge, or punishment upon a person with whom the actor is involved in an intimate relationship . . . [i.e.,] between spouses, former spouses, past or present unmarried couples or persons who are both the parents of a child regardless of whether the persons have been married or have lived together at any time. (CRS, Sec. 1, 18–6–800.3)

While physical injury is often lethal and should be responded to as a crime, one should never underestimate the power of a threat. Initial threats of violence lay a foundation of fear and, left unchecked, are very likely to inevitably accelerate into physical violence. Threats made by the perpetrator, after he has used violence, verify the survivor's belief that he will indeed carry out his threats. She believes that if he used violence once, and threatens to use it again, he will. She is right. When his threats put her in fear for her safety or the safety of her family, children, or property, he has committed a crime (e.g., harassment, assault, and reckless endangerment). As with threats and physical violence to a person, destruction of property or violence toward pets is to also be taken seriously.

The destruction of property or pets is symbolic. It is a threat. It is violence. He may destroy or harm the object or pet for revenge, punishment, or coercion. Some common targets include her clothes, pictures of her family, wedding gifts, schoolbooks, record albums–anything she values. The destruction of property or harm to pets also acts as an "as if" message. For instance, the message might be:

> I am destroying the picture of your parents (or kicking your dog, or smashing a hole in the wall, or poking the eyes out of the picture of the baby, etc.). If I do not like what you do (say, look like, cook, etc.), I will be more violent to you and/or to them.

Or,

> I'm cutting the crotch out of all your panties. If I do not like how I feel about you sexually, I will use these scissors on you.

Intermittent Reinforcement

Intermittent reinforcement is a social-learning theory asserting that behavior that has been intermittently reinforced is the most difficult behavior to extinguish. In a battering relationship, the batterer increases his ability to gain more power by intermittently reinforcing the behavior of the survivor (Walker, 1990).

Likewise, his behavior intermittently reinforces itself. According to Ewing, "the man who batters is rarely in touch with any feeling other than anger (1984; p. 3). Therefore, when he, consciously or subconsciously, experiences unacceptable feelings or thoughts, he transforms those thoughts and feelings into feelings of anger/rage. Because he believes that violence is a legitimate and appropriate response to anger, he uses violence. Thus, his violence is reinforced by his belief in the "rightness" of his violence and the relief he feels when he no longer experiences the precipitating thoughts and feelings.

Because the batterer is typically responding to feelings and thoughts that he does not know he has, and is therefore not discussing his distress with the survivor, his behavior appears random and unpredictable. The apparent "randomness" and "unpredictability" of his behavior serves as intermittent reinforcement for the survivor. The battered woman never knows when he will respond negatively or positively toward her or the children.

Because of our cultural belief that a person can "cause" someone else to think or feel a particular way (i.e., jealously, cheerfully) or to behave in a particular way (violently, sexually), the battered woman translates the batterer's negative or positive responses into: "I must have done something to cause him to behave the way he does." He, too, points out what she has done to "set him off" or "push his buttons." So, when he participates in loving, caring, exciting sex one time, and violently rapes her the next, they both believe that it is her behavior causing his responses. She believes her happiness (and ultimately her life) depends on her ability to please and "fix" him. The "good" responses serve as intermittent reinforcement to stay in the relationship.

Learned Helplessness

Learned helplessness is a psychological theory that describes what happens when cognitive and the emotional understanding do not match. Learned helplessness is a "survival focused" (as opposed to an "escape focused") adaptation to repeated, intermittent abuse such as domestic violence. This theory proposes that when a battered woman believes intellectually that she is the cause of her and her batterer's behavior, while emotionally she knows that her behavior has no effect on his behavior, she learns that

. . . she is unable to predict the effect her behavior will have. . . . People suffering from learned helplessness are more likely to choose behavioral responses that will have the highest predictability of an effect within the known, or familiar, situation; they avoid responses–like escape, for instance–that launch them into the unknown . . . she believes the demons she knows well are probably preferable to the demons she does not know at all. (Walker, 1990; p. 50–51)

As the battering and isolation increase, a shift in her comprehension of the situation occurs. She increasingly perceives escape as impossible. While she may continue to work at her paid job, eat, clean house, take care of the children, laugh with coworkers, and appear self-confident and independent, at home, *surviving* the battering relationship becomes the focus of her life.

In her eyes, he becomes more and more powerful. She sees police and other agencies as less and less able to help (Browne, 1987; Kelly, 1989; Seligman, 1975; Walker, 1979; Walker, 1990). She feels trapped and alone. She will likely develop a variety of coping mechanisms she believes will help her and her children stay alive. These mechanisms may include withdrawal, asking permission to do even trivial things, compulsiveness, manipulation, substance abuse, and asking that charges be dropped.

Posttraumatic Stress Disorder (PTSD)

PTSD is a syndrome many battered women develop. A single severe, traumatic event may bring on this disorder. Repeated trauma most assuredly will. Some key symptoms of repeated abuse include "learned helplessness," avoidance of reminders of the trauma, disruption in sleep patterns, insomnia, nightmares, flashbacks to battering episodes, depression, eating disorders, hyper-vigilance, exaggerated startle response, and panic (American Psychiatric Association, 1989).

Stockholm Syndrome

Another common consequence of domestic violence is the Stockholm syndrome–originally coined to describe the reaction of hostages to their captors (Graham et al., 1989), it has more recently been applied to battered women (Russell, 1982). The identifying reaction is characterized by a strong emotional bond between the two involved in a severe power imbalance–captor/hostage or batterer/survivor. The two depend upon each other: the captor for his feelings of power and dominance, the victim for her life.

The survivor develops feelings of fear and hopelessness about her situation. This is especially true for women who have the additional terror that he will rape and attack people she loves, and, for women who sought help from

the criminal justice system only to have them fail to respond to her pleas. The survivor attempts to increase the batterer's "love" behavior and decrease the aggressor response. Since batterers/captors have the ability to kill, they are seen as gracious for sparing the survivor's life. Even though he is the one who initiated the violence, the batterer is the only one there to console the survivor after threatening or abusing her.

The survivors grow to fear change and outside interference. Hostages fear situations like shoot-outs and battered women fear more beatings. The fear of what happens if they don't comply with the aggressor keeps them from reaching out.

Coercion

What does it take to produce Learned Helplessness, PTSD, and/or the Stockholm syndrome? According to Biderman (1967) and Romero (1985), it takes three coercive elements: dependency, debilitation, and dread. Although it is true that the life experience of the victim/survivor prior to contact with the batterer has a significant impact on her perception of the situation and her survival adaptations, most battered women develop at least some level of these three characteristics. Debilitation may result from deprivations occurring individually, serially, or simultaneously. The most common deprivations are food, sleep, and human contact. When a battered woman experiences significant deprivation, she becomes paradoxically dependent on [her] torturer for these things. The only person who can provide this relief is the torturer, and in the induced abnormal environment where deprivation and stress are the norm and other social contacts are withdrawn, the victim becomes dependent on him as the sole source of support. Occasional unpredictable brief respites, when among other things the torturer becomes a sympathetic listener, make the victim obligated toward him. (Bettelheim, 1947; p. 46)

According to Russell (1982) it is not very common for a man to physically lock up his female partner, or tie her up, or deprive her of food, but it is common for him to deprive her of sleep and contact with other people. His physical ability to overpower her, his psychological abuse, deprivation and isolation, combined with the societally perpetuated debilitating factors (economic, cultural, and psychological), increase the dependency of women on men in relationships, and increases the likelihood that she will stay with him and comply with his demands. Dependency is culturally driven. In much the same way that guards and prisoners of war experience a power differential when they are thrust into those positions, husbands in traditional patriarchal marriages are attributed much power and authority–historically by law and currently by custom. Therefore, husbands need apply little or no manipula-

tion or coercion in order for a considerable power and resource differential to exist between them. In such marriages, dependency is a given.

Even today, with increasing egalitarian values, great power, resource, and status differences exist between men and women. These differences are continually reinforced through a variety of formal and informal sanctions. Debilitation leads to dependency, and dependency leads to dread. The feeling of dread is consuming. It becomes an involuntary response that strikes at the very core of the survivor. It is not just a fear of death. If it were only a fear of death, many would eagerly choose death and be done with it. Indeed, many survivors pray for death. Many commit suicide. The feeling of dread is a spontaneous reflex—a knee jerk reaction—that catapults the woman into survival behavior. Therefore, noncompliance to the batterer's demands becomes less and less possible, and psychological "symptoms" become more pronounced.

After one or more attacks, the survivor can be reminded of the incident by the batterer giving a particular look, word, nod of the head, facial movement, or gesture. These signs may trigger the same psychological and physiological response in the survivor as if she were being physically attacked again. These factors—dependency, debilitation, dread—when executed in the proper measure over time, significantly alter a person's self-perception and lead to psychological and behavioral adaptations described above. When a survivor is no longer subjected to these factors, she regains her previous self-perception.

CONTRIBUTING FACTORS

Why does domestic violence exist? There is a risk in asking such a question. The risk is generating an endless list of "becauses" that only perpetuate the invisibility of domestic violence and provide potential excuses for its existence. From our earliest learning, we are led to believe that the "why–because" method of thinking will lead us to *the answer,* and thus, to the "cure" or "fix" for *the problem.* The intent of this section is to describe some elements within a complex matrix of cultural, community, familial, and personal factors creating and perpetuating (domestic violence. It is intended to shed light on the "why" of domestic violence as a process, rather than isolated or discrete events (see McIver, 1973, for a discussion of the "why of process and events").

Cultural Context: Sex/Gender Role Socialization

All societies have clear expectations of individual and group behavior based on sex. Society assigns males and females different expectations for personality traits, expressions of emotion, behaviors, and occupations. Boys are taught to be aggressive, competitive, and winners. They are taught that they are superior to girls. Girls, on the other hand, are taught to be passive, submissive, caretakers, and inferior to boys. These values—reinforced by adolescent rituals, the media, popular press, and many adults—are carried by these children into dating relationships and adulthood.

> This [sex role] differentiation ranks the sexes in such a way that women are unequal in power, resources, prestige, or presumed worth. At the same time, both women and men are denied the full range of human and social possibilities. The social inequalities created by sex differentiation have far-reaching consequences for the society at large. (Eitzen, 1988; p. 352)

Not surprisingly, one of these far-reaching consequences has to do with sex roles. As more people believe in traditional sex roles, the more likely they are to support a male using violence toward a female in an intimate relationship (Finn, 1986).

Cultural Context: Learned Aggression

While male/female sex roles lay the foundation for dominance/submission, it does not explain violence. People must be taught the appropriate time, place, method, and object of violence as well as rationalizations and excuses for violence. Most domestic violence is not the act of a "deviant" or "pathological" or "perverted" man (Lindsey, 1990; Sonkin, 1982). It is the act of a person whose belief system is firmly grounded in our culture. Male violence toward women has existed for millennia. It has been an accepted, even expected, part of the family system. Although acceptance of wife abuse is waning, still reflected in our culture and social institutions are much of the ideology and many of the institutional arrangements which support male violence through the subordination, domination, and control of women and children. The spanking and hitting parents use on their children as well as the adult-to-adult violence that children observe teaches them three lifelong lessons:

1. Those who love you the most are also those who hit you;
2. There is a moral right to hit other members of the same family; and
3. When all else fails, use violence. (Straus et al., 1981; p. 102–104)

Children also hear fairy tales, watch television and go to the movies where they learn that violence is necessary, legitimate, exciting, and fun. These portrayals of violence primarily depict males being violent toward other males and females.

Isolation: Geography, Mobility, Family, and Community

People need reference points: anchors where they can feel a sense of safety, sameness, consistency, and stability. They need contact with friends and family as a "reality check." They need to experience changes with significant others over a period of time. Increasingly, people are isolated from communities or groups with whom they have a history and a future. Most people live far away from their hometown or family of origin. Over half of all mothers and fathers work outside the home. The divorce rate is now around 50 percent. Increasing numbers of women remain unmarried after divorce–working long hours inside and outside the home in order to support themselves and their children. Fewer than 50 percent of all people court ordered to pay child support, do so (Chesler, 1987). Second and third marriages often result in blended or reconstituted families–bringing groups of strangers together to live as a single unit. Often this involves a change in housing, work, school, and geographic location. People living in rural areas or in urban areas where they may be afraid to associate with other people, lack personal contacts and social support networks that could help them develop healthy perceptions of adult-to-adult interactions or provide support in time of need. Contributing to this lack of connection is economic mobility. Because of shifts in the U.S. economy, a significant percent of the population moves at least once every five years. The result is isolation: personal and familial. Because there are fewer long-term experiences that allow a person to truly understand how people change and how they feel, there is an increased reliance on public, external, surface presentations of how people should look, act, feel, think, and function. This results in unrealistic expectations of self and others and a disconnection from self, others, family and community.

Drug Abuse

Drug and alcohol use/abuse does not cause domestic violence. It does, however, occur in a large number of cases where domestic violence is present (Coleman and Straus, 1979), because we tend to excuse the behavior of people who claim that they would not have been violent had they been sober. Experience shows that this is not true. Many people who use/abuse drugs and alcohol are not violent; likewise, many people who are violent do not use drugs or alcohol (Ganley and Harris, 1978; Roberts, 1984). Consequently, many people are still violent long after they are no longer using/abusing drugs or alcohol. Therefore, stopping drug abuse will not stop domestic violence; however, stopping domestic violence will go a long way toward reducing drug abuse (Gelles & Straus, 1988). Others have also found substance abuse among domestic batterers (Schumacher, et al., 2001). Suffice it to say that while there is an association between domestic violence and substance abuse (drugs and alcohol), this relationship falls short of being a causal one.

Myths

Many myths are associated with domestic violence. Myths serve to explain some phenomenon by diverting attention from the most pressing issues. Eradication of myths and myth debunking will help focus on the reality of domestic violence (Adapted and expanded from Walker 1979):

MYTH 1: Only a few people are affected by domestic violence. Not only are over 50 percent of all couples (males and females) involved in domestic violence sometime during their lives, but children are also involved, as are friends, family, and neighbors. Each year over 15,000,000 women, children, and men are directly involved in adult-to-adult domestic violence. If we add "community costs"–such as health care, school programs, bankruptcy, civil and criminal justice expenditures, foreclosures, etc.–everyone is affected in some way and everyone pays either directly or indirectly.

MYTH 2: Battered women are masochistic. Battered women do not want to be beaten. Often, battered women have asked their batterer to stop his abuse, have asked for help, and have tried to leave. People who label battered women as masochistic are either discounting the physical and emotional trauma she has experienced and/or do not have information about all the ways in which she has tried to stop the violence and the threats. What is seen as masochism is an adaptation for survival.

MYTH 3: Batterers and battered women are crazy, lower class, minority, uneducated people with few social or job skills and no religious beliefs. Domestic violence is an equal opportunity crime. Perpetrators and victims/survivors come from every category listed above as well as their opposite and everywhere in between.

MYTH 4: Love and violence cannot exist together in a relationship. Most batterers and survivors love each other. Many batterers act in loving, caring ways most of the time. Most survivors love the batterer–and they want the battering to stop. Over time, love may change or fade as physical damage, learned helplessness, PTSD, and the Stockholm syndrome take their toll.

MYTH 5: Once a battered woman, always a battered woman. Women who receive positive intervention move past the victim stage, rebuild their sense of self, and rarely choose another battering relationship. It should be noted, however, with 50 percent of all relationships experiencing domestic violence, there are many batterers in our society. Women do not "choose batterers." They choose men who present themselves as kind, loving, caring, thoughtful people. In most cases, it is only later that his facade crumbles–exposing his violent behavior. There is some likelihood that a battered woman will choose another partner who turns out to be a batterer–not because of a "defect" or "problem" with her, but because there are so many men who use violence against their partners.

MYTH 6: Once a batterer, always a batterer. Although the prognosis for change is dim (Gallup, 1990), some men do stop their violent behavior. Men have more success at stopping physical violence than they do at stopping verbal and emotional violence. It is estimated that it will take between three to five years of weekly therapy for a man to make a significant, lasting change in all aspects of his violent behavior.

MYTH 7: "I just lost it." When a person faints or has a seizure (i.e., epilepsy) there is a loss of control. The person will be unable to speak, move, or in some cases, control their bladder or bowel. The person will be unable to direct violence toward another person. In other cases, batterers will say that, while this was not like a seizure, they could not stop themselves. Most men who batter use other methods of dealing with frustration, anger, or "provocation" when it is convenient for them to do so. When he feels angry he does not beat up his boss, his secretary, the neighbor, a stranger on the street, or children playing in the next yard. It is only in the privacy of his own home, or when he perceives he will receive no negative consequences, will he choose to use violence toward his female partner–and possibly his children and, in the vast majority of cases, no one else (Ewing et al., 1984; Ptacek, 1988; Stordeur et al., 1989). When the perpetrator uses violence it is because he has made an assessment of the situation and has determined that:

1. What I am doing is not wrong;
2. If it is wrong, I will not get caught;
3. If I get caught, I can talk my way out;
4. If I cannot talk my way out, the penalties will be minor–I will decide what the penalties are. (Lindsey, 1990)

In these "I just lost it" episodes of violence, batterers say and do things they know will hurt their victim. They yell obscenities and threats. They may kick the pregnant woman in the stomach. They may hit the victim in places that will be seen or hidden, depending on the message to be delivered by the violence. Batterers use violence because they know they can.

MYTH 8: Battered women can always leave. Two major concerns block women from leaving: financial and emotional. Financially, most battered women have not been allowed access to information about finances or control of assets–including their own, if they work. In a society where the average woman earns $.70 for every $1.00 the average man earns, even if she has marketable skills, she is likely to have great difficulty supporting herself and her children. Emotionally, because of the violence, she has probably been isolated from friends and family—leaving her with few, if any, emotional support systems. In addition, the batterer has, in the vast majority of cases, threatened that he will kill her, the children, her parents, her friends, her boss, himself—anyone who she cares for. Because he has been violent in the past, she has good reason to believe he will not only continue to use violence, but also to escalate that violence. Therefore, she may stay with him and endure the violence so that he will not kill the people she loves. She perceives that it is better to sacrifice herself than to live in guilt if he kills someone when she leaves. Research on the dynamics of domestic violence and the issue of why women simply don't leave the abusive situation demonstrates that there are often substantive reasons for staying. These are grounded in family theory and research. When a woman decides not to leave the household, she may be defined as "deviant" by experts (Loseke and Cahill, 1984).

MYTH 9: Children need their father, even if he is a batterer. Male children who see their father beat their mother are seven times more likely to be violent as adults than those who did not witness such violence (Straus et al., 1981). Children need healthy role models. Unhealthy role models damage children now and in the future. Therefore, the presence of an abusive family in lieu of no father at all defies common sense.

MYTH 10: Stress causes violence. Neither stress nor drugs nor heredity cause domestic violence. Domestic violence is "caused" by a person choosing to use violence as a means by which to relieve stress and frustration. That person has learned from his culture and interpersonal relations that his behavior is legitimate, necessary, and/or appropriate at that moment in time. Like drug and alcohol abuse, many people use stress as an excuse to be violent. Many people who feel stress *do not* use violence. When a person feels stress there are a myriad of options for dealing with that stress, and violence is an inappropriate option.

CHARACTERISTICS AND DYNAMICS OF PERPETRATORS

There is no "typical" batterer, victim, or survivor. While many men who batter love their partners and do not want to use violence, others do not love their partners, feel comfortable using violence, and do not care whether their partners stay or leave. Likewise, most battered women love the man who is beating them, do not want to see him hurt, and just want him to stop the beatings. Others hate their batterer and would like to kill him.

Characteristics

Although we cannot talk about *the* batterer or *the* victim/survivor, there are some general patterns and characteristics that have emerged in the literature. The purpose of this section is to understand batterers within the context of how their behavior impacts their victim/survivor/family. Most of the information in the literature about batterers is from victims and survivors. Some information about their behavior is provided by batterer treatment programs. Gathering information from and about batterers is difficult. Batterers typically do not like to discuss the battering incidents and will often evade questions or deny any memory of the incident. The relationship batterers crave and create is filled by extremes of action and emotion that every day lives seldom match. The relationship they crave is the opposite of the one they create. Confronted by the inconsistency, they escalate the violence. As they escalate their violence, what they crave becomes increasingly illusive.

Because he feels insecure, frightened, and has a low self-esteem, the man who batters fears that his partner will leave/abandon him. Therefore, he demands attention and creates crisis situations that remain more immediate, tangible, real, and compelling than the surrounding "ordinary" stimulation. Instilling such immediacy in the survivor is mostly accomplished through (Ewing et al., 1984):

- Violence
- Lavishing affection and gifts
- Isolation
- Creating crisis and chaos

Jealousy

The batterer is jealous to the point of intrusion into every aspect of his partner's life, and yet, remains insecure about her love and loyalty. He may continue to be suspicious of her possible relationships with others. He will eventually isolate her from all her support systems: not allowing her to work or if she does he monitors her every move. He blocks her making friends or continuing relationships with family.

Overkill

His excessive behavior carries over into other areas. When he is trying to be nice or affectionate, he typically lavishes his partner with large quantities of the biggest and best, even if he cannot afford it. Likewise, when he uses violence, he far exceeds that which even he perceives is necessary to "get his point across." Often his intention, when he hits his partner, is to "teach her a lesson." What begins as "a good smack or two," finishes as slapping interspersed with punches and kicks, and, may continue until she is badly injured. When substance abuse is involved, his violence is even worse since the drugs dull his perception of when to stop.

Generational Cycle of Abuse

Violence is learned behavior. A man who saw his father beat his mother will likely batter. If the man was also beaten as a child, the likelihood that he will batter increases again (Bowker, Arbitell, and McFerron, 1988; Straus et al., 1981). With the addition of societal reinforcement of violent behavior, the likelihood of generational violence is once again increased. As Widom and Maxfield (2001) note, "being abused or neglected as a child increased the likelihood of arrest as a juvenile by 59 percent, as an adult by 28 percent, and for a violent crime by 30 percent." (p. 10).

Charming and Manipulative Personality

Many batterers are very charming, personable, calm, and controlled when they are not being violent. They have effectively learned that presenting this persona allows them to get what they want and to "talk their way out" of situations that could have negative consequences for them.

Avoiding Feelings

The batterer is unable to identify the majority of his feelings. This is combined with his inability to express his feelings within a society that does not encourage men to express feelings—except anger. While anger is a normal emotion, a batterer tends to turn all emotions into anger and then is unable to express his anger in a nonviolent way (Ewing et al., 1984). There are occasions, especially immediately after he has been violent to his partner, that he may actually express guilt, shame, fear, and/or remorse. He may even cry. While he may allow himself these momentary flashes of feelings, he soon suppresses them and returns to his previous, relied on, method of coping.

Dynamics: Why He Batters

This discussion of why men batter is not a list of excuses, reasons, causes, justifications, denials, or abusive behavior or the basis for forgiveness. It is a presentation of salient issues surrounding their violence. The reasons why men batter are also instructive of why women stay. Male violence is learned behavior that can be modified and changed. The key to changing behavior is found in the identification and containment of immediate, consistent messages and consequences for the batterer. Men use violence against their female partners and their children because, in the short term, it works. Although the violent explosions mask and repress his feelings, the batterer believes that violence "releases" or "fixes" them. Violence also results in a change in behavior of the individual at whom the violence is directed. The results: a deeply embedded cycle of violence.

> Violence is men's response to pain, via a circuitous, sometimes hidden, route. The man who batters is rarely in touch with any feelings other than anger. Anger is men's easy emotion. Anger is always there, ever present, as the emotion which veils hurt, fear, pain, loss and anxiety. Literally speaking, there is no "reason" that men batter . . . there is only the violence at the moment, when unresolved feelings and cognition, covered with hurt-become-anger become rage, explode in an irrational act of "control." What [he perceives] is out of control, the batterer will beat into control. Violence controls; therefore in the short run, violence works. It serves us better therefore to list simply and straightforwardly the unresolved feelings and cognition of men who batter. (Ewing et al., 1984; p. 3–4)

His Unresolved Feelings

Victimization. "The batterer is in some way still imprisoned in his own developmentally frozen child-victim experience" (Ewing et al., 1984; p. 4). Emotional and physical assaults during his childhood have left lasting impressions, which he translates into control through violence as an adult.

The Primary Relationship: Filling the Void. Unresolved emotional issues in childhood may be conceptualized as emotionally deep, infected wounds that have not healed. When such a wounded man enters a primary relationship, he looks for his partner to fill the void and fix the wound. Because of his unwillingness/inability to communicate the nature of the wound, he sees her only hurting him more. He feels the pain of the original wound, the pain of the increased infection caused by hiding the wound, and betrayal that she will not fix him. When the survivor threatens to leave or leaves the batterer, "he experiences major disorientation, becomes suicidal, and sometimes becomes homicidal, hunting down his victim-partner" (Ewing et al., 1984; p. 4), the children, and frequently, her friends and family.

Avoiding Feelings. Some men enjoy feeling angry. To a man who lives in an emotional void, anger may feel good. Although other men may not like to feel angry, it is a familiar feeling; one with which the batterer feels a certain level of comfort. He may believe he is at least good at feeling one emotion.

Typically the batterer turns fear, sadness, even joy, into anger.

His inability to express those feelings, compounded by his living in an environment which does not support men's expression of feelings, has crippled him . . . the man who batters . . . has compressed the entirety of his denied emotional life into hurt-becomes-anger-becomes-rage. (Ewing, 1984; p. 5)

Isolation. Men who batter use intimidation, violence, and chaos to create emotional and physical distance. He creates multiple, unrealistic expectations, all of which demand considerable attention. He deals with this chaos by working harder, demanding more–of himself and others–bargaining, lying, denying, forcing, cutting corners, in short, creating chaos.

Subsequently, he is often friendless or relates to other men [and women] in very shallow ways, and very conscious of and deliberate about his behavior and demeanor in relation to the world from which he is actually disconnected . . . he narrows and narrows the confinement of meaning to the battering relationship itself. (Ewing et al., 1984; p. 5)

Fear and Inadequacy. Underneath it all, batterers typically feel frightened and inadequate (Ewing et al., 1984). They also feel shame and guilt about their inadequacy. As these feelings intensify, the batterer transforms them into anger, rage, and violence. After the violent explosion, shame, guilt, fear, and inadequacy return–the emotional circle is complete. The feelings he was trying to avoid reemerge to propel him into repeating his pattern: hurt-into-anger-into-rage-into-violence.

His Childhood

It is likely that he came from a violent home where his father abused his mother and he may have been beaten or mistreated. At the very least, the batterer probably experienced some type of emotional deprivation. Moreover, there may have also been a general lack of respect for women and children in his home. Given these factors, he learned that under certain circumstances, it is legitimate and necessary to use violence at home.

His Beliefs about Women

He is likely to look at women as possessions, and he is likely to look on his "possession" of a woman as a symbol of power. An assumption may be made that having a relationship with a woman will help him be less afraid, insecure and lonely. He believes his wife, his children, his money, his marriage, her income, his house, his car, are all his property. To lose any one part, is to lose everything. He may believe that he must control her in order to keep her.

His Fears

His fear is that she will abandon him, and tell family, friends and neighbors of his behavior. This threatens his sense of security, power, and the behavioral facade he has attempted so hard to maintain. He is afraid that he will lose the children if she leaves. He may also be economically dependent on her and see no real alternative. He may further believe that if they separate or divorce, she will "take him to the cleaners" and ruin whatever financial worth he may believe he has. Thus, in his eyes, he must control her in any way he can to maintain his economic security. He fears that she will expose him as the inadequate failure he secretly believes he is.

CHARACTERISTICS AND DYNAMICS: VICTIMS/SURVIVORS

Characteristics

Any woman can be the victim of domestic violence, just as anyone can be the victim of any other crime. Therefore, there is no profile of a woman who is more, or less, likely to be abused. However, from studies of battered women, we have derived some common characteristics.

Low Self-Esteem

Battered women typically underestimate their abilities. The batterer repeatedly tells her she is incompetent and unable to function on her own. Because women often define themselves more by their success or failure as a partner and/or mother, when things are not going well at home, it adversely affects their self-esteem. A battered woman assumes guilt for her man's behavior. Society's belief is that he would change if only she would change, i.e., if she could stop making mistakes and do things right, his behavior would improve.

Traditional Beliefs

Typically, battered women feel that a woman's role in a relationship is to nurture the man, maintain the household, and take care of the relationship. She may continue her job out of economic necessity, and/or because she loves it. It may be the only respite from her husband's constant monitoring of her behavior. However, she may feel guilty about her choice. Conversely, she may give her job up either willingly or unwillingly because of her feelings about the relationship: hoping that giving up the job will give him some security and he will then be happy. Frequently, this creates real economic hardship on the family—adding further stress. Some battered women will turn their paycheck over to their partner who will take over decisions about how family income is spent. She may be perceived as holding the entire family together emotionally, and maybe even financially. Nevertheless, he is still seen as the head of the house. She is also a woman who sometimes hides money so that she can leave the marriage. Whether she leaves or not, the secreted money helps her cope.

Stress Reactions Resulting in Psychological and Physiological Problems and Complaints

Battered women complain of a variety of minor ailments such as fatigue, restlessness, sleep problems (disruption, inability to sleep), and headaches. They complain of depression and anxiety, and they are generally suspicious. The suspicion and secretiveness is well founded and helps them cope by increasing their perception of control over their lives and the batterer, avoiding beatings and obtaining a few moments of privacy from their excessively intrusive men.

Minimizing the Violence

Battered women tend to minimize the amount and intensity of the violence. This may involve elaborate processes of rationalization and justification, which excuses the amount of harm inflicted.

Believes She Deserves the Punishment She Receives

Because she believes what her parents told her, e.g.:" I am spanking you for your own good," "I would not hit you if you didn't deserve it," "Stop that! Don't make me hit you," "I only hit you because you did what I told you not to do" and because the batterer is saying the same things to her, she tends to merge her parents' teaching with his violence.

Dynamics: Why She Stays

Increasingly, women do not stay. Even in cases where it appears as if she stays—or leaves only to return time and time again—she is usually preparing to leave. Women leave an average of five to seven times before they change their living arrangements. Because of the nature and intensity of the batterer's violence and threats, the battered woman leaves in stages: testing the environment to see if she and her children can safely escape and survive. For those women who stay or who take longer to leave, it is the dynamics of a violent relationship, the failure of society to exert negative sanctions toward the perpetrator and provide her with positive role models and options that keeps them trapped in the cycle of violence. After considering the dynamics of domestic violence and the social barriers to leaving, along with the physical, emotional, and psychological consequences, the fact that so many women do leave inspires amazement.

Frequency and Severity of the Battering

Each battering incident may occur over a relatively short period of time . . . like a hit and run driver or a terrorist attack. He may tell her, and she may be convinced, that this battering incident is the last. Generally, the less severe and less frequent the incidents, the more likely she will stay. She may have a disability resulting from previous battering, or have a disability from another source. If so, she may not be mentally (head injury, developmentally disabled, etc.) or physically able to leave under her own power. She may be physically restrained (wheel chair taken away, doors locked and phone disconnected if she is blind, etc.). He may be over or under medicating her to restrain her. If she is elderly, the physical injuries may be more; extensive and perceived as more lethal than when she was younger. Additionally, she, like the woman with a disability, may be physically restrained (i.e., tied up) or medicated to the extent that she cannot leave.

Her Childhood

She may have lived in a home where her father beat her mother, and expects or accepts it as natural or normal. The more she was hit by her parents and/or siblings, the greater the probability she will stay in the present abusive situation. In other words, she learned at an early age that it is okay to hit someone you love when they have done something defined as "wrong." She or one of her siblings may be a survivor of child abuse–including child sexual assault.

Economic Dependence

She may be economically dependent on her spouse/partner and see no real alternative. In her eyes, it may be worth putting up with abuse in order to maintain economic security for herself and the children. Economic conditions today afford a woman with children few viable options. She often has no (or low level) marketable skills. Government assistance is very limited and many women know that welfare is an option affording little hope for the future. Even when she does have marketable skills, women still earn about $.70 for every dollar earned by a male. Not only will she earn less, now she must totally maintain a separate household for her children and herself–batterers may resist paying child support because it requires payment without control. Additionally, he may use every opportunity to bring her back into court over and over again; thus, causing her to incur tremendous legal fees or lose the children, the house, car, or anything else she values. If children need special attention (physical or behavior problems) she is rarely able, on her own, to provide funds for these needs. He may try to control all of their money. She may have no access to cash, credit cards, checks, or important documents. If she has a disability or other problem that will require long-term medical intervention, he may have the only health insurance from which medical bills are paid. She fears inability to take care of the children, bankruptcy, institutionalization, or death if she does not stay with him. As an elderly spouse abuse survivor, she may be relying on his pension and other retirement funds in order to live. She fears that he will cut her off and she will live in poverty, become a homeless "bag lady," be institutionalized by the state, or die.

Fear

If she has experienced the cycle of violence many times (especially if police have been called and did not arrest him), she believes her husband to be omnipotent. She sees no way to protect herself from him. She does not believe anyone else can or will protect her either. Many of her fears are justified: the violence exhibited is terrifying and lethal. This is exemplified by the case in which a battered woman shot her husband multiple times with a shotgun; she still thought he was not dead and would get up to come after her (Walker, 1990). She is likely to believe that if she, or even a neighbor, reports him to the police, he will take revenge upon her, the children, friends, family, pets . . . anyone or anything important to her. She may believe that if she stays with him he will hurt only her. In her mind, she is sacrificing herself so that others may live.

Some women are afraid that if they report the crime to tell of the abuse, her husband might lose his job . . . the only source of income and medical insurance for the family. She is likely to be afraid that no one will believe the true extent of his violence. She is afraid she may be blamed for his violence. She is afraid that she might lose the children, because she could not stop his violence and is, therefore, a bad mother. Some women are afraid of incurring the wrath of the extended family or their particular community if they break up with him or report him. She may have some "hidden" event in her past that, if brought into the open, would focus unwanted social or criminal action upon her, i.e., drug abuse, sexual behavior, writing bad checks, etc.

If an undocumented person, she may fear arrest and deportation . . . perhaps having to leave the children behind. If a woman of color or a lesbian, she may fear that the system will treat her unfairly, possibly taking her children or putting her in jail. If he is a man of color undocumented person, non-American, or lower class, she may fear that the police will beat or kill him. While she wants him to stop the violence, she usually does not want him hurt or killed. She may be afraid that if she leaves, he will commit suicide. Generally, she does not want him dead but wants him to stop his violence. In some cultures, the police and social services are seen as the enemy, an agent of the government to be feared. Only under the most extreme conditions would the battered woman, family members or neighbors call the police. Often they do not call the police until a death occurs. In rural areas, she may fear neighbors will talk about the battering if they find out. Additionally, there are fewer resources in rural areas to address domestic violence. An elderly person or a person with a disability may believe that others will see her as incompetent or incapable of getting the story straight. Often an elder abuse survivor will experience barriers to reaching out to services that can provide help, based on pride or ignorance of the system and how to use it.

Isolation

Often he has become her only psychological and emotional support system after having systematically destroyed her other friendships. Friends and family feel uncomfortable around his intimidation, hostility, or violence and withdraw from them. This isolation supports her feeling of his omnipotence. She has no one else (except perhaps the children) to validate her feelings and her perception of reality . . . neither does he. The children act out what they see and experience at home. Neither the survivor nor the batterer may know of services to help those experiencing domestic violence (if there are services). Where services exist, many people would never ask for help from "social services," "charity," or the "government" because "what happens in the family stays in the family."

Service providers, including health care providers, do not seek accurate information about injuries. When presented with an unbelievable story about the injury, many just let the matter drop. She may leave the batterer an average of five to seven times before she finally leaves for good. Relatives, friends, police, and service providers may fail to understand that she develops strengths and resources each time she leaves. They become tired of helping her, only to see her return to the batterer. They become decreasingly willing to be resources upon which she can rely. They may also be afraid of him or in a state of denial as well. They may blame her for his violence and tell her that she is a bad mother if she does not protect the children.

He often threatens to kill her, the children, and anyone else she involves if she leaves him. In response, she usually cuts off communication with potential helpers. In her mind, she would rather take the beatings than "cause" others to be hurt. Having no one to talk to, they rarely see themselves as battered women or batterers. Some batterers do not know how to relate without using intimidation and violence. The couple may realize they have problems, but may not identify the battering as being the main problem. Often, batterers and survivors identify the "real problem" as his drinking or, more commonly, something she is doing.

Some women and men believe that outsiders should not be involved in the affairs of a family. Some battered women abuse alcohol and other drugs. Typically, as battering increases, substance abuse increases. Thus, the isolation associated with battering is multiplied with increased substance abuse. Some women who go to a doctor or psychiatrist, complaining of physical and emotional problems are given drugs to "calm them down." This action by the doctor tells her that there is something wrong with her and, in conjunction with the effects of the drug itself, decreases her ability to access appropriate services.

Her Beliefs about the Batterer

She often still loves him and is emotionally dependent on him. Often, motivated by pity and compassion, she feels she is the only one who can help him overcome his problem (alcohol, violence, depression, etc.). When he is also abusing alcohol and/or other drugs, she believes that he will stop battering her if he stops the substance abuse. If he is elderly or has a disability, she may think that he will die without her.

Her Religious Beliefs

While increasing numbers of clergy are gaining an awareness and understanding of domestic violence, many clergy believe and perpetuate the myths of domestic violence and counsel the woman to be a better wife, mother, and nurturer. The more a woman internalizes the tenets espoused by some clergy concerning the traditional, submission role of women, the more likely she is to stay (Fortune, 1987).

The Cycle of Violence

Although not the same in all relationships where domestic violence exists, the cycle of violence typically consists of three phases: increased tension, battering incident, and calm respite (Walker, 1979). This process has been an established theoretical position in understanding domestic violence (Widom and Maxfield, 2001). It should be noted that the calm or honeymoon phase does not exist in all relationships and in other relationships decreases and disappears over time as the man begins to feel that power and control are achieved by violence.

ABUSE PHASES AND LETHALITY

While there are "lethality checklists" (Denver and Aurora, Colorado Police Departments, 1990) recognizing that a perpetrator will typically increase the frequency and severity of violence each time the cycle is repeated, *there are no guarantees* he will not use lethal force the first time he uses violence, or the second or the third and so on. Therefore, every domestic violence incident must be considered potentially lethal.

PHASE 1: TENSION OR BUILD UP

This phase may last a week, months, or years. It will usually occur more frequently as the cycle repeats itself. It is characterized by increasing verbal and minor physical abuse, and a decrease in loving communication. This is a time when the survivor may be amenable to resources in the community and may even seek them by way of visits to clergy, physician, and other authority figures she trusts. The batterer feels increased tension, but will deny this to himself and others. It is this denial to himself that is the basis for his inability to identify that "the problem" is within him. It is also the basis for his unwillingness to access help–he thinks he can handle anything if he is "just man enough" to control himself and his environment.

PHASE 2: BATTERING INCIDENT–
INTERMITTENT REINFORCEMENT

The tension has exceeded the batterer's ability or desire to suppress his feelings. If he has battered before, he knows that his "stress" seems to "vanish" when he uses violence. If he has not battered before, he will learn that violence works to "decrease his stress," and "change her behavior." Thus, the acute battering phase begins. It is important to note that either partner may "initiate" the battering phase. This is different from "asking for it" as the common myth suggests. Rather, if the survivor "initiates" the battering phase, she creates the illusion of controlling the place and time of the event. In this situation, she hopes that if he batters her now, the violence will relieve his tension before the tension is so great that he becomes lethal. It is after this phase that the batterer and the survivor are highly susceptible to intervention. She is frightened. He often feels guilty, humiliated, and ashamed.

PHASE 3: CALM OR HONEYMOON–
POSITIVE INTERMITTENT REINFORCEMENT

In this phase there is a perception of reconciliation and resolution. This phase tends to be shorter than the tension phase and may disappear over time. The man is usually contrite, justifies his behavior by blaming the victim/survivor, offers excuses such as drinking, and promises that it will never happen again—and he means it until the next time. The survivor is least likely to be amenable to intervention at this time, particularly if the cycle has not had many repetitions (intermittent reinforcement). The batterer may be more amenable to intervention at this time because, typically, he is remorseful and wishes to please (keep and to maintain control over) his partner. Later in the phase, if he believes that he has again "won over" his partner, he is less and less amenable to intervention. During the height of this phase, both parties minimize the violence and will actually forget and distort what happened. When that occurs, repetition of the cycle is surely inevitable. It is impossible for people to consciously change their behavior if they do not remember it . . . they cannot learn from past experience if they do not know what they did, thought, or felt. In Phase 1, neither partner addresses the violence because they hope that if they ignore it, it will go away. The survivor may feel that things are already too tense. If she just behaves right, things will be "okay." The batterer feels that his partner is really pushing him. He also believes that if she behaves right, he will be okay. In Phase 2, neither partner is in any condition to discuss things logically and rationally. In Phase 3, both partners think circumstances are getting better. If both ignore the problem, they believe it will get better. They see the honeymoon phase as evidence of that. They both think that if she would only be more sensitive, giving and understanding and not "push his buttons," he would not "lose it" and hit her. They minimize the damage he has done and fantasize that the honeymoon will last forever.

THE CRISIS INTERVENTION PROCESS

Family violence (child abuse, spouse abuse, and elder abuse) is one of the only crimes in which the perpetrator voluntarily remains at the scene. Not only is he likely to stay on the scene, he is also likely to challenge anyone who suggests that he is doing anything "wrong" or criminal. Therefore, the crisis intervention process in these cases must include the perpetrator as well as the survivors and other family members. The focus of this section is the adult survivor and perpetrator who are on the scene.

Domestic violence is a crime. Arrest is a frequent and, in 99.9 percent of the cases, one of the desired outcomes. Because studies show a decreased recidivism rate (Berk and Newton, 1985; Breslin, 1983; Edwards, 1989; Jaffe, et al., 1986; Parnas, 1971; Scott, 1981; Sherman and Berk, 1984) and an increase in the quality of life of the survivor (Calhoun-Stuber and Mickish, 1990) when an arrest is made, jurisdictions are increasingly requiring "probable cause" arrests. When the offender repeats his violent behavior, it is considered necessary to rearrest him, as one would continue to arrest other criminal offenders, such as bank robbers and arsonists who refuse to discontinue their criminal behavior.

The goal of crisis intervention in domestic violence cases is to insure the safety of the survivors and to contain/arrest the perpetrator. Increasingly, police officers are being met with three situations when they arrive at a domestic violence crime scene:

1. The survivor asks the police to arrest the perpetrator.
2. The survivor is physically defending herself—leaving physical marks on her attacker.
3. The perpetrator is showing the police the marks left by the self-defending survivor and claiming that he is the true victim.

The ability to perceive danger, to select appropriate intervention/control strategies, and to communicate effectively is of paramount importance in domestic violence cases. To fail at any one of these tasks is to prolong or escalate the violence.

The crisis intervention steps—assessment, information gathering, control/direction, referral, and disposition—will assist in achieving this goal. These steps are to be considered general guidelines; each situation requires that the intervener use general knowledge of the dynamics of domestic violence presented here and safety techniques found within various departments and criminal justice agencies. Specifically, there are several model domestic violence response programs which have been made available for modeling purposes and adaptation to local domestic violence concerns (Bureau of Justice Assistance, 1993). Moreover, others have presented effective strategies and considerations when intervening with assaulted women

(Pressman, Cameron, and Rothery, 1989) with the information below. The first consideration in a domestic violence case is assessment.

Assessment

Assessment is essential. Domestic violence is a crime. If it is determined that a crime has been committed, mediation is no more appropriate here than it is in cases of bank robbery or burglary. To ask someone to sit down and talk rationally and effectively with someone who has just beaten and/or threatened him or her verbally and/or with a weapon is outrageous, unrealistic, and dangerous. If mediation is attempted, the result will typically be that the survivor learns that the police do not understand the terror she is experiencing and that the batterer will again be able to talk his way out of negative consequences for his violence. As the honeymoon phase begins (if it has not been extinguished in this relationship), the batterer will apologize and promise to do whatever the officers and/or his partner suggests. The survivor, terrified, traumatized, and hopeful, complies. The cycle is thus sanctioned and perpetuated.

Information Gathering

Information gathering before arrival on the scene involves determining whether a restraining order exists. If a restraining order does exist, the intervener should determine the nature, extent, and type of order as well as the authority of the responding officers to enforce the order. It may be possible that eviction, no contact provisions, child custody orders, visitation orders, or other provisions may also be in place (Finn and Colson, 1990). Whether a restraining order exists (or some other type of condition) or whether the responding officers have the authority to enforce it, a thorough investigation is essential. Other crimes may also have been committed (i.e., harassment, breaking and entering, destruction of property, etc.) and the intervener must be cognizant of all possibilities.

Because domestic violence involves more than physical violence (i.e., destruction of property, threats, etc.), on-site information gathering must include the appearance and demeanor of all parties. The appearance of the inside and outside of the house/apartment, and vehicles or other valuables owned by either party is equally important.

Neighbors or children may also have been threatened or abused by the perpetrator–they are therefore also victims. By virtue of the fact children witness domestic violence, they are affected and they are secondary victims of the assault. Questioning children and neighbors should be conducted in the same manner as questioning the identified/presenting victim.

Control-Direction

In domestic violence cases, the crime scene is unpredictable. The survivor, several children, the perpetrator, and even extended family members or friends may all be present. Upon entering and assessing the situation, the intervener may need to call for assistance so that (1) the situation does not escalate given limited crisis management, (2) the survivor or the perpetrator is not left to manage the children—who are also in crisis, (3) accurate information is obtained from those present, and (4) when children are present, someone is there to transport them to child protection services if necessary.

Using information from the cycle of violence, learned helplessness, PTSD, Stockholm syndrome, and profile of the batterer, we know that the parties may be in denial and uncooperative immediately after the violence. The perpetrator does not want to be arrested. He may have threatened his wife and children that, if anyone reveals anything he has done, he will harm or kill them. He may have made those threats in conjunction with his assurances that "this time" he will go into couples or family counseling, after all it was she who "pushed *his* buttons."

The survivor and children may be in a daze or still feel panic and emotional escalation. They take his threats seriously and may cling to his promises of reform as a way to feel safer. Children may have attempted to step in to help their mother, or are beginning to side with the perpetrator. Children often side with the person who they perceive has power—power to protect as well as power to kill. Therefore, they may be helpful in providing essential information, or they may be a potential threat to the safety of the intervener and survivor.

Because the survivor has probably been physically attacked, and because the perpetrator is subconsciously gathering "evidence" to justify repeating his attacks, physical contact between the intervener and the survivor or batterer should be kept to an absolute minimum—regardless of whether the intervener is male or female. Light touching may be appropriate. However, using a "cattle herding" technique and other body and hand movements may prove more appropriate and less likely to escalate the situation. Occasionally physical force must be used.

In this circumstance the intervener should use the least amount of force necessary to effect control. Modeling is important since the intervener demonstrates behavior that is expected from [those present]. If the intervener acts calm (and talks softly) . . . [others] will eventually modulate their own hostility (Hendricks, 1985, p. 73)

While it is important that the intervener show support and understanding for the concerns of both the survivor and perpetrator, it is never appropriate for the intervener to suggest in any way that illegal behavior (i.e., abuse) is or was an appropriate response to the situation. This can be done in a clear, direct way without ridicule or harassment. Saying such things as "I know that the dinner is burned, I would feel upset too. Hitting your wife is illegal and not the solution to your problems" does not help in such instances.

In the event that anyone at the scene begins "blowing off steam," be alert. Identifying people by demeaning terms reinforces hostility and objectification of others. It is easier to use violence toward a disgusting "object" such as a bitch or whore, than it is toward Fran or Mary. Additionally, the perpetrator may be attempting to signal the survivor and the children that he will escalate his violence if they cooperate with the police. His words may constitute harassment or assault.

The police role is to control the situation and assess whether a crime has been committed. Attempting to determine the etiology of the domestic violence is not productive: the "cause" of his violence is a mix of the perpetrator's unresolved feelings in conjunction with societal permission for him to use violence and, possibly, substance abuse by him. However, providing both the perpetrator and survivor an opportunity to talk about the violence may help the officers secure trust and rapport so that immediate safety is enhanced and further action can be taken with minimal force.

Referral–Disposition

Increasingly, disposition means arrest of the alleged perpetrator. When an arrest is made, it is essential that the officers inform both the alleged perpetrator and survivor that

1. The alleged behavior (e.g., hitting, kicking, breaking and entering) is a crime; and therefore,
2. The police are making the arrest for the citizens of that jurisdiction–the survivor is not making an arrest nor can she change the process.

This accomplishes two purposes. First, it serves as a notice to the family that abusive behavior will result in negative consequences. Second, it shifts the focus for the violence (and its consequences) away from the survivor and places it on the police and the alleged perpetrator. The alleged perpetrator now has less reason to threaten the survivor (she cannot drop charges) and more reason to work with the criminal justice system to insure that he will not receive more negative sanctions. This strategy is designed to provide batterers with incentive to change their behavior.

Discussion about the realities of domestic violence, safety plans, and referrals are an integral part of the crisis intervention process. It is essential that questions about the law, the legal process and options, the children, safety, and her future be discussed with the survivor. This includes a discussion of the cycle of violence and the availability of domestic violence services.

Because the criminal justice system is increasingly part of a community effort to stop domestic violence, there is a strong likelihood that local domestic violence programs have printed material the interveners can leave with the survivor. If such material is not available, the intervener should write down essential resource information and leave it with the survivor. In many cases, the intervener can facilitate survivor contact with appropriate referral sources before leaving the scene.

CONCLUSION

Domestic violence is a crime—a dangerous crime consuming resources and destroying individuals, families, and communities. While individual perpetrators and survivors/victims come from every socioeconomic, racial, ethnic, and mental health category, and may, therefore, have individual problems or behavior disorders, domestic violence is a power-based control mechanism, founded upon and perpetuated by societal permission and conditioning. As a result, there are many identifiable similarities in perpetrators, survivors/victims and patterns of abuse.

The emphasis of the criminal justice system has shifted from insuring a man's right to use violence, to treating the perpetrator like other criminals, enforcing the survivor's rights to police action, opening her legal options, and protecting her and her children from further harm.

CHAPTER QUESTIONS

1. What is domestic violence?
2. Is domestic violence a serious problem? Explain.
3. List three reasons lawsuits were brought against the police and discuss three administrative responses.
4. List and describe three social factors contributing to the perpetuation of domestic violence?
5. Discuss the "I just lost it" myth in relation to the crisis intervention process.
6. List and discuss three characteristics of a) perpetrators b) survivors/ victims.
7. List and discuss three reasons why a man might batter.
8. Do battered women stay in battering relationships? Explain.
9. List and discuss five reasons a woman might stay in an abusive rela-

tionship.

10. Describe the cycle of violence.
11. List, describe and explain the importance of the crisis intervention steps used in domestic violence cases.

SIMULATED EXERCISES

Simulated Exercise 1

You are called to an apartment complex where you observe:

1. An adult male pushing an adult female up the stairs.
2. He is yelling at her that she is once again late fixing his dinner.
3. Smeared blood is on the back of his hand.
4. Her nose is bleeding and she is crying.
5. He has a slight scratch (not bleeding) on his face.
6. No weapons are visible.
    a. List 3 realistic options you have in dealing with this case.
    b. State chronologically, in detail, what you believe you should do.
    c. Explain why you chose the options you did.

Simulated Exercise 2

You are dispatched to a "domestic in progress" in a fashionable neighborhood. Upon arrival you see that the three car garage doors are open, the windows on the east side of the house are smashed and a small fire is burning in the front yard. Upon closer inspection you find that the fire smells of lighter fluid and that some women's clothes and pictures are burning. When you knock on the door a woman's voice yells at you to go away.

1. List 3 realistic options you have in dealing with this case.
2. State chronologically, in detail, what you should do. Stop your chronology if and when you are admitted to the house.
3. Explain why you chose the options you did.

Simulated Exercise 3

In the above cases, you are admitted to the dwelling where you observe the following:

1. The adult male is standing behind his three children (one male: 10; two females: 4 and 6).
2. The adult female's eyes are red—red from crying and one is bright red from blood collecting in it—probably from a blow to the head.

3. The adult female has a very red neck–streaks of red–a tinge of black and blue beginning to form in spots.
4. The adult male shows you long, deep scratches on the back of his hands. He says that she attacked him for no apparent reason and he slightly pushed her to defend himself. He says she is on medication for her nerves and that sometimes, she just goes crazy.
5. The two girls are shaking and crying. The boy is trying to hold back tears and is asking if he can go watch TV now that it's all over. He says there is a good Rambo movie he wants to watch.
6. Several small items (vase, picture with frame, coffee cup) are lying broken on the floor. A pair of scissors is stuck in the top of the coffee table.
7. The adult male is an attorney.
8. The adult female is a Ph.D. economist.
9. Police once before responded to a "disturbance" call at this residence. There is no record of the events or disposition.
   a. List 3 realistic options you have in dealing with this case.
   b. State chronologically, in detail, what you should do.
   c. Explain why you chose the options you did.

APPENDIX A

Additional Internet Resources

For further information regarding domestic violence visit these sites:

National Coalition Against Domestic Violence:
    http://www.ncadv.org/
Institute on Domestic Violence in the African American Community:
    http://www.dvinstitute.org/
Defense Task Force on Domestic Violence:
    http://www.dtic.mil/domesticviolence/
Partnership Against Domestic Violence:
    http://www.padv.org/
Family Violence Prevention Fund:
    http://endabuse.org/
National Domestic Violence Hotline:
    http://www.ndvh.org/index.html
National Resource Center on Domestic Violence:
    http://www.nrcdv.org/
National Center on Domestic and Sexual Violence:
    http://www.ncdsv.org/
Faith Trust Institute:
    http://www.faithtrustinstitute.org/
The Silent Witness National Initiative:
    http://www.silentwitness.net/
The Domestic Abuse Project (DAP):
    http://www.mndap.org/
National Latino Alliance for the Elimination of Domestic Violence:
    http://www.dvalianza.org/home.htm
Break the Cycle:
    http://www.breakthecycle.org/
Violence Against Women Online Resources:
    http://www.vaw.umn.edu/
Minnesota Center Against Violence and Abuse:
    http://www.mincava.umn.edu/
Domestic Abuse Helpline for Men:

http://www.batteredmenshelpline.org/

REFERENCES

American Psychiatric Association. (1989). *Diagnostic and statistical manual of mental Disorders* (3rd Edition) Revised. Washington, D.C.: American Psychiatric Association.

Aurora Police Department. (1990). *Policies and procedures for handling domestic violence cases.* Aurora, CO: Aurora Police Department.

Bachman, R. (1994). *Violence against women: A national crime victimization report.* Washington, DC: U.S. Dept. of Justice. U.S. Government Printing Office.

Bae, R.P. (1981). Ineffective crisis intervention techniques: The case of the police. *Crime and Justice, 4,* 61–82.

Bannon, J.D. (1975, August). Law enforcement problems with intra-family violence. Paper presented at the Annual Meeting of the American Bar Association, Montreal.

Bard, M. (1971). *The study and modification of intrafamilial violence: The control of aggression and violence.* New York: Academic Press.

Berk, R. & Newton, P.J. (1985). Does arrest really deter wife battery? *American Sociological Review, 50,* 253–262.

Bettelheim. (1947). Individual and mass behavior in extreme situations. In T.M. Newcom and E.L. Hartley (Eds.), *Readings in social psychology.* New York: Holt, Rinehart and Winston.

Biderman, A.D. (1967). Captivity love and behavior in captivity. In G.H. Grosser, H. Wechler, & Greenblatt, M. (Eds.), *The threat of impending disaster.* Cambridge, MA: MIT Press.

Bowker, L.H., Arbitell, M. & McFerron, R. (1988). On the relationship between wife beating and child abuse. In Y. Kerti & M. Bograd (Eds.), *Feminist perspectives on wife abuse.* Newbury Park, CA: Sage.

BLPC (Boston Lesbian Psychologies Collective). (1987). Urbana/Chicago: University of Chicago.

Breslin, W.J. (1983). Police intervention in domestic confrontations. *Journal of Police Science and Administration, 6,* 293–320.

Browne, A. (1987). *When battered women kill.* New York: Free Press.

Bruno v. Codd, 47 NY 2d 528, 1979.

Bureau of Justice Assistance. (1993). *Family violence: Interventions for the justice system.* Washington, D.C.: U.S. Department of Justice. U.S. Government Printing Office.

Buzawa, E.S. & Buzawa, C.G. (1996). *Domestic violence: The criminal justice response* (2nd Edition). Thousand Oaks, CA: Sage.

Buzawa, E.S. & Buzawa, C.G. (Eds.) (1992). *Domestic violence: The changing criminal justice response.* Westport, CT: Auburn House.

Calhoun-Stuber, S. & Mickish, J. (1990, February). Effects of criminal justice system intervention in domestic violence cases: The next step. Paper presented at the Annual Meeting of the Academy of Criminal Justice Sciences, Denver.

Cardarelli, A. (ed.). (1997). *Violence between intimate partners: Patterns, causes and effects.* Boston: Allyn and Bacon.

Carmody, D.C. & Williams, K.R. (1987). Wife assault and perceptions of sanctions. *Violence and Victims, 2,* 1, 25–38.

Chesler, P. (1987). *Mothers on trial.* Seattle, WA: Seal Press.

Clunis, D.M. & Green, D.G. (1988). *Lesbian couples.* Seattle, WA: Seal Press.

Cohen, M. (2000). Measuring the costs and benefits of crime and justice. National Institute of Justice. Washington: U.S. Government Printing Office.

Coleman, D.H. & Straus, M.A. (1979, August). Alcohol abuse and family violence. Paper presented at the American Sociological Association, Boston.

CRS, Colorado Revised Statutes, Sec. 1, 18–6–800. 3.

Denver Police Department. (1990). *Domestic violence manual.* Denver, CO: Denver Police Department.

Dobash, R.E. & Dobash, R. (1979). *Violence against wives.* New York: Free Press.

Edwards, S. (1989). *Policing 'domestic' violence: Women, the law and the state.* Newbury Park, CA: Sage.

Eisenbertg, S.E. & Micklow, P.L. (1976). The assaulted wife: 'Catch 22' revisited. *Women's Rights Law Reporter, 3,* 138–161.

Eitzen, D.S. (1988). *In conflict and order: Understanding society.* Boston: Allyn and Bacon.

Elk, R. & Johnson, C.W. (1989). Police arrest in domestic violence. *Response to the Victimization of Women and Children, 12,* 4, 7–13.

Ewing, W., Lindsey, M. & Pomerantz, J. (1984). *Battering: An amend manual for helpers.* Denver, CO: Abusive Men Exploring New Directions.

FBI. (1989). *Uniform crime reporting handbook.* Washington, D.C.: U.S. Government Printing Office.

Fields, M.D. (1978). Wife beating: Government intervention policies and practices. In *Battered women: Issues of public policy.* Washington, D.C.: U.S. Commission on Civil Rights.

Finn, J. (1986). The relationship between sex role attitudes and attitudes supporting marital violence. *Sex roles, 14,* 5/6, 235–245.

Finn, P. & Colson, S. (1990). *Civil protection orders: Legislation, current court practice, and enforcement.* Washington, D.C.: U.S. Department of Justice. U.S. Government Printing Office.

Fortune, M.M. (1987). *Keeping the faith: Questions and answers for the abused woman.* NY: Harper and Row.

Gaines, K., Mickish, J. & Haack, D. (1991). *Domestic violence: A guide for health care providers.* Colorado Domestic Violence Coalition and Colorado Department of Health (2nd ed). Denver, CO: CDVC and CDLI.

Gallup, R. (1990). Executive Director, Abusive Men Exploring New Directions. Interview.

Ganley, A. & Harris, L. (1978, August). Domestic violence: Issues in designing and implementing programs for male batterers. Paper presented at the American Psychological Association Annual Meeting, Toronto, Canada.

Gelles, R.J. (1979). *Family violence.* Beverly Hills, CA: Sage.

Gelles, R.J. & Cornell, C.P. (1990). *Intimate violence in families.* Newbury Park, CA: Sage.

Gelles, R.J. & Straus, MA. (1988). *Intimate violence: The definitive study of the causes and consequences of abuse in the American family.* New York: Simon and Schuster.

Gilles & Mederer. (1985, November). Comparison or control: Intervention in the cases of wife abuse. Paper presented at the annual meeting of the National Council on Family Relations, Dallas, Texas.

Graham, D.L.R., Rawlings, E. & Rimini, N. (1989). Survivors of terror: Battered women, hostages and the Stockholm Syndrome. In K. Yllo and M. Bograd (Eds.), *Feminist perspectives on wife abuse.* Newbury Park, CA: Sage.

Harway, M. & O'Neil (eds.) (1999). *What causes men's violence against women?* Thousand Oaks, CA: Sage.

Hamberger, K. (1990). The impact of mandatory arrest on domestic violence perpetrator counseling services. *Family Violence Bulletin, 6,* 1, 11–12.

Hickman, S. (1990). Executive Director, Domestic Violence Initiative for Women With Disabilities. Interview.

Hendricks, J.E. (1985). *Crisis intervention: Contemporary issues for on-site interveners.* Springfield, IL: Charles C Thomas, Publisher, Ltd.

Herskowitz, L. (1966). Tort liability between husband and wife: The interspousal immunity doctrine. *Miami Law Review.*

Island, D. & Letellier, P. (1991). *Men who beat the women who love them: Battered gay men and domestic violence.* Binghamton, NY: Haworth.

Jacobson, B. (1977). Battered women–the fight to end wife beating. *Civil Rights Digest, 9,* 13.

Jaffe, P., Wolfe, D.A., Telford, A. & Austin, G. (1986). The impact of police charges in incidents of wile abuse. *Journal of Family Violence, 1,* 1, 37–49.

Jensen, RH. (1978). Battered women and the law. *Victimology, 2,* 585–590.

Johnson, J. (1981). Program enterprise and official cooperation in the battered women's shelter movement. *American Behavioral Scientist, 24,* 6, 827–842.

Kelly, L. (1989). How women define their experiences of violence. In K. Yllo and M. Bograd (Eds.), *Feminist perspectives on wife abuse.* Newbury Park, CA: Sage.

Klaus, PA. (1994). *The costs of crime to victims.* Washington, D.C.: U.S. Department of Justice. U.S. Government Printing Office.

Kuhl, A.F. (1983). Community responses to battered women. *Victimology, 7,* 49.

Langley, R. & Levy, R.C. (1978). Wife abuse and the police response. *FBI Law Enforcement Bulletin, 4,* 6.

Lerman, L .G. (1981). *Prosecution of spouse abuse: Innovations in criminal justice response.* Washington, D.C.: Center for Women Policy Studies.

Lerman, Landis & Goldzweig. (1981). State legislation on domestic violence. *Research on Violence and the Family, 4,* 1.

Lerman, L.G. (1986). Prosecution of wife beaters: Institutional obstacles and innovations. In M. Lystad (Ed.), *Violence in the home: Interdisciplinary perspectives.* New York: Brunner/Mazel.

Lindsey, M. (1990). Founder, Abusive Men Exploring New Directions. Interview.

Lobel, K. (Ed.). (1986). *Naming the violence: Speaking out about lesbian battering.* Seattle,

WA: Seal.

Loseke, D.R. & Cahill, S.E. (1984). The social construction of deviance: Experts on battered women. *Social Problems, 31,* 3, 296–310.

Martin, D. (1976). *Battered wives.* San Francisco, CA: Glide.

Martin, D. (1978). Overview–scope of the problem. In *Battered women: Issues of public policy.* Washington, D.C.: U.S. Commission on Civil Rights.

Mclver, R.M. (1973). *Social causation.* Gloucester, MA: Peter Smith.

Meuer, T., Seymour, A. & Wallace, H. (2000). *Domestic violence.* United States Department of Justice, Office of Victims of Crime. Washington: U.S. Government Printing Office.

NCWFL (National Center on Women and Family Law). (1989). Resource List-Battered Women-Litigation. Item No. 24.

National Institute of Justice. (1984). *Family violence.* Washington, D.C.: U.S. Department of Justice. U.S. Government Printing Office.

National Institute of Justice. (1986). *Confronting domestic violence: A guide for criminal justice agencies.* Washington, D.C.: U.S. Department of justice. U.S. Government Printing Office.

National Institute of Justice. (1986). *Preventing domestic violence against women.* Washington, D.C.: U.S. Department of Justice. U.S. Government Printing Office.

National Institute of Justice. (1988). *Establishing and expanding victim-witness assistance programs.* Washington, D.C.: U.S. Department of Justice. U.S. Government Printing Office.

NIJ/CDC (2000). *Extent, nature, and consequences of intimate partner abuse: Findings from the national Violence Against Women Survey.* United States Department of Justice. Washington: U.S. Government Printing Office.

Parnas, R.I. (1970). Judicial response to intrafamily violence. *Minnesota Law Review, 54,* 585–644.

Parnas, R. (1971). Police discretion and diversion of incidents of intrafamily violence. *Law and Contemporary Problems, 36,* 546.

Potter, J. (1978). Police and the battered wife: The search for understanding. *Police Magazine, 1,* 41–50.

Pressman, B., Cameron, G. & Rothery, M. (Eds.). (1989). *Intervening with assaulted women: Current theory, research, and practice.* Hillsdale, N.J.: Lawrence Erlbaum Associates.

Ptacek, J. (1988). Why do men batter their wives? In K. Yllo and M. Bograd (Eds.), *Feminist perspectives on wife abuse* (pp. 133–157). Newbury Park, CA: Sage.

Renzetti, C. (1988). Violence in lesbian relationships. *Journal of Interpersonal Violence, 3,* 4, 381–399.

Roberts, A.R. (Ed.). (1984). *Battered women and their families: Intervention strategies and treatment programs.* New York: Springer.

Romero, M. (1985). A comparison between strategies used on prisoners of war and battered wives. *Sex Roles, 13,* 9/10, 537–547.

Roth, J.A. (1994). *Understanding and preventing violence.* Washington, D.C.: U.S. Department of Justice. U.S. Government Printing Office.

Russell, D.E. (1982). *Rape in Marriage.* New York: Macmillan.

Saathoff, A.J. & Stoffel, E.A. (1999). Community-based domestic violence services. *Domestic Violence and Children, 9,* 3, 97–110.

Schecter, S. (1982). *Women and male violence: The visions and struggles of the battered women's movement.* Boston, MA: South End Press.

Schumacher, J.A., Feldbau-Kohn, S., Slep, A.M.S. & Heyman, R.E. (2001). Risk factors for male-to-female partner physical violence. *Aggression and Violent Behavior 6,* 2–3, 281–352.

Scott, E.J. (1981). *Calls for service: Citizen demand and initial police response.* Washington, D.C.: U.S. Department of Justice. U.S. Government Printing Office.

Seligman, M.E. (1975). *Helplessness: On depression, development, and death.* San Francisco, CA: W.H. Freeman.

Sherman, L.W. & Berk, R. (1984). The Minneapolis domestic violence experiment. *Police foundation reports.* New York: Police Foundation.

Sonkin, D.J. (1987). *Domestic violence on trial: Psychological and legal dimensions of family violence.* New York: Springer.

Sonkin, D.J. & Durphy, M. (1982). *Learning to live without violence.* San Francisco, CA: Volcano Press.

Sonkin, D.J., Martin, D. & Walker, L. (1985). *The male batterer.* New York: Springer.

Stordeur, R.A. & Stille, R. (1989). *Ending men's violence against their partners: One road to peace.* Newbury Park, CA: Sage.

Straus, M.A., Gelles, R.J. & Steinmetz, S.K. (1981). *Behind closed doors: Violence in the American Family.* New York: Anchor Books.

U.S. Attorney General's Task Force on Family Violence. (1984, September). *Final Report.* Washington, D.C.: U.S. Dept. of Justice. U.S. Government Printing Office.

U.S. Commission on Civil Rights. (1978). *Battered women: issues of public policy.* Washington, D.C.: U.S. Commission on Civil Rights.

U.S. Commission on Civil Rights. (1982a). *The federal response to domestic violence.* Washington, D.C.: U.S. Government Printing Office.

U.S. Commission on Civil Rights. (1982b). *Under rule of thumb: Battered women and the administration of justice.* Washington, D.C.: U.S. Commission on Civil Rights.

U.S. Department of Justice. (1980). *Intimate victims: A study of violence among friends and relatives.* Bureau of Justice Statistics, Bulletin. Washington, D.C.: U.S. Government Printing Office.

U.S. Department of Justice. (1986). *Danger to police in domestic disturbances—A new look.* Washington, D.C.: National Institute of Justice. U.S. Government Printing Office.

U.S. Surgeon General's Workshop on Violence and Public Health. (1985). *Final Report.* Washington, D.C.: U.S. Government Printing Office.

Walker, L.E. (1990). *Terrifying love.* New York: Harper and Row.

Walker, L.E. (1979). *The battered woman.* New York: Harper and Row.

Widom, C.S. & Maxfield, M.G. (2001). An update on the 'Cycle of Violence.' *National Institute Research in Brief.* Washington: U.S. Government Printing Office.

Chapter 4

POLICE RESPONSE TO DOMESTIC VIOLENCE

MICHAEL G. BRECI

INTRODUCTION

The police are the gatekeepers to the criminal justice system. They are the first responders to problems that occur in the community. How they handle a problem determines how involved other branches of the criminal justice system will become. To illustrate; a police officer observes a car going back and forth over the centerline. The officer stops the car and determines the driver is intoxicated. At this point, the officer has several options. First, the officer may decide to take no action, in which case the driver has been deflected away from the system. Second, the officer could write the driver a citation for a reduced charge, such as reckless driving. In this case, the driver will have limited contact with the system. Finally, the officer could arrest the driver for driving under the influence of intoxicants. In this instance, the offender will appear in court and face further contact with the system. In this scenario, the initial decision by the officer determined the level of involvement of the criminal justice system. The same applies to police response to domestic violence.

The police are usually the first agency to respond to families experiencing crises. In fact, the police spend a considerable amount of their time responding to these types of calls. Nationwide, 15 to 40 percent of all calls for police assistance are family disturbances (U.S. Commission on Civil Rights, 1982), and as Sherman (1992) states, "Up to eight million times each year, this nation's police are confronted with a victim who has just been beaten by a spouse or lover" (p. 1). In Atlanta, 60 percent of the calls on the night shift are domestic dispute calls (Hyde and Rosenberg, 1980). Family disturbances range from the very trivial to being deadly. The majority of the disputes, however, do not involve situations where the police often have the authority to make an arrest. For example, Hirschi and Hutchison (1987) estimate 75 percent of family disturbance calls involve situations where probable cause does not exist to show a crime has been committed. In cases that do involve violence, the decisions officers make affect how involved disputants will become in the criminal justice system. The decision to arrest or not reflects the formal and informal policies of law enforcement agencies. There is yet another dramatic statistical finding on domestic violence and the police. Between 1987 and 1996, there was a 121 percent increase in the number of people arrested for "offenses against family and children" in the United States (Sourcebook of Criminal Justice Statistics, 1997, p. 333).

Over the last thirty years, these policies have changed dramatically. This chapter will examine the evolution of the police response to family disturbances. The changing police response involves three stages: the traditional response (prior to the mid 1970s), the service response (1970s–1980s), and the arrest response (1980s). For each of these stages, the research, implementation, and critique will be reviewed. To conclude, we discuss the form police response has taken in the 1990s and into the new millennium. In this chapter female pronouns will be used to refer to spouse abuse. This does not imply chauvinism, but rather reflects the fact that the majority of spouse abuse victims are female.

TRADITIONAL POLICE RESPONSE

Prior to the mid 1970s, the prevailing response by police officers to family disturbance calls was to "cool" the situation down and then leave as quickly as possible. The philosophy behind this response was that outside agencies should not get involved in family affairs. The participants themselves best worked out family problems. As a result, the traditional police response could be described as one of "noninvolvement."

Research

In the 1950s and 1960s, family violence was not defined as a social issue within the United States. In fact, the typical family was believed to be like those portrayed on television shows such as "Leave It to Beaver" or "Father Knows Best." These types of shows fostered the image that the husband and wife without police intervention could address problems in the middle-class family calmly and rationally. In the 1970s, researchers "discovered" a seamier side to the American family (Dobash and Dobash, 1979; Martin, 1976; Walker, 1979). They found family violence was pervasive in our society.

Moreover, it occurred among all races, social classes, and in every section of the country. Family violence was not a new problem, however, but one may say that it was discovered during the decade of the seventies.

Violence within the family has been common throughout most of recorded history. Under the guise of patriarchy (male domination), males have had power and authority over their wives and children. Over the last 2000 years of western history, societies have enacted laws protecting males' rights to control and punish their wives. In the United States, it wasn't until 1871 that attention was focused on the "ancient privilege" of wife beating when two states, Alabama and Massachusetts, rescinded statutes protecting males who beat their wives. Since then, all the states have changed their laws on wife beating; however, the attitudes and values underlying patriarchy have been slower to change (Pagelow, 1984). The police were aware that problems existed in the family long before researchers discovered it. Since the development of the modern police in 1829, officers have been responding to domestic disputes. Their perceptions of the causes for the problems occurring in the family were influenced, however by the attitudes and beliefs held within society. Thus, their interventions reflected societal values on male/female relationships. Viewed in this light, it is not too surprising that an officer's response was one of nonintervention. They believed that the family best handled problems occurring within the family.

Interviews with police officers lend credence to this justification for nonintervention. Davis (1981) found that officers developed stereotypes of domestic disturbances and then based their response on these conceptions. According to Davis, officers believed that fights in the family were natural and to be expected; consequently, arrest was avoided in favor of non-legal remedies. These officers contended responding to domestic disturbances was not "real" police work. As a result, they were less likely to become involved. Similarly, Burns and Jaffe (1983) speculated police officers do not get involved in family disputes because they perceive violence to be a normal male response to stress. Consequently, violence within the family was condoned as long as it remained within the family's private domain. As recently as 1994, victims of domestic violence reported that the matter was personal or private as an important reason for not reporting instances to the police (U.S. Dept. of Justice, 1994). Police departments assigned low priority to family violence. This reinforced officer's attitudes that the police should not be involved in family affairs. As social awareness of the problem of family violence spread in the 1970s, the police were severely criticized for their failure to adequately respond to domestic violence (Martin, 1976). Researchers charged that police officers were not only inadequately trained to address and manage family violence situations but were also given little guidance from their departments other than that "arrest should be exercised as a last resort" (Field and Field, 1973; p. 228).

Contributing to this problem was the ambiguous nature of the role of the police at domestic disputes. Should they respond as "law enforcers" or "peace keepers"? This uncertainty left officers with a considerable amount of discretion for handling family disputes (Pahl, 1982). With little training to guide them, officers relied on their own attitudes and values about family relationships. As Martin (1976) pointed out, most police officers were male, and they believed in the traditional attitudes that a man's home was his castle. As a result, officers were willing to accept "spousal violence as long as it is within certain limits" (Bae, 1981; p. 70). Compounding this factor was the lack of adequate, germane training for the law officer in how to address domestic crisis intervention situations (Schwartz, 1975).

Implementation

Prior to 1966, there were no police departments in the United States providing training for crisis management in domestic disturbances (Liebman and Schwartz, 1972). In fact, few departments had written policies or guidelines concerning family violence situations. As a result, police officers learned to handle these calls "on the job," from experienced officers as part of their professional socialization. The traditional response was passed down from veteran to rookie, with new officers interpreting the techniques based on their own attitudes and values. Walter (1981) demonstrated the influence of such beliefs in a study of small city police officers. The predominant attitudes held by the police toward family disturbance calls were "dislike, frustration, and anger" (Walter, 1981; p. 260). They disliked responding to family fights more than any other calls. They felt family fights were dangerous and should be avoided. The officers felt they had no legitimate role at domestic disturbances because they were private matters falling outside the realm of legal intervention. Walter traced these feelings back to the belief that nothing could be done successfully with a family fight call. As a result, the predominant response was minimal contact. Research examining the effect of situational determinants on an officer's decision to arrest at family fights illustrates the influence of their attitudes and beliefs. Berk and Loseke (1981) contended police officers responding to domestic disputes construct a picture of what happened based on their own prior experiences. For example, if a female is unwilling to sign an arrest warrant, the officer concludes from prior experiences that she will not follow through if the male is arrested. Therefore, the officer decides not to arrest. The decision to arrest is not based on whether or not a law has been violated. Rather, it is based on how the officer interprets the situation. Smith and Klein (1984) specified the situational determinants that influence officer decisions to arrest. The most important

factor was victim preference for arrest. Following victim preference in determining arrest were previous contact with the disputing parties, offender
antagonism toward the police, and drinking by the offenders. The traditional response was characterized by discretion. This discretion gave officers the
power to determine their response based on extralegal criteria. Beliefs, personal experiences, and situational determinants became the deciding factors
influencing officers' decisions at family fights. A more recent study also high-
lights the importance of victim preference as this factor may influence officer discretion. Buzawa and Austin (1993), in an extensive study of domestic
violence, examined reports in domestic cases and conducted follow-up interviews with some 90 victims. In the final analysis, Buzawa and Austin (1993)
found that victim preference for arrest was one important factor, among
three, which influenced an officer's decision to arrest. The other two factors
were the presence of bystanders and whether the victim lived with the
offender. The presence of bystanders increased the likelihood of arrest, as
did instances where the victim and offender lived with each other (Buzawa
and Austin, 1993; p. 613–614).

Critique

The battered women's movement focused attention on the plight of battered women which enabled family violence to emerge as a "high priority
social issue" (Gelles, 1980; p. 144) in the late 1970s. The rise in awareness of
family violence reinforced critics assertions that the police response to
domestic disputes was deficient (Bard, 1973; Field and Field, 1973; Martin,
1976). Studies of battered women portray the ineffectiveness of the traditional response. Brown (1984) interviewed 84 battered women residing in a shelter home for abused women who indicated that despite the physical violence
inflicted upon them by their husbands, the police rarely made an arrest and
seldom referred them to other agencies for help. Similarly, Pahl (1982) questioned 42 battered women who contended the police were the least helpful
of all the agencies they turned to for help. The victims said that the police
were unwilling to get involved even when asked to or when the extent of
injuries would seem to have made legal actions appropriate" (Pahl, 1982; p.
341). Research in the 1970s suggested domestic disputes accounted for a high
percentage of police deaths and injuries (Bard and Zacker, 1985). As a result,
departments focused on safety measures for officers which reinforced the
philosophy of nonintervention in domestic cases or calls (Bae, 1981). Garner
and Clemmer (1986) examined this relationship between response and
police injury and concluded "domestic disturbances account for only a small
proportion of all police deaths" (Garner and Clemmer, 1986; p. 2). They
contend that domestic violence calls are not a major cause of mortality to the

police; therefore, police agencies should switch their focus from officer protection to improving police effectiveness in response to domestic disturbances.

SERVICE PERSPECTIVE

In the 1970s, researchers and advocates for battered women demanded police accountability when responding to family fights. Critics claim: "the ineffective police response to domestic violence has at its roots inadequate training" (Hendricks, 1985; p. 52). Police agencies responded by instituting domestic violence training for officers. The philosophy guiding this approach was that trained law enforcement officers would act as practitioners mediating violent family situations. To facilitate their role as practitioners, officers would develop skills and techniques that would enable them to fashion an intervention that best fit the needs of the participants involved. This approach, the service perspective, gained momentum in the mid 1970s and continued into the 1980s.

Research

The idea of training police officers to handle family disturbance calls was popularized by Morton Bard in the early 1970s. Bard developed an experimental project, which provided officers with the skills and insight necessary to improve their effectiveness when responding to family crisis situations. The findings from this study were promising (Bard, 1969; Bard and Zacker, 1985; Bard, 1980) and led to the rapid development of police training programs in the United States.

The early training programs implemented by police departments had four major goals:

1. Officer safety
2. To improve the relationships between social service agencies and the police
3. To develop the skills necessary for officers to deal with family disputes
4. To improve the attitudes of police officers toward their role in family crisis intervention (Buchanan & Chasnoff, 1986)

The amount and type of training officers received varied based on the degree of specialization departments employed in handling domestic violence. Bard (1973) developed a typology to illustrate the different forms of family crisis intervention training:

1. *Generalist* is where all patrol officers are trained in domestic crisis intervention.

2. *Specialist* refers to a small group of selected officers trained to respond only to domestic dispute calls.
3. *Generalist-specialist* trains a select number of officers to mainly handle domestic disputes, but they are also assigned to other duties.

Bard used the *Generalist-Specialist* model for his project; however, the Generalist model has been the most widely used by police departments in this country (Buchanan and Chasnoff, 1986).

Training provided by the department-influenced officers' attitudes and response to domestic disputes. Breci and Simons (1987) found the training offered by departments was an important predictor of the type of response employed by officers handling family fights. Departments that stressed a service response provided training that gave officers the types of skills and knowledge necessary to provide services to disputants, whereas departments that favored a law enforcement approach were less likely to provide training and more likely to encourage nonintervention or arrest.

Implementation

The training model developed by Bard (1969) offered police officers intensive training in practical techniques for handling disturbances as well as a theoretical understanding of the dynamics involved in violent relationships. The project had five interrelated content areas: crisis intervention, interpersonal conflict management, and theory on the structure and dynamics of the family, intervention methods, and referral networks. Eighteen police officers were trained at the City College of New York and then paired up and instructed to handle all of the family disturbance calls on their tour of duty. In a twenty-two-month period, they engaged in 1,388 interventions with 962 families. An evaluation of the experiment showed there was a reduction in the number of family assaults in the precinct. Bard noted the favorable attitude families had toward the officers' intervening and concluded:

"Attitudes toward police will change when the police are seen as performing in ways consistent with principles of human psychology and when they are given realistic training to render professional police services with dignity" (Bard, 1969; p. 249). The positive results generated by this experiment led Bard (1980) to conclude that the police should not be limited in their use of discretion when responding to family fight calls. Bard contended that single alternatives, such as mandatory arrest, were too simplistic in scope to solve such a complex problem as domestic violence. In contrast, police trained to implement skilled interventions not only have the power to arrest, but also can employ any number of interventions that would best meet the needs of the family involved.

Training programs developed in the 1970s were strongly influenced by

Bard's ideas with departments throughout the country adapting the model to fit the needs of their own agency. Some departments developed innovative variations to the Bard model that emphasized collaboration between police officers and social workers. A project in Illinois had social workers placed in police departments to follow up with those families identified by the police as high risk (Treger, 1975) of having domestic conflicts. In Ft. Lauderdale, Florida, social workers were teamed with police officers to provide on-the-scene crisis intervention (Higgins, 1978), while in Erie, Pennsylvania, social workers trained police officers to intervene skillfully in domestic disturbances. Ann Arbor, Michigan developed a program to improve the linkages between community social service agencies and the police (Hanewicz et al., 1982). Reportedly the first program, one in Richmond, took a generalist approach to crisis intervention in domestic violence cases (Schwartz, 1975). Regardless of the form of the training program, a major goal was to raise the consciousness level of officers regarding the dynamics of family violence. Workshops were designed to dispel the myths about wife beating and to encourage cooperation between law enforcement, social agencies, and women's groups (McShane, 1979). Crisis training sessions, involving role-played domestic disputes, gave officers insight into the feelings and motivations of disputants. Presentations by community agencies, such as battered women's shelters, counseling agencies and family court provided officers with an understanding of the social network they operated within and the community's social services. By and large, these programs were successful in sensitizing officers to the plight of battered women as well as changing officers' attitudes toward family violence (Schreiber, 1975; Buchanan and Perry, 1985; Levens and Dutton, 1985; Bandy et al., 1986; Breci, 1989).

Critique

Interest in training programs peaked in the 1970s and then began to decline in the 1980s. The decline can be attributed to "the lack of empirical evidence to support the claims made by these programs" (Buchanan and Chasnoff, 1986; p. 161) and to criticisms leveled at police for not protecting battered women. A multiyear study of domestic violence led Bell (1985) to conclude the police were contributing to the perpetuation of family violence by not taking decisive action at these calls. Of the 128,171 domestic disputes reported in Ohio between 1979 and 1981, victims were either injured or killed in 41 percent of the cases, but an arrest was made by the police only 14 percent of the time. Bell claimed the police were failing to make justifiable arrests, and thus failing to provide legal coverage to victims of domestic violence. Oppenlander's (1982) analysis of the 1977 Police Services Study led to similar conclusions reached by Bell, in that the police were not doing their jobs when responding to domestic violence situations. In the Police Services Study, trained observers rode with the police in 24 communities recording officer response to complaints. Six findings emerged from this study:

1. The police were slower to respond to family fights than other types of disputes, for example, bar fights.
2. The police were more concerned with the suspect and less concerned with the needs of the victim.
3. The most common strategy used by officers was nonintervention.
4. Few of the officers who used mediation and counseling had been trained in counseling techniques.
5. Ninety percent of the officers were familiar with referral agencies, but in only 4 percent of the domestic disturbances was a referral made.
6. Disputants saw the police as authority figures there to enforce the law, not as facilitators providing on the scene counseling.

Based on these findings, Oppenlander devalues the service perspective and police training: "Arrest at least offers greater potential than make shift psychological palliatives for reducing family violence" (Oppenlander, 1982; p. 463). Wermuth (1982) was also critical of the training approach. She contends programs based on Bard's model assume violence within the family is not a criminal matter but an interpersonal problem. Police interventions are then based on the precept that both participants were equal partners and, therefore, both responsible for the violence. As a result, criminal sanctions, though warranted, were seldom considered. Instead of focusing on the causes of violence against women, the criminal justice system mystified the problem: "Violence becomes a symptom of weakness and illness, rather than of power and force" (Wermuth, 1982; p. 43). According to Wermuth, the police had to start taking responsibility for protecting the victims of violent domestic abuse and to begin treating it [domestic violence] in the same manner as other violent crimes.

ARREST PERSPECTIVE

The arrest perspective developed as a reaction to police under enforcement in violent family situations. Activist groups wanted to reduce or eliminate the discretion officers possessed in handling family violence calls by developing guidelines specifying arrest when violence occurred in the family. Two types of arrest policies evolved in the 1980s. *Preferred arrest* policies raised the presumption that an offender should be arrested when certain criteria were met. *Mandatory arrest* policies *required* the arrest of an offender if the criteria were satisfied. The difference between the two policies revolves around the degree of officer discretion allowed. Mandatory arrest mandates an arrest, which limits an officer's discretion. Preferred arrest suggests that an arrest might be an appropriate action with the presence of certain criteria, giving the officer more freedom to interpret the situation (Hutchison and Hirschel, 1990).

Research

The movement toward adoption of arrest as the primary response to family violence was fueled by the Minneapolis Police Project. Sherman and Berk (1984) hypothesized that police officers have three options for handling a misdemeanor domestic disturbance case:

1. Forced separation to achieve short-term peace;
2. Mediation as a means of getting to the underlying cause of the dispute; or
3. Arrest the assailant to protect the victim.

They devised an experiment in which officers randomly used one of these three options when responding to family disputes. They evaluated the dependent variable in the experiment by recording the number of callbacks to a particular residence in a six-month period. They also interviewed the victims to ascertain the success of the intervention. Analysis of the results led Sherman and Berk to conclude that arrest produced less recidivism than separation or mediation. Following the publication of this study, researchers criticized Sherman and Berk's conclusions. According to the critics, there were numerous problems regarding the methodology and the validity of their statistical analysis (Binder and Meeker, 1988). Despite the criticisms, this study received unprecedented national media attention, and was credited with the implementation of arrest policies in many police departments around the country (Sherman et al., 1986).

Two attempts at replicating the Minneapolis Project provided mixed support. The first attempted to replicate the findings. Berk and Newton's (1985) analysis of 783 wife battering cases in California generally supported arrest as a deterrent in wife abuse cases. There was a conditional effect, however, in that arrest was most effective for batterers the police would normally arrest. In an actual replication of the Minneapolis experiment in Omaha, Nebraska, arrest was found to be no more effective than separation or mediation (Dunford, Huizinga and Elliott, 1989). In a more recent study of the deterrent effect of arrest, Berk et al. (1992) found some support that arrest was a deterrent to future domestic violence, but they caution as follows:

> . . . there is some evidence that arrest works better for some suspects [those who are employed] than others. However, the case is hardly overwhelming, and it's meaning unclear. Therefore, we believe there are no direct policy

implications except for the general warning that a particular arrest will not necessarily lead to a beneficial outcome. The findings [of the present study] do not provide a sound rationale for abandoning arrest, even presumptory arrest, as a policy *option*. (p.706)

The Minneapolis study, and other related research, has had a significant impact in the formation of public policy in the 1980s, but of equal importance was the advocacy of the feminist movement. Feminist groups helped to raise public consciousness about the conditions battered women endured. The growing awareness of women's rights led to several celebrated lawsuits against police departments. In these cases, the courts found the police violated battered women's due process rights by failing to make an arrest when an assault occurred (for example, *Thurman v. City of Torrington*, 1984; *Balistreri v. Pacific Police Department*, 1988; *Ross v. Gaston* (Indiana), 1999; *Fajardo v. County of Los Angeles*, 1999). The lawsuits provided the impetus for state legislatures to pass laws requiring arrest in family violence situations and for police departments to implement arrest guide lines for officers (Zalman, 1990; Lemon, 2001). Additional evidence in support of possible arrest guidelines may be culled from the work of Eigenberg and Moriarty (1991). These researchers found that a sample of Texas peace officers were largely unaware of the legal criteria under which police could make a warrantless, discretionary arrest in domestic violence cases.

Implementation

By 1988, ten states had passed mandatory arrest laws to guide officers responding to family violence situations (Hutchison and Hirschel, 1990). One of the first was the state of Washington. Six months after the passage of the state law, the number of arrests in Seattle had increased by 520 percent with a corresponding 300 percent increase in the number of prosecutions (Ferguson, 1987). Likewise, arrests have been shown to increase under mandatory arrest policies especially when a restraining order was in place (Mignon and Holmes, 1995). Similar results were noted in other departments following the implementation of arrest guidelines (Burns and Jaffe, 1983; Quarm and Schwartz, 1985; Rowe, 1985; Jaffe et al., 1986; Davis, 1987). Nationally, the passage of state laws and the implementation of departmental policies in the 1980s resulted in "more men than ever before . . . being sanctioned by the Criminal Justice System for the crime of domestic violence" (Hamm, 1989; p. 41).

Police officers' reactions to the enactment of arrest guidelines have varied. Officers in Indiana are encouraged to make arrests when probable cause exists that an assault has occurred within the family. Ford (1987) found

Indianapolis police officers were not opposed to arresting males who beat their wives, but due to the nature of the relationship (being spousal), were more likely to look for alternatives to arrest. Michigan's state laws also allow officers to make warrantless arrests at domestic violence situations. Detroit police officers' response to the new law was to decrease the number of arrests at family fight situations. Officers stated they were willing to intervene, but they perceived arrest as a last resort (Buzawa, 1982) which was reminiscent of police attitudes and practices of a decade before. A survey of police officers in Sioux Falls, South Dakota, found 85 percent favored the new domestic violence laws that gave officers the power to make probable cause arrests. The majority of officers (65%) felt there should be an arrest when violence occurred in the family, even if the officer had not observed it (Green, 1986). In comparison, 15 percent of Detroit's police officers thought the police shouldn't even respond when the violence occurred before the police were notified, while 39 percent felt they should refer the parties elsewhere (Buzawa, 1982). The Minneapolis police department implemented a mandatory arrest policy after publication of the Sherman and Berk study. Three years after implementing the guidelines Minneapolis police officers indicated they favored the policy and were making arrests when warranted. Moreover, the officers felt that mandatory arrest was an effective deterrent in reducing future family fights (Breci, 1990b).

The attitudes police officers hold are instrumental in determining the effectiveness of arrest guidelines. Saunders and Size (1986) compared the attitudes of battered women with police officers and found the majority of victims (63%) favored arrest, in contrast, only four percent of the officers felt arrest was an appropriate response to family violence. Breci (1987) compared the attitudes of officers with different educational levels. Officers with higher levels of education felt mandatory arrest laws would not provide long-term solutions for reducing violence in the family. Rather, they believed officers should respond to family violence situations using an eclectic approach. This type of response would give officers a number of interventions to choose from to best meet the needs of the participants involved. In contrast, officers with less education were more likely to see mandatory arrest laws as a long-term solution to family violence. Victim perceptions also matter. Smith (2000) in a multistate study of domestic violence victims found that favorability for mandatory arrest must be considered in light of other issues. While her subjects tended to support mandatory arrest laws, few believed the laws were of direct benefit to them. Moreover, the findings also suggest that mandatory arrest laws might reduce the chance of victim reporting in future domestic violence incidents (Smith, 2000).

Critique

State law and department policies have been combined to direct and guide officers in the handling of domestic violence calls. The intent of these guidelines is to limit officer discretion. The majority of domestic disputes, however, do not require an arrest. As a result, in cases that do require an arrest, officers have a great deal of discretion, which enables them to classify events as either fitting or not fitting the guidelines. To illustrate, the Phoenix police department adopted an arrest policy to coincide with Arizona's preferred arrest law. Ferraro (1989) reports that despite the policy, arrests were made in only 18 percent of the battering incidents responded to by the Phoenix police. Discretion allows officers to interpret the situation in such a way as to reinforce their attitudes regarding the avoidance of arrest.

Hutchison and Hirschel (1990) examined the effect of state law on police policy regarding arrest in domestic violence. Twenty-five police departments in 25 states were surveyed. Seven of the states had mandatory arrest laws. The departments in these states had aggressive policies requiring arrest when violence occurred. The other 18 states had preferred arrest policies. Departments in these states developed guidelines that paralleled those states with mandatory arrest in cases where *serious* violence occurred. However, in preferred arrest states, the majority of the departments allowed officer discretion in cases of minor injury. Hutchison and Hirschel (1990) point out only a very small number of domestic violence calls involve serious injury. For the majority of family violence calls, officers in states with preferred arrest policies are given too much discretion. They argue states with preferred arrest policies should be changed to mandatory arrest, because they are "better equipped to capture the real range of abusive behavior and to treat it seriously" (Hutchison and Hirschel, 1990; p. 24). Further, other researchers have called into the question the usefulness of mandatory arrest policies (Gelles, 1993; Mills, 1998; Schmidt and Sherman, 1993).

There are three factors associated with officer acceptance of preferred arrest policies. First, an officer's values toward domestic violence affects whether or not arrest policies will be followed. Second, female officers are generally more supportive of arrest policies than male officers. And finally, training affects officers' attitudes toward arrest (Hutchison and Hirschel, 1990). Training has the most potential for changing officers' traditional values and influencing the acceptance of arrest policies. Arrest policies should not be "viewed as a panacea for the problem of the abuse of women" (Hutchison and Hirschel, 1990; 26). Spouse abuse is a complex problem that requires societal-based solutions. The following six factors illustrate the scope of the problem:

1. Most domestic disputes do not involve situations that allow the police

to make an arrest.

2. On the scene arrest is not an option in many states when the abuser leaves before the police arrive. In these situations, the female must sign out a warrant.

3. The arrest movement was fueled in the 1980s by one experiment, the Minneapolis Study. Replications in other cities have not found support for the conclusion that arrest reduces recidivism or serves as an effective specific deterrent to domestic violence.

4. Arrest means different things in different communities. It may mean one hour in jail or a weekend. There is no evidence to show the effect of different levels of incarceration on the offender.

5. There is great variation in individuals that are abusive. Some have been arrested many times; others are first-timers. Arrest will have varying degrees of impact depending on the person's involvement with the criminal justice system.

6. Abuse is a societal problem requiring changes in societal values and attitudes.

Hutchison and Hirschel point out: "It is myopic to think that this rather straightforward action by the police will have a long-term impact on the overall problem" (Hutchison and Hirschel, 1990; p. 28).

Other, more recent research on deterrence, domestic violence, and arrest echoes some of the same sentiments. While Berk et al. (1992) maintain support for domestic violence arrest options and simultaneously provide important policy caveats, others, most notably Peter K. Manning, have been quite critical of criminal justice arrest policies on theoretical, philosophical, and deterrent grounds. Manning (1993) maintains that current arrest policies directed at domestic violence cases are bereft of significance given the differing meanings that "arrest" may have in domestic violence situations and that arrest policies cater merely to "crime control" preferences in society and the criminal justice system. Stark (1993) argues, in part, that ". . . the wisdom of arrest should be assessed in terms of its effect on violent behavior; *whatever they are.* To do this, we need to conceptualize the presumed object of the arrest policy—woman battering—and unpack the 'demand' that arrest is designed to satisfy" (p. 654).

POLICE RESPONSE IN THE 1990s

Police response over the last two decades has been strongly influenced by societal priorities. Social awareness of the incidence and the dysfunctional nature of family violence resulted in the service perspective of the 1970s. The conservative philosophy of the 1980s advocated a "get tough" stance with law violators, which led to arrest guidelines being implemented by state legislators and police departments. The two perspectives provided police with the awareness and the power to protect family violence victims, but the perspectives, in and of themselves, did not go far enough.

The Attorney General's Task Force on Family Violence (1984) recommended that "every law enforcement agency should establish arrest as the preferred response in cases of family violence" (1984; p. 17). Further, the Task Force stated law enforcement officers should be "well trained in diagnosis, intervention and referral of family violence victims and perpetrators" (1984; p. 77). In essence, the Task Force recommended combining the arrest and service perspectives. Thus, the awareness offered by the service perspective and the power to protect offered by the arrest perspective would increase the effectiveness of the officers responding to family disturbances in the 1990s.

The combination of the arrest and the service perspectives reflect the general public's desire for a more effective police response to domestic disturbances. To illustrate, a random sample of Minnesota residents were surveyed on their perceptions of the police role at family violence calls. Minnesota residents were strongly in favor of mandatory arrest laws but also wanted police officers to provide services to disputants, such as helping them work through disputes or referral to agencies that can help (Breci, 1990a). On the surface, this may seem contradictory, but in reality it is not. When an assault has been committed, an arrest should be made. However, most family disturbance calls do not involve physical violence. For the majority of disputes, officers who are trained can help disputants or refer them to someone who can. By training officers to provide services, the police may help to prevent situations from becoming violent in the future.

Combining the arrest and the service perspectives will improve police response, but even that does not go far enough. The most promising strategies for the 1990s involve coordinating the efforts of the police with other community agencies (Rowe, 1985). Steinman (1990) found the enforcement of arrest policies reduced the recidivism rate of family violence offenders when police action was coordinated with community interventions, such as pretrial diversion programs, men's anger control groups, alcohol and drug referral agencies, and the prosecutor's office. Dutton (1988) indicates court mandated treatment for males who assault their spouses aids in the reduction of recidivism. The actions of the police are reinforced when the courts and treatment agencies take the crime of spouse abuse seriously and follow up with the offender who has been arrested.

Community mobilization offers concrete strategies for combating family violence in the 1990s. But even these efforts do not go far enough. Family violence is endemic to American society. It is a complex societal problem that requires complex solutions that address the very nature and structure of our society. A similar point is made in the conclusion of Sherman's (1992) work *Policing Domestic Violence* when he writes: "If this book proves anything, it is that 'getting tough' [in response to domestic violence] in a simplistic way like mandatory arrest offers no guarantee of winning a 'war' on crime, any more than getting tough will win a 'war' on cancer. It should also demonstrate that domestic violence, like all crime, is as complex as cancer, and equally difficult to treat. . ." (p. 266).

CONCLUSION

This chapter reviewed the evolution of the police response to family violence. Prior to the 1970s, the most common strategy used by police officers responding to family disturbance calls was "noninvolvement." This response failed to protect victims of spouse abuse, so in the 1970s, departments implemented training that focused on the dynamics of family violence. Training provided officers with skills to help families experiencing crises. In the 1980s, the police were criticized for failing to arrest abusers. State legislatures and police departments responded by developing policies requiring officers to arrest spouse abusers, which were based on popular, and limited, research.

Neither of these solutions, by themselves, have provided a panacea for police agencies or society. The problem was too complex for simple solutions. However, police experiences over the last twenty years offer insight for developing policies in the 1990s. Research indicates combining the arrest and service perspectives will increase the effectiveness of the police. Further, coordinating police action with other community agencies will enable a more efficient and focused approach to handling family violence in the community.

CHAPTER QUESTIONS

1. What factors affect a police officer's decision to arrest at domestic disturbances?
2. How does patriarchy influence family relationships?
3. Describe the traditional response used by police officers to respond to family disputes.
4. What effect do situational determinants play in an officer's decision to arrest?
5. What is the philosophy behind the service response?
6. What is the difference between mandatory arrest policies and preferred

arrest policies?
7. How do you think police officers should respond to family disturbances in the future?

SIMULATED EXERCISES

Simulated Exercise 1

You and your partner arrive at the Smith residence. It is apparent Mr. and Mrs. Smith have both had too much to drink. Mrs. Smith contends Mr. Smith hit her in the stomach, and she wants him out. Mr. Smith denies hitting Mrs. Smith, and says she is an alcoholic and has delusions when she drinks too much. Both Mr. and Mrs. Smith are very upset. Which of the following solutions would you use and Why?

1. Arrest only Mr. Smith.
2. Arrest only Mrs. Smith.
3. Arrest both Mr. and Mrs. Smith.
4. Tell them to call back when they are sober.
5. Have Mr. Smith leave for the night.
6. Calm the situation down then leave.
7. Help them to work out their problems.
8. Refer them to social agencies for help.

Simulated Exercise 2

You and your partner are called to the Brown residence. Mrs. Brown (age 60) claims Mr. Brown (age 65, recently retired) sits around the house all day and verbally harasses her. She states he has not laid a hand on her, but she fears for her safety because of his deep depression and constant drinking. She says he will not listen to her and she does not know what to do. Mr. Brown refuses to talk to you and your partner. What are you going to do?

1. Arrest Mr. Brown.
2. Tell Mrs. Brown to call back when he gets violent.
3. Tell Mr. Brown to leave.
4. Calm Mrs. Brown down then leave.
5. Help Mr. and Mrs. Brown to work the problem out.
6. Refer them to a social agency for help.

Simulated Exercise 3

The neighbors call the police and complain about the fighting going on at the Mars residence. You and your partner arrive and find Mr. and Mrs. Mars in the front yard hitting each other. Both have visible cuts and bruises. It is apparent both have been drinking, but neither is intoxicated. Both are very excited. They begin screaming at you that this is their problem and they do not want you interfering. What are you going to do?

1. Leave.
2. Arrest Mr. Mars only.
3. Arrest Mrs. Mars only.
4. Arrest both Mr. and Mrs. Mars.
5. Have either Mr. or Mrs. Mars leave.
6. Calm them both down, and then leave.
7. Help them to work out their problems.
8. Refer them to social agencies for help.

Simulated Exercise 4

You and your partner arrive at the Jones residence. Mrs. Jones is standing over Mr. Jones with a frying pan in her hand screaming at Mr. Jones. Mr. Jones has a large gash in his head and appears to be dazed. Mrs. Jones is very upset, she claims he can't do anything right, he burned the meat loaf. What are you going to do?

1. Arrest Mrs. Jones.
2. Have Mrs. Jones leave for the night.
3. Calm the situation down, then leave.
4. Help them to work through their problems.
5. Refer them to social agencies for help.

APPENDIX A

Additional Internet Resources

For further information about police response to incidents of domestic violence visit the following websites.

National Association of Domestic and Child Abuse Investigators:
  http://www.nadcai.org/
National Center for State Courts, The Center
for Family Violence and the Courts:
  http://www.ncsconline.org/famviol/index.html
The Greenbook Initiative:
  http://www.thegreenbook.info/
Minneapolis Domestic Violence Experiment Summary:
  http://www.policefoundation.org/pdf/minneapolisdve.pdf
Metropolitan Nashville Police Department, Domestic Violence Division:
  http://www.police.nashville.org/bureaus/investigative/domestic/default.htm
Safe State, California Attorney General's Crime and Violence Prevention Center:
  http://safestate.org/index.cfm?navid=221
Partnership Against Violence Network:
  http://www.pavnet.org/
Institute of Law and Justice, Domestic Violence Resource Page:
  http://www.ilj.org/dv/
The Battered Women's Justice Project:
  http://www.bwjp.org/
ABA Commission on Domestic Violence:
  http://www.abanet.org/domviol/home.html
Office for Victims of Crime:
  http://www.ovc.gov/
Office of Violence Against Women:
  http://www.ojp.usdoj.gov/vawo/
WomensLaw.Org:
  http://www.womenslaw.org/index.htm

REFERENCES

Attorney General's Task Force. (1984). *Family violence.* Washington, D.C.: U.S. Government Printing Office.

Bae, R.P. (1981). Ineffective crisis intervention techniques: The case of the police. *Journal of Crime and Justice, 4,* 61–82.

Bandy, C., Buchanan, D.R., & Pinto, C. (1986). Police performance in resolving family disputes: What makes the difference? *Psychological Reports, 58,* 743–756.

Bard, M. (1969). Family intervention police teams as a community mental health resource. *The Journal of Criminal Law, Criminology and Police Studies, 60,* 247–250.

Bard, M. (1973). *Early crisis intervention: From concept to implementation.* Washington, D.C.: U.S. Department of Justice Law Enforcement Assistance Administration.

Bard, M. (1980). Functions of the police and the justice system in family violence. In Green (Ed.), *Violence and the Family.* Boulder: Westview.

Bard, M. & Zacker, J. (1985). The prevention of family violence: Dilemmas of Community intervention. *Journal of Marriage and the Family, 31,* 677–682.

Bell, D.F. (1985). The police response to domestic violence: A multiyear study. *Police Studies, 8,* 58–63.

Berk, S.F. & Loseke, D.R. (1981). Handling family violence: Situational determinants of police arrest in domestic disturbances. *Law and Society Review, 15,* 317–346.

Berk, R.A. & Newton, P.J. (1985). Does arrest really deter wife battery?: An effort to replicate the findings of the Minneapolis spouse abuse experiment. *American Sociological Review, 50,* 253–262.

Berk, R.A., Campbell, A., Klap, R. & Western, B. (1992). The deterrent effect of arrest in incidents of domestic violence: A Bayesian analysis of four field experiments. *American Sociological Review, 57,* 698–708.

Binder, J. & Meeker, J.W. (1988). Experiments as reforms. *Journal of Criminal Justice, 16,* 347–358.

Breci, M.G. (1987). Police officers' values on intervention in family fights. *Police Studies, 10,* 192–202.

Breci, M.G. (1989). The effect of training on police attitudes toward family violence: Where does mandatory arrest fit in? *Journal of Crime and Justice, 12,* 35–49.

Breci, M.G. (1990a). When to call the cops: Public views on police involvement in family disturbances. Paper presented to the Academy of Criminal Justice Sciences, Denver.

Breci, M.G. (1990b). Police officers' perceptions of mandatory arrest guidelines. Paper presented to the Midwest Criminal Justice Association, Chicago.

Breci, M.G. & Simons, R.L. (1987). An examination of organizational and individual factors that influence police response to domestic disturbances. *Journal of Police Science and Administration, 15,* 93–101.

Brown, S.E. (1984). Police responses to wife beating: Neglect of a crime of violence. *Journal of Criminal Justice, 12,* 277–288.

Buchanan, D.R. & Chasnoff, P. (1986). Family crisis intervention programs: What works and what doesn't. *Journal of Police Science and Administration, 14,* 161–168.

Buchanan, D.R. & Perry, P.A. (1985). Attitudes of police recruits towards domestic disturbances: An evaluation of family crisis training. *Journal of Criminal Justice, 13,* 561–572.

Burns, C.A. & Jaffe, P. (1983). Wife abuse as a crime: The impact of police laying charges. Canadian *Journal of Criminology, 25,* 309–318.

Buzawa, E.S. (1982). Police officer response to domestic violence legislation in Michigan. *Journal of Police Science and Administration, 10,* 415–424.

Buzawa, E.S. & Austin, T. (1993). Determining domestic response to domestic violence victims: The role of victim preference. *American Behavioral Scientist, 36, 5,* 610–623.

Davis, P.W. (1981). Structured rationales for non-arrest: Police stereotypes of the domestic disturbance. *Criminal Justice Review, 6,* 8–15.

Davis, R.C. (1987). The domestic violence prevention project: A proactive response to familial abuse. *The Police Chief 54,* 42–44.

Dobash, R.E. & Dobash, R. (1979). *Violence against wives: A case against patriarchy.* New York: The Free Press.

Dunford, F.W., Huizinga, D.E., & Elliott, D.S. (1989). *The Omaha domestic violence police experiment.* Washington, D.C.: National Institute of Justice.

Dutton, D.G. (1988). *The domestic assault of women.* Boston: Allyn and Bacon.

Eigenberg, H. & Moriarty, L. (1991). Domestic violence and local law enforcement in Texas: Examining police officers' awareness of state legislation. *Journal of Interpersonal Violence, 6, 1,* 102–109.

Ferguson, H. (1987). Mandating arrests for domestic violence. *FBI Law Enforcement Bulletin, 56,* 6–11.

Ferraro, K.J. (1989). Policing woman battering. *Social Problems, 36,* 61–74.

Field, M.H. & Field, H.F. (1973). Marital violence and the criminal process: Neither justice nor peace. *The Social Service Review, 47,* 22 1–240.

Ford, D.A. (1987). The impact of police officers' attitudes towards victims on the disinclination to arrest wife batterers. Paper presented to the Third National Conference for Family Violence Researchers, University of New Hampshire.

Garner, J. & Clemmer, E. (1986). *Danger to police in domestic disturbances: A new look.* Washington, D.C.: National Institute of Justice.

Gelles, R.J. (1993). Constraints against domestic violence. *American Behavioral Scientist, 36, 5,* 575–586.

Gelles, R.J. (1980). Violence in the family: A review of research in the seventies. *Journal of Marriage and the Family, 42,* 143–155.

Green, D. (1986). Police Chief's Survey of Sioux Falls, South Dakota Police Officers.

Hamm, M.S. (1989). Domestic violence: Legislative attitudes toward a coherent public policy. *Journal of Crime and Justice, 12,* 37–59.

Hanewicz, V.P., Cassidy-Riske, C., Fransway, L.M. & O'Neill, M.W. (1982). Improving the linkages between domestic violence referral agencies and the police: A research note. *Journal of Criminal Justice, 10,* 493–503.

Hendricks, J.E. (1985). *Crisis intervention: Contemporary issues for on-site interveners.* Springfield, IL: Charles C Thomas, Publisher, Ltd.

Higgins, J. (1978). Social services for abused wives. *Social Casework, 59,* 266–271.

Hirschel, J.D. & Hutchison, I.W. (1987). Experimental research on police response to spouse assault: The Charlotte project. Paper presented to the American Society of Criminology, Montreal, Canada.

Hutchison, I.W. & Hirschel, J.D. (1990). A Critical analysis of the movement toward preferred arrest policies in spouse abuse cases. Paper presented to the Academy of Criminal Justice Sciences, Denver.

Hyde, J.S. & Rosenberg, B.G. (1980). *Half the human experience.* Lexington, KY: Heath.

Jaffe, P., Wolfe, D.A., Telford, A. & Austin, G. (1986). The impact of police laying charges in incidents of wife abuse. *Journal of Family Violence, 1,* 37–49.

Lemon, N.K.D. (2001). *Domestic violence law.* St. Paul: West Group.

Levens, B.R. & Dutton, D.G. (1980). *The social service role of police: Domestic crisis intervention.* Ontario: Minister of Supply and Services.

Liebman, D.A. & Schwartz, J.A. (1972). Police programs in domestic crisis intervention: A review. In Snibbe and Snibbe (Eds.), *The urban policeman in transition.* Springfield, IL: Charles C Thomas, Publisher, Ltd.

Manning, P.K. (1993). The preventive conceit: The black box in market context. *American Behavioral Scientist, 36,* 5, 639–650.

Martin, L. (1976). *Battered wives.* New York: Pocket Books.

Mignon, S.I. & Holmes, W.M. (1995). Police response to mandatory arrest laws. *Crime and Delinquency, 41,* 4, 430–442.

McShane, C. (1979). Community services for battered women. *Social Work, 24,* 34–39.

Mills, L.G. (1998). Mandatory arrest and prosecution policies for domestic violence. *Criminal Justice and Behavior, 25,* 3, 306–318.

Oppenlander, N. (1982). Coping or copping out. *Criminology, 20,* 449–465.

Pagelow, M.D. (1985). *Family violence.* New York: Praeger.

Pahl, F. (1982). Police response to battered women. *Journal of Social Welfare Law, 82,* 337–343.

Quarm, D. & Schwartz, M.D. (1985). Domestic violence in criminal court: An examination of new legislation in Ohio. *Women and Politics, 4,* 29–45.

Rowe, K. (1985). The limits of the neighborhood justice center: Why domestic violence cases should not be mediated. *Emory Law Journal, 34,* 856–910.

Saunders, D.G. & Size, P.B. (1986). Attitudes about woman abuse among police officers, victims and victim advocates. *Journal of Interpersonal Violence, 1,* 25–42.

Schmidt, J.D. & Sherman, L.W. (1993). Does arrest deter domestic violence? *American Behavioral Scientist, 36,* 5, 601–609.

Schreiber, F.B. (1975). Crisis intervention training for police using civilian instructors. *The Police Chief, 42,* 254–258.

Schwartz, J.A. (1975). Domestic crisis intervention: Evolution of a police training program. *Crime Prevention Review, 2,* 4, 9–16.

Sherman, L.W. & Berk, R.A. (1984). The specific deterrent effects of arrest for domestic assault. *American Sociological Review, 49,* 261–272.

Sherman, LW., Cohn, E.G., & Edwin, E. (1986). *Police policy on domestic violence: A national survey.* Washington, D.C.: Crime Control Institute.

Sherman, L.W. (1992). *Policing domestic violence: Experiments amid dilemmas.* New York:

The Free Press.

Smith, A. (2000). It's my decision, Isn't it?: A research note on battered women's perceptions of mandatory intervention laws. *Violence Against Women, 6,* 12, 1384–1402.

Smith, D. & Klein, J.R. (1984). Police control of interpersonal disputes. *Social Problems, 31,* 468–481.

Stark, E. (1993). Mandatory arrest of Batterers: A reply to its critics. *American Behavioral Scientist, 86,* 5, 651–680.

Steinman, M. (1990). Does arrest coordinated with other criminal justice interventions lower rates of woman battering? Paper presented to the Academy of Criminal Justice Sciences, Denver.

Sourcebook of Criminal Justice Statistics. (1997). National Institute of Justice. Washington, DC: U.S. Government Printing Office.

Treger, H. (1975). *The police-social worker team.* Springfield, IL: Charles C Thomas, Publisher, Ltd.

United States Commission on Civil Rights. (1978). *Battered women: Issues of public policy.* Washington, D.C.: U.S. Government Printing Office.

United States Department of Justice. (1994). *Violence against women: A national crime victimization survey report.* Washington, D.C.: U.S. Government Printing Office.

Walker, L. (1979). *The battered woman.* New York: Harper and Row.

Walter, F.D. (1981). Police in the middle: A study of small city police intervention in domestic disputes. *Journal of Police Science and Administration, 9,* 243–260.

Wermuth, L. (1982). Domestic violence reforms: Policing the private? *Berkeley Journal of Sociology, 27,* 27–49.

Zalman, M. (1990). The courts response to police intervention in domestic violence. Paper presented to the Academy of Criminal Justice Sciences, Denver.

Chapter 5

CHILD ABUSE AND NEGLECT

BARBARA A. CARSON and BRUCE K. MACMURRAY

INTRODUCTION

Intervention into child abuse cases, whether they involve physical abuse, neglect, or sexual abuse, presents unique dilemmas for professionals. First, there are critical and immediate decisions that must be made. It must be determined whether or not a child has been injured, and, if so, a decision must be made concerning the likelihood that the child may experience future, or further, injury. At the same time that a crisis intervention team is attempting to make these decisions, it often must also be determined if a criminal offense has taken place. Therefore, the role of interveners in child abuse and neglect cases is often twofold: investigatory and protective.

It is important that intervention in child abuse cases be made by professionals who are sensitive to the type of world in which the typical abused child lives and recognize the political realities of agencies designated with the duty of protecting children from their abusers. Research on the subject is very clear in demonstrating how improper intervention into these cases can drastically increase the trauma experienced by both the child victim and other family members, a process called *secondary victimization.*

Such responses may be immediate, for example, where parents, upset by the accusation of child maltreatment, take revenge on the child shortly after caseworkers leave the house. More frequently, the term secondary victimization refers to the suffering experienced by the victims of child abuse as they are processed through the official intervention agencies. The effects of the intervention process may have long-ranging negative consequences for future family relations. Even in cases where parental rights to custody are terminated, the consequences for involved members can be extremely devastating. Intervention into child abuse cases is further complicated by the fact that few communities have the necessary services for child victims and thus, the range of options for deciding how to intervene in these cases may be severely limited.

While it is necessary to have general guidelines on how different types of cases are approached, flexibility is also needed in making decisions for intervention on individualized bases. The present chapter provides a brief background on what is known about child abuse, including physical abuse, neglect, and sexual abuse. Goals of intervention by professionals in the criminal justice system as well as for social services are then reviewed and general guidelines for intervention are provided.

DEFINITIONS

Physical child abuse is typically defined as the use of force against a child by a parent or guardian that results in death, permanent or temporary disfigurement, or impairment of any bodily organ (Besharov, 1978). All 50 U.S. states have laws prohibiting the intentional injury of children. Likewise, each of the states has laws regarding the neglect of children, which typically focus on parents or guardians failing to provide the necessities of life appropriate to the upbringing of children. Included here are needs such as health, nutrition, shelter, education, supervision, affection, and protection.

All states also have laws stating that emotional or psychological abuse is illegal but there is considerable diversity in what is covered by these laws. Emotional abuse may include any or all of the following behaviors: torturous restriction of movement; habitual patterns of belittling or denigrating a child; using deprivation of food, shelter, or sleep as a form of punishment; threatening a child with physical or sexual abuse. Some states also include issues of emotional neglect which include behaviors such as: providing inadequate affection to a child, having a child exposed to chronic spouse abuse, or encouraging a child to participate in illegal drug use or trafficking.

While some definitions of emotional harm specify concrete, observable behaviors, others are difficult to document. As such, it is relatively rare that cases involving solely allegations of emotional injury are processed by the criminal justice system (Melton and Corson, 1987; Melton and Davidson, 1987).

At present, complete consensus regarding a definition of sexual abuse does not exist even though all states have laws prohibiting and proscribing such behavior. This term has been used to denote a broad range of behaviors, often with considerable variation in the type of physical contact and the degree of force. A broad, straightforward definition of sexual abuse is a sexual act that is inappropriate for a child's age, level of development, or role within the family (Brant and Tisza, 1977).

Within the research literature on sexual abuse, several elements are particularly important for the definitional question: (1) the upper age limit of the victim; generally this ranges from 15 to 17 years old (Peters et al., 1986), (2) the types of sexual behavior that are involved: (a) actual penile penetration or intrusion, whether this intrusion is oral, anal, or vaginal; (b) molestation with genital contact where there is no penetration (e.g. kissing or fondling of genitals or masturbation); and (c) other forms of sexual abuse where there is either no contact (e.g., exposure or nudity) or acts which do not involve actual genital contact (e.g., fondling of breasts or buttocks) (National Center of Child Abuse and Neglect (NCCAN), 1988), and (d) whether the experience was considered abusive (Finkelhor, 1984; Finkelhor et al., 1986), unwanted (Russell, 1983), coercive (Wyatt, 1985), or the result of pressure or force by the offender.

EXTENT OF THE PROBLEM

In a nationally representative study where over 2,000 parents were interviewed through anonymous telephone calls, Straus and Gelles (1986) found that 620 children out of every 1,000 between the ages of 3 and 17 were physically abused during a one-year time period. One hundred seven per thousand (107 per 1,000) children suffered severe attacks such as kicking, biting, punching, hitting with an object, beating, threatening or using a gun or knife. Comparing this to an earlier study conducted in 1975, it appears that the number of children in the U.S. who are being abused is decreasing slightly.

Cases reported to official agencies present a different trend. Analyzing data from 1986 (one year after the Straus and Gelles study), the National Center on Child Abuse and Neglect (1988) found that more than one and one-half million children were officially reported and confirmed victims of abuse or neglect. This suggests that 25 out of every 1,000 children in the U.S. were substantiated as victims. This is a 66 percent increase over the number of cases reported in 1980.

Of the cases reported in 1986, the National Center on Child Abuse and Neglect study (also referred to as NCCAN) found that the majority involved neglect (63%), although close to half involved physical abuse (43%). The increase in reports between 1980 and 1986 was primarily due to a 58 percent increase in the number of physical abuse cases and a 300 percent increase in the number of reported and substantiated cases of sexual abuse.

According to the 1999 National Report Series publication "Children as Victims" (OJJDP, 2000), the number of child abuse victims in the United

States nearly doubled between 1986 and 1993. This finding was obtained through the third National Incidence Study of Child Abuse and Neglect (or NIS-3). Respondents included child protection agencies, criminal justice agencies, and community institutions. Consistent with previous research, far more children are victims of neglect than any other form of abuse. In 1993, 70 percent of the known cases of child maltreatment were classified as "neglect" (OJJDP, 2000). However, children often experience more than one type of maltreatment. This is evident when examining the categories of maltreatment. The study results appear as follows:

- Physical neglect (47%)
- Physical abuse (22%)
- Emotional neglect (21%)
- Emotional abuse (19%)
- Sexual abuse (11%)
- Educational neglect (14%)

Gender influenced the type of maltreatment. Females were three times more likely to be victims of child sexual abuse and emotional abuse was more common among males (OJJDP, 2000). The reported incidence of child maltreatment was also dependent on gender. Between 1986 and 1993, reports of male child abuse increased by 102 percent and the increase for females was 68 percent (OJJDP, 2000).

The National Child Abuse and Neglect Reporting System provide an additional, and more common, source of data on child maltreatment in the United States. Data from this source reveals the following:

- Of the estimated 2,974,000 referrals received, approximately three-fifths (60.4%) were transferred for investigation or assessment and two-fifths (39.6%) were screened out.
- More than half of child abuse and neglect reports (54.7%) were received from professionals. Nonprofessionals, including family and community members submitted the remaining 45.3 percent of reports.
- Most States have established time standards for initiating the investigation of reports. The average response time to initiate investigating reports was 63.8 hours.
- Slightly less than one-third of investigations (29.2 %) resulted in a disposition of either substantiated or indicated child maltreatment. More than half (54.7%) resulted in a finding that child maltreatment was not substantiated.
- The average annual workload of CPS investigation and assessment

workers was 72 investigations.
(http://www.acf.dhhs.gov/programs/cb/publications/cm99/high.htm)

In summary, it is unclear if the overall occurrence of child abuse in the U.S. is decreasing. However, it is clear that the number of reports of child maltreatment being made to official agencies is increasing at an overwhelming rate. This trend is likely to continue in the near future because, in part, research indicates that many cases of abuse, particularly sexual abuse, are still not reported to official agencies (Finkelhor and Hotaling, 1983). In the world of public opinion, there is support for the notion that the problem has gotten worse. According to a 1993 Harris Poll (NIJ, 1994), 75 percent of their respondents indicated that they thought the problem of child abuse had gotten worse compared to when they were children.

CHARACTERISTICS OF VICTIMS

Generally, as children get older they are more likely to be victims of physical abuse (NCCAN, 1988) as well as sexual abuse (Kilpatrick, 1997). However, children under the age of six are at the highest risk of being injured (Straus et al., 1979; National Center on Child Abuse and Neglect, 1988). Moreover, in 1999, "Children younger than a year old accounted for 42.6 percent of the fatalities, and 86.1 percent were younger than 6 years of age." (National Center on Child Abuse and Neglect, 2000). Additionally, "Maltreatment deaths were more often associated with neglect (38.2%) than with any other type of abuse." (National Center on Child Abuse and Neglect, 2000). This probably occurs because younger children are physically more fragile and more susceptible to injury. This factor may also account for the higher mortality rates from abuse for infants than for older children. Generally, children between the ages of 8 and 12 years are most vulnerable to sexual abuse (Finkelhor, 1984; Russell, 1983; Wyatt, 1985).

Research further suggests an increase in risk for children ages 6–7 years and those between ages 10 and 12 years, with the latter age group victimized at twice the average rate (see Finkelhor and Baron, 1986). The NCCAN study (1988) found only a marginal age trend for sexual abuse with the single statistically significant finding being that children between the ages of birth to two years old were less likely to be sexually abused than older children. Overall, females are more likely to be victims of physical abuse than males (NCCAN, 1988; OJJDP, 2000; Straus et al., 1980). Males are most at risk when they are younger and during adolescence but females at all age levels are still more likely to be victimized (Straus et al., 1980). However, more recent research has concluded that determining characteristics and risk factors for sexual abuse is difficult. The number of reported cases impacts our ability to accurately discuss these factors (Black, Heyman, and Slep, 2001).

Among the most consistently supported findings in research on sexual abuse is the higher rate of abuse for females than for males (OJJDP, 2000). For those surveys which have used random sample procedures, the average ratio of 2.5 female victims to each male victim suggests that about 71 percent of all sexual abuse victims are females, while about 29 percent are males (Finkelhor and Baron, 1986). The National Center on Child Abuse and Neglect (1988) found an even higher ratio among reported cases, where females were sexually abused at a rate nearly four times that of males (3.5 females compared to 0.9 males per 1,000) nationwide. Overall, these figures translate into an estimate of 30,400 boys and 107,000 girls being confirmed victims of sexual abuse in 1986. It is quite likely that this difference between agency and community surveys is largely a result of the underreporting of sexual abuse cases involving male victims in comparison to females (Finkelhor and Baron, 1986; Wood and Dean, 1984).

Studies examining ethnicity for sexual abuse victimization find no differences in the rates of white and black children being victimized (NCCAN, 1988; NCCAN, 1981; Russell, 1986; Trainor, 1984; Wyatt, 1985). This has also been found elsewhere (NIJ, 1994). For other ethnic groups, however, there is some evidence of differential victimization. For example, Kercher and McShane (1984), in a Texas sample, found Hispanic females face higher risks, and Russell (1986) found lower risks of abuse for Asian and Jewish females as compared to other groups in her San Francisco-based survey.

Despite anecdotal evidence suggesting higher risks for children raised in rural areas, there is mixed support. Finkelhor (1984) found higher rates of abuse for females who had grown up in rural locales, but Wyatt (1985) found higher rates for females from urban or suburban areas. Other evidence does not support any rural-urban differences (NIJ, 1994). For other measures of social isolation there is much stronger support (Finkelhor and Baron, 1986). First, sexual abuse victims tend to be isolated from peers. Second, females who live without their natural mothers or fathers are more vulnerable to sexual abuse, and mother's employment outside of the home is more characteristic of such families. Third, one of the most consistently supported findings is that victims generally have poor relationships with their parents. This has also been found for cases for child neglect (Schumacher, Slep, and Heyman, 2001). Fourth, sexual abuse victims are also particularly likely to have parents who do not get along well or are involved in conflict with each other.

Despite the strength and consistency of the findings that families where sexual abuse occurs are generally families with poor relationships between members, it is difficult to determine whether this situation is a precursor to, or consequence of, the abuse (Finkelhor and Baron, 1986). Poor intra-familial relations is also a possible contributor in cases of child psychological abuse (Black, Slep, and Heyman, 2001) and child physical abuse tends to be related to lower levels of family social support (Black, Heyman, and Slep, 2001).

CHARACTERISTICS OF PERPETRATORS

Parents are most typically the perpetrators of child abuse (OJJDP, 2000; Straus et al., 1980), younger parents more often than older parents (Lauer, 1974; Smith, 1975), and birth parents tend to be the most common abusers (OJJDP, 2000). Eighty percent of all perpetrators are parents to the child abuse victim (OJJDP, 2000). Mothers are more likely to be perpetrators than fathers are; however, since mothers spend more time with children, this is not unexpected. Research further indicates that there is a higher rate of abuse by fathers in families where the father is disabled or not currently employed, and thus, presumably spending more time at home with the children (Straus et al., 1980). However, and regardless of gender, children in single parent households are more likely to be abused (NCCAN, 1999; OJJDP, 2000).

It is clear that for physical abuse, families that are experiencing multiple problems are more likely to be abusive towards their children. Such problems include inadequate income (Straus et al., 1980; NCCAN, 1988; Hampton and Newburger, 1985), frequent unemployment (Steel and Pollock, 1974), lower levels of education (Straus et al., 1980), and large families (Gil, 1970; Light, 1973). As was discussed in terms of victims, perpetrators of child maltreatment tend to be socially isolated (Smith, 1975; Gaudin and Polansky, 1986; Polansky, 1985). For example, one study found that these parents generally do not have close ties to their extended family, neighbors, community groups, or religious organizations (Garbarino and Crouter, 1978). Additionally, it has been shown that perpetrators tend to be the heads of large households and have annual incomes under $15,000 per year (NCCAN, 1999; OJJDP, 2000).

Common sense thinking often states that both child abuse, generally, as well as sexual abuse, more specifically, is most likely to occur in lower or working class families. While research has established some support for this finding for physical abuse (OJJDP, 2000; Pelton, 1981; Straus et al., 1980), studies have found no relationship between socioeconomic class and sexual abuse (Finkelhor, 1984; Russell, 1986). This finding from community surveys is in sharp contrast with the experience of official agencies where class is consistently related to reported cases of sexual abuse (NCCAN, 1988; H.H.S., 1981; Trainor, 1984). This difference suggests that many cases involving higher social classes may not be known to official agencies.

Knowledge about victims of sexual abuse is not nearly as well balanced as the research on perpetrator characteristics. One important factor related to sexual abuse, which is well supported in the literature, is the presence of a stepfather (or nonbiologically related father) to the child. In opposition to cultural stereotypes of "dirty old men," or "friendly strangers," the majority of perpetrators of sexual abuse are related and/or known to the victim (NIJ, 1992; Mrazek, 1983; De Francis, 1969; Garbarino and Gilliam, 1980). Estimates suggest that approximately 77 percent of all reported sexual abusers are parents, 57 percent of whom are natural parents to the victims, while other relatives are responsible for 16 percent of these cases (H.H.S., 1982). Similarly, males are the abusers in 80–95 percent of reported cases (H.H.S., 1982; NCCAN, 1982; Conte and Berliner, 1982). In general, research suggests that sexual perpetrators show an unusual pattern of sexual arousal toward children, that such abusers are often "blocked" psychologically in their heterosexual and other social relationships, that alcohol is clearly a disinhibiting factor important in many sexual abuse situations, and that a substantial number of sexual abuse perpetrators were victims of sexual abuse themselves when they were younger (Finkelhor and Baron, 1986). However, when compared to other child abuse victims, child sexual abuse victims seem to be less likely to demonstrate a cycle of perpetration in later years (NIJ, 1992).

THE CHILD RAPE VICTIM

According to the Bureau of Justice Statistics (BJS, 1994), there were a total of 109,062 forcible rapes of females reported to the FBI Uniform Crime Reporting Program in 1992. Out of an interest in the ages of female victims, BJS initiated a survey among states in order to determine victim ages. It was revealed that 36 states did not keep data on victim ages while 14 states and the District of Columbia did. Of the jurisdictions maintaining such records, 15 in all, they reported victim characteristics on a total of 26,427 cases, or about 25 percent of the total population of reported rapes in the U.S. during that year.

These data reveal interesting and startling insight concerning the child rape victim. Of twelve states supplying data sufficient to distinguish victims by age, 51 percent of the victims within those states were under the age of 18. During the same year, 1992, females under age 18 made up only 25 percent of the female population within the United States. Due to design features of both the FBI Uniform Crime Reports and the BJS National Crime Victimization Survey, no sufficient data exists concerning child rape victims. However; estimates derived from the limited data obtained from the 15 jurisdictions indicate that one in six rape victims may be under the age of 12 and as many as 17,000 girls under the age of 12 may have been raped in 1992 (NIJ, 1994).

Possibly the most pronounced finding by BJS concerning child rape victims is the victim-offender relationship. Like other forms of child abuse, child rape victims typically are victimized by family members, acquaintances, or friends based on state level data and surveys of imprisoned rapists (NIJ, 1994).

GOALS OF INTERVENTION

Several authors and organizations have investigated the importance of child abuse and neglect intervention and the appropriateness of various intervention strategies (Budd, et al., 2001; Hershkowitz, 2001; Martin and Besharov, 1991; National Council on Crime and Delinquency, 1999; NIJ, 1992; OJJDP, 2001; Resick and Schnicke, 1990; Salter et al., 1985; Salter et al., 1985; Slep and Heyman, 2001; Whitcomb, 1992; Whitcomb et al., 1994; Widom, 1991). There are three primary goals for intervention in cases of child abuse. First, the immediate safety of the child must be established. Second, help and support need to be provided to the entire family unit experiencing the crisis. Third, it must be determined if a criminal act has occurred and whether or not an arrest is necessary. This mixture of goals is largely the reason why most communities authorize at least two distinct agencies to intervene in cases of child abuse: police and related criminal justice agencies and child protective or social service agencies.

Safety and Welfare of the Child

When intervening in child abuse crises, it is paramount to investigate and ensure the safety and welfare of all children in the home. Initially, it must be determined if these children are in need of special emergency services such as medical treatment or psychological counseling. The future safety of the children must also be assessed. It must be determined if it is safe to leave children in the home environment. This is an extremely critical decision point, because it may involve preventing the death of a child. Yet, it is difficult to evaluate whether or not future violence will take place. As much information as possible must be evaluated to make this decision as well as keeping in mind the general characteristics of victims and abusers of child maltreatment (as discussed earlier). The importance of this decision is intensified because, as will be discussed shortly, the intervention process itself may create further harm to the children.

Helping Troubled Families

A second goal of intervention is to reduce the trauma of the immediate situation and orient the family towards interactional patterns that will prevent acts of violence from reoccurring. It may be extremely painful for family members to acknowledge to outsiders that there are severe problems in their household. This alone can increase the trauma for all. Yet, if handled carefully, intervention can be a great opportunity for change, leading to greater understanding and willingness to improve relations among family members (Boergman et al., 1979).

Some theorists in the area of crisis intervention suggest focusing on the immediate situation rather than long term personal or interactional pathologies (Lukton, 1982; Kaplan, 1962; Caplan, 1964). However, in dealing with child abuse cases, it is probably more useful to focus on the crisis as part of a long-term pattern. Research indicates that there is a high probability that investigated abuse patterns have probably occurred repeatedly in the past, and are likely to occur again in the future (Straus et al., 1980). In addition, family ties last a lifetime, and the effects of abuse, as well as the intervention, are likely to influence family relationships and dynamics for extended periods of time.

It may be more useful to view the crisis as suggested by Brown (1980), namely a situation where ordinary people have reached a point in their lives where they are ineffective in coping with their own problems and possibly become dangerous to others around them. Typically, child abuse takes place at a time when parents are confronted with situations of stress and have few resources available. These parents are probably involved in almost constant crisis and the episode of child abuse may represent a life-threatening response to these circumstances.

The research on the multitude of problems experienced in abusive families supports this type of analysis. As such, one way to help terminate the crisis and to prevent future episodes of violence is to approach the intervention as the beginning of a process of providing support and services to troubled families.

Assessing Criminal Behavior

A final goal of intervention into child abuse cases is to determine whether or not there has been a violation of the criminal code and if someone should be arrested. There is considerable variation between states as to whether child maltreatment cases are processed in civil court, where a preponderance of evidence is needed, or if these cases proceed through criminal court where the highest standard of proof (that beyond a reasonable doubt) is needed

(Duncan, 1973). Previous research suggests criminal action and prosecution are relatively rare events for child abuse (Finkelhor, 1983; MacMurray, 1988; Rogers, 1982). Typically, only cases of sexual assault and child homicide are processed in criminal courts.

Prior research also indicates that there are many problems in pursuing legal action and criminal prosecution for child abuse cases (see MacMurray and Carson, 1991). These problems include such issues as: very young child victims are not yet verbal and thus unable to testify; even slightly older children may not be evaluated as credible witnesses; concerns about victim/witness cooperation; the sufficiency of available evidence; the nature of the family situation; and feelings among many involved in the criminal justice system that child-parent relationships should not be dealt with in the public sector.

Berliner and Barbieri (1984) describe several reasons why it is also difficult to prosecute cases of child sexual abuse. First, adults, be they investigators, lawyers, judges, or juries, are skeptical that the incident described actually took place. There is always the concern that children may be lying. Second, many adults believe that perpetrators are mentally ill, thus they are in need of services, not legal prosecution. Third, adults believe that children will be traumatized by legal proceedings. Fourth, prosecutors, in particular, fear that children will not be good witnesses. Berliner and Barbieri (1984) cite evidence demonstrating that these four factors are all myths but nevertheless have an important impact on legal action taken in such cases.

In summary, there are three distinct goals that must be met in crisis intervention of child abuse cases. While these goals are extremely important, their specific content makes the actual process of intervention very difficult. For example, there are clearly conflicting concerns when intervention workers are attempting to provide support to a family in crisis but at the same time are deciding whether or not a child should be removed and whether or not criminal charges should be initiated. It is also extremely difficult to get family members to be open and responsive to crisis workers when what they say may incriminate them. These tasks are even further complicated in that the action involved in the intervention itself can increase the trauma experienced by the child (Whitcomb et al., 1985). The clinical literature has focused on the potential trauma for child victims as related to the criminal investigation process in terms of retardation, developmental immaturity, language and learning disabilities, fabrication and parental indoctrination, and post-traumatic stress disorder symptoms for child witnesses. This is particularly problematic for cases involving parent disputes related to divorce, custody, and/or visitation issues (Nurcombe, 1986; Quinn, 1986; Terr, 1987; Yates, 1987). This concern, called either "secondary victimization" or "system induced trauma" (Wolfe et al., 1987) has resulted in some changes in criminal proceedings and also has important implications for the crisis intervention process as will be discussed shortly.

TOWARD CRISIS INTERVENTION

The following section reviews the steps involved in the crisis intervention process for cases of child abuse. In the United States, laws regarding child abuse are state-level statutes and most social service agencies are regulated by state-level policies. Thus, while general guidelines for intervention can be provided, some of the tasks, especially those involving criminal investigation, may vary depending upon local jurisdiction. Perhaps this is most clearly suggested in policies on mandatory reporting.

Toward Intervention: Reporting Requirements and Responsibilities

With the enactment of The Child Abuse Prevention and Treatment Act of 1964, each of the 50 states passed legislation requiring that all forms of suspected child abuse is officially reported. While the range of mandated reporters varies somewhat by state, they minimally include physicians, nurses, teachers, and social workers. Some states extend this to require all adults who suspect child abuse to make a report. Regardless of their specific content, mandatory reporting laws are based on the view that children, due to their immaturity, are unable to make reports for themselves. The burden is placed on adults in the community to notify authorities of any improper treatment of children. The majority of states have criminal penalties for the failure to report abuse and some specify general statutory provisions establishing criminal liability. A few states have penalties ranging from $100 to $1,000 and/or jail imprisonment and some have specified statutory provisions establishing civil liability for not reporting cases of child maltreatment. Stevenson and Grauerholz (1993) maintain that reporting practices in child maltreatment cases may be enhanced by community crisis intervention centers.

Toward Intervention: Those Responsible For Receiving Reports of Child Abuse

States vary on who receives reports of suspected cases of child abuse. In some states, reports are made to the police, while in others they are provided to social or child protective service agencies, and in still others they are made to both. In some states, serious cases (e.g., sexual assault, death and serious physical injuries) are also reported to prosecutor's offices (MacMurray, 1988). Some professions are legally responsible to report suspected cases of child maltreatment. For example, certain mental health professionals, social service workers, and school personnel are often required to report cases to investigative agencies (OJJDP, 2000). Yet other states require that anyone, regardless of profession or status, report suspected cases.

THE CRISIS INTERVENTION PROCESS IN CHILD ABUSE AND NEGLECT CASES

Initial Contact

States also differ on who is assigned to conduct the initial investigation after a report is received. The police may conduct an investigation, by social workers in child protective services offices, or by both. Regardless of who is designated to respond to the emergency, most typically the investigation is required to take place within 21 to 48 hours of the initial report of alleged abuse.

Ideally, it is useful if representatives from both social services and the criminal justice system are actively involved in the initial contact (Cesnik and Pulls, 1977). Social service agents, most typically social workers, may need help from the criminal justice system in order to conduct their investigation. For example, meeting suspected abusive parents can be personally dangerous for social workers in situations where they are investigating cases of incest, the death of children, or in households characterized by abusive relationships among family members. In addition, there are times when the only way to obtain services for a family is to either secure a juvenile or family court's mandate and often this action can only be initiated by the police.

Similarly, law enforcement officers can benefit from working in conjunction with social workers. Social workers typically have more training in working with family conflict as well as with interviewing children. The necessity of these skills has led to some police departments employing, within their own ranks, individuals with social work training to serve in a position of victim advocate or to coordinate case investigations with other service agencies.

Because there are frequently two agencies responding to child abuse situations, and since each of these agencies tends to have different goals and approaches to intervention, it is not surprising that, at times, there is disagreement between the agencies concerning how to handle a particular case (Craft and Clarkson, 1985; Whitcomb et al., 1985). Some communities have found it helpful to formalize guidelines concerning how to proceed during times when professionals disagree. This may involve consulting supervisors or having policy dictate solutions. For example, in the State of New Jersey, it is written policy that during conflicts between agencies regarding the appropriate action for a family, the "welfare of the child" should be the paramount goal. Clearly, this policy does not resolve all problems, but it does establish guidelines on priorities as determined by the state. Other jurisdictions have adopted multiagency child protection teams or child resource centers with the responsibility of investigating child maltreatment cases with the express purpose of benefiting from each other's expertise and to share information across agency boundaries.

The initial work of intervention into child abuse cases requires interviewing the alleged child abuse victim and the parents as well as the alleged perpetrator, if this individual is someone other than a parent. In most cases it may also be helpful to interview others who may have witnessed the abuse or who have relevant knowledge about the family including siblings, extended family members, teachers, and neighbors. Usually, the first step is to speak with the child who is reported to be the victim. The National Institute of Justice (1992) has provided information on interviewing child victims. The Office of Violent Crime (OVC) of the U.S. Justice Department offers training materials for this purpose. Finally, various organizations such as the National Center for Child Abuse and Neglect and the national office of the Court Appointed Special Advocate Program (CASA) encourage proper training.

Interviewing Child Victims

The interview with the child generally should *not* be conducted in the presence of the parents. If the initial report originates with the school system, it may be helpful to make arrangements to schedule the initial interview to take place in the school. If such arrangements cannot be made, it is best to conduct the interview in an environment that is familiar and safe to the child.

It is likely that victimized children will be hesitant to talk to outsiders, particularly if they think they may be endangering the safety of their parents. Thus, it is important to establish a friendship-like rapport with the child. With many children it may also be useful to have a support person present during the interview. This should be someone whom the child knows and feels comfortable around, but someone who has no connection with the abusive incidents. In a number of jurisdictions, special facilities have been created to help reduce the trauma of interviews for children as well as for providing a setting conducive to investigations. These include special playrooms, anatomically complete or correct dolls, and the utilization of art materials (Cramer, 1986; Wolfe et al., 1987). Another important effort involves the employment of the child/victim/witness advocate, a person working in either the police department, for the prosecutor, or for the courts, and who is specifically trained to conduct interviews and work with children throughout criminal case processing (Whitcomb, 1985).

For cases involving allegations of sexual abuse or other forms of serious abuse, it is particularly crucial to be concerned about the issue of interviewers (or any adult present during the interviews) "prompting" or "suggesting" to children when they describe the alleged incidents. Hershkowitz (2001) in a study of interviews with child sexual abuse victims, found that "open-ended" questions or prompts tend to yield the most promising victim narratives from children. However, there is a thin line between trying to be supportive and encouraging victims to be as open and complete in their disclosure as possible, and having the interviewer "lead" the child into making certain statements during the interview. This is a problem that hampered the prosecution in the highly publicized McMartin day-care case in California. Similarly, whenever possible, the number of different interviews (and interviewers) should be minimized as much as possible in order to reduce the trauma the child experiences over the abuse. The use of a coordinated social service/criminal justice team to interview the child can help to eliminate this problem.

In the interview with the child it is crucial to establish who did what to whom. Generally, direct questions work best with children of all ages (Germain et al., 1985). For social service purposes, the collected information must be evaluated in order to substantiate the original allegation of child abuse. Typically, for consideration of criminal action, more rigorous criteria must be met. The interview with the victim in this context must reveal as accurately as possible: all of the incidents involving possible criminal abuse, clear and detailed information about the specific forms of behavior involved, the perpetrator(s) of such abuse, dates, times, and places where abusive episodes occurred, as well as any information about witnesses, participants, or other individuals who are aware of the abuse.

Photographing the victim's injuries is important, and these photographs must also be well documented. All pictures must be labeled and dated by the photographer. If injuries are in the genital area it is important to have a member of the same sex as the child present during inspection of the injuries. For alleged sexual abuse cases, a medical examination as well as psychiatric or counseling reports on the victim is often useful as supportive evidence.

Research in developmental psychology suggests that the statements of very young children (as young as four years of age according to Melton, 1985) can be as reliable and valid as those of adults. Research on memory, suggestibility, and cognitive abilities as they relate to legal testimony suggests far greater similarities than differences between children and adults (Goodman, 1984; Melton, 1985; Nurcombe, 1986). However, while social scientists indicate that the testimony of young children is credible local sitting judges do not always recognize this. Thus, when attempting to determine criminal responsibility, attention must be paid to local practices.

As discussed previously, intervention into a family crisis may pose a threat to the emotional health of child victims. However, the interview process also has the potential to help the child psychologically (Pyroos and Eth, 1984; Terr, 1986). The establishment of rapport between the crisis intervener and the child victim, if handled appropriately, can reduce the negative impact of the maltreatment the child has experienced (Germain et al., 1985). Attempts can be made to help build a positive self-concept for the child. The very act of children being able to communicate to a listener concerning how others have violated them can have the impact of developing trust and empowering child victims. This can also serve as a learning time as the children probably need information on what is acceptable caregiver behavior, that is, on what is appropriate and what is inappropriate.

Interviewing the Perpetrator

The interviewing of alleged perpetrators of abuse is similarly a very complex and delicate process. As is the case for interviewing victims, the concerns of social service and criminal justice agency representatives are related but distinct. For child protective workers, the primary issues relate to evaluating the issue of safety for the child and the potential risk of revictimization in the future. Yet, in cases where there are to be criminal charges filed against the perpetrator or a court petition filed for the provision of "protective services," the line of questioning must not violate legal procedures as defined by each state's criminal code.

Understandably, most adults will not be receptive to being interviewed about whether or not they have abused children, and this reaction may be particularly strong if the alleged perpetrator is the parent of the victimized child. A wide range of reactions by alleged perpetrators may occur. There is likely to be anger directed at the person who is "tampering in family matters," anger directed at whoever made the initial report of abuse, and anger directed at the victim(s)/survivor(s). There is often fear of official action. In addition, perpetrators may have tremendous problems in trying to understand their own behavior. They may feel genuinely guilty about what they have done. Many abusive parents love their children and may not be able to understand why they have abused their children. They may be very fearful that they are bad parents. Many may also be afraid that they may commit similar acts again (Borgman et al., 1979; Brown, 1980).

In spite of the range of potential reactions by perpetrators (often there is a mixture of reactions), certain facts must be established during the initial interview. It must be determined if the alleged perpetrator is aware of the incidents that have been reported. It must also be determined if the perpetrator's description of prior events is consistent with information the intervention workers have already collected. It must further be determined if there is evidence sufficient for criminal processing.

Regardless of the determination of criminal behavior, the immediate welfare of the child must also be assessed. The prior behavior of the alleged perpetrator, as well as his or her reaction to being accused of child abuse, can be used to determine whether or not the child is at risk of further harm. This involves evaluating whether or not the perpetrator may seek revenge upon the child at a later time, or whether the alleged abuser is in such despair that the care of the child may be in jeopardy.

Interviewing Nonaccused Parents

The initial intervention into child abuse cases also must include an interview with the victim's parent(s) not directly involved in the allegation of abuse. It must be established if these adults were also involved in the abuse incident(s). If they were not involved in the abuse, or if the alleged perpetrator is not a direct family member or someone living in the same household as the child, it is possible that the nonaccused parents will be extremely cooperative and will actively seek the best solution for their children. However, as stated earlier, parents inflict the majority of all abuse. Thus, while the collection of information from the nonabusing parent is essential, it must be recognized that the network of relationships of those involved may be complicated.

The initial assumption should be that the nonaccused parent is probably aware that abuse has been occurring. The reaction of this parent to the initial investigation may be a good indicator of the extent of his or her awareness. If this parent is indignant, horrified, and angry with the perpetrator, or, if it was this parent who initiated the formal report, it is possible that he or she was not previously aware of the abuse. Yet, simply because these reactions are exhibited, it should not be assumed that the children will be safe if they remain in the custody of these adults.

More commonly, the scenarios are very complex. Typically, the nonaccused adult has an intimate relationship with the alleged perpetrator; usually they are married. As such, the allegiance of the nonaccused parent may be divided between that of the child victim and the adult perpetrator. These parents may attempt to mediate the crisis in an attempt to preserve family relations. These efforts may be so strong that the nonaccused adults may deny the child's allegations even though they know they are true.

This mixture of reactions by the nonaccused parent makes documentation of facts difficult when trying to substantiate a case. More importantly, however, this situation also has implications for determining the future safety and welfare of the children. Sometimes, in spite of evidence to the contrary, the nonaccused parent refuses to acknowledge that abuse has occurred. In these cases, it must be inferred that the nonaccused parent will not be effective at preventing future violence. This presumption may have strong implications for decisions made by crisis intervention workers concerning how to resolve the emergency situation.

Investigation for Supporting Evidence

Often in cases involving allegations of child abuse, individuals other than the victim, the alleged perpetrator, and the child's parents need to be contacted as part of the investigation process. In many instances, such individuals can serve an invaluable role in helping to clarify, validate, and refine information gathered via the original abuse report and the initial interviews. In cases where siblings, other peers or friends, neighbors, teachers, physicians and nurses, as well as other relatives or household members have information relevant to the allegations of abuse, it is important to interview these individuals in a setting that is separate from the victim and the immediate family. As discussed in the previous sections on interviews, the primary focus for these discussions should concern what the witness knows about the alleged abusive incidents and how this individual knows this information. This information may be useful in assessing the validity of the victim's allegations for substantiation assessments. It may also aid in determining whether or not these reports describe behaviors that fit the legal definition of criminal abuse (or battery), neglect, or sexual abuse. Also significant in this sense is the issue of whether testimony by these individuals can be used in court for the prosecution of the cases, and related legal concerns of hearsay and corroboration.

Outcome Options

In the most serious cases, it must be determined if the child needs to be removed from the home on an emergency basis as a result of the current injuries. All states authorize police to take this action without court orders, and approximately half of the states allow child protective service workers to do so as well. In all child abuse cases, it must be determined if the child will be safe in the near future if he or she remains in the home. In these cases, it must subsequently be determined whether the process for permanent removal of the child from the home should be initiated.

The removal of the child from the home, for either temporary or permanent placement, should not be hastily adopted nor frequently used. For a number of reasons, there is the very real possibility that the out-of-home placement may promote more harm to the child than the original abuse that instigated the official intervention. Again, this may result in secondary victimization of the child abuse victim.

There are several ways in which the removal of a child from the home can increase the harm done to the child. First, many communities do not have adequate facilities for emergency placement of children. As such, sometimes, victimized children are sometimes placed in facilities such as juvenile detention centers or in local hospitals. These types of placements might cause serious trauma for a child who is already suffering considerably. Second, some communities have service networks that require a child to be transferred between numerous agencies and/or foster homes. Such constant moving also causes long-term harm to the child. Third, the intervention of public agencies into the family network is one that causes severe family strain, and this adds strain to a family that is already experiencing severe problems.

If the child or children are to be removed from the home, one must remember that the event may be extremely traumatic for both the parents and the children. Borgman et al. (1979) indicates that this may well induce a crisis in itself. They recommend that every effort be made to involve the parents in the decision regarding emergency placement. It is also important to consult and include the child or children in this decision as well. Placement with familiar friends or relatives is usually preferable as compared to foster care involving a stranger. Whatever the choice, the children need to feel that they will be in a secure environment. Many of these children experience extreme guilt, believing they are at fault for their removal from the home or for the arrest of their parents. Intervention workers need to realize these fears are common and efforts should be made to assure the children that they are not responsible for the violence, the arrest, or the out-of-home placement. If emergency placement is necessary, allowing the child to take familiar possessions (e.g., toys, clothing, pictures, etc.) will help ease the trauma of leaving. If at all possible, efforts should be made to keep siblings together when out-of-home placements are necessary.

In the majority of cases, removing children from the home is not the best alternative. One must then decide what should be done, both to end the immediate crisis and to set the precedent for longer-term intervention and recovery. To resolve the immediate crisis, there are several options. One may be to separate the children from the alleged perpetrator. This can occur by having the perpetrator move out of the house or by having the parents agree to a voluntary placement of the children in the custody of extended family members or close friends (MacMurray, 1988).

After determining a resolution to the immediate crisis, more long-range plans should be established. These plans must coincide with available community services. Such services may include: individual or family therapy, parenting education programs, substance abuse programs, protective day-care or restrictive access of the perpetrator to the children. The crisis intervention workers may have considerable leverage over soliciting family members' agreement to engage in services at this point because of the threat of more intrusive intervention. Allowing the family members to participate in the long-range planning will help establish a commitment within the family to actually seek solutions to their problems.

Service and/or treatment strategies, be they immediate or long-term, should include all family members. If treatment programs are deemed necessary for the victim (Salter et al., 1985), it is important to consider the possibility of also including any other children who are in the household (Paluszny et al., 1989). It may be difficult to substantiate that they too were actual victims of abuse by official criteria but they are clearly children who have been living in a malfunctioning household along with the identified victim and may very well have been affected either directly, or indirectly, by the abusive incidents. Furthermore, even the nonaccused parent is experiencing trauma and they too are probably in need of services (Paluszny et al., 1989; Salter et al., 1985).

During this planning stage, the crisis intervention workers can be supportive and sympathetic to the problem of the family, but they must also make it clear that they do not approve of how the family has been treating the children. Likewise, the intervention can be supportive of the family attempting to determine what type of long-term intervention is most appropriate, but the case workers should also clarify that the family will continue to be monitored in order to ensure that future abuse does not occur.

At all stages of the intervention into child abuse cases, be it substantiating abuse, determining what services are necessary, or removing the children from the home, it must be recognized that there are considerable differences between families and how they will respond to intervention. As has been discussed by several analysts of various practices (Bourne, 1984; Newburger, 1985; Valentine et al.), tasks such as assessing the safety of children, are difficult to determine when the lifestyle of the family under investigation is different from that of the investigators. Issues of social class are particularly relevant here. Although analyses of reports from official agencies indicate that lower class families are more commonly reported, this does not imply that all poor families mistreat their children.

Diversity Issues in Child Abuse Intervention

Crisis intervention workers must also be respectful of cultural variations between families. While it is essential to determine that children are safe and being cared for, it also must be recognized that there is variation in how these criteria are met. The decisions on how to intervene in child abuse cases, especially for drastic actions such as out-of-the-home placements, must be made wisely with a thorough review of the implications of making such decisions. Cultural groups vary on their understanding of the child welfare system in the United States. It is critical that the intervener understand and appreciate that child protective services is a cultural construct found in western society and that this concept may not be common knowledge to those with diverse backgrounds.

The Aftermath of Intervention

Once the immediate crisis has been resolved, the investigation and intervention with the family should not be terminated. For those families who have been referred to services, there needs to be continued monitoring to determine if the family is actually receiving (or attending) these services. They must also be supervised in terms of how they are responding to these services. If the services are having no impact, the safety of the children again becomes an important issue. The effectiveness and eventual impact of actions taken in a case may be minimal or even counterproductive resulting in secondary victimization, unless the intended service, disposition or program is being delivered appropriately to the family involved.

Similarly, judgments about the ability of differing approaches to effect change in individual families can only be reached if there is careful and continual monitoring of such program implementation and its effects. Parenthetically, for many cases in which criminal justice action occurs, an informal disposition along with a requirement to partake in, or obtain, certain services is the prescribed action in a case. The coordination of services and the follow-up of whether or not such services are actually being utilized, and are having the intended impact, are crucial.

In many cases, decisions concerning whether to handle child abuse cases as matters requiring only child protective social services or only criminal justice action are extremely difficult and complex. Often such judgments are determined on the basis of discretionary evaluations having little or nothing to do with the specific facts of the abuse. Instead, such decisions are based on the availability of services, resources, and staff to handle such cases, the particular family situation, the age and developmental maturity of the victim, or other related factors. However, if action for child abuse cases is to occur in an organized and appropriate fashion with an aim toward achieving a positive outcome, the integration of criminal justice and social service goals and interests must be taken into consideration. Among the important steps necessary to such an approach is active networking between the various agencies and personnel involved in handling and rendering decisions about these cases (Cesnik and Puls, 1977; Martin and Besharov, 1991; Whitcomb, 1992).

One technique used in a number of jurisdictions to help accomplish this task is that of multidisciplinary teams (Cohn, 1982; Mac Murray, 1988; Whitcomb, 1992). These teams are generally composed of representatives of both criminal justice agencies (e.g., law enforcement, prosecutors, victims' advocates) and social service agencies (e.g., case workers and administrators) as well as, in some cases, counselors, treatment specialists, or medical personnel. The purpose of these teams is to discuss the available information for a specific case and to coordinate the process of decision making and formulating recommendations for action in cases. Such procedures can be useful throughout the crisis intervention process in establishing joint or collateral investigations, consolidating information about families, and in furthering a mutual understanding and respect between agencies for their work in particular cases. It is also an effective means by which to assess current services available in the community and initiate action to provide increased services if necessary.

CONCLUSION

This chapter has sought to indicate the critical importance of crisis intervention for cases of child abuse. The available research literature suggests that such abuse in its various forms—physical, emotional, sexual, and neglect—is a major social problem in the United States today. This research further indicates that child abuse affects significant numbers of victims and families and that the number of cases reported to official agencies continues to increase each year. While there are specific risk factors for child abuse victimization and perpetration, there is wide variability in the types of family situations where abuse occurs.

The crisis intervention process for child abuse is crucial as a key decision-making stage for how these cases will be handled by official agencies and the resulting outcomes for the involved individuals, families, and communities. These decisions involve identifying, investigating, and providing services for child abuse on the basis of concerns about the safety of the child victim and other potential victims, the present situation and needs of troubled families, and any possible criminal activity that occurred. The resulting actions taken by agencies may include a provision of social services (including medical, financial, and psychological services) and removal of the child from the family through the full range of formal and informal criminal justice sanctions.

Careful judgments determining the most appropriate and beneficial services for families, the abilities of communities to provide and deliver such services, and follow-up monitoring of their use and effectiveness are critical to the full impact of crisis intervention for child abuse. Implemented properly, these actions can provide a vital social safety net helping involved families to prevent future abuse and develop more functional family systems. Conducted improperly, however, these same actions have the potential to do extensive harm and further traumatize victims and families.

CHAPTER QUESTIONS

1. Define Child Abuse in its various forms: physical abuse, neglect, emotional or psychological abuse, and sexual abuse.
2. What is known about the extent of child abuse in the U.S. in its various forms? What research methodologies have been utilized to develop such estimates? What discrepancies appear to be present for the extent of child abuse based upon data from official reports in comparison to community or national surveys? What summary conclusions can be drawn from this information about the extent of child abuse in the United States?
3. Discuss the common characteristics research has revealed about the:
   (a) victims of child abuse, and (b) abuse perpetrators.
4. What are the three primary goals for intervention in cases of child abuse? How do these goals fit with the mandate of different agencies that intervene in child abuse cases? What assessments and decisions must be made in order for each of these goals to be reached?
5. What problems or obstacles make these goals difficult to accomplish?
6. What similarities and differences exist between state laws on mandatory reporting of child abuse cases? What is the guiding rationale behind mandatory reporting laws of child abuse?
7. What are the important benefits that result from the coordination of child abuse investigations between social service and criminal justice agencies? What problems may result from this combination of agencies? What are some of the ways in which interagency coordination problems can be overcome?
8. What are the major issues raised in the interviewing of victims in the investigation process? In interviewing alleged perpetrators? In interviewing parents of abuse victims?

9. What issues are important for the actions, which follow the investigation process for cases of child abuse?
10. What conclusions can be drawn from this discussion? What are the implications of these conclusions for social policy and action for child abuse generally? For policy and action in your local community?

SIMULATED EXERCISES

Simulated Exercise 1

As a child protective services worker, you receive a call from a second grade teacher about an 8-year-old boy who has cigarette burn marks on his stomach. The teacher warns you that the boy is extremely shy and does not like to talk about his family. How would you approach interviewing this child?

Simulated Exercise 2

As a police officer, a child's aunt calls you, reporting that she suspects her 10-year-old niece may be sexually molested by her mother's live-in boyfriend. You go to the house and the only person home is the mother. You start to ask her questions and she firmly denies that her boyfriend would ever do such a thing and that if it were actually happening, her daughter would surely tell her. She claims her daughter has a vivid imagination. How would you proceed with the interview of the mother?

Simulated Exercise 3

As a crisis intervention worker in your community, you respond to a report that a father of two pre-teenagers is "wildly shooting a gun in the house." Police officers at the scene arrest the father. What do you need to do to determine what should be done with the children?

Simulated Exercise 4

As the same crisis intervention worker in Exercise 3, you decide that the children must be temporarily removed from the home. How do you best implement this decision?

APPENDIX A

Additional Internet Resources

For more information regarding child abuse and neglect, and the role of crisis intervention regarding this issue, visit the following websites.

Administration for Children and Families:
   http://nccanch.acf.hhs.gov/
Abuse and Neglect, International Journal via ScienceDirect:
   http://www.sciencedirect.com/science?_ob=JournalURL&_cdi=5847&_auth=y
   _acct=C000027161&_version=1&_urlVersion=0&_userid=537414&md5=d7eb2a
   e20eddd1a15f61aa74b72ea6e5
National Data Archive on Child Abuse and Neglect:
   http://www.ndacan.cornell.edu/
Childhelp USA, Treatment and Prevention of Child Abuse:
   http://www.childhelpusa.org/
Susan K. Smith, Attorney/Mediator, Mandatory Reporting Facts:
   http://www.smith-lawfirm.com/mandatory_reporting.htm
The National Academies Press:
   http://www.nap.edu/openbook/0309048893/html/
Child Abuse and Neglect Learning Modules:
   http://www.vcu.edu/vissta/training/va_teachers/introduction.html
Medline Plus, Child Abuse:
   http://www.nlm.nih.gov/medlineplus/childabuse.html
National Clearinghouse on Family Violence:
   http://www.phac-aspc.gc.ca/ncfv-cnivf/familyviolence/nfntsnegl_e.html
Child Abuse: Statistic, Research and Resources:
   http://www.jimhopper.com/abstats/
National Exchange Club Foundation:
   http://www.preventchildabuse.org/
   http://www.preventchildabuse.org/learn_more/research_docs/
   cost_analysis.pdf
Child Abuse Prevention Network:
   http://child-abuse.com/
Center on Child Abuse and Neglect:
   http://ccan.ouhsc.edu/

State of Connecticut Department of Children and Families:
   http://www.state.ct.us/dcf/hotline.htm
Medem, Medical Library:
   http://www.medem.com/MedLB/article_detaillb.cfm?article_ID=ZZZ3S3DRU
   DC&sub_cat=355
Child Abuse and Neglect Disability Outreach Project
   http://disability-abuse.com/cando/
Washington Council for Prevention of Child Abuse and Neglect (WCPCAN):
   http://www.wcpcan.wa.gov/
National Association of Counsel for Children:
   http://naccchildlaw.org/childrenlaw/childmaltreatment.html
The Future of Children:
   http://www.futureofchildren.org/pubs-info2825/
   pubs-info_show.htm?doc_id=75332

REFERENCES

American Humane Association (AHA). (1982). *Estimated maltreatment victims in the United States: Child protective services.* Denver, CO: AHA.

American Humane Association. (1981). *National study on child neglect and abuse reporting.* Denver, CO: AHA.

Berliner, L. & Barbieri, M.K. (1984). The testimony of the child victim of sexual assault. *Journal of Social Issues, 40,* 125–137.

Besharov, D.J. (1978). *The abused and neglected child: Multi-disciplinary court practices.* Practicing Law Institute.

Black, D.A., Heyman, R.E., & Slep, A.M.S. (2001). Risk factors for child physical abuse. *Aggression and Violent Behavior, 6,* 2–3, 121–188.

Black, D.A., Heyman, R.E., & Slep, A.M.S. (2001). Risk factors for child sexual abuse. *Aggression and Violent Behavior, 6,* 2–3, 203–229.

Black, D.A., Slep, A.M.S., & Heyman, R.E. (2001). Risk factors for child psychological abuse. *Aggression and Violent Behavior, 6,* 2–3, 189–201.

Borgman, R., Edmunds, M., & MacDicken, R.A. (1979). *Crisis intervention: A manual for child protective workers.* National Center on Child Abuse and Neglect, Washington: DHEW Publication.

Bourne, R. (1985). Family violence: Legal and ethical issues. In E. Newburger & R. Bourne (Eds.), *Unhappy Families* (pp. 39–46). Littleton, MA: PSG Publishing.

Brandt, R. & Tisza, V. (1977). The sexually misused child. *American Journal of Orthopsychiatry, 44,* 80–87.

Brown, J.A. (1980). Child abuse: An existential problem. *Clinical Social Work Journal, 8,* 2, 108–115.

Budd, K.S., Poindexter, L.M., Felix, E.D., & Naik-Polan, A.T. (2001). Clininal assessment of parents in child protection cases: An empirical analysis. *Law and Human Behavior, 25,* 1, 93–108.

Bureau of Justice Statistics (BJS). 1994. *Sourcebook of criminal justice statistics,* 1993, edited by K. Maguire & A.L. Pastore. Washington, D.C.: U.S. Dept. of Justice.

Caplan, G. (1964). *Principles of preventive psychiatry.* New York: Basic Books.

Cesnik, B.I., & Puls, M. (1977). Law enforcement and crisis intervention services: A critical relationship. *Suicide and Life-Threatening Behavior, 7,* 211–215.

Cohn, A.H. (1982). Organization and administration of programs to treat child abuse and neglect. In E.H. Newberger (Ed.), *Child abuse* (pp. 89–103). Boston, MA: Little, Brown.

Conte, J.R. & Berliner, L. (1981). Sexual abuse of children: Implications for practice. *Social Casework, 62,* 601–606.

Craft, J.L. & Clarkson, C.D. (1985). Case disposition recommendations of attorneys and social workers in child abuse investigations. *Child Abuse and Neglect, Special issue: C. Henry Kempe Memorial, 9,* 2, 165–174.

Cromer, R. (1986). A community approach to child sexual abuse: The role of the office of the district attorney. *Response to the Victimization of Women and Children, 9,* 10–13.

DeFrancis, V. (1969). *Protecting the child victim of sex crimes committed by adults.* Denver, CO: American Humane Association.

Duncan, E.G. (1973). Recognition and protection of the family's interest in child abuse proceedings. *Journal of Family Law, 13,* 803–817.

Finkelhor, D. (1983). Removing the child and prosecuting the offender in cases of sexual abuse: Evidence from the national reporting department for child abuse and neglect. *Child Abuse and Neglect, 7,* 195–205.

Finkelhor, D. (1984). *Child sexual abuse. New theory and research.* New York: Free Press.

Finkelhor, D. & Baron, L. (1986). High-risk children. In D. Finkelhor, S. Araji, L. Baron, A. Browne, S. Doyle Peters, & G.E. Wyatt (Eds.), *A source book on child sexual abuse.* Beverly Hills, CA: Sage.

Finkelhor, D. & Hotaling, G. (1983). *Sexual abuse in the national incidence study of child abuse and neglect.* Report to national center on child abuse and neglect.

Garbarino, J. & Grouter, A. (1978). Defining the community context of parent-child relationships: The correlates of child maltreatment. *Child Development, 49,* 604–616.

Garbarino, J. & Gilliam, G. (1980). *Understanding abusive families.* Lexington, MA: Lexington Books.

Gaudin, J. & Polansky, N. (1986). Social distancing of the neglectful family, Sex, race, and social class influences. *Children and Youth Services Review, 8,* 1–12.

Germain, R.G., Brassard, M., & Hart, S.N. (1985). Crisis intervention for maltreated children. *School Psychology Review, 14,* 3, 291–299.

Gil, D.G. (1970). *Violence against children: Physical child abuse in the United States.* Cambridge, MA: Harvard UP.

Goodman, G. (1984). The child witness: Conclusions and future directions for research and legal practice. *Journal of Social Issues, 40,* 157–175.

Hampton, R. & Newberger, E. (1985). Child abuse incidence and reporting by hospitals: Significance of severity, class, and race. *American Journal of Public Health, 75,* 56–69.

Hershkowitz, I. (2001). Children's responses to open-ended utterances in investigative interviews. *Legal and Criminological Psychology, 1,* 49–63.

Kaplan, D.A. (1962). A concept of acute situational disorders. Social Work, 7, 15–23.
Kercher, G. & McShaney, M. (1984). The prevalence of child sexual abuse victimization in an adult sample of Texas residents. *Child Abuse and Neglect, 8,* 495–502.

Kilpatrick, D.G & Saunder, B.E. (1997). *Prevalence and consequences of child victimization: Results from the national Survey of Adolescents, Final Report.* United States Department of Justice. Washington, DC: U.S. Government Printing Office.

Lauer, B. (1974). Battered child syndrome: Review of 130 patients with controls. *Pediatrics, 54,* 67–70.

Light, R.J. (1973). Abused and neglected children in America: A study of alternative policies. *Harvard Education Review, 44,* 551–598.

Lukton, R.C. (1982). Myths: Realities of crisis intervention. *Social Casework, 6,* 32, 276–285.

MacMurray, B.K. (1988). The nonprosecution of sexual abuse and informal justice. *Journal of Interpersonal Violence, 3,* 12, 197–202.

Mac Murray, B. & Carson, B. (1991). Legal issues in violence toward children. In R.T. Ammerman and M. Herson (Eds.), *Case studies in family violence.* New York: Plenum Press.

Martin, S.E. & Besharov, D.J. (1991). *Police and child abuse: New policies by expanded responsibilities.* Washington, D.C.: U.S. Dept. of Justice.

Melton, G.B. & Davidson, H.A. (1987). Child protection and society: When should the state intervene? *American Psychologist, 42,* 2, 172–175.

Melton, G.B. & Gorson, J. (1987). Psychological maltreatment and the schools: Problems of law and professional responsibility school. *Psychology Review, 16,* 2, 188–194.

Melton, G.B. (1985). Sexually abused children and the legal system: Some policy recommendations. *American Journal of Family Therapy, 13,* 1, 61–67.

Mrazek, P. (1983). Sexual abuse of children. In B.B. Lahey & A.E. Kazdin (Eds.), *Advances in Clinical Child Psychology* (pp. 199–215). New York: Plenum Press.

National Center on Child Abuse and Neglect (NCCAN). (1982). *Profile of child sexual abuse.* Rockville, MD: Clearinghouse on child abuse and neglect information.

National Council on Crime and Delinquency. (1999). *New approach to child protective services: Structured decision making.* Madison, WI: Author.

National Center on Child Abuse and Neglect (NCCAN). (1999). *National study of the incidence and prevalence of child abuse and neglect.* Washington, D.C.: U.S. Dept. of Health & Human Services.

National Center on Child Abuse and Neglect. (1988). *National study of the incidence and prevalence of child abuse and neglect.* Washington, D.C.: U.S. Dept. of Health & Human Services.

National Center on Child Abuse and Neglect. (1981). *Study findings: National study of incidence and severity of child abuse and neglect.* Washington, D.C.: Department of Health, Education, and Welfare.

National Institute of Justice (NIJ). (1994). *Child rape victims, 1992.* Washington, D.C.: U.S. Dept. of justice.

National Institute of Justice (NIJ). (1992). *New approach to interviewing children: A test of its effectiveness.* Washington, D.C.: U.S. Dept. of Justice.

Newburger, E.H. (1985). The helping hand strikes again: Unintended consequences of child abuse reporting. In E. Newburger & R. Bourne (Eds.), *Unhappy families* (pp. 171–178). Littleton, MA: PSG Publishing.

Nurcombe, B. (1986). The child as witness: Competence and credibility. *Journal of the American Academy of Child Psychiatry, 25,* 4, 473–480.

OJJDP. (2001). *Keeping children safe: OJJDP's child protective division.* United States Department of Justice, Office of Juvenile Justice and Delinquency Prevention. Washington, DC: U.S. Government Printing Office.

OPJJDP. (2000). *Children as victims.* United States Department of Justice, Office of Juvenile Justice and Delinquency Prevention. Washington, DC: U.S. Government Printing Office.

Paluszny, M., Cullen, B.J., Funk, J., Liv, P. & Goodhand, J. (1989). Child abuse disposition: Concurrence & differences between a hospital team, child protection agency, and the court. *Child Psychiatry and Human Development, 20,* 1, 25–38.

Pardeck, J.T. & Nolden, W.L. II. (1985). An evaluation of a crisis intervention center for parents at risk. *Family Therapy, 12,* 1, 25–37.

Pelton, L.H. (Ed.). (1981). *The social context of child abuse and neglect.* New York: Basic Books.

Peters, S.D., Wyatt, G.E. & Finkelhor, D. (1986). Prevalence. In D. Finkelhor, S. Araji, L. Baron, A. Browne, S. Doyle Peters & E. Wyatt (Eds.), *A Sourcebook on child sexual abuse.* Beverly Hills, CA: Sage.

Polansky, N., Gaudin, J., Ammons, P., & Davis, K. (1985). The psychological ecology of the neglectful mother. *Child Abuse and Neglect, 9,* 265–275.

Pynoos, R. & Eth, S. (1984). The child as witness to homicide. *Journal of Social Issues 40,* 87–108.

Quinn, K.M. (1986). Competency to be a witness: A major child forensic issue. *Bulletin of American Academy of Psychiatry and the Law, Special issue: Child Forensic Psychiatry, 14,* 311–321.

Resick, P.A. & Schnicke, M.K. (1990). Treating symptoms in adult victims of sexual assault. *Journal of Interpersonal Violence, 5,* 4, 488–506.

Rogers, C.M. (1982). Child sexual abuse and the courts: Preliminary findings. *Journal of Social Work and Human Sexuality, 1,* 145–153.

Russell, D.E.H. (1986). *The secret trauma: Incest in the lives of girls and women.* New York: Basic Books.

Russell, D.E.H. (1983). The incidence and prevalence of intrafamilial and extrafamilial sexual abuse of female children. *Child Abuse and Neglect, 7,* 133–146.

Salter, A.C., Richardson, C.M., & Kairys, S.W. (1985). Caring for abused preschoolers. *Child Welfare, 64,* 4, 343–356.

Salter, A.C., Richardson, C.M. & Martin, P.A. (1985). Treating abusive parents. *Child Welfare, 64,* 4, 327–341.

Schumacher, J.A., Slep, A.M.S. & Heyman, R.E. (2001). Risk factors for child neglect. *Aggression and Violent Behavior, 6,* 2–3, 231–254.

Slep, A.M.S. & Heyman, R.E. (2001). Where do we go from here?: Moving toward an integrated approach to family violence. *Aggression and Violent Behavior, 6,* 2–3, 353–356.

Smith, S.M. (1975). *The battered-child syndrome.* London: Butterworth.

Steel, B. & Pollock, F.C. (1974). A psychiatric study of parents who abuse infants and small children. In R. Heifer & C. Kempe (Eds.), *The battered child.* Chicago: University of Chicago Press.

Stevenson, D.G. & Grauerholz, E. (1993). The role of crisis centers in defining and reporting child abuse. *The Journal of Contemporary Human Services,* April, 221–225.

Straus, M.A. & Gelles, R.J. (1986). Societal change and change in family violence from 1975 to 1985 as revealed by two national surveys. *Journal of Marriage and the Family, 48,* 465–479.

Straus, M.A., Gelles, R.J., & Steinmetz, S. (1980). *Behind closed doors.* Garden City, NY: Anchor Press.

Terr, L.C. (1986). The child psychiatrist and the child witness: Traveling companions by necessity, if not by design. *Journal of the American Academy of Child Psychiatry, 25,* 462–472.

Trainor, C. (1984). Sexual maltreatment in the United States: A five-year perspective. Paper presented at the International Congress on Child Abuse and Neglect, Montreal.

Valentine, D.P., Acuff, D.S., Freeman, M.L., & Andreas, T. (1984). Defining child maltreatment: A multidisciplinary overview. *Child Welfare, 63,* 6, 497–509.

Whitcomb, D. (1992). *When the victim is a child, Second Edition.* Washington, D.C.: U.S. Dept. of Justice.

Whitcomb, D., Goodman, G.S., Runyan, D.K., & Hoak, S. (1994). *The emotional effects of testifying on sexually abused children.* Washington, D.C.: U.S. Dept. of Justice.

Whitcomb, D., Shapiro, E.R., & Shellwagen, L.D. (1985). *When the victim is a child: Issues for judges & prosecutors.* Washington, D.C.: U.S. Department of Justice.

Widom, C.S. (1991). The role of placement experiences in mediating the criminal consequences of early childhood victimization. *American Journal of Orthopsychiatry, 61,* 2, 195–209.

Wolfe, V.V., Las, L. & Wilson, S.K. (1987). Some issues in preparing sexually abused children for courtroom testimony. *Behavior Therapist, 10,* 5, 107–113.

Wood, S.C., & Dean, K.S. (1984). *Final report: Sexual abuse of males research project* (90 CA/812). Washington, D.C.: National Center on Child Abuse and Neglect.

Wyatt, G.E. (1985). The sexual abuse of Afro-American and white American women in childhood. *Child Abuse and Neglect, 10,* 231–240.

Yates, A. (1987). Should young children testify in cases of sexual abuse? *American Journal of Psychiatry, 144,* 471–480.

Chapter 6

CHILDREN IN CRISIS

CINDY S. HENDRICKS

A six-year-old boy faces a crisis: his father is having chest pains. As the boy calls 911 for help, his hysteria escalates. The dispatcher tries to calm the child so that crucial information may be obtained. In another part of town, a young girl watches, helplessly, as her parents engage in a variety of forms of domestic violence. She hears the sounds of sirens in the distance. She knows that the police car will soon be arriving in front of her house. Meanwhile, across the street, the children are being abused and neglected. A social worker is inside talking to the parents while the children sit outside on the porch; their physical scars are visible while the emotional scars remain hidden.

In each of the aforementioned situations, there are similarities. All of the scenarios involve children facing a crisis situation. Hendricks and McKean (1995, p. 6) explain that, "A crisis occurs when unusual stress brought on by unexpected and disruptive events render an individual either physically or emotionally disabled because their usual coping mechanisms prove ineffective." Dixon (1979, p. 15) noted that a crisis can be characterized by, "The existence of a subjectively defined precipitating event, unusual personality disorganization and impaired social functioning, debilitating emotional responses, and resolution within four to six weeks."

Another similarity among each of the scenarios is that each child needs some type of assistance: someone to intervene on the child's behalf. These professionals, whose goal is "to assist crisis victims to return to their pre-crisis levels of functioning and to seek avenues for positive change" (Hendricks and McKean, 1995, p. 11), are crisis interveners. Johnson (1989) suggests that young people in crisis need supportive, normalizing, and affirming contact if they are to move beyond the crisis.

A dispatcher, a police officer, and a social worker came to the aid of the children in the vignettes. Professionals such as firefighters, correctional workers, emergency medical personnel, ministers, probation officers, parole agents, victim advocates, teachers, school counselors, and others who come into contact with children in crisis may also be called upon to act as a crisis intervener. "During most of our existence, crisis intervention was provided by family members who would comfort their relatives and offer assistance, understanding, and support. As urbanization and technology advanced, people became more mobile. . . . A need then developed for someone or something to provide these helping services" (Hendricks and McKean, 1995, p. 3).

The nature of the crisis is another similarity in the vignettes. Erickson (1959, 1963) identified two types of crises that people may face: maturational-developmental and accidental-situational. Maturational-developmental crises occur during a transitional period of a person's life; these periods are characterized by cognitive or affective upsets. Such crises for children may include, but are not limited to, moving to a new neighborhood, school situations (beginning kindergarten, moving from elementary to middle school or from middle school to high school), peer pressure, dating, relationships, prejudice, cultural differences, ethnic group mistrust and misunderstanding, nontraditional home environments, physical maturation, and the search for identity. Each of the children in the vignettes faced an accidental-situational crisis. This type of crisis is characterized by periods of psychological and behavioral upsets that are precipitated by unexpected life hazards, usually involving a significant loss. For children, these crises occur frequently. Potential accidental-situational crisis situations confront children on a daily basis: substance abuse, illness, death, divorce, disabilities, crime, domestic violence, hate crimes, gang violence, and child abuse and neglect.

The major difference in the scenarios is the extent to which the children are victimized. In the first situation, the father is the victim. The child is involved in an accidental-situational crisis, but is not in any physical danger. While his fears and hysteria may be of primary concern, it is the father who is of immediate concern to the intervener. In the second scene, the parents are each other's victims. The child could be a victim as a result of interfering with the parents' dispute, or could be another victim for either parent. The intervener must be concerned with the parents' situation, and should also attend to the child's needs. In the last scenario, the children are the victims. The intervener's first priority is the children who are being abused and neglected by their parents.

A crisis intervener approaching any one of the aforementioned scenarios must determine whether the children involved in the crisis situation are the primary victims or secondary victims to perform the task of crisis intervention effectively. The term *primary victim* refers to the child who is the victim, such as the children in scenario three. The crisis intervener's immediate concern should be with the primary victim. The term *secondary victim* identifies situations in which the primary victim is not the child, but the crisis situation impacts on the child, illustrated by scenarios one and two. Although the children in these two scenarios are secondary victims in need of attention, the intervener's immediate responsibility is to the primary victim.

PRIMARY VICTIMIZATION

The National Institute of Justice (1992, p. 1) explains: "Any crime that can be committed against an adult can be perpetrated as easily (if not more so) upon a child. What is perhaps even more appalling is the fact that so little is known about the incidence and types of crimes committed against children." The Bureau of Statistics (U.S. Department of Justice, 1994) reported that in a study of three states, police investigators determined that only four percent of the rape victims younger than 12 years old were attacked by strangers. All the other assailants were either family members (46%) or acquaintances or friends (50%). Twenty percent were raped by their fathers. Among 12- to 17-year-old victims, 20 percent were raped by family members, 65 percent by an acquaintance or friend and 15 percent by a stranger. Among those 18 years old or older, 12 percent were raped by a family member, 55 percent by an acquaintance or friend and 33 percent by a stranger. In a recent study, participants who did not report abuse during childhood cited the following reasons: fear of the abuser, fear of negative reactions from family members, fear that no one would believe them, belief that they deserved the abuse, and lack of awareness that abuse was wrong (Palmer, Brown, Rae-Grant, and Loughlin, 1999).

Children become primary victims whenever a crime is committed against them by someone, including parents, such as sexual violations, child abuse, child neglect, hate crimes, gang violence, robbery, harassment, or homicide. In their 1997 article, Marans and Berkman reported that, in 1994, almost 2.6 million children ages 12 to 17 were victims of crime (assaults, rape, and robbery). They reported homicide as the leading cause of death among African American males ages 15 to 24 while Doerner and Lab (1995) reported that for all children under the age of 14, homicide is the fourth leading cause of death. Marans and Berkman (1997) also reported that, in a survey of inner-city high school students, 45 percent had been threatened with a gun, or shot at, and one in three had been beaten up on their way to school.

In 1992, nearly three million children were reported as abused and/or neglected (U.S. Department of Health and Human Services, 1993). Over half of the reported cases involved abuse, with physical abuse being the most frequently reported type of abuse, followed by sexual abuse and emotional abuse (American Humane Association, 1994). Marans and Berkman (1997) reported a similar number of cases in 1994 (3.1 million) with nearly 33 percent of the cases substantiated. In a report based on data from law enforcement agencies of 12 States which covers the years 1991 through 1996, Snyder (2000) reported that of the incidents of forcible rape and other sexual assault (forcible sodomy, sexual assault with an object, and forcible fondling), 14 percent of the victims were between the ages 18 and 24. The remainder, over two-thirds (67%) of all victims of sexual assault reported to law enforcement agencies, were juveniles (under the age of 18 at the time of the crime). More than half of all juvenile victims were under age 12. That is, 33 percent of all victims of sexual assault reported to law enforcement were ages 12 through 17 and 34 percent were underage 12. Most disturbing is that one of every seven victims of sexual assault (or 14 percent of all victims) reported to law enforcement agencies were under age 6. Sechrist (2000) estimates that the annual number of child maltreatment deaths is approximately 2000 per year: 5 children per day.

The Child Abuse Prevention and Treatment Act (Public Law 100–294) defines child abuse and neglect as: "the physical or mental injury, sexual abuse or exploitation, negligent treatment or maltreatment of a child by a person who is responsible for the child's welfare, under circumstances which indicate that the child's health or welfare is harmed or threatened thereby." Public Law 98–457 (The Child Abuse Amendments of 1984) expanded the definition to include the withholding of medical treatment to an infant with a life-threatening health condition or complication.

While some people and organizations favor broad definitions of child abuse and neglect, others prefer to define the terms more specifically, providing definitions for the major types of abuse (physical, sexual, emotional) and neglect (physical, educational, emotional):

1. *Physical abuse:* physical injury such as beating, punching, kicking, bruising, burning, etc., perpetrated upon a child by a caretaker. The degree of such abuse, the age of the abused, and the harm to the child as a result are all considered in defining the act as physical abuse,

2. *Sexual abuse:* sexual acts perpetrated upon a child by a parent or caretaker, such as fondling, intercourse, incest, sodomy, and sexual exploitation,

3. *Psychological or Emotional abuse:* acts or injury by the parent, guardian, or caretaker that cause or could potentially cause serious behavioral, emotional, cognitive or mental disorders to the child,

4. *Physical neglect:* abandonment, inadequate health care, nonsupervision, forcing the child to leave home,

5. *Educational neglect:* condoning truancy or failure to see to the child's educational needs,
6. *Emotional neglect:* failure to meet the child's psychological needs, allowing the child to witness domestic violence, condoning drug use by the minor (Flowers, 1994, pp. 6–7).

Children typically notify a family member of abusive situations first (58% of the cases studied by the U.S. Department of Justice, 1994); however, children also report abusive situations to professionals such as physicians, nurses, teachers, school administrators, clergy and social workers. All states have laws requiring certain persons (law enforcement personnel, probation officers, criminal prosecutors, juvenile rehabilitation or detention facility employees, health care workers, mental health professionals, social workers, teachers and other school personnel, child care workers and administrators, foster parents, commercial film and photo processors) to report suspected abuse or neglect of children and youth under the age of 18. These laws were enacted to provide a mechanism for investigating suspected child maltreatment and intervening where necessary to protect children and youth who are at risk for abuse. Typically, the mandated reporter should contact either a designated child protection agency (such as a Department of Social Services) or a law enforcement agency to report any suspected child abuse, including sexual abuse, physical abuse, and/or neglect (U.S. Department of Justice, 1995). The U.S. Department of Justice (1994) reported that in the sexual abuse cases they investigated, 51 percent were first reported to a social service agency; 49 percent were first reported to law enforcement officers.

States also differ as to who conducts the initial investigation. Cesnik and Puls (1977) suggest it is beneficial if representatives from both social services and the criminal justice system are actively involved in the initial contact with the child. Carson and MacMurray (1996) claim that most communities authorize at least two different agencies to intervene in cases where children are primary victims such as child abuse. Combinations of agencies may include: police and related criminal justice agencies and child protective or social service agencies.

SECONDARY VICTIMIZATION

Children can be influenced, often in negative and unforeseen ways, by events that occur within families and communities. Marans and Berkman (1997) reported that in a Boston City Hospital primary care clinic, one out of every ten children had witnessed a shooting or a stabbing before the age of six (50% in the home and 50% in the streets). Marans and Berkman also reported that in a study of sixth, eighth and tenth grade students, 40 percent witnessed at least one violent crime in the previous year. Results from another survey of fifth and sixth grade students in Washington, D.C., indicated 31 percent witnessed a shooting; 17 percent witnessed a murder, and 23 percent had seen a dead body. Marans and Berkman (1997) reported the results of another survey in which 21 percent of males in some high schools reported seeing a person sexually assaulted; 82 percent had witnessed a beating or mugging in school; 46 percent had seen a person attacked or stabbed with a knife; and 62 percent had witnessed a shooting. These events, as well as substance abuse, death, and divorce can negatively affect children even though they are not the primary victims.

Domestic violence also places children in secondary victimization situations. The most common type of domestic violence is spousal abuse, which occurs in all socioeconomic, ethnic, racial, and age groups. Hendricks (1985, p. 48) states, "Research indicates that violent families are the breeding grounds for juvenile delinquency, alcohol and drug abuse, and intergenerational violence. Many of the children within these violent families become violent adults and violent parents." Horowitz, Boardman and Redlener (1994, p. 85) add." . . . children in poorly functioning homes or highly stressed families learn to be aggressive and develop destructive conflict resolution patterns . . . destructive patterns of problem solving and conflict resolution that begin in the home are maintained in other relationships." The violence used on children (spanking and hitting) as well as the violence observed by children (adult-to-adult) teaches them three lifelong lessons:

1. Those who love you the most are also those who hit you;
2. There is a moral right to hit other members of the same family; and
3. When all else fails, use violence. (Mickish, 1995)

Mickish (1996, p. 55) also expresses concern regarding children in violent homes:

The cost to children is immediate and cumulative. The vast majority of children living in a household where their mother is abused are aware of or witness the physical abuse. To compound the child's trauma, the adult male who is beating his female partner is, typically, also beating his children. The immediate cost is loss of a sense of safety. Children's behavior may "regress." They may get poor grades because they are unable to concentrate in school or do their homework. They may act out violent behaviors toward objects, animals, siblings, and schoolmates.

Additional behavioral and psychiatric ramifications which may be observed in a child victim, particularly in intra-familial child sexual abuse cases, may include affective problems (guilt, shame, anxiety, fear, depression, anger, low self-esteem, negative self-concept), physical complications (injuries, pregnancy, diseases), cognitive changes (short attention span), behavioral problems (misbehavior, antisocial behavior, isolation, delinquency, stealing, tantrums, substance abuse, withdrawal), self-destructive behaviors (mutilation, suicide), psychopathological behaviors (neurosis, multiple personalities), sexual behaviors (excessive masturbation, repetition of sexual acts with others, atypical sexual knowledge), social problems (interpersonal relationships), and Post-Traumatic Stress Disorder (Berliner and Wheeler, 1987; Lusk and Waterman, 1986; Mickish, 1995).

Family and friends are a child's world and when a friend or family member becomes a victim of violence or any other type of crime, a crisis situation evolves for the child. According to the National Clearinghouse on Child Abuse and Neglect (1999), "Since families are systems, what affects one member of a family affects other members" (p. 1). Doerner and Lab (1995, p. 45) suggest that in addition to the physical injury and/or property loss or damage sustained by adult victims, "They also endured emotional anguish and interpersonal complications with family members." Thus, a child, although not directly involved, also becomes a victim, a secondary victim, when parents are victimized. "Surprisingly, information is not available about the proportion of the U.S. population that has been indirectly victimized" (Kilpatrick, Amick & Resnick, 1990, p. 1). Rasinski and Gillespie (1992, pp. 4–5) state:

> Children have difficulty dealing with the trauma in their lives . . . often, children have less access to help in making it through such crises. Children can often mask their suffering from others, and adults can easily assume that children either do not understand the emotional impact of the crisis or are resilient enough to be unaffected.

UNDERSTANDING CHILD DEVELOPMENT

A child's understanding of a crisis situation, whether the child is a primary or secondary victim, is primarily determined by the developmental age of the child. "A child of four and an adolescent of 17 have radically different faculties for dealing with information and reacting to events. Differences in cognitive, social, and emotional development mean that they will respond differently to events . . ." (Sandoval, 1985, p. 264).

To effectively intervene in crisis situations involving children, the crisis intervener must draw from two bodies of knowledge: knowledge of the profession, and knowledge of child development. Without knowledge of child development, a crisis intervener may expect too much of a child, or not fully anticipate the child's reaction to a crisis. Similarly, those who interview child victims may not understand what the child is/is not able to communicate regarding the victimization. Maddox (1994, p. 7) suggests: "The unique vulnerability of children mandates extreme caution on the part of police personnel responding to an emergency at a care facility. . . . Officers and administrators who are involved in any police action at a child care facility need to prepare for intensely emotional responses from the children."

Not only do crisis interveners need to be aware of the emotional responses of children, they also need to know what information children are and are not capable of providing in instances where children are primary and/or secondary victims. Gullo (1994, p. 19) acknowledges the importance of increasing law enforcement officers' knowledge of child development:

> Law enforcement officers often respond to incidents that involve children, including calls that require emergency placement, social service referrals, and criminal investigations . . . officers who deal with child abuse cases should have a fundamental understanding of child development . . . interviewers need to learn as much as possible about how children think and develop. . . . Basic knowledge in the area of child development helps to build a foundation for successful interviews of children.

Investigators who understand how children develop can more effectively choose appropriate methods to gain information and assess the child's response during the interview process. To assist crisis interveners in understanding the development of children, Gullo (1994) identifies five stages of child development. The stages and their characteristics are:

1. Infancy (birth to two): unable to form concepts, self-centered, learning to trust;
2. Early childhood (ages 2–4): develop basic language skills, engage in imaginative behavior, gather information from senses and environment, learning independence;
3. Preschool (ages 4–6): primarily use language to communicate, do not understand abstract concepts, verbal skills may imply more comprehension than they possess, memorize without comprehension, spotty memories, can distinguish some fact from fantasy, capable of lying to get out of a problem situation;
4. School (ages 6–11): continue to master language, develop group loyalty (usually with own gender), seldom lie about major issues; and
5. Adolescent (ages 12–18): undergo profound physical and emotional changes, minimal rapport with adults (at least outwardly), question the values and beliefs they have been taught, may be shy in some settings while

outgoing in others, capable of deception and manipulation, may use outward shows of bravado or hostility to cover feelings of shyness and inferiority.

A key factor in interpreting the developmental stages of children is an understanding that the ages and characteristics are approximations. Many factors, such as circumstances surrounding the birth of the child, parents, schooling, socioeconomic status, etc. influence how slowly or rapidly children develop.

Norton (1999, pp. 5–44) provides a more detailed explanation of the language, cognitive, personality and social development of children from ages two to twelve (see Table 1, Appendix A). According to Norton (1999), children, ages two to three, experience rapid language growth (approximately 900 words in their vocabularies). They can identify and name the action they see in pictures (walking, running, swimming, eating, etc.), as well as identify large and small body parts. It is important for crisis interveners to understand that, even though children might have extensive speaking vocabularies, they may not know what the words being used mean. They may merely be imitating words that have been used in their presence. Cognitively, children at this age learn to organize and classify their worlds by grouping similar items. Their personalities are such that they believe they have identities separate from other family members. Socially, these children imitate the actions and behaviors they see and tend to transfer things into make-believe. In cases of violent crimes, "children focus on the central action and disregard other details. For example, in all his accounts, one three-year-old boy repeated the phrase, "Daddy squished mommy's neck" (Pynoos and Eth, 1984, p. 92). Goodman also suggests that, at this age, a child's language may inhibit investigations:

> A child 3 years of age, who had been abducted from her home by a strange man, described . . . how the "Gordle pushed [her] and made [her] bleed" and how the gordle scratched [her] arm." In their report, the police wrote that she said "him pushed me and made me bleed." But screening of the audio taped interview by an expert in children's testimony and consultation with the child's mother revealed that "gordle" was this 3-year-old's word for girl. The possibility therefore arose that the man who kidnapped her had an accomplice. (1984b, p. 164)

This example demonstrates how children attempt to provide crucial details, but people who lack training in child development could easily fail to understand them.

Children, ages three to four, continue to experience rapid growth in their language (vocabularies of approximately 1500 words). Again, even though they may be able to repeat words that they have heard, they may not have attached meaning to these words. Their speech becomes more complex as they develop the ability to use past tense. Cognitively, they develop an understanding of how things relate to each other, how parts make a whole, and spatial relations. They can classify objects, and understand the concepts of bigger and smaller. Their personalities can be characterized by the development of self-concept. At this age, children tend to hide from unhappy situations by withdrawing, suggesting that problems do not exist or blaming others. Socially, they realize that others have feelings, enjoy playing with others, enjoy group games and activities, and develop strong attachments to other children. Determining others' feelings through the use of facial expressions is also characteristic of this age group (Norton, 1999). Most children in this age group tend to express themselves more non-verbally, through play, rather than verbally. An example of how a three-year-old used play to recount her abduction was explained by Goodman, (1984a, pp. 1–2):

> Three-year-old Lori Poland was playing in the front yard of a neighbor's home when a man pulled up in an orange Datsun and ordered her inside. Several children playing near Lori at the time reported later to the police that the man said, "Take your pants off and get in the car," and Lori did. . . . When found, she was able to tell the police that the "bad man" hit her and put her "in the hole." . . . With the aid of props and anatomically correct dolls, Lori was able to describe to a psychiatrist details of the kidnapping, sexual assault, and attempted murder.

In a case of "observed parental homicide, a four-year-old girl carefully painted her hands red and acted at a game of stabbing herself with a paint brush" (Pynoos and Eth, 1984, p. 92). Pynoos and Eth (1984, p. 100) describe another similar example, "Julie, a four-year-old girl, was the only witness to her divorced mother's fatal stabbing. . . . In describing the event she consistently placed her father at the scene, described significant portions of the central action, and recounted her father's efforts to clean up prior to leaving." Later, Julie began stabbing a pillow, crying, "Daddy pushed mommy down" (Pynoos and Eth, 1984, p. 100).

Children, ages four to five, have vocabularies in excess of 2500 words; however, the number of words for which they have meanings may be significantly smaller. Their language is more abstract and more complex. They begin to produce grammatically correct sentences. Cognitively, they can remember up to three items in sequence, can retell short stories, can group objects by characteristics and pretend to tell time. Their personalities continue to be of egocentrism, tending to talk in first person. They improve their ability to handle their emotions productively; however, the fear of the unknown can cause them to lose confidence and control of their emotions. They begin to respond to intrinsic motivation. Socially, they try to avoid aggression when they are angry, tending to seek compromises. At this age, the children are frequently bossy and prone to alibis. They understand the consequences of good and bad behavior and test adults. They have an understanding of the roles people play. These children seldom play by themselves, and exhibit unreasonable fears (Norton, 1999). Many children, at this age, do not understand the permanence of death. They also tend to believe that bad things happened because they behaved badly and exhibit "big man/big woman" syndrome which means that they believe that somehow they could have prevented something from happening (Froggee, 1994). Johnson and Foley (1984, p. 34) suggest that children under the age of five" . . . do not deal with memory tasks in a strategic fashion (do not rehearse, generate images or other mediators, spontaneously organize, etc.)" and "may not have the relevant prior knowledge that would allow them to organize disparate elements into a cohesive whole or to relate one set of events to another." For example:

> Five-year-old Jimmy and his mother were taken by force to a motel room by her estranged boyfriend, Mike. There the mother was brutally beaten to death. . . . Jimmy observed the beating. . . . On the witness stand . . . Jimmy responded, "Mike hit mommy." He later added, "He pulled on her legs to the bathroom." . . . The district attorney then began a series of questions which confused Jimmy, and his responses were inconsistent. For example, Jimmy was asked how many times Mike had hit his mother, "More than five, more than ten?" As he did not know how to count past five, Jimmy repeatedly answered, "I don't know." He was also asked . . . where she was standing–by the bed, the closet, or the bathroom. Jimmy became flustered at having to choose the specific location in an unfamiliar hotel room. (Pynoos and Eth, 1984, p. 102)

The vocabularies of children, ages five to six, contain nearly 6000 words, many of which have meaning for the children. They use more sophisticated grammar, enjoy dramatic play and enjoy producing dialogue about everyday events. Children in this age group are also increasing their cognitive abilities. They can count, identify colors, distinguish between a lot/a little and smallest/largest, and have vague concepts of time; however, they are very literal minded. The personalities of children in this age group tend to be outgoing, sociable and friendly. Socially, the children like to help parents around the house. They develop a protective instinct for younger siblings as well as others. They exhibit dependable behavior; take pride in their work, school and possessions; enjoy dressing up; and engage in role playing and creative play. Children of this age continue to have unreasonable fears (Norton, 1999). Typically, children do not understand the permanence of death; they equate bad behavior with bad events, and display characteristics of the "big man/big woman" syndrome. An example of the literal mindedness of this age group is exemplified in the following example from Berliner and Barbieri (1984, p. 132):

> In the following case example, a five-year-old child, on direct examination, told the jury about her father putting his penis in her mouth. On cross-examination by the father's defense attorney, the following exchange took place:
> Defense Attorney: And then you said you put your mouth on his penis?
> Child: No
> Defense Attorney: You didn't say that?
> Child: No
> Defense Attorney: Did you ever put your mouth on his penis?
> Child: No
> Defense Attorney: You didn't say that?

At this point, it seemed as if the child had completely recanted her earlier testimony about the sexual abuse and had only fabricated the story. . . . However, the experienced prosecuting attorney recognized the problem and clarified the situation:

> Prosecuting Attorney: Jennie, you said that you didn't put your mouth on daddy's penis.
> Is that right?
> Child: Yes
> Prosecuting Attorney: Did daddy put his penis in your mouth?
> Child: Yes

Had the prosecuting attorney not recognized the literal mindedness of the child, the father might not have been convicted. Another example involves a case where a child answered "no" to the question, "Were you in the man's house?" but answered "yes" to the question, "Were you in the man's apartment?" (Goodman, Golding and Haith, 1984, p. 144).

The language development of children, ages six to eight, continues to expand. Vocabularies are increased as are their abilities to use complex sentences. Cognitively, children are learning to read and write. They enjoy reading easy books, demonstrating their reading abilities, and creating their own stories. Emotional instability characterizes the personalities of children at this age. They show more tension, which may result in them lashing out at someone. As this age group develops socially, they may defy parents when they are under pressure and have difficulty getting along with younger siblings. They respond to teachers' help/praise and try to conform to please the teacher. Children in this age group enjoy listening to stories read at school, at home, or the library. They have definite inflexible ideas of right and wrong, and become curious about the differences between boys and girls (Norton, 1999). Children may engage in "magical thinking" at this age. If they wished that something would happen, and it did, they may believe that they are responsible for the situation. At this age, children begin to understand the concepts of time, which is important for interviewing children in crisis situations. According to Pynoos and Eth (1984, p. 92), children may involve their school friends in re-dramatizations or trauma-related games. "A seven-year-old girl, whom we interviewed one month after she witnessed her father strangulate her mother and then carry the body to the bedroom, forces all her friends to play the 'mommy game.' 'In the mommy game, you play dead, and I pick you up.'"

According to Berliner and Barbieri (1984, p. 133), "When a child first reveals that there has been sexual abuse, the content and manner of the revelation is often striking in its clarity and ring of truth." For example, "one seven-year-old girl said casually to her father: 'Daddy, does milk come out of your wiener? It comes out of Uncle Bob's and it tastes yukky'" (Berliner & Barbieri, 1984, p. 133). According to Berliner and Barbieri, "There could be little doubt that the child making such a startling statement has been sexually abused" (1984, p. 133).

From ages eight to ten, children's language development grows more complex, while their reading ability improves rapidly. The ability to comprehend what is read and use meaningful vocabulary increases. Children at this age tend to be interested in literature above their reading ability. There is an increase in the ability to remember objects as they learn to attend to certain stimuli while ignoring others. Cooperation is a highly valued personality trait. While they may have fewer fears about possible dangers, they may have strong fears about remote or impossible situations. Children learn to be more flexible regarding the issues of right and wrong, taking the situation into consideration. Peer influence begins and children also begin to understand other people's points of view (Norton, 1999). They also understand time and can put events in sequential order, which should be of assistance to interviewers of victims this age.

From the ages of ten to twelve, children continue to experience increases in language and cognitive development. They can apply logical rules, reasoning, and formal operations to solve abstract problems. Their personalities are characterized by the belief that they are in control of what happens to them, assuming responsibility for their successes and failures. They value independence. Physical changes in their appearance may influence their behaviors. Socially, at this age, children have developed racial attitudes. Other social characteristics include wanting to do jobs well, feeling inferior or inadequate if they believe they cannot meet their own expectations, increasing conformity to peer groups while decreasing conformity to parents which may lead to challenging parents (Norton, 1999). Interviewing children of this age is enhanced because, like the previous age group, they understand time and can place events in sequential order.

Gullo (1994, p. 20) believes that "while understanding the development of young children is important, investigators should not neglect to educate themselves on the developmental stages of adolescents as well." Davidson and Koppenhaver (1993) believe adolescents face extraordinary changes from their younger counterparts (see Table 2, Appendix A). Not only does the language development of adolescents continue to grow, but the gap that exists between those who have mastered the language and those who have not also continues to grow. Children at this age have a wide variety of experiences to share with others. The physical changes experienced by adolescents impact on their perceptions of themselves and others. Davidson and Koppenhaver (1993, p. 14) state: "Much less is known about the unfolding of their thinking than about their physical growth. . . . In any given classroom the students' cognitive and linguistic abilities will be as diverse as their relative levels of physical and emotional maturity."

Adolescents experience several major changes. Cognitively, these changes include developing the ability to hypothesize and predict. They begin to define their interests and strengths and may seek employment and/or instruction to pursue goals in their chosen area of interest. Adolescents have the ability to compare and integrate information from their own experiences and learning, and to make inferences based on that knowledge (Davidson and Koppenhaver, 1993). Pynoos and Eth (1984) characterize adolescents' reactions to homicide as rage, shame and betrayal. These teens may be considered rebellious and may participate in unusual antisocial acts: "One day after her mother was shot, a 13-year-old girl stole a piece of jewelry from her aunt, and then returned it the next day accompanied by a sorrowful note of apology" (Pynoos and Eth, 1984, p. 93). Adolescents may also engage in reenactment behaviors. According to Pynoos and Eth (1984, p. 93), "One mother shot her estranged husband after he broke the arm of their 17-year-old boy who was trying to protect her from abuse. On the first anniversary of the shooting, the boy suddenly returned home, and, in an unprecedented rage, attempted to shoot his mother."

Young (1989) believes that older children tend to exhibit different, yet equally challenging, developmental patterns. For instance, pre-adolescents may have a fairly sophisticated vocabulary; however, they may use words and phrases they do not fully understand. Puberty makes the children in this age group more vulnerable to sexual abuse. Adolescents tend to become self-centered, private and secretive. Pynoos and Eth (1984) suggest that adolescents are capable of giving a full account of the victimization, but may first appear uncooperative, suspicious, and guarded. Acting out in inappropriate or socially unacceptable ways is common in cases of pre-teen and teenage sexual abuse (Young, 1989). Gullo (1994) believes that interviewers armed with the information that teenagers frequently mask their true feelings with humor or denial can approach the interview by first developing a rapport with them to put them at ease. Teenagers at ease with their interviewers are much more likely to share their experiences and feelings.

Johnson and Foley (1984, p. 45) summarize their thoughts regarding children, their development and their recollection of events:

> Children will typically produce less detailed testimony in the courtroom, although not necessarily for all aspects of an event. For example, it is not clear whether children should be expected to be any worse than adults in recalling spatial arrangements of objects and people, or the temporal order and frequency of events. Our own work suggests that even young children may be able to recognize who did what. On the other hand, recall of complex events that children do not understand (e.g., adult conversations) would show a marked developmental trend.

Similarly, Waterman (1986) explains three types of child development issues that are important when allegations of sexual abuse arise: the child's developmental level relative to other children in his or her age group, the child's developmental level with regard to sexuality (pre-schoolers are curious about the origin of babies and show some interest in physical differences between the sexes; young children engage in self-stimulatory behavior or exhibitionism; discussions of intercourse and other adult sexual behaviors are inappropriate for this age), and the child's ability to respond adequately to interviews and to testify in court. Waterman (1986) remind adults who work with children that (1) children think in concrete terms; (2) children do not organize their thoughts logically; (3) children have a limited understanding of space, distance, and time; (4) children have a complex understanding of truth and lying; (5) children see the world egocentrically; (6) children have a limited attention span, and (7) children have varying degrees of comfort with strangers.

Chance and Goldstein (1984, p. 70) summarize research related to a child's ability to identify an assailant, "A child might be as capable as an adult of accurately identifying a familiar face, but be at a disadvantage in identifying a stranger's face." Additionally, they state (1984, p. 78):

> Preschool children made fewer accurate identifications of classmates than older children, strongly suggesting that children's processing of familiar faces becomes more efficient and better organized with increasing age. . . . Immediate memory for unfamiliar faces among children from 6 to 16 as a func-

tion of changes in facial expression and changes in "paraphernalia"–presence or absence of hats, shirts, scarves, necklaces, eyeglasses, wigs–shows a steady improvement between the ages of 6 and 10, but little change thereafter.

Developmentally, according to Pynoos and Eth (1984, pp. 98–99), children differ in their responses to homicide:

> Confronted with an immobilized preschool child, most police officers are unfamiliar with the developmental processes at work, and unaware that it may be premature to ask a mute child to verbalize or reenact the episode. . . . After a delay, the child may first describe the crime to a trusted adult for example, a week after her mother's brutal murder, one little girl spontaneously told her great-grandmother the details of the crime. . . . School-age children risk being coerced into an accomplice role. They may be forced to tell an agreed-upon lie, to remain silent, or to be otherwise uncooperative with the police . . . an 8-year-old boy . . . told the police a rehearsed story of his father's efforts to revive his drunken wife. Within minutes, however, he drew a picture of a man being arrested for killing an unprotected woman . . . adolescents . . . understand that they can, without lying, make one parent appear to be at fault by overlooking or reporting certain facts. For example, we interviewed two teenagers from a divorced family who had resided with different parents and who colored their accounts accordingly. The boy neglected to mention having seen his father load the gun, whereas his sister's account included this fact but omitted her mother's defiant taunt, "Okay, show what a big man you are. Shoot."

Goodman (1984b, p. 162) summarizes findings regarding other developmental issues which may affect child victims; he suggests that younger children ". . . have great difficulty reporting events on a purely verbal basis. Moreover, their reports tend to be less rationally ordered than adults' and typically present a less coherent whole." He suggests that children may know more than they can spontaneously recall or coherently report. Goodman (1984b, p. 162) states that props may be useful in ". . . providing a context to maximize narrative detail in children's accounts." For example:

> Suppose a four-year-old girl witnessed her mother's murder in the parking lot of a shopping mall. The child might be able to say only that a man killed her mother. But provided with a toy shopping mall, a toy parking lot, and dolls representing her mother, herself, and the murderer, she might be able to reenact many of the events that led up to and followed the homicide. (Goodman, 1984b, p. 163)

Goodman (1984b) also suggests that taking the child back to the scene of the crime could facilitate reports from children who may otherwise be considered too young to testify.

TRADITIONAL INTERVENTION PROCEDURES

Carson and MacMurray (1996) identify two primary goals of traditional intervention once the safety of the child has been established: (1) Determine if a criminal act has occurred, and (2) Provide help and support for the entire family unit. Additionally, Carson and MacMurray (1996) suggest that, once the immediate crisis has been resolved, there needs to be continued monitoring to determine if the family has received services and how they are responding to the services. According to the National Institute of Justice (1992):

> Essentially, there are two "gatekeepers" in the child protection system. First is the intake worker who receives the initial report, typically on a telephone hotline, and determines whether the report deserves further investigation. Second is the investigative caseworker who follows up on the reports that survive the first level of screening to determine whether the reported child is at risk. (p. 5)

One of the most common criteria for screening is custody disputes: "about 2–10 percent of all family court cases involving custody and/or visitation disputes also involved a charge of sexual abuse" (NIJ, 1992, p. 7). Additional criteria for screening include: repeated unfounded allegations, truancy or educational neglect, incomplete information, no indication of harm or risk of harm, failure to mention a specific incident or pattern of incidents, and maltreatment by a non-caretaker.

The initial contact with the child victim usually takes the form of an interview. Before the interview begins, the interviewer should develop a positive rapport with the child. The interviewer must realize that, "When children become victims or witnesses of violence or sexual abuse, they are thrust into an adult system that traditionally does not differentiate between children and adults" (NIJ, 1992, p. 15).

Mickish (1995) acknowledges the importance of the child's developmental stages as she outlines guidelines for interviewing child victims. After appropriate background information is obtained, the interviewer should prepare for the interview by determining "the child's general developmental status" (p. 191). During the interview, while trying to obtain the *what, who, when, where,* and *coercion,* the interviewer should "use language appropriate to the child's level; be sure the child understands words. Watch for signs of confusion, blankness, or embarrassment; be careful with words like incident, occur, penetration, prior, ejaculation, etc." (Mickish, 1995, p. 192). Age-appropriate interviewing strategies to determine whether or not a criminal act has occurred may include the use of anatomically correct dolls (first used in the late 1970s according to White, 1988) as well as art work (Cromer,

1986; Wolfe, Las and Wilson, 1987).

Establishing who should be with the child during the interview (caregivers, teachers, social workers, support persons, etc.) and where the interview should be conducted (school, home, police station, social worker's office, special play rooms, etc.) are also important considerations. Interviewers must realize that during the interview, there are two essential goals: collecting data, and minimizing or reducing the trauma experienced by the child.

While Germain, Brassard and Hart (1985) believe that, generally, direct questions are more effective than indirect questions with children of all ages, Stafford (1962, p. 314) warns interviewers, "Questions should be kept within the grasp of the child's mind. Interrogators should remember that questions which seem simple and direct to them may be confusing or absolutely meaningless to a child." Gullo (1994) believes that when interviewing children, crisis interveners who are familiar with the developmental stages of children can better judge whether the child is likely, given the age of the child, to comprehend the questions, as well as whether the child can successfully communicate thoughts and feelings:

> For example. investigators who know that children between the ages of 4 and 6 do not generally comprehend such major concepts as time, space, and distance, avoid asking questions such as "What time did your daddy touch you?" Instead, they frame their questions around times familiar to children, such as dinner, or bed time. (p. 20)

One major issue that interviewers should consider is the memory capacity of children. The National Institute of Justice (1992, pp. 24–25, 59–60, 62) summarized the research on children's memories:

1. Children are less skillful than adults in reproducing events using free recall (i.e., in responding to open-ended questions like, "What did you do in school today?").
2. When answering specific open-ended questions, children do provide less information than adults, but what they say is generally accurate.
3. When there are errors in children's memories, they are more likely to be errors of omission (i.e., forgetting) than commission (i.e., adding new or inaccurate information).
4. Like adults, children have stronger memories for central events than for peripheral details.
5. All but the youngest children (roughly pre-school years) generally perform on a par with adults when (1) identifying persons from pictures or lineups (2) responding to suggestive questioning about central events that are understandable or interesting to them (provided there has not been a lengthy

delay since the event occurred), and (3) distinguishing between memories originating from an actual experience and those from an imagined experience.

6. It may be fair to say that young children cannot independently fabricate truly credible descriptions of events outside of their experience.

Johnson and Foley (1984) suggest that when children are asked to testify about activities with which they are quite familiar, their memories can be expected to be at least as good, and on occasion better, than those of adults.

The second goal, that of providing help and support for the entire family unit and continued monitoring of services provided to the family, is dependent upon an understanding of the eight common traits of social and domestic violence which "weave a network of trauma and disruption" (Warner, 1981, p. 4). Warner believes, although their signs and symptoms may vary, all victims experience or deal with each of the following traits:

1. *Victim/Perpetrator Relationship:* In cases when the individual who is victimized knows the perpetrator, trust, along with personal faith and belief in someone, is destroyed. In place of trust, feelings of doubt, fear, and anticipatory anxiety develop.

2. *Victim/Perpetrator Personal Feelings:* Perpetrators often say the victim triggers the violence-release mechanism through an action or comment or by nothing more than being present.

3. *Self-Image:* A victim's self-image is injured because of the apparent vulnerability, the inability to abort the attack, and the resulting disgrace. The question of physical/emotional strength is frequently raised when the victim wonders how he/she could have prevented the attack.

4. *Guilt:* The victim tends to redirect feelings inward, which build into tremendous waves of guilt. The victim tends to accept the blame for the incident.

5. *Denial:* This tendency to hide from the fact that an act of violence has occurred becomes an automatic reflex. Embarrassment over the awareness that he/she had been victimized causes the individual to try to block the incident, to hide it from others, and to not report it.

6. *Long-Term Impact:* With the build-up of such feelings as guilt and denial comes a cancerous form of growth which eats away at, and eventually destroys, the family unit in general and the victim in particular.

7. *Intervention:* If the person is unwilling to share his/her feelings and/or discuss the situation with an uninvolved, helping person, and begin to develop a feeling of trust, recovery and re-growth will not occur. It is understandable that due to the nature of the violence and its accompanying feelings of embarrassment, guilt, pain, and isolation, it is extremely difficult to talk freely to an outsider. The first step toward intervention, that of open communication and honesty, is frequently overwhelming and very frightening, yet it is the only way the involved parties can honestly address all the issues

and visualize the scope of the problem.

8. *Legal System:* The process of legal recourse and correction, by the mere lack of its complexities, poses tremendous barriers for many people. The automatic tendency is to forget the entire issue, and not to face additional trauma. Along with the overwhelming process itself is the tendency for the victim to be re-victimized. The rehashing and reliving of a horrible experience is often as traumatic as the original incident. (Warner, 1981, pp. 4–9)

Warner (1981) believes that first responders, armed with the knowledge that people are most responsive while the crisis is still in process, should help link the victims to appropriate support systems as soon as possible. To accomplish the task of linking victims to support systems in a more effective and efficient manner, Cesnik and Puls (1977) recommend that representatives from both social services and the criminal justice system be actively involved in the initial contact with the child victim. These two agencies with their specialized skills, working in tandem, provide the most appropriate intervention for the child victim.

Helping children overcome the trauma of victimization can be accomplished through the use of victim-witness assistance programs or victim advocate programs. Over 7,000 communities throughout the United States offer some type of victim assistance program (NIJ, 1992). The purpose of these programs is to minimize witness discontent with the way they are treated by the criminal justice system and social services. Prosecutors are urged "to communicate more closely with victims, seek greater victim input, protect them against any harassment, honor scheduled case appearances, return property promptly, and improve the overall quality of client services" (Doerner and Lab, 1995, p. 51). The services that victim/witness assistance programs provide fall within eight stages of the criminal justice process: (1) emergency response, (2) victim stabilization, (3) resource mobilization, (4) after arrest, (5) pre-court appearance, (6) court appearance, (7) pre-sentence, and (8) post-sentence. At each stage, a victim/witness assistance program can provide the following types of services: emergency services, counseling, advocacy, claims assistance, court-related services, and system-wide services (U.S. Department of Justice, 1995). Doerner and Lab (1995) report that in one jurisdiction, a victim-witness program was developed for only child sexual abuse cases. The victim's counselor would meet several times with the victim to establish a rapport with the child and to evaluate the validity of the complaint. Anatomically correct dolls were available so the child could explain what had happened to him or her. When cases went to the grand jury, judges allowed the victim counselor to take the place of the child on the witness stand and explain the details of the case.

Specialized victim-witness assistance programs, traditional victim-witness assistance programs and victim advocate programs provide a variety of services which include crisis intervention and follow-up counseling. According to the Federal Rules of Criminal Procedure (Victims of Child Abuse Act of 1990), specific "rights" for children, never before legally recognized in federal court, have been established. Some of the accommodations include:

1. Using multidisciplinary teams to provide medical and mental health services to child victims, expert testimony, case management, and training for judges and court personnel;
2. Using appointed guardians ad litem to protect the best interests of child victims;
3. Using multidisciplinary teams and specialized "counseling centers to improve the investigation and prosecution of child abuse cases;
4. Using the Court-Appointed Special Advocate program.

Victim advocates may assist prosecutors in preparing children for courtroom testimony by using multilingual coloring books/children's books to acquaint the children with courtroom procedures and/or by taking children on a tour of the courtroom and introducing them to some of the personnel who will be involved (NIJ, 1992). Unfortunately, Doerner and Lab (1995, p. 45) report, "Even though many social service agencies were in operation, victims remained largely unaware of service availability. As a result, relatively few victims received help coping with their crime-induced problems."

After the initial crisis, long-range plans for continued assistance should be developed for the child victim. Because the acceptance rate for prosecution of sexual abuse cases with child victims is relatively low (61%, according to the U.S. Department of Justice, 1994) and because of the trauma associated with children who are victims of abuse, it is important that intervention with the children be undertaken by professionals who are sensitive to the child's developmental needs, and knowledgeable about the agencies available to assist the child. Services such as individual or family therapy, parenting education programs, substance abuse programs, and protective day-care may be deemed necessary by the intervener. Active networking between the various agencies and personnel involved in handling these cases is essential. However, after a review of research related to crisis intervention, Doerner and Lab (1995, p. 153) concluded: "Perhaps the most notable result of intervention studies is the almost universal finding that more services are needed than are typically available. . . . Among the needs most often cited are the needs for . . . extended treatment and counseling."

INNOVATIVE INTERVENTION PROCEDURES

Many changes are being made in the techniques used in cases when children are victims. In 1994, the U.S. Department of Justice introduced two types of reforms on behalf of children: courtroom reforms and system reforms.

> Courtroom reforms include efforts to shield the child from direct confrontation by the accused by using closed-circuit television, videotape technology, or opaque screens. Other courtroom reforms include efforts to limit the courtroom audience, special hearsay exceptions for sexually abused children, and elimination of special competency examinations for child witnesses. By definition, courtroom reforms are available only to children whose cases go to trial. By contrast, system reforms benefit every child whose abuse is disclosed to authorities. Although many system reforms do not require statutory authorization and no threat to constitutional protections, they may be as difficult to implement as courtroom reforms because implementation depends on cooperation among multiple agencies. Among the most popular system reforms are provision of a support person for the child, assignment of a guardian ad litem, reducing delay, multidisciplinary case review, and streamlining the system by reducing the number of interviews and appearances required of the child. (U.S. Department of Justice, 1994, p.11)

Other changes involve interviews with child victims. These include, but are not limited to:
1. Videotaping interview sessions to eliminate multiple interviews;
2. Drawing interviews in which the child constructs pictures to explain graphically what happened to him or her;
3. Using puppet shows and/or role playing;
4. Designating special rooms for conducting interviews with children.

Changes in the approaches to crisis intervention have also occurred. Such changes include parent and family counseling, crisis conflict and crisis resolution programs, and intrapsychic humanisim, described as ". . . a compassionate and rigorously scientific reconceptualization of child development, psychopathology, and treatment . . ." (Tyson, 1999, p. 64). There are now a variety of public and private agencies whose purpose is to provide medical, emotional, and legal support to children and youth, including child protection agencies, victim assistance agencies, mental health centers, medical facilities, runaway shelters, drop-in centers, outreach projects, independent or transitional living programs, and youth services programs (U.S. Department of Justice, 1995).

Another change in practice is the use of multidisciplinary teams. Carson and MacMurray (1996, p. 132) state:

One technique . . . is that of multidisciplinary teams. These teams are general-ly composed of representatives of both criminal justice agencies (e.g., law enforcement, prosecutors, victims' advocates) and social service agencies (e.g., case workers and administrators) as well in some cases counselors, treatment specialists, or medical personnel. The purpose of the teams is to discuss the available information for a specific case and to coordinate the process of deci-sion making and formulate recommendations for action in cases.

The federal Victims of Child Abuse Act directs the court and attorneys for the government to work with state and local governments that have estab-lished multidisciplinary teams to assist young victims and witnesses. As of December 1993, thirty-one states had enacted statutes mandating or author-izing the creation of multidisciplinary child protection teams. Such teams are defined to include representatives from health, social service, law enforce-ment, and legal service agencies. The role of multidisciplinary teams is to provide a range of services to young victims as witnesses, including: medical diagnoses and evaluation services; telephone consultations in emergencies; medical evaluations related to abuse or neglect; psychological and psychi-atric diagnoses and evaluations; expert medical, psychological, and related professional testimony; case service coordination and assistance; training for judges, litigators, court officers and others. Where there is no existing multi-disciplinary team, the U.S. Attorney General Guidelines accompanying the Victims of Child Abuse Act instructs federal investigators to coordinate with existing child protective service agencies (U.S. Department of Justice, 1995). Many multidisciplinary teams meet on a regular basis to discuss new cases, progress of ongoing cases, and proposals for improvements in the delivery of services to the victim. "In some jurisdictions, interviews with child victims are scheduled to coincide with the team meetings to enable the various agency representatives to participate in, or contribute to, the ques-tioning" (NIJ, 1992, p. 138). In Madison County, Alabama, a residential building was converted to a Children's Advocacy Center. The Center hous-es specialists from each of the relevant agencies so that children may remain in one building while being interviewed by all the necessary parties (NIJ, 1992). Other teams have followed Madison County's lead by creating simi-lar centers for children.

BIBLIOTHERAPY AND CRISIS INTERVENTION

Naitove (1978), Green (1978), and Pardeck (1990) agree that traditional therapies in the treatment of child abuse may not be successful because chil-dren perceive the conventional methods of assessment and treatment as threatening; abused children may not have the emotional and cognitive development requisite to benefit from conventional therapy, and abused children fear being abused by others. Lindeman and Kling (1969) stress that bibliotherapy can be used with emotionally troubled clients, individuals with minor adjustment problems, and children with growth and developmental needs while Hollander (1989, p. 187) claims "children's books are neutral vehicles for teaching about specific, often-embarrassing topics such as the proper terminology for body parts, bodily functions, private zones, uncomfortable touching, and fondling."

While bibliotherapy may be useful to children in resolving crisis situations, it is important to note that there are limitations as to when bibliotherapy is appropriate within the legal system. To understand when bibliotherapy is appropriate, it is necessary to first understand the legal system with reference to children as primary victims. Imagine the following scenario: Uncle Bob and Aunt Mabel live in Somewhere County, Iowa, just three blocks from their niece and nephew, whom they suspect are being abused by one of the parents. They report their suspicions to the intake worker at the Somewhere County Child Protection Services Office (They could have reported their suspicions directly to law enforcement officers, who, in turn, would have reported the case to Child Protection Services). The intake worker determines whether the report deserves further investigation. If further investigation is warranted, an investigative caseworker determines, based on the evidence provided, whether the case is assigned a one-hour priority status (sexual abuse, physical abuse, danger to the child), a twenty-four-hour priority status (all other parent abuse cases, severe/acute neglect), or a five-day priority status (educational neglect, etc.).

At this point, the caseworker begins the investigation by conducting a background check, cross referencing data basis, and conducting interviews. The investigative caseworker must talk face to face with the victim. The caseworker in Somewhere County is also required to contact two non-associated professionals, the parent(s), siblings, and perpetrator, if it is not a parent. Law enforcement officials are consulted if they are needed, and crosschecks are made to avoid the duplication of interviews. All the investigative work (summaries of interviews conducted by the Child Protective Services caseworker and law enforcement officials) are sent to prosecutor, who decides whether to prosecute.

Regardless of prosecution, the investigative caseworker determines what type of services are needed. Even though the caseworker does not believe services are necessary, he/she still provides information to the victim and the family regarding the services that are available to help resolve the crisis such as mental health agencies (parenting, counseling for parents), comprehensive mental health providers (parenting classes, counseling for parents and child, and family counseling (child and parents). If the caseworker determines additional services are needed, he/she makes referrals to the appropriate agencies. In Somewhere County, parents sign an informal adjustment which means they agree to take the child to the appropriate agency for assistance. If there is not an agreement, or the parents don't take the child, a petition is filed in court and the court makes a ruling regarding the use of support services.

In this case, there are two courts involved: criminal court and family court. The criminal court may prosecute the parent, while the family court may need to make a decision as to whether the children should be removed from the home, or have the parent removed. A great many differences exist between these two courts (see Table 3, Appendix A). "Additionally, the rules of evidence and procedures are more relaxed in child protection proceedings: the courtroom is closed to the public; hearsay restrictions are less prohibitive; in most jurisdictions, children may not be required to testify at all; and when they do testify, it often takes place in the judge's chambers" (Whitcomb, Goodman, Runyan and Hoak, 1994, p. 5).

Of particular importance are the techniques by which evidence was gathered. The criminal court requires first-hand statements from the victim; in family court, however, the child may testify, a therapist may testify for the child or may testify on behalf of the child. In criminal court, if the child is reluctant to talk about the abuse, then the likelihood of conviction is lessened. Any type of coercion of the victim by prosecutors or victim advocates (which may include bibliotherapy) could confound the issues and lead to the case being dismissed. However, in family court, if the child is not willing to talk about the abuse, then informational resources such as children's books and videotapes may be used to try to encourage the child to talk about what happened. In this scenario, then, if the children volunteered information about the abuse, then charges may be filed in criminal court. The use of bibliotherapy would only provide the parent with probable cause for dismissal, claiming the children are simply recalling a story read to them. However, in determining whether the children should be removed from the home, bibliotherapy, as well as other techniques such as showing the children videotapes, may be used to encourage children to verbalize what happened to them.

Currently, the only acceptable situation for using bibliotherapy in a criminal court case is in preparing children for testimony. Using a bibliotherapeutic approach, with books such as *Carla Goes To Court* (Beaudry & Ketchum, 1983), *The Judiciary, Laws We Live By* (Summer & Woods, 1992), and *To Tell the Truth* (Ogawa, 1988), may assist in acquainting the child with the courtroom, the proceedings and personnel involved in a trial. For example, in Carla Goes To Court, the main character, Carla, witnesses a burglary.

She tells her story to the police and then is asked to identify the suspect from a lineup. The story takes readers through the entire process from answering questions during the preliminary interviews to testifying at a preliminary hearing and a jury trial. Carla's feelings are also clearly explained which provides the opportunity for bibliotherapeutic techniques to be used. Once charges are filed and statements are recorded (written, videotaped, etc.), social workers and therapists may use bibliotherapy to help the child resolve the crisis situation.

However, when a child is a secondary victim, social service providers may begin bibliotherapy almost immediately. For example, Allison's mother has just informed her that Mary, her best friend who lives across the street, has been sexually abused by a man in the neighborhood. Allison is devastated by the news. She is afraid to go outside and cries at night. Her mother decides to take her to a social worker to help Allison understand what has happened and what will happen to Mary and the man in the neighborhood. The social worker, familiar with bibliotherapy and children's books related to sexual abuse, initiates a discussion with Allison. She recommends a carefully-selected story for Allison to read at home. She schedules a return visit so they can discuss the book. During the next session, the social worker discusses the book with Allison. She determines whether or not Allison could identify with the character and situation in the story, and interpret the relationships between characters and their motives. The catharsis should occur during the discussion of the book. The therapist should monitor the child's reaction to the literature, the degree of similarity between the child's own emotional experience and the problem being considered, and the emotional experiences of the child through his or her identification with the story character. The final step would be developing insight into the problem, possibly trying to encourage Allison to understand what her friend, Mary, may be going through and how she may be feeling.

CONCLUSION

In her article, entitled "The Cycle of Violence," Cathy Spatz Widom presents some startling information:

> In one of the most detailed studies of the issue to date, research sponsored by the National Institute of Justice (NIJ) found that childhood abuse increased the odds of future delinquency and adult criminality overall by 40 percent . . . being abused or neglected as a child increased the likelihood of arrest as a juvenile by 53 percent, as an adult by 38 percent, and for a violent crime by 38 percent . . . being abused or neglected in childhood increased the likelihood of arrest for

females. . . . The physically abused (as opposed to neglected or sexually abused) were the most likely to be arrested later for a violent crime. Notably, however, the physically abused group was followed closely by the neglected group. (1992, pp. 1–3)

This information leads to the conclusion that strategies and practices currently employed to help children in crisis situations are not as effective as they might be. Children who are primary victims have a more urgent need for intervention than their secondary victim counterparts; however, interveners must realize that children who are secondary victims also need assistance in resolving their crises. Hendricks (1985, p. 33) states, "Individuals have two main concerns when they approach a conflict. One of these concerns is people, both themselves and other people. The second, and equally important concern, is for the resolution of the conflict." For crisis interveners to successfully assist child victims in resolving conflicts, they need to be aware of the developmental strengths, weaknesses and characteristics of children. An increased awareness of child development provides crisis interveners with essential information from which to develop appropriate questions for interviews and to make decisions about appropriate intervention strategies.

When children become victims, they are thrust into an adult system that traditionally does not differentiate between children and adults (NIJ, 1992). Perhaps one of the problems of the current system is that once children are referred to other agencies, they are forgotten as are many adults. Establishing multidisciplinary teams to streamline cases involving child victims might reduce the possibility of this happening. With a cooperative group effort, teamwork may lessen the chance that a child will miss out on services that are essential to a healthy resolution. Current courtroom reforms, such as providing a support person for the child, assigning a guardian ad litem, reducing the number of interviews and courtroom appearances, may also help make what appears to be a hostile adult environment more hospitable toward children.

Another way in which crisis interveners may help make the adult criminal justice system work for children is to continue to seek alternative strategies for assisting the child. The American Bar Association, the Attorney General's Advisory Board on Missing and Exploited Children and the President's Child Safety Partnership endorse the following four reforms: obtaining children's testimony via closed-circuit television or videotape, using anatomically correct dolls to help children communicate, employing a team approach to investigation and prosecution and using specialized victim assistance or advocacy programs (NIJ, 1992). Whitcomb, Goodman, Runyan and Hoak (1994, p. 6) suggest "since maternal support was consistently found to be an important factor contributing to children's psychological well-being, it follows that if personnel in the justice system direct greater attention to the mothers' needs, the mothers, in turn, will be better able to support their children." It would seem reasonable, then, that victim advocate programs of the future should involve the child victim and the mother.

An additional strategy which may be incorporated as an intervention strategy is bibliotherapy. Bibliotherapy helps the child victim realize that he/she is not alone. Many other reported benefits of bibliotherapy have been documented. For instance, James Baldwin (1964) claimed that books taught him the things that tormented him most were the very experiences that connected him with others both alive and dead. Cardenas' reflections (1980) provide additional support for bibliotherapy, ". . . if those who read look back into their experiences, surely they will conclude that the printed word has affected them changed them, mellowed them. They will indeed testify to the understanding and value of bibliotherapy" (p. 3).

Bibliotherapy could provide a link between the child victim, the mother, and the victim advocate. If mothers and children were reading together, spontaneous discussions regarding the victimization could enhance both the victim's and mother's understanding of the crisis situation and the effects it may or may not have on each of them. The use of bibliotherapy, as a way to get uncommunicative children to reveal information related to abuse, is questioned in criminal courts as it may confound the issues; however, it may be used in family courts. When the judicial system is willing to accept the notion that all but the youngest children (roughly pre-school years) can distinguish between fact and fantasy, then bibliotherapy will be an innovative addition to the existing repertoire of intervention strategies. Rubin (1978, p. 18) states "Bibliotherapy clearly is—and should be further developed as—an interdisciplinary field." Social workers have begun to endorse this strategy, and it is time for those involved in crisis intervention to explore the multiple uses of children's books as a way to resolve children's crises.

CHAPTER QUESTIONS

1. In your own words, explain the different types of abuse and neglect identified by Flowers (1994).
2. List 5 reasons why it is important for crisis interveners to understand child development.
3. Define "bibliotherapy" in your own words.
4. Identify the major stages of bibliotherapy.
5. Rubin (1978) states, "Bibliotherapy clearly is—and should be further developed as—an interdisciplinary field." Explain in your own words what this means as it applies to crisis intervention.

SIMULATED EXERCISES

Simulated Exercise 1

Based on your knowledge of child development, develop a set of questions you would use if you were interviewing a ten-year-old whom you suspect is being physically abused.

Simulated Exercise 2

Choose a book on bibliotherapy. Apply the criteria established by Jalongo (1983) to determine if the book is appropriate for bibliotherapy. Then, identify how you would use the book for bibliotherapy.

Simulated Exercise 3

A seven-year-old has been recommended to you for bibliotherapy. Outline the procedures you would use to conduct bibliotherapy with the child.

APPENDIX A

Table 1. The Language, Cognitive, Personality and Social Development of Children Ages 2–12

	Language	*Cognitive*	*Personality*	*Social*
Ages 2–3	Rapid language growth Vocabulary = 900 words Identify and name actions in pictures Identify large and small body parts	Learn new ways to organize and and classify by putting things together they perceive to be alike Remember 2–3 items	Think that they have an identity separate from family members Need for security	Organize and represent their worlds; Imitate actions and behaviors Transfer things into make-believe
Ages 3–4	Vocabulary = 1,500 words Play with sound and rhythm of language Develop the ability to use past tense Use language to find out about the world Speech becomes more complex	Develop understanding of how things relate to each other; how parts go together to make a whole; and how they are arranged in space in relation to each other Understand relationships and how to classify things Understand how objects relate to each other in in number and amount Compare two things and tell which is bigger and smaller	Developed a fairly steady self concept Have sets of feelings about themselves Require warm and secure environments Hide from unhappy situations by withdrawing, suggesting problems do not exist or blame others Become aware of cultural heritage	Realize that others have feelings Enjoy playing together Develop strong attachment to other children Enjoy participating in group games, activities Identify others' feelings by observing facial expressions

184

**Table 1 (con't.). The Language, Cognitive, Personality and
Social Development of Children Ages 2–12**

Ages 4–5	Language is more abstract Grammatically correct sentences Vocabulary = 2,500 words Understand some prepositions Ask questions: why, how why, how	Remember 3 things told to them or retell a short story if the material is presented in a meaningful way Improve in their ability to sequence Increase ability to group objects according to important characteristics Pretend to tell time	Continue egocentrism Talk in first person Consider themselves the center of the world Improve ability to handle their emotions in productive ways Fear of unknown causes them to lose confidence and control of their emotions Respond to intrinsic motivation Require warm and secure environments	Avoid aggression when angry and look for compromise Frequently bossy, assertive Understand consequences of good/bad and may engage in unacceptable behaviors to elicit reactions Seldom play alone Work by themselves Increased awareness of the roles people play Exhibit unreasonable fears (dark, thunder)
Ages 5–6	Use complex sentences Correct pronouns and verbs in present and past-tense Vocabulary = 6,000 words Enjoy dramatic play and producing dialogue about every day activities Curious about the written appearance of their own language Vague concepts of time	Learn to follow one type of classification through to completion without changing the main characteristic Discriminate 10 objects and counts to 10 Identify primary colors Learn to distinguish between a lot and a little Require trial and error in arranging things from smallest to largest	Outgoing, sociable and friendly Stable and adjusted in emotional life Developing confidence in others and self-assurance Require warmth and security in adult-relationships	Like to help parents around the house Developing dependable behavior Protect younger siblings and others Proud of accomplishments Take pride in school and possessions Show anxiety and unreasonable fear Enjoy playing outside Enjoy excursions to new

**Table 1 (con't.). The Language, Cognitive, Personality and
Social Development of Children Ages 2–12**

				and familiar places Enjoy dressing up, role playing, and creative play
Ages 6–8	Language development continues Larger vocabularies Complex sentences Average oral sentence length is 7 1/2 words	Learning to read and Enjoy reading easy books and demonstrating new abilities Learning to write and enjoy creating their own stories Enjoy longer stories Attention span increasing Base rules on on immediate perception and learn through real situations Develop a new set of rules, called groupings, so they don't have to see all objects to group Understand relationships among categories	Not as emotionally stable as before; they show more tension and may strike out Seek independence from adults but continue to require warmth and security from adults	May defy parents when under pressure Difficulty getting along with younger siblings Want to play with other children but frequently insist on being first Respond to teachers' help or praise Try to conform to please teachers Enjoy sitting still and listening to short stories read at school, at home or in the library Have definite inflexible ideas or right and wrong Curious about the differences between boys and girls

Table 1 (con't.). The Language, Cognitive, Personality and Social Development of Children Ages 2–12

Ages 8–10	Relate concepts to general ideas Use of subordinating conjunctions Use of more complex grammar Average sentence length is 9 words	Reading skills improve rapidly Wide variations in reading ability Level of interest in literature is still above reading level Memory improves as children learn to attend to certain stimuli and ignore others	Cooperation is highly valued in 4th graders but declines in later years Fewer fears about immediate and possible dangers but may have strong feelings about remote or impossible situations (ghosts)	Concepts of right and wrong more flexible; the situation is taken into consideration Peer group influence begins Thinking is becoming socialized-children can understand other's viewpoints Reasoning and solutions to problems should agree with others
Ages 10–12	Use complex sentences Use auxiliary verbs	Develop an understanding of the chronological ordering of past events Apply logical rules, reasoning, and formal operations to abstract problems	Internalize their control; believe they are in control of what happens and assume personal responsibility for successes and failures Value independence Rapid change in physical growth may cause children to become self-conscious and self-critical	Develop racial attitudes Want to do jobs well Sense of justice Strong peer influence May have feelings of inferiority and inadequacy if they don't measure up to own standards Accept opposite sex identity Conformity to parents decreases

Table 2. The Language, Cognitive, Personality and Social Development of Adolescents

Language	*Cognitive*	*Personality*	*Social*
Language development continues	Abilites are more diverse	Chronological age is poor indicator of physical maturity	Cultural understanding
New strategies are learned	Gain the ability to hypothesize and predict	Physical changes impact their perceptions of themselves and others	Interests and strengths are defined
Literacy learning occurs in context	Relate thoughts to the larger world around them	Emergence of secondary sex sex characteristsics	Am I normal?
Abilities are diverse			Compare, contrast and weigh their own morals and values, along with those of their parents, against those of their friends
Increased knowledge of vocabulary and concepts			Closely connected to family
Awareness of the multiple meanings of words			Increasing autonomy and responsibility for personal behavior and goals
Realize ordering of words can change meanings of words			
Realize ordering of words can change meaning			
Compare and integrate information from their own experiences and learning, and to make inferences based on that knowledge			

Table 3. Comparison of Criminal Court and Family Court

	Criminal Court	*Family Court*
Purpose	Is the defendant guilty of abuse? Is the defendant innocent of abuse?	Is it likely abuse occurred? Does child remain at risk? Is protective action necessary?
Focus	Offender-oriented	Child-centered
Goal	Resolution of the case	Resolution of the case, in a way that serves the best interests of the child
Outcome	Defendant's liberty	Most severe outcome: removing the child or parent from the home
Rights	Guaranteed to defendants by the U.S. Constitution	No rights according to the U.S. Constitution
Burden of Proof	Beyond a reasonable doubt	A preponderance of evidence
Evidence	Victim must have volunteered freely, first-hand	From child, from child information through therapist, from therapist
Bibliotherapy	Not permitted except to prepare child for court or after criminal process is completed Depends on court preference	May be used before, during and after process Depends on court preference

APPENDIX B

Additional Internet Sources

The following websites will help you to gain more in-depth knowledge about children in crisis, as well as the role of service professionals in this difficult subject.

Coordinating Council for Children in Crisis:
  http://www.ccccnh.org/
Lifeskills, Inc.:
  http://www.lifeskills.com/crisis-services.htm
Citizens Against Sexual Assault, Child Assault Prevention Project (CAP):
  http://www.casaonline.net/cap.htm
The National CASA Association - Court Appointed Special Advocates:
  http://www.nationalcasa.org/index-1.htm
National Exchange Club Foundation:
  http://www.preventchildabuse.com/abuse.htm
National Council on Child Abuse & Family Violence:
  http://www.nccafv.org/
World Health Organization:
  http://www.who.int/topics/child_abuse/en/
Understanding Child Abuse and Neglect, Iowa State University:
  http://www.extension.iastate.edu/Publications/PM1478X2.pdf
Child Abuse and Neglect Prevention Task Force:
  http://www.childabuseprevention.com/links.html
Prevent Abuse Now (PAN):
  http://www.prevent-abuse-now.com/stats.htm
Abuse and Neglect Links:
  http://travel.state.gov/family/services/abuse/abuse_581.html
U.S. Department of Health and Human Services, Crisis Intervention in Child Abuse and Neglect:
  http://nccanch.acf.hhs.gov/pubs/usermanuals/crisis/crisis.pdf
Child Development Institute:
  www.childdevelopmentinfo.com/
Foundation for Child Development:
  http://fcd-us.org/
National Center for PTSD:
  http://www.ncptsd.va.gov/facts/specific/fs_child_sexual_abuse.html

Internet School Library Media Center's (ISLMC) Bibliotherapy Page:
  http://falcon.jmu.edu/~ramseyil/bibliotherapy.htm
Bibliotherapy Page:
  http://www.sas.upenn.edu/~weinberg/Bibliotherapy.html
Understanding and Dealing with Child Abuse, by Michael G. Connor, Psy.D.:
  http://www.crisiscounseling.com/AbuseViolence/ChildAbuse.htm
Childabuse.com:
  http://www.childabuse.com/capubs.htm
National Association of School Psychologists:
  http://www.nasponline.org/NEAT/crisismain.html

REFERENCES

Aiex, N. (1993). Bibliotherapy. *ERIC Digest.* (ERIC Document Reproduction Service No. ED 357 333).

Alston, E. (1962). Bibliotherapy and psychotherapy. *Library Trends, 11,* 166–167.

American Humane Association. (1994). *Child abuse and neglect data. AHA fact sheet #1.* Englewood, CO: American Humane Association.

Arbuthnot, M. & Sutherland, Z. (1972). *Children and books* (4th Edition). Glenview. IL: Scott, Foresman.

Association of Hospital and Institution Libraries. (1971). *Bibliotherapy: Methods and materials.* Chicago: American Library Association.

Baldwin, J. (1964, June 1). Television Narrative. WNEW-TV. New York City.

Beaudry, J. & Ketchum, L. (1983). *Carla goes to court.* New York: Human Sciences Press.

Berliner, L. & Barbieri, M. (1984). The testimony of the child victim of sexual assault. *Journal of Social Issues, 40,* 2, 125–137.

Berliner, L. & Wheeler, J. (1987). Treating the effects of sexual abuse on children. *Journal of Interpersonal Violence, 2,* 415–434.

Bernstein, J. (1977). *Books to help children cope with separation and loss.* New York: Bowker.

Bernstein, J. (1983). *Books to help children cope with separation and loss.* (2nd Edition). New York: Bowker.

Bodart, J. (1980). Bibliotherapy: The right book for the right person at the right time, and more! *Top of the News, 86,* 183–188.

Bowker, R.R. (2001). Children's books in print. New Providence, NJ: R.R. Bowker.

Bryan, A. (1939). Can there be a science of bibliotherapy? *Library Journal, 64,* 773–776.

Cardenas, M. (1980). *Bibliotherapy: Good book or media selection plus individual guidance plus a definite goal.* (ERIC Document Reproduction Service No. ED 191–484).

Carson, B. & MacMurray, B. (1996). Domestic violence–Child abuse. In J.E. Hendricks & B. Byers (Eds.), *Crisis Intervention in Criminal Justice/Social Services* (2nd Edition) (pp. 113–138). Springfield, IL: Charles C Thomas, Publisher, Ltd.

Cesnik, B. & Puls, M. (1977). Law enforcement and crisis intervention services: A critical relationship. *Suicide and Life-Threatening Behavior, 7,* 211–215.

Chance, J. & Goldstein, A. (1984). Face-recognition memory: Implications for children's eyewitness testimony. *Journal of Social Issues, 40,* 2, 69–85.

Cionciolo, P. (1965). Children's literature can affect coping. *Personnel and Guidance Journal, 48,* 897–903.

Cohen, L. (1987). Bibliotherapy: Using literature to help clients deal with difficult problems. *Journal of Psychosocial Nursing, 25,* 20–24.

Cromer, R. (1986). A community approach to child sexual abuse. The role of the office of the district attorney. *Response to the Victimization of Women and Children, 9,* 10–13.

Davidson, J. & Koppenhaver, D. (1993). *Adolescent literacy: What works and why* (2nd Edition). New York: Garland Publishing.

Delaney, S. (1938). The place of bibliotherapy in a hospital. *Library Journal, 68,* 305–308.

Dixon, S. (1979). *Working with people in crisis: Theory and practice.* St. Louis: C.V. Mosby Co.

Doerner, W. & Lab, S. (1995). *Victimology.* Cincinnati, OH: Anderson Publishing.

Dreyer, S. (1993). *The bookfinder.* Circle Pines, MN: American Guidance Service.

Erickson, E. (1959). Identity and the life cycle. *Psychological Issues Monographs.* New York: International Universities Press.

Erickson, E. (1963). *Childhood and society* (2nd Edition). New York: W.W. Norton.

Flowers. R. (1994). *The victimization and exploitation of women and children: A study of physical, mental and sexual maltreatment in time United States.* Jefferson, NC: McFarland & Co.

Froggee, S. (1995, March). Children and grief. Paper presented at the Indiana Victims' Assistance Network. Indianapolis, Indiana.

Germain, R., Brassard, M. & Hart, S. (1985). Crisis intervention for maltreated children. *School Psychology Review, 14,* 291–299.

Giblin, P. (1989). Use of reading assignments in clinical practice. The American *Journal of Victim Therapy, 17,* 219–228.

Gladding, S. & Gladding, C. (1991). The abc's of bibliotherapy for school counselors. *The School Counseling, 8,* 7–13.

Glazer, J. (1981). *Children's literature for early childhood.* Columbus, OH: Merrill.

Good, C. (1973). *Dictionary of education.* New York: McGraw-Hill.

Goodman, G. (1984a). The child witness: An introduction. *Journal of Social Issues, 40,* 2, 1–9.

Goodman, G. (1984b). The child witness: Conclusions and future directions for research. *Journal of Social Issues, 40,* 2, 157–175.

Goodman, G., &.Golding, J. & Haith, M. (1984). Jurors' reactions to child witnesses. *Journal of Social Issues, 40,* 2, 139–156.

Gottschalk, L. (1948). Bibliotherapy as an adjunct in psychiatry. *American Journal of Psychiatry, 104,* 632–637.

Green, A. (1978). Psychopathology of abused children. *Journal of the American Academy of Child Psychiatry, 17,* 92–103.

Gullo, D. (1994, January). Child abuse: Interviewing possible victims. *FBI Law*

Enforcement Bulletin, pp. 19–22.

Hendricks, J. (1985). *Crisis intervention: Contemporary issues for on-site interveners.* Springfield, IL: Charles C Thomas, Publisher, Ltd.

Hendricks, J. & McKean, J. (1995). *Crisis intervention: Contemporary issues for on-site interveners* (2nd Edition). Springfield, IL: Charles C Thomas, Publisher, Ltd.

Hollander, S. (1989). Coping with child sexual abuse through children's books. *Elementary School Guidance & Counseling, 23,* 183–193.

Horowitz, S., Boardman, S., & Redlener, I. (1994). Constructive conflict management and coping in homeless children and adolescents. *Journal of Social Issues, 50,* 85–98.

Huck, C. (1976). *Children's literature in the elementary school* (3rd Edition). New York: Holt, Rinehart & Winston.

Hynes, A. & Hynes-Berry, M. (1986). *Bibliotherapy–the interactive process: A handbook.* Boulder, CO: Westview Press.

Jalongo, M. (1983, July). Using crisis oriented books with young children. *Young Children, 38,* 29–35.

Johnson, K. (1989). *Trauma in the lives of children.* Claremont, CA: Hunter House.

Johnson, M. & Foley. M. (1984). Differentiating fact from fantasy: The reliability of children's memory. *Journal of Social Issues, 40,* 2, 33–50.

Karlin, A. & Bruneau, O. (1985, March). Child abuse: Helping children through bibliotherapy. Paper presented at the annual meeting of the Texas State Council of the International Reading Association, Dallas, TX. (ERIC Document Reproduction Service No. ED 268 487)

Kilpatrick, D. Amick, A. & Resnick, H. (1990). *The impact of homicide on surviving family members.* Charleston, SC: Medical University of South Carolina. (National Institute of Justice Grant No. 87–IJ–CX–0017)

Lindeman, B. & Kling, M. (1969). Bibliotherapy: Definitions, uses, and studies. *Journal of School Psychology, 7,* 36–41.

Lusk, R. & Waterman, J. (1986). Effects of sexual abuse on children. In K. MacFarlane & J. Waterman (Eds.), *Sexual Abuse of Young Children* (pp. 15–29). New York: Guilford Press.

Maddox, J. (1994, October). Police intervention at child day care centers. *FBI Law Enforcement Bulletin,* pp. 6–8.

Manning, D. & Manning, B. (1984). Bibliotherapy for children of alcoholics. *Journal of Reading, 27,* 720–725.

Marans, S. & Berkman, M. (1997). Child development-community policing: Partnership in a climate of violence. http://www.ncjrs.org/txtfiles/164380.txt

Martin, M., Martin, D. & Porter, J. (1983). Bibliotherapy: Children of divorce. *The School Counselor; 30,* 312–315.

McInnis, K. (1982). Bibliotherapy: Adjunct to traditional counseling with children of stepfamilies. *Child Welfare, 61,* 153–160.

Menninger, K. (1930). *The human mind.* New York: Alfred A. Knopf.

Menniner, W. (1937). Bibliotherapy. *Bulletin of the Menninger Clinic, 1,* 263–273.

Mickish, J. (1996). Spousal abuse. In J.E. Hendricks & B. Byers (Eds.). *Crisis Intervention in Criminal Justice/Social Services* (2nd Edition) (pp. 53–91). Springfield.

IL: Charles C Thomas, Publisher, Ltd.

Mickish, J. (1995). Child abuse and neglect. In J.E. Hendricks & J. McKean (Eds.), *Crisis intervention: Contemporary issues for on-sight interveners* (2nd Edition) (pp. 162–198). Springfield, IL: Charles C Thomas, Publisher, Ltd.

Mikulas, W. (1985). Behavioral bibliotherapy and games for testing fear of the dark. *Child and Family Behavior Therapy, 7,* 1–7.

Naitove, C. (1978). Research and special projects: Protecting our children: The fight against molestation. *Arts in Psychotherapy, 12,* 115–116.

National Clearinghouse on Child Abuse and Neglect. (1999). Crisis intervention assessment. Available: http://www.calib.com/nccanch/pubs/usermanuals/crisis/assess.htm.

National Institute of Justice. (1992). *When time victim is a child* (2nd Edition). Washington, D.C.: U.S. Department of Justice.

Newhouse, R. (1987). Generalization fear reduction in second-grade children. *Psychology in the Schools, 24,* 48–50.

Norton, D. (1999). *Through the eyes of a child: An introduction to children's literature* (5th Edition). New York: Merrill.

Ogawa. B. (1988). To tell the truth. Wailuku, HI: Victim Witness Assistance Program.

Ogles, B., Lambert, M. & Craig, D. (1991). Comparison of self-help books for coping with loss: Expectations and attributions. *Journal of Counseling Psychology, 38,* 387–393.

Ouzts, D. (1994). Bibliotherapeutic literature: A key facet of whole language instruction for the at-risk student. *Reading Horizons, 35,* 161–175.

Palmer, S., Brown, R., Rae-Grant, N. & Loughlin, J. (1999). Responding to children's disclosure of familial abuse: What survivors tell us. *Child Welfare, 78,* 259–282.

Pardeck, J. (1991). Using books to prevent and treat adolescent chemical dependency. *Adolescence, 26,* 201–208.

Pardeck, J. (1990). Bibliotherapy with abused children. *Families in Society: The Journal of Contemporary Human Services, 71,* 229–235.

Pardeck, J. & Pardeck, J. (1986). *Books for early childhood: A developmental perspective.* Westport, CT: Greenwood Press.

Pardeck, J. & Pardeck, J. (1985). Bibliotherapy using a new-Freudian approach with children of divorced parents. *The School Counselor, 32,* 313–318.

Pardeck, J. & Pardeck, J. (1984). *Young people with problems: A guide to bibliotherapy.* Westport, CT: Greenwood Press.

Penny, R. (1966). *Practical care of the mentally retarded and mentally ill.* Springfield, IL: Charles C Thomas, Publisher, Ltd.

Pomeroy, E. (1937). Bibliotherapy-A study in results of hospital library service. *Medical Bulletin of the Veterans Administration, 13,* 360–364.

Pynoos, R. & Eth, S. (1984). The child as witness to homicide. *Journal of Social Issues, 40,* 2, 87–108.

Rasinski, T. & Gillespie, C. (1992). *Sensitive issues: An annotated guide to children's literature K–6.* Phoenix: Oryx.

Rubin, R. (1978). *Using bibliotherapy: A guide to theory and practice.* Phoenix: Oryx.

Rudman, M., Gagne, K. & Bernstein, J. (1993). Books to help children cope with separation and loss: An annotated bibliography (3rd Edition). New Providence, NJ: R.R. Bowker.

Rudman, M., Gagne, K. & Bernstein, J. (1994). *Books to help children cope with separation and loss: An annotated bibliography* (4th Edition). New Providence, NJ: R.R. Bowker.

Rudman, M. & Pearce, A. (1988). *For love of reading: A parents guide to encouraging young readers from infancy through age 5.* Mount Vernon, NY: Consumers Union.

Sandoval, J. (1985). Crisis counseling: Conceptualizations and general principles. *School Psychology Review, 14,* 257–265.

Sechrist, W. (2000). Health educators and child maltreatment: A curious silence. *Journal of School Health, 70,* 241–243.

Sheridan, J., Baker, S. & deLissovoy, V. (1984). Structured group counseling and explicit bibliotherapy as in-school strategies for preventing problems in youth of changing families. *The School Counselor, 32,* 134–141.

Shrodes, C. (1949). *Bibliotherapy: A theoretical amid clinical experimental study.* Berkeley, CA: University of California.

Smith, A. (1989). Will the real bibliotherapist please stand up? *Journal of Youth Services in Libraries, 2,* 241–249.

Snyder, H. (2000, July). *Sexual assault of young children as reported to law enforcement: Victim, incident, and offender characteristics.* Washington, D.C.: National Center for Juvenile Justice.

Stafford, C. (1962). The child as a witness. *Washington Law Review, 37,* 303–324.

Sullivan, J. (1987). React aloud sessions: Tackling sensitive issues through literature. *Journal of Reading, 30,* 874–878.

Summer, L. & Woods, S. (1992). *The judiciary: Laws we live by.* Madison, NJ: Raintree/Steck Vaughn.

Tews, R. (Editor). (1962). Bibliotherapy. *Library Trends, 11.*

Tyson, K. (1999). An empowering approach to crisis intervention and brief treatment for preschool children. *Families in Society: The Journal of Contemporary Human Services, 80,* 64–77.

U.S. Department of Health and Human Services. (1993). *National Child Abuse and Working Paper #2-1991 Summary Data Component.* Washington, D.C.: Government Printing Office.

U.S. Department of Justice. (1995). *Child sexual exploitation: improving investigations and protecting victims.* Washington, D.C.: U.S. Department of Justice.

U.S. Department of Justice. (1994). *Half of women raped during 1992 were younger than 18 years old.* Washington, D.C.: Bureau of Statistics.

U.S. Department of Justice. (1994). *The child victim as a witness.* Washington. D.C.: Office of Juvenile Justice and Delinquency Prevention.

Warner, C. (1981). *Conflict intervention in social and domestic violence.* Bowie, MD: R.J. Brady Co.

Waterman. J. (1986). Developmental considerations. In K. MacFarlane & J. Waterman (Eds.), *Sexual Abuse of Young Children* (pp. 15–29). New York: Guilford Press.

Watson, J. (1980). Bibliotherapy for abused children. *The School Counselor, 27,* 204–208.

Webster, J. (1961). Using books to reduce fears of first grade children. *The Reading Teacher, 14,* 159–162.

Whitcomb, D., Goodman, G., Runyan, D., & Hoak, S. (1994, April). The emotional effects of testifying on sexually abused children. *National Institute of Justice: Research in Brief.* Washington, D.C.: U.S. Department of Justice.

White, S. (1988). Should investigatory use of anatomical dolls be defined by the courts? *Journal of Interpersonal Violence, 3,* 471–475.

Widom, C. (1992. October). The cycle of violence. *National Institute of Justice: Research in Brief.* Washington, D.C.: U.S. Department of Justice.

Wolfe, V.V., Las, L. & Wilson, K. (1987). Some issues in preparing sexually abused children for courtroom testimony. *Behavior Therapist, 19,* 107–113.

Young, M. (1989). Working with victims who are children or adolescents: Using the lessons of child development with young trauma victims. *NOVA Newsletter, 13.*

Chapter 7

ELDER MISTREATMENT

BERNARD E. BLAKELY and RONALD DOLON

INTRODUCTION

The late Claude Pepper first directed national attention to the problems of elder abuse, neglect, and exploitation when he chaired the House Select Committee on Aging in 1978. Findings by the House Select Committee revealed that approximately one million elderly people were being victimized by these problems annually (U.S. House of Representatives, 1981). Awareness of the prevalence of elder mistreatment led to the introduction of federal legislation to provide financial assistance for state governments so they could establish agencies to identify and treat elderly victims. To qualify for federal support under the proposed legislation, states were required to enact laws which mandated the reporting of elder mistreatment. As of 1990, 42 states and the District of Columbia had enacted mandatory reporting statutes on behalf of the elderly (U.S. House of Representatives, 1990). Today, all states have some type of elder abuse or adult protective services (APS) law. Unfortunately, the proposed federal legislation has never been passed, and specific appropriations to the states for the purposes of identifying, treating, and preventing elder mistreatment were not forthcoming during the 1980s. However, in late 1998 the federal government created the National Center on Elder Abuse (NCEA). This organization, along with the existing National Committee on the Prevention of Elder Abuse (NCPEA) formed in 1987, help to dissemination information on elder abuse.

States have found it difficult to secure adequate funding for programs to protect elders from abuse, neglect, and exploitation. A recent report by the Subcommittee on Health and Long-Term Care of the Select Committee on Aging (U.S. House of Representatives, 1990) illustrates the financial constraints which have plagued these programs. In 1989 the states spent an average of $3.80 on protective services for each elderly resident within their borders. During the same year, the states spent an average of $45.03 on protective services for each child. With so few dollars available to serve elderly adults, the Subcommittee's report indicates that rates of elder mistreatment are growing in most areas of the nation and that only one out of every eight cases is reported to designated authorities. Unless additional resources are committed to the problem, the suffering of millions of elderly citizens is likely to continue with little hope of detection or treatment.

The need for action is not predicated solely upon the prevalence of elder mistreatment. Case histories provide chilling accounts of the severity of abuse, neglect, and exploitation. Victims of abuse and neglect may have experienced starvation, dehydration, beatings, burns, and prolonged isolation. They may also be found lying in their own excrement with untreated broken bones, maggot-infested wounds, or large decubitus ulcers that have eroded skin tissue all the way down to the bone. Victims of exploitation may lose their homes, their savings, and other possessions as a result of unlawful manipulations by relatives or caregivers (U.S. House of Representatives, 1990). Such losses are particularly devastating to elders, because their hopes and their independence can disappear along with their assets.

While anecdotal case information can provide a glimpse into the work of elder mistreatment, this cannot replace the statistical picture. While some have suggested that the number of elder mistreatment cases may be as high as "one million per year," recent research on confirmed cases of elder mistreatment suggest that there may be as many as 551,000 cases annually in the United States according to the National Elder Abuse Incidence Study or "NEAIS" (NEAIS, 1998). Given the scope and severity of elder mistreatment and the limited resources that have been allocated to society's response systems, social workers, police, and other professionals who encounter the problem should have a base of theoretical and practical knowledge to help them in shaping appropriate interventions. Workers should be aware of the types of elder mistreatment, the cultural, social and situational dynamics of mistreatment, and models, which are used to conceptualize mistreatment. Contacts with elderly victims are likely to be more effective when workers are informed about methods of detection, assessment techniques, and treatment, which can be applied in a particular situation. The purpose of the present chapter is to provide the reader with theoretical and practical information about elder mistreatment and possible intervention options.

TYPES OF ELDER MISTREATMENT

Intuitively, most people have a sense as to what constitutes elder abuse, neglect, and exploitation. However, consistent views of the forms of mistreatment do not exist in the research literature or in the wording of state laws. For instance, in a pioneering study of elder mistreatment, Block and Sinnott (1979) investigated occurrences of physical and psychological abuse, exploitation, and medical abuse. In another well-known inquiry, Douglass, Hickey, and Noel (1980) examined instances of active and passive neglect, verbal or emotional abuse, and physical abuse. However, Hudson (1989) does attempt to provide empirical referents for elder mistreatment, which might be used by researchers and practitioners in defining and addressing elder abuse and neglect. Psychological abuse, a particularly difficult type of mistreatment to define and address, is not a form of elder mistreatment according to the law in the state of Iowa, but it is included in the Alabama state statute (Fulmer and O'Malley, 1987). Depending upon the state, abandonment, sexual abuse, self-abuse, self-neglect, confinement, and hazardous living conditions may or may not be incorporated into the legal definition of mistreatment (Traxler, 1986; Byers and Lamanna, 1993).

When concepts of elder mistreatment vary from study to study and from state law to state law, a considerable amount of confusion results. The task of generalizing from research becomes more difficult because researchers may not be looking at the same types of behavior. Moreover, the statistics compiled by states cannot simply be added to produce a meaningful picture of how much elder mistreatment occurs nationally. Adjustments must be made to reflect differences among the states in what is or is not considered to be elder mistreatment. Self-neglect or self-abuse is very common (Byers, 1993; Byers and Hendricks, 1990; Byers and Lamanna, 1993; McCuan and Jenkins, 1992). However, not all jurisdictions consider self-neglect a type of elder mistreatment. Therefore, not only are there problems with defining abuse, but there are also considerable problems with measurement (Wolf and McCarthy, 1991).

To prepare individuals in a variety of geographic locations for future work with the elderly, it is heuristic to offer a broad-based review of the types of elder mistreatment. The three main categories of mistreatment are abuse, neglect, and exploitation. Physical and psychological abuse are both included in the first category. Physical abuse involves acts of violence against an elderly person. Researchers typically include physical abuse in their studies of elder mistreatment (Hudson, 1986), and nearly all of the states accept reports of physical abuse of the elderly (U.S. House of Representatives, 1990). Psychological abuse involves the use of humiliation, threats, intimidation, or other verbal devices in such a way as to produce fear, suffering, or distress on the part of an elderly person (Galbraith, 1986; Giordano and Giordano, 1984; Johnson, 1986). This form of mistreatment is examined in many studies of abuse (Hudson, 1986) and is defined as a form of elder abuse in more than 20 states (Fulmer and O'Malley, 1987; Traxler, 1986). National estimates suggest that there may be upwards of 402,000 cases of elder "abuse" annually (NEAIS, 1998).

Elder neglect occurs when food, medical and hygienic care, human companionship, clothing, and other necessities which are needed to maintain physical and mental health are withheld from an elderly person (American Medical Association Council on Scientific Affairs, 1987; Douglass, Hickey and Noel, 1980). Neglect may constitute 182,000 elder mistreatment cases per year. Another type of neglect, "self-neglect," is characterized by an elder living in filth and squalor. Typically, the elder is living in conditions that create safety and/or health risks. Estimates of this type of mistreatment, although not at the hands of another, suggest that there may be some 139,000 self-neglect cases annually in the United States (NEAIS, 1998). Exploitation is present when an elderly person's money or other properties are unlawfully misused or misappropriated (Block and Sinnott, 1979; Giordano and Giordano, 1984). There are no readily available and accurate data on the number of exploitation cases annually. Exploitation, especially financial abuse, is easy for perpetrators to hide. Neglect and exploitation are common themes in the research literature and are identified as forms of elder mistreatment in a majority of the states (Fulmer and O'Malley, 1987; Traxler, 1986).

In the preceding discussion of the definitions of abuse, neglect, and exploitation, no mention has been made of the characteristics of perpetrators. Consequently, it might be assumed that an act of exploitation has taken place when a stranger has stolen an elderly woman's purse. While it is clear that a crime has taken place according to criminal statutes, an act by a stranger would usually not be considered as a case of elder mistreatment under adult protective services laws. These laws pertain to self-victimization by the elderly or to abuse, neglect, and exploitation by relatives or other caregivers. Most of the crimes which strangers commit against the elderly fall within the jurisdiction of local law enforcement officials. Elder mistreatment cases may be investigated by local law enforcement officials, area agencies on aging, state departments of human services, state mental health departments, or other entities which have been designated by the states (Elder Abuse Project, American Public Welfare Association, 1986). In contrast to the situation in which a stranger commits a crime, the emphasis in elder mistreatment cases is not on criminal prosecution (Block and Sinnott, 1979). Intervention strategies are designed instead to introduce services and support to elderly victims, and, when possible, to alter the caregiving behaviors of perpetrators (Kinney, Wendt and Hurst. 1986).

One further issue needs to be addressed in our discussion of what does or does not constitute elder mistreatment. Imagine an elderly man who lives with his fifty-year-old son. An adult protective services investigator discovers that the father is malnourished and seems to be suffering from an untreated respiratory infection. The home, which is shared by the father and son, is cluttered with old newspapers, rotting food scraps, and other garbage. Mice droppings are scattered about the flooring of the house, and roaches can be seen scurrying up and down the walls and furniture. During a conversation with the elderly man, the investigator learns that when the son has too much to drink he sometimes beats his father.

Given the obvious signs of abuse and neglect, the investigator talks to the elderly man about possible treatment options, such as homemaker services, visiting nurses, home-delivered meals, protective orders, counseling, and guardianship. The elderly man appears to fully comprehend what services are available, and indicates that he doesn't want any assistance. According to the elderly man, he's quite content with his current living arrangement and his relationship with his son. In this situation, the existing dilemma is to risk the death of the elderly man by leaving him alone, or to force him to accept help against his will. The investigator might make further attempts to provide services, but ultimately he must recognize that the intent of adult protective services laws is not to violate the rights of the elderly to live as they choose. Interventions are to be imposed involuntarily only when individuals are incapable of making their own decisions. Since competent elders are free to refuse the protection of the state, they can defeat the investigative process before acts of mistreatment are substantiated. In these cases, acts of abuse, neglect, or exploitation may be excluded from official counts of elder mistreatment. Whatever the case, however, intervention should be the "least restrictive" possible. In a word, intervention should allow as much client independence as possible while simultaneously providing assistance and protection to the elder. This principle applies to the voluntary and involuntary client.

This section of the chapter has attempted to provide readers with an awareness of the types of elder mistreatment and problems which are due to the variable definitions that appear in research and state laws. It should also be apparent that in addition to the age of victims, other attributes of elders and perpetrators affect decisions as to whether mistreatment has taken place, who conducts investigations, and what approaches to treatment will be utilized.

CULTURE, SOCIETY AND ELDER MISTREATMENT

An instructor in a sociology class recently asked his students why acts of elder mistreatment occur. The students had little difficulty in identifying elder dependency, caregiver stress, abuse of alcohol, a lack of education, and mental illness as potential causal factors in cases of elder mistreatment. Certainly the physical and mental characteristics of elders and their caregivers cannot be dismissed in a discussion of the causes of elder mistreatment. In a recent study of caregiver violence and violent feelings, Pillemer and Suitor (1998) examined similar correlates. Among many findings, they reveal that violence from the care recipient increased caregiver violent feelings and living with the care recipient (dependence) also increased violence feelings among caregivers (Pillemer and Suitor, 1998). Overall, the authors note that elder abuse is often not caused by one single factor. Rather, the phenomenon is the result of a variety of complex factors. Pillemer (1986) has also found:

- [Elder] Spouse abuse is much more common than the public perceives, yet is rarely ever detected or reported. It remains a largely ignored problem.
- When adult children are the abusers, they usually are heavily dependent on the victim, are substance abusers, and have a history of violence, arrests or psychiatric hospitalization.
- When black elders are abused, 80 percent of the abusers, usually heavily dependent children or grandchildren, were found to be drug abusers.
- Among white elder abusers, 57 percent had alcohol problems and 11 percent were drug abusers.
- Among Asian elderly abusers, only 11 percent were alcohol abusers and 11 percent drug abusers, and caregiver stress was a major cause.
- When the elderly person has Alzheimer's disease, violent or disruptive outbursts from the patient are most often the root cause of caregiver abuse, not caregiver "burnout."

Along with the work of Pillemer, Tatara (1999), Montoya (1997), and Anetzberger et al. (2000) have also recognized the importance of understanding minority populations when confronting elder abuse.

It is also important to consider the general nature of the cultural and social environment that gives rise to abuse, neglect, and exploitation. One feature of this environment, which contributes to elder mistreatment, is the existence of widespread ageism or prejudicial attitudes toward the elderly (Butler, 1969; Hendricks and Hendricks, 1986). Feelings of prejudice and negative stereotypes create expectations that the elderly are helpless, sick, childlike, irritable, and unproductive creatures who no longer deserve our attention or respect (McTavish, 1971; Viano, 1983). Prolonged exposure to such beliefs tends to lower the self-esteem of elderly persons and to increase their isolation, their sense of powerlessness, and their vulnerability (Davidson, Hennessey and Sedge, 1979; Ward, 1984). Even when elders find someone to listen to their troubles, there is a risk that they won't be taken seriously. For instance, Block and Sinnott (1979) found in one state that reports of elder mistreatment which were made to public agencies rarely produced action to assist victims.

It might be argued that the findings by Block and Sinnott (1979) were obtained in a decade when neither the public nor professionals who worked with the elderly knew very much about elder mistreatment. Since the problem has been more widely researched and publicized during the 1980s, it would be expected that professionals would now be more responsive to victims. Regrettably, however, recent studies show that professionals still fail to meet the needs of the elderly. According to a national survey of adult protective services workers by Dolon and Blakely (1987), only a few occupational groups, such as visiting nurses, were considered to be at least somewhat helpful in discovering and/or treating victims of elder mistreatment. Police, clergy, nursing home personnel, physicians, lawyers, and other professionals were perceived as not being particularly helpful in dealing with victimization of the elderly. Among the various occupational groups, the performance of physicians in many areas of the country has been especially disappointing (Traxler, 1986). For example, in the state of Alabama, Daniels, Baumhover, and Clark-Daniels (1989) found that a majority of physicians who are mandated to report elder mistreatment did not know how or where to make a report. Perhaps, as Crystal (1987) contends, physicians pay too little attention to the professional obligations and the penalties, which so often are as mild as infractions, for noncompliance which are specified in mandatory reporting statutes.

Victims and potential victims of elder mistreatment aren't served much better by policymakers than they are served by many professionals. As noted in the introduction to this chapter, adult protective services programs continue to be enacted without adequate funding from the states or direct support from the federal government. Congress has also failed to provide funding for a national clearinghouse to disseminate information on the prevention of domestic violence, for emergency shelters for elderly victims, or for demonstration projects to provide other types of assistance (U.S. House of Representatives, 1990). The inaction by the federal government would be insufficient enough if the national incidence of elder mistreatment was expected to remain constant. The truth is that the incidence of elder mistreatment is likely to increase. The basis for this prediction lies in demographic trends, which are reshaping the structure of our society.

These demographic trends show that the number and proportion of elderly people in our population will grow substantially during the next 50 years. Currently, the fastest growing segment of our population is the group of individuals who are 85 years of age or older. According to the U.S. Bureau of the Census, the number of Americans in this age group will triple by the year 2020 (Longino, Soldo and Manton, 1990). Assuming that the very old will be the ones who will be most in need of long-term care, the projected growth in this age group suggests that there will be a corresponding increase in the number of persons who must provide care. As the burdens of care fall on more and more families and other caregivers, the opportunities for elder mistreatment will multiply accordingly.

THE SITUATIONAL DYNAMICS OF MISTREATMENT

A potential danger in talking about national population trends and millions of cases of mistreatment is that large numbers may not convey the reality of the problem to readers. Students who have little or no experience with the responsibilities of caring for the elderly may lack an understanding of the situational dynamics that result in mistreatment. These students may simply attribute mistreatment to alcoholism, mental illness, greed, ignorance, or other faults on the part of perpetrators. Before you join the ranks of those who categorically condemn those who commit acts of elder mistreatment, project yourself forward in time forty years or so. You and your spouse are paying off the last of the debts you incurred when your children were in college. You are thinking of early retirement and travel to the places you've always dreamed of visiting. At this stage of your life, you receive news that your father-in law has died. Your mother-in-law is seventy-nine years old and has no one else to look after her. Your hopes and plans will have to be put on hold.

When your mother-in-law moves into your home, you begin to realize how much care she will require. She no longer drives an automobile. Walking is difficult for her and she has a restricted diet. A medical problem necessitates frequent monitoring by a physician, and she is still grieving over the loss of her husband. You attempt to help her as much as you can, but your job, children, and grandchildren already make heavy demands upon your schedule. At the cost of considerable personal effort, you struggle to satisfy the needs of your mother-in-law (day after day and week after week). After four years of managing the caregiver role, no end appears to be in sight.

At this point, the pressures begin to escalate. Your spouse has major surgery and is incapacitated indefinitely. The medical expenses for the operation consume the last of your savings. While you are busy caring for two people, the condition of your mother-in-law further deteriorates. Her mental acuity and her physical strength diminish, and she remains in bed most of every day. She cannot make it to the table for meals, and it is necessary for you to help her to and from the bathroom. When you are not immediately available, she wets the bed. Your patience, energy, and health are being consumed rapidly, and you do not perceive alternative ways of handling the situation. With luck, you'll be able to maintain enough self-control so that you do not resort to physical or verbal outbursts to release your frustrations. Such outbursts could be defined as elder mistreatment.

As the above example illustrates, well-intentioned family members can be overwhelmed by the stress of long-term caregiving. In light of this possibility, stress has been commonly featured in theoretical models and empirical investigations of elder mistreatment (e.g., Block and Sinnott, 1979; Phillips, 1986; George, 1986; Giordano and Giordano, 1984; O'Malley et al., 1979; Pillemer, 1986; Sager, 1986; Steinmetz, 1981). According to this body of literature, there is little doubt that family caregiving for an elder tends to be a stressful undertaking. Frequently, the tasks associated with caregiving are disproportionately allocated so that one person ends up with the majority of the responsibility (Steinmetz, 1983). Many of the duties performed by caregivers, such as dispensing medication or providing bathroom assistance, cannot be deferred, and may have to be performed at various times around the clock. In addition to the tasks which are merely time consuming, others require higher levels of skill and knowledge which caregivers may not possess. For instance, caregivers may be poorly prepared to cope with the needs of elders who are afflicted with Alzheimer's disease or other severe mental and physical impairments. In such situations, the demands of providing care may be sufficient in and of themselves to produce physical and psychological exhaustion, and many caregivers also have careers and responsibilities to other family members.

The pressures associated with excessive work may be a secondary source of frustration compared to the family conflicts that can arise during the course of caregiving. Other relatives of the dependent elder may disagree with the caregiver's decisions and behaviors. Sources of interference rather than of help frequently emerge from the structure of extended families. Within the caregiver's immediate family, one's spouse and offspring can become increasingly resentful when the time devoted to an elder is subtracted from the time available for them. Unsatisfied demands for attention may compound other strains that are already present within the immediate family. Existing strains might include those due to financial loss, poor health, infidelity, substance abuse, or unemployment. To further complicate matters, studies show that relationships between caregivers and dependent elders are also prone to conflict.

In an investigation of adult children who were caregivers for their elderly parents, Steinmetz (1981) found that each person attempted to gain control over the other. Yelling, hitting, and slapping were controlling techniques which were used by both the adult children and their elderly parents. However, the elderly parents were the ones who were far more likely to hit or slap. Moreover, dependent parents pouted, refused food and medication, threw objects, and cried in order to manipulate their caregivers. Elderly parents can also belittle the accomplishments and efforts of their adult children, renew old battles concerning the life choices of their offspring, and otherwise spawn feelings of guilt, anger, and resentment (Quinn and Tomita, 1986). Whether caregivers are adult children or not, activities and relationships outside the home tend to be affected by the responsibilities of providing care. Vacations, trips, and other recreational diversions often have to be canceled, and there is less time to spend with friends. Consequently, outlets which caregivers might normally use to cope with strains and frustrations may no longer be available to them. Some fortunate caregivers have access to adult day-care centers or to respite-care programs, so they can obtain temporary relief from their duties. Others are required to manage with little or no assistance from formal or informal sources of support.

In spite of all of the attention which researchers have given to caregiver stress and elder mistreatment, questions remain about the precise nature of the relationship between these two variables. To illustrate existing concerns about the relationship between stress and mistreatment, let's consider an example. Adult protective services workers around the nation have indicated that stress and family conflict contribute to instances of elder abuse much more commonly than substance abuse, dependency, or other factors (Dolon and Blakely, 1989a). While this finding appears to be plausible, it seems reasonable to assume that many of the caregivers who do not abuse elders also experience stress and family conflict. Consequently, other variables are needed to differentiate abusers from nonabusers. Some of these variables may be found in a study of elderly residents in the Boston metropolitan area by Pillemer and Finkelhor (1989). Self-reports from the elderly respondents showed that spouses were much more likely to be perpetrators of abuse and neglect than were adult children who functioned as caregivers. Moreover, comparisons between those who had been abused or neglected and those who had not revealed that physical, mental, and other problems on the part of perpetrators were the best predictors of mistreatment. Thus, the investigation teaches us to look at other situations in addition to those in which stressed caregivers, usually adult children, abuse or neglect dependent elders. A rogue's gallery of perpetrators must leave room for portraits of spouses and other relatives who are afflicted with physical or psychological disorders and who are dependent upon their elderly victims for care and/or financial support.

While researchers disagree as to which family members are most likely to commit acts of elder mistreatment, there is agreement that many perpetrators are the spouses of their victims (U.S. House of Representatives, 1981; Wolf, Strugnell, and Godkin, 1982). However, a recent national study conducted by Tatara (1993) revealed that most abusers were adult children of the abused and spouses were the second most likely abusers, but their involvement only constituted half of that of adult children (p. 47). When attention shifts from adult children to the spouses of victims, there is less support for the idea that stress leads to violence or neglect. George (1986) offers evidence that spouses generally do not look upon caregiving in the same way as adult children. Spouses are inclined to consider caregiving as an accepted commitment of marriage. Even when spouses must care for husbands or wives with dementia, they feel that the job of caregiving rightfully belongs to them. Adult children, on the other hand, have not entered into an agreement with their parents which is analogous to a marital contract and are not required by law to accept responsibilities for parental care. Hence, adult children who act as caregivers have a tendency to perceive their efforts as one-sided performances which are beyond the call of duty. This sense of sacrifice can easily turn to resentment when the demands of caregiving interfere with career and obligations to one's own spouse and children. These stressors are not as likely to apply when spouses assume the role of caregivers.

If spouses are not as susceptible as adult children to many of the stresses of caregiving, then other causes must be sought to explain those instances in which spouses engage in elder mistreatment. One possible cause is presented by Quinn and Tomita (1986) in a discussion of learned violence. According to these authors, spouses may periodically abuse their mates over a span of decades. Since there is no guarantee that abusive behaviors will end when couples reach a particular age plateau, elder mistreatment may be an extension of normative patterns from earlier phases of marital relationships. When long-term abuse has occurred within a marriage, a revenge factor can also become operative. In the event that a former abuser is debilitated by old age or disease, a former victim may resort to violence in retaliation for previous wrongs. Although this hypothesis is usually reserved for cases in which adult children are caregivers (Breckman and Adelman, 1988), it may be equally applicable to situations in which formerly abused spouses assume control over their formerly abusive partner. Finally, senile dementia or other psychological breakdowns can alter the judgment and behavior of an aged spouse and precipitate acts of mistreatment.

The task of finding determinants of elder mistreatment which pertain exclusively to spouses is complicated by the fact that adult children can also be advanced in age and suffer from the same maladies as those who are married to their victims. Perpetrators from either of these groups may have problems of substance abuse, histories of violent behavior, and mental or physical infirmities (Pillemer and Finkelhor; 1989). Chronic disorders can incapacitate spouses and adult children and place them in the position of care recipients rather than of caregivers. A potential response to dependency among spouses and adult children is to compensate for feelings of powerlessness by striking out against the persons who attend to their needs (Finkelhor, 1983). In these cases, the "whipping boys" who are available are not boys but elderly members of one's own family. Abusive behaviors directed against elderly caregivers constitute acts of elder mistreatment.

PRACTICAL AND THEORETICAL MODELS

By now, readers of this chapter should recognize that elder mistreatment is due to a wide variety of societal and situational circumstances. Perpetrators may occupy a number of different positions within or outside of families. Mistreatment may be triggered by stress or motivated by powerlessness, resentment, revenge, or ageism. Both perpetrators and victims can be afflicted with distress, alcoholism, psychiatric disorders, and other pathologies. Physical infirmities and numerous other variables can also contribute to instances of mistreatment. The range of possibilities is so enormous that practitioners who work with the elderly and researchers need some means of organizing information about elder mistreatment. To accomplish this end, practitioners can use assessment protocols to document relevant characteristics of their clients, to pinpoint causes of existing mistreatment, and to produce informed estimates of the risks for future abuse, neglect, and exploitation (Kosberg, 1988). The advantages of assessment protocols are not merely organizational. Systematic analysis of "risk factors" facilitates early identification of vulnerable elders and presents practitioners with the opportunity of preventing elder mistreatment before victimization actually occurs.

Instead of assessment protocols, researchers tend to use theories to organize their knowledge about elder mistreatment. One of the theories which is currently in vogue is *social exchange theory* (Phillips, 1986). This theoretical perspective views social interaction as an exchange of rewards and punishments. Individuals who engage in interaction attempt to maximize rewards and to minimize punishments or costs. When the costs a person sustains in social relationships outweigh the rewards he or she receives, inequities are perceived. Perceived inequities promote feelings of resentment and anger. These feelings, in turn, can prompt individuals to punish those parties who are felt to be guilty of violating the norms of social interaction.

The theory provides a framework for understanding relationships between caregivers and dependent elders. Caregivers tend to accumulate an excess of costs over rewards. The growing deficit produces a sense of inequity, and caregivers may vent their anger by punishing or mistreating their elders. Given the isolation and the power differences which characterize relations between caregivers and recipients, caregivers may feel that they have very little to lose when they do resort to mistreatment.

Additional scenarios can be derived from the exchange model to describe the positions of elderly recipients of care. In environments that are nurturing and are free of abuse, care recipients may be content because they are accumulating a surplus of rewards. However, complications can arise even when caregivers do their best to satisfy the needs of the dependent elderly. Recipients of care may experience an overwhelming sense of loss (cost) due to widowhood, infirmity, or other factors. As a result, recipients can become frustrated, depressed, or rebellious and display maladaptive behaviors. In such cases, the exchange model can then be utilized as a basis for predicting the responses of caregivers.

As the above discussion illustrates, the exchange model can help researchers to conceptualize processes of interaction that lead to elder mistreatment. The model also has potential value in the analysis of interpersonal contacts between professional workers and elderly clients and other social relationships, which are germane to the phenomenon of mistreatment. Hence, it is likely that future researchers will try to expand the model's sphere of application. It is further expected that systematic tests will be conducted to determine how accurately the model can predict human behaviors. Presently, however, not enough testing has been completed to gauge the effectiveness of the model either in prediction or explanation.

Another promising theory available to researchers is the *environmental press model* proposed by Ansello, King, and Taler (1986). This theoretical perspective focuses on the fit between an individual and the demands or "press" of her or his environment. When environmental demands exceed the individual's capacity to successfully respond, then stress, burnout, and aggression are likely consequences. These outcomes appear to be consistent with the experiences of many overworked caregivers. Conversely, an individual's environment can become stale, unchallenging, and repetitive as in the case of assembly-line workers in a factory. Just as too little stimulation can cause factory workers to be apathetic or embittered, elderly recipients of care may withdraw into a world of fantasy or become antagonistic toward their caregivers. Whether dependent elders spend their days dreaming about the past or arguing and fighting with caregivers, the same end is served. That is, the elderly have used diversions to cope with a dull, unrewarding environment.

Use of the environmental press model is not limited to the conceptualization of conditions which cause elder mistreatment. The model can also assist practitioners in designing interventions. For instance, temporary relief might be prescribed for an overworked caregiver in much the same manner as "time-out" may be prescribed for a child who is overstimulated by her or his environment. Training, counseling, and other methods can be employed to increase the caregiver's capacity to meet environmental demands. At the same time, measures can be taken to create a more favorable environment for care recipients in order to help them adjust more effectively to their surroundings. In spite of the insights the model provides, it has generally been ignored by researchers in empirical studies of elder mistreatment.

Researchers are not the only ones who have been less than attentive to the basic propositions of the environmental press model. Professionals who work with the elderly are rarely heard discussing the finer points of this model or other theoretical perspectives. These practitioners tend to have more urgent concerns, such as finding immediate solutions to problems that can destroy the health and the lives of their clients. Consequently, professional workers may not have the time or the inclination to read about tests of abstract theories or other findings of empirical investigations. By the same token, individuals who construct and test theories may not take the time to learn about the special needs of potential consumers of scientific information in applied settings. These scientists may examine issues of questionable interest to practitioners and present the results of their studies in ways that are difficult for practitioners to understand. So long as practitioners and scientists continue to move in their own separate ways, the gap between theory and practice is not likely to be bridged, and progress in combating elder mistreatment will be more difficult to achieve. However, research in the field of elder abuse and neglect has always contained an applied dimension, while some very recent research has focused particularly on the research and practice connection (Byers and Hendricks, 1993).

DETECTION OF ELDER MISTREATMENT

Police, nurses, physicians, clergy, social workers, and representatives of many other occupational groups have contacts with victims of elder mistreatment (Crouse et al., 1981; Douglass, 1983; O'Malley et al., 1979). Most of these individuals are responsible only for reporting an occasional case of suspected abuse, neglect, or exploitation that they have encountered. Others have responsibilities for mobilization of community resources to assure that cases will be reported and for subsequent investigations to determine if maltreatment has taken place. In some areas of the country, adult protective services workers are charged with each of these latter duties. To accomplish these dual missions, adult protective services workers must be aware of barriers to reporting elder mistreatment, methods for conducting outreach with professionals and the public, and interaction strategies to facilitate communication with perpetrators and victims. In other words, these practitioners must know how to gain the support of the community and the cooperation of the elderly in order to detect cases of elder mistreatment. This section of the chapter will be presented with these objectives in mind. For purposes of illustration, let's create an adult protective services worker, David Myers, who has just been hired. David is a retired police officer who doesn't have much prior experience with protective services programs. Before he starts his work assignment, he receives a few days of training so he can perform the tasks that lie ahead. From his instructor, David learns about studies, which describe the tendencies of professional workers and the general public to report suspected cases of elder mistreatment. The results of the studies do not give David reasons to be optimistic about the amount of support he can expect from the community.

According to Morris and Blakely (1990), only one adult in every 20 knows where to report abuse, neglect, or exploitation. Doctors may be only slightly more knowledgeable than other citizens about correct reporting procedures (Daniels, Baumhover and Clark-Daniels, 1989). Home health and community-health nurses generally know how to report cases of mistreatment, but many of these nurses feel that reports do more harm than good. That is, reports may anger perpetrators, and authorities may not take any action to assist victims (Clark-Daniels, Daniels and Baumhover, 1990). Police departments frequently do not know how many reports of elder mistreatment they receive, and officers may not even be aware of the statutes which pertain to the problem (Plotkin, 1988). In addition to these difficulties, the elderly aren't likely to report that they are being victimized because of isolation, infirmity, fear, embarrassment, and other factors (Hudson, 1986).

David agrees with Salend et al. (1984) that publicity and outreach will be needed to increase the probability that cases of elder mistreatment will be reported. However, his instructor indicates during a training session that no money has been allocated so David can publicize adult protective services in the community. Television, radio, newspapers, and billboards can be used to increase awareness of how, where, and when to report mistreatment only if these resources are available without cost. As David starts thinking about ways of obtaining free coverage by the media, he is further advised about the dangers that are present when the public is too well-informed about elder mistreatment. Some protective services programs have been flooded with so many reports of suspected cases that they have been forced to curtail operations (U.S. House of Representatives, 1990). In the absence of better alternatives, David plans to draw some funds out of his secretarial budget in order to print brochures which can be distributed to the public at senior citizens' centers, doctors' offices, and other locations.

While the brochures are likely to be helpful, they cannot supply all of the information which will be needed by doctors, visiting nurses, police, case managers, and others who work with elderly. These professionals should know about their obligations and safeguards under mandatory reporting laws, how to recognize the signs of mistreatment, what services are available for victims and perpetrators, the rights of victims and what to do when abuse, neglect, or exploitation are suspected. In order to educate workers in the community, David recognizes that it will be necessary to establish in-service training programs for a variety of agencies, departments, and professional associations. When he conducts training, he will also be able to meet with community leaders and key personnel in hospitals, agencies, and other organizations. If enough skill and effort are devoted to outreach activities, David can build a network of concerned and knowledgeable professionals to assist him in detecting cases of elder mistreatment. Of course, it will be difficult to find much time for outreach. David's other duties will include taking reports of suspected cases, conducting investigations, appearing in court, arranging for services, and monitoring interventions.

When a professional or private citizen calls to report a case of suspected mistreatment, David learns that he will have to do much more than to simply write down information about the reporter, the suspected victim, and the alleged mistreatment. Many callers will describe situations which do not fall under the jurisdiction of adult protective services so screening devices will have to be used to determine which cases should be referred elsewhere. Screening and referral should not be taken lightly. The worker can ill-afford to waste time on cases that should be handled by other agencies. At the same time, he does not wish to alienate other agencies by sending individuals to them who waste their time and resources. In the interests of maintaining good relations in the community and satisfying the needs of callers, the worker will have to know which agency is the most appropriate one to contact for a particular service. Whenever possible, the worker should supply a caller with the telephone number of that agency and the name of a person in the agency who can provide assistance. When extra steps are taken to satisfy callers, a worker can create an image of competence and concern for others, which will help him to gain public support for adult protective services.

In those cases in which callers do describe conditions of elder mistreatment, a protective services worker must decide whether or not their allegations can be accepted at face value. A neighbor, a landlord, or a relative may be prompted by a dispute with a caregiver to make a report just to irritate a caregiver. Probing questions about the reasons for a call can help a worker to identify those reports which can be attributed to greed, revenge, or other selfish motivations. Callers should also be asked to provide the names of other people who might have knowledge of the alleged mistreatment. Substantiation by these witnesses can alleviate any lingering doubts about spurious reports and provide a more complete picture of the types of mistreatment that may be taking place.

From the case information, the worker will have to decide if a situation warrants his immediate attention. When a condition of crises does not exist, the worker may defer a visit to the home of an alleged victim until s/he has served other elders who may be at greater risk. That is, the workers must *triage* his/her cases based on urgency, immediacy, danger, and efficiency. In any event, before a home visit is made, the worker should have assembled enough facts concerning a case to determine if he is likely to be harmed by an alleged perpetrator or anyone else at the scene. Insofar as David is concerned, his past experiences as a police officer will help him to remain calm in the face of danger. Nevertheless, he will be more than willing to request assistance from the police or a sheriff when he anticipates violence during a home visit.

The worker's success during a home visit will depend heavily on his/her skills in communication and impression management. His/her first task will be to gain entry into a household. For David, this was seldom a problem when he was a police officer. Now he can no longer rely on a uniform, weapons, and a warrant to secure admittance. As a protective services worker, he must have permission from the occupants of a dwelling in order to obtain entry. In difficult cases, the presence of a police officer or possession of a court order are possible means of obtaining access to suspected victims of mistreatment. However, these measures should be used only when other alternatives have been exhausted or victims arc perceived to be in imminent peril. In other situations, the worker can ask a neighbor, a relative, or another professional to introduce him/her to the residents of a house or apartment so they will allow him/her to come inside. S/he can also gain acceptance by appearing as a potential friend who can help the elderly to qualify for needed services (Quinn and Tomita, 1986).

Inside the households of alleged victims, the worker will encounter highly variable conditions. In one instance, an elderly client might live alone without enough food to eat. This elderly client might be very happy that the worker has come for a visit. However, her or his ability to converse may be hampered by partial deafness. The next client may be the victim of physical mistreatment at the hands of her spouse. He may be suffering from dementia, and she may be intimidated by her spouse so much that she refuses to speak to the worker. Within a worker's overall caseload, home visits are likely to reveal numerous barriers to communication including a host of physical ailments and impairments, mental incapacities, and psychological disturbances. Some barriers to communication can be overcome by the creativity and the interpersonal tactics of the protective services worker. By presenting him/herself as a helper rather than as a threat, s/he can break down the resistance of both victims and perpetrators. For example, s/he might open a conversation with a suspected perpetrator by stating that most people do not know how difficult caregiving can be. This display of empathic understanding gives the suspected perpetrator an opportunity to express agreement and to talk about problems which he or she may be experiencing. In general, a gentle, reassuring stance by a worker will be more persuasive than the authoritarian postures, which are the products of moralizing, lecturing, or blaming (Hepworth and Larsen, 1986).

While a worker is interviewing clients in their places of residence, s/he should also be an active observer. Nonverbal cues may send messages that are inconsistent with the verbal reports made by clients. A perpetrator might hover over a victim and refuse to leave her or him alone so the worker can get responses to questions without interference. A victim might avert eye contact, turn away, or exhibit nervous gestures when inquiries are made about mistreatment. While these cues do not provide direct evidence of abuse, neglect, or exploitation, they can arouse a worker's suspicions and establish a focus for detailed investigations during later processes of assessment.

A survey of the home environment can also provide considerable information about the occupants and their patterns of behavior. The labels on prescription bottles can show a worker what medications his/her clients are taking. Prescription dates and unused capsules or pills can be used to determine whether or not medication is being consumed according to a doctor's instructions. The availability of food can be checked by a quick look in the refrigerator and cupboards. The condition of bedding and clothing, which may be lying around, can suggest how long it has been since the items were cleaned. The protective services worker can also look for spots of dried blood, broken furniture, and other possible signs of past violence.

During initial home visits, the worker will usually try to learn as much as s/he can by paying attention to what s/he sees rather than to conduct a thorough inspection of the premises. In the course of his/her conversation with clients, the worker can establish a rationale for moving from one room to another by asking how well appliances are working, posing other questions about a house or apartment, or requesting a drink of water. At this stage of contact, the worker should be particularly sensitive to indicators of crisis or emergency whether they are due to the actions of perpetrators or hazardous living conditions within the home.

At this time, David has a sense of all that must be accomplished to properly set the stage for comprehensive assessments of clients. Public and professional assistance will be needed in order to detect cases of elder mistreatment. However, support from the community will not come automatically. David will have to design and implement publicity campaigns and outreach programs so that suspected instances of mistreatment will be reported to adult protective services. In spite of the importance of building a solid foundation for community action, very little time and money are likely to be available to achieve this objective.

David also knows that tact, creativity, and skill will be required when individuals phone him to report suspected mistreatment, and when he makes his initial visits to the homes of clients. Callers on the telephone may describe conditions that should be investigated by other agencies, so David will have to learn how to make appropriate referrals. He will also have to learn how to use information provided by callers to sort out spurious reports of mistreatment, cases which require immediate attention, and cases in which violence might be directed against a protective services worker. Initial visits to the homes of clients will be particularly challenging. During these visits, David will have to gain the trust of clients, overcome a wide range of barriers to communication, and use his powers of observation to help him detect signs of crisis or mistreatment and hazards in the home environment. With the many and diverse obstacles that lie ahead, David wonders how well he can fill the role of an adult protective services worker.

ASSESSMENT OF ELDER MISTREATMENT

The preceding section of the chapter showed how cases of suspected mistreatment are reported and some of the strategies which a protective services worker might employ during initial contacts with clients. Crisis conditions observed at these times may require an immediate response by a protective services worker. A victim of abuse or neglect might be taken to a hospital for emergency treatment, or a court order might be obtained to remove a perpetrator from a home. However, even in these instances, comprehensive assessments of clients will be needed so that plans for effective, long-term treatment can be devised. Comprehensive assessments are not based on suspicions or conjecture. In addition to the facts which a protective services worker can compile on his own, assessments will frequently incorporate diagnoses by physicians, psychiatrists, and other experts. Consequently, assessments can be viewed as the result of the efforts of a team of professionals rather than as the work of a single individual.

Our fictional protective services worker, David Myers, affords a means of illustrating why accurate, detailed assessments are necessary. In his first week on the job, David encounters an elderly woman who has been beaten by her husband. With her permission, David takes her to the hospital to determine the extent of her injuries and to obtain treatment. Provided that the woman is mentally competent, she will be free to return to her home at the end of her stay in the hospital. If her spouse is mentally competent, he could be there to greet her and abuse could recur.

The protective services worker can begin seeking answers to questions of mental competency by consulting with the client's physicians or by administering mental tests to the perpetrator and the victim. Possible tests include the Dementia Scale (Kahn et al., 1960) and the Mini-Mental Status Examination (Folstein, Folstein and McHugh, 1975). Either of these tests can show that a client is disoriented with regard to time and place, and demonstrate the need for a complete mental and psychiatric evaluation. Moreover, there are other instruments for assessment available to the worker (McKean and Wilson, 1993). In the abuse case that David is currently investigating, a finding of mental incompetency could lead to involuntary confinement of the woman or her husband in a nursing home or some other protective environment. Thus, one potential result of the assessment process is that individuals may be judged to be incapable of exercising the right to choose where and how to live.

In the case at hand, David discovers that the female victim is in full possession of her mental faculties. Since she is able to decide what services will be accepted, David requests her permission to evaluate her physical capabilities. He points out that the purpose of the evaluation is to determine what kinds of assistance she will need when she leaves the hospital. With the woman's consent, David begins an assessment of her physical condition.

David learns from the woman's doctor that no permanent disabilities were caused by her injuries. She will be stiff and sore for a few weeks and should remain in bed as much as possible. He also asks the woman if she was functionally impaired in any way prior to the incident with her husband. The woman reports that she had no trouble bathing, dressing, cooking, going to the bathroom, or walking. Her responses are consistent with the worker's limited observations of the woman and with reports supplied by her neighbors. Based on the available evidence, the worker concludes that home-delivered meals, some help from a home-health aide, and monitoring by a visiting nurse would facilitate the woman's recovery. If the woman agrees, the worker will contact the required agencies to see if her needs for services can be accommodated.

The protective services worker will not be able to focus all of his attention on the victim. If the actions of the husband cannot be attributed to mental incapacity, then additional steps should be taken to find out why he was abusive. As a result of further inquiries, the worker may discover that the man has a history of substance abuse or marital violence. It might also be that the man is suffering from a serious physical ailment, a major financial setback, or the death of a close friend. On the surface, it would appear that the worker could easily narrow down the list of possible explanations for the man's abusive behavior and establish a possible cause. However, there is no assurance that the perpetrator, the victim, or anyone else will cooperate with the worker's investigative efforts. Hence, errors in diplomacy can be as damaging as flaws in procedure. In either event, mistakes by the investigator can lead to an incomplete or incorrect assessment of the man's condition, and nullify his chances for effective treatment.

Each time that David conducts an investigation, he is very concerned about the impact of his findings on the lives of his clients. In most instances, David believes that the assessment process should guide the worker to the least-restrictive solution for client problems (Quinn and Tomita, 1986; Salem and Favre, 1993). That is, a client should not be confined in a nursing home if the person can survive with assistance in her or his own environment. A perpetrator should not be jailed if counseling or other therapeutic measures can be used to alter maladaptive behaviors. David does not wish to disrupt elderly clients anymore than is necessary to restore conditions of health and safety; herein lies the principle of least restrictiveness. However, in practice, least-restrictive solutions also have drawbacks. Although abusers may receive therapy, they can abuse again. A decision to defer institutionalization of a victim of self-neglect can contribute to the decline or the death of the client. As a protective services worker, David's role is to enforce the will of the state by protecting those who cannot protect themselves. If David is too heavy-handed in discharging this role, he can take away the prerogatives of clients when other options are available. If he is too permissive, he can leave clients at risk. During assessment, David will endeavor to avoid these extremes so that he can effectively serve the interests of his clients. There are many factors and participants in the protective service case which will come to bear on his decision.

In the preceding discussion, readers have been presented with an opportunity to observe some of the ideal characteristics of assessments. These characteristics can be summarized as follows:

1. Assessments should be comprehensive in scope. Significant details should not be overlooked by the investigator.
2. Assessments require teamwork. Diagnoses should be obtained from doctors, psychiatrists, and other professionals whenever these diagnoses are needed.
3. Assessments should be accurate. Every effort should be made to replace guesswork with facts.
4. Assessments should be able to resolve issues of mental competency.
5. Assessments should include evaluations of the physical capabilities of clients.

6. In assessments, investigators should utilize diplomacy. Otherwise, investigators may not be able to investigate.

7. Assessments should be responsive to the needs and interests of clients within the limits specified by the state.

Identification of these seven characteristics provides one with a general sense of what assessments ought to be. This knowledge does not offer much insight into the specific methods which can be used to achieve desired results. One might consult *Crisis Intervention with the Elderly* by Losee et al. (1988) for additional direction in crisis assessment specific to this client group. Without additional guidance, a novice protective services worker might test for mental competency in one case and forget to carry out this procedure in the next. Similarly, he or she might do a good job of documenting a case of abuse and overlook indications of exploitation, which are also present. As the caseload of the novice worker grows, it will be more and more difficult to remember which procedures were carried out and which ones were omitted in a particular investigation. To avoid such problems, the worker needs some way of standardizing the assessment process and of assuring the quality of investigative efforts. The worker's needs may be at least partially satisfied by a formal assessment protocol. In particular, the works of Bookin and Dunkle (1989), Fulmer (1989), and Phillips (1989) all found within *Elder Abuse: Practice and Policy* edited by Filinson and Ingman (1989), Miller (1998), and the work of Dozier (1984) should be helpful to those attempting to develop elder abuse assessment skills.

A formal assessment protocol lists the steps that should be carried out during an investigation and shows how each step can be completed. Tomita (1982) provides an example of a formal protocol which can be used in cases of suspected abuse and neglect. In addition to instructions on how to conduct tests for mental competency and evaluations of physical capabilities, this protocol offers detailed information about many other facets of an investigation. When a worker utilizes the protocol, he or she learns how to arrange interviews with clients and what questions should be asked. The worker also learns how to estimate the time when an injury occurred by looking at the color of a victim's bruises, how to document injuries with a camera and a tape measure, and how to seek information from physicians, neighbors, and other people who know the clients. Finally, the Tomita protocol presents treatment options for both victims and perpetrators.

While formal assessment protocols can assist in standardizing and upgrading the performances of workers, they also have limitations. For instance, the Tomita protocol does not contain information about investigations of exploitation. Furthermore, it may prescribe techniques that are inconsistent with local standards of investigation. Consequently, it may be necessary for a worker to review several different protocols, such as those which are provided by

Ferguson and Beck (1983), Fulmer and Cahill (1983), Hwalek and Sengstock (1986), and Kosberg (1988). During this review, the worker can select those procedures that are suited to his/her particular purposes. This process of review and selection appears to be particularly advisable for novice investigators. These individuals cannot wait for experience to teach them how to do assessments. The needs of elderly clients will be too urgent to be professionally appraised and resolved at some unspecified time in the future.

METHODS OF INTERVENTION

The previous section of the chapter demonstrated that interventions may begin before assessments have been completed. The section also described some of the interventions that may be carried out by practitioners. However, before describing the various types of interventions which may be possible, it might be instructive to distinguish between *crisis intervention* and *protective services* as these apply to the elder abuse client (Bergman, 1989). Crisis intervention normally refers to immediate person-to-person assistance needed in order to resolve a hazardous or threatening situation, while protective services may be in response to both acute and chronic situations. Protective services are those steps taken by adult protective services and others, which are intended to remedy an abusive, exploitative, or neglectful situation. Protective services, then, depending on the variety and form, may be implemented in response to an acute crisis situation or the chronic case. Crisis intervention, on the other hand, tends to be more immediate and is intended to establish relief, control, and stability within a dangerous, hazardous or otherwise crisis producing situation.

Relief may be sought for clients in a number of ways, and the following discussion is primarily focused on protective service interventions. One avenue is court intervention. Doctors can provide medical treatment in or out of hospitals. Counselors can alter the behavior of victims and perpetrators, and agencies can provide services to assist clients in managing activities they cannot manage by themselves. In earlier discussions, these treatment options were presented by way of example rather than as part of an overall plan of treatment. In order to design a treatment plan, a protective services worker needs to be aware of all of the tools which are available for use during intervention. The worker's tool kit should include a variety of therapeutic remedies, legal remedies, and client services. He or she will have to decide which ones can be employed to deal with client problems in a given case of elder mistreatment.

Medical services are probably the most frequently prescribed therapeutic remedies in cases of abuse and neglect. Normally, protective services workers do not have much trouble in obtaining a client's consent for medical services, or in arranging for a client to be treated. When a client does refuse medical treatment, it may be necessary for a worker to seek an emergency protective order from a judge. If this order is granted, the client can be required to submit to treatment for his own good whether s/he wishes medical assistance or not (Quinn and Tomita, 1986). Obtaining medical care for homebound clients can present additional difficulties for protective services workers. It may be awkward or inadvisable to transport a homebound client to a medical clinic or a hospital for diagnosis and treatment. Another way of handling these situations is to persuade physicians to visit the homes of clients. In fact, programs can be set up with private physicians or medical schools so that doctors routinely reserve time to make house calls to the clients of protective services workers (Dolon and Blakely, 1989b).

Education, counseling, and support groups can be utilized to provide cognitive and emotional therapies to victims and perpetrators of elder mistreatment. When protective services workers encounter victims of mistreatment, their attention tends to be drawn to the physical damages which have been incurred by victims. The emotional or psychological wounds which victims have suffered may be less visible. Even those who have been trained in psychiatry can erroneously attribute psychological disturbances in elderly patients to senility and consider the elderly to be too old to be candidates for therapy (Waxman, Carner and Klein, 1984).

A more helpful stance by protective services workers and other professionals is to be alert to psychological reactions to victimization which may appear in both older and younger victims. Studies suggest that victims of violence or adversity tend to blame themselves for their misfortune, feel that the world can no longer be understood, and experience losses in self-esteem and perceived control of their personal destinies (e.g., Janoff-Bulman and Frieze, 1983; Miller and Porter, 1983; Perloff, 1983; Peterson and Seligmann, 1983). Moreover, victims may selectively focus on life's blessings and compare themselves to others who are less fortunate (Taylor, Lichtman and Wood, 1984). Collectively, these symptoms can defeat attempts by workers to convince clients that problems requiring treatment exist. Consequently, the process of overcoming psychological denial or reluctance on the part of clients is viewed by Breckman and Adelman (1989) as the first step in their staircase model of intervention. With the assistance of protective services workers or counselors, clients' feelings of reluctance can gradually dissipate. In the next stage of intervention clients are able to recognize the serious implications of mistreatment. In the final stage of intervention, clients are willing to participate in interventions, which can rebuild or improve the conditions of their existence. Breckman and Adelman also apply the staircase model to interventions with perpetrators of mistreatment. Once again, the task of the practitioner is to guide the clients through stages of reluctance, recognition, and rebuilding. However, this may be easier said than done.

While protective services workers are not likely to be attorneys, they will need to possess a working knowledge of the law. When therapeutic techniques do not succeed in changing the behaviors of perpetrators or victims of mistreatment, legal proceedings may be required to insure the safety, possessions, and health of clients. The most restrictive legal solutions occur in cases in which clients are found to be mentally incapable or incompetent. This finding enables a judge to appoint a conservator or guardian who thereafter becomes a substitute decision-maker for the client. At the same time, the client can be stripped of her or his rights to manage property, to enter into contracts, to refuse medical treatment, or to make any other legally binding decisions (Regan, 1978).

A protective services worker may feel compelled to petition for a guardianship in a client's behalf when the client seems to be unable to make rational decisions and is endangered by his own actions or those of a caregiver. A potential shortcoming of guardianships is that a client who is of sound mind can be judged to be mentally incapable by the courts. A mistake in judgment is all the more likely when a client is not represented by counsel or informed that a court hearing is taking place (Quinn and Tomita, 1986). Because of the possibility that court procedures and decisions might be biased, a protective services worker should be extremely cautious about seeking guardianships for elderly clients. The worker should consider whether an emergency protective order, a power of attorney, or some other less-restrictive device would be sufficient to protect the client's welfare. If these are not viable options, then the worker should be informed about safeguards to clients, which may be written into state guardianship laws. These might include provisions for limited guardianships, court supervision of financial transactions by guardians, and periodic reviews by the courts to terminate guardian-ships when they are no longer needed. In an era in which the courts are being presented with growing numbers of petitions for guardianships, a protective services worker is likely to become actively involved in such proceedings (Quinn, 1989). On these occasions, the worker must remember that his/her duty is not only to protect the health and the lives of his clients, but also to uphold their rights to due process.

In addition to guardianship laws, other statutes are applicable to cases of elder mistreatment but vary substantially from state to state. For example, in New York a protective services worker might seek criminal prosecution of an abuser under the harassment section of the criminal code. Since a comparable law does not exist in California, protective services workers in that state must invoke other laws to prosecute those who abuse the elderly (Breckman and Adelman, 1988). According to the statutes of Indiana, protective services workers are attached to the offices of county prosecutors, or they may fall under contract with a local social service agency. However, in most instances within Indiana, workers are sworn prosecutor's investigators. As members of these offices, protective services workers can easily initiate the steps which are necessary to petition for subpoenas so they can gain access to financial records in suspected cases of exploitation. In most other states, protective services workers are not employees of law enforcement agencies. Hence, these workers may have to overcome a number of bureaucratic entanglements in order to get a petition for a subpoena into the hands of a judge.

Knowing how local laws and procedures operate with regard to guardianships, criminal prosecutions, and subpoenas do not exhaust the supply of legal information which will be needed by protective services workers. They will be required to learn how to obtain emergency protective orders in crisis situations so that clients who are unable to give informed consent can receive medical treatment or other forms of assistance. A worker might also seek a restraining order to remove an abuser from the household of her or his victim. However, along with other legal devices, restraining orders should be used with caution. It may be unreasonable to expect an elderly victim to call the police if an abuser violates the order and enters the home. If the abuser is angered by the order, s/he may decide to take out that anger on the unprotected victim.

Another device which is not totally free of risk is employed by protective services workers when clients are physically or mentally unable to manage the checks which they receive from the Social Security Administration or other branches of the federal government. In these instances, a worker can request that the required government agencies establish representative payees to receive and use the checks in behalf of the clients. Byers and Hendricks (1990) describe the effectiveness of one such program as a protective service approach. Unfortunately, representative payees occasionally forget the intended purpose of the arrangement and withhold funds that should be available to clients (Quinn and Tomita, 1986). Protective services workers do not have to remain passive and wait for government agencies to discover exploitation by representative payees. Workers can anticipate conflicts of interest when relatives or other parties become representative payees and monitor these situations to see that clients are receiving the benefits to which they are entitled.

Given the fact that state legal systems do not provide uniform approaches to problems of mistreatment, protective services workers might hope to find a higher degree of consistency in the ways in which human services are distributed to the elderly. In one sense these hopes have been fulfilled. According to the provisions of Older American Acts, which have been enacted by the federal government, a national aging network has been established to deliver human services to the elderly. At state and local levels, area agencies on aging play key roles in this network. Human services which might be available to the elderly through a particular agency on aging include case management, legal assistance, advocacy, day care, home-health care, telephone reassurance, housekeeping, home-delivered meals, victim assistance, and counseling (Atchley, 1988; Fallcreek and Gilbert, 1981). When so many services can be obtained through an area agency on aging, the task presented to a protective services worker appears to be a simple one. All the worker has to do is to refer an elderly client to the appropriate agency on aging. A case manager in the agency will determine what services the client needs and will then attempt to provide them. At least from the perspective of the protective services worker, this scenario represents an ideal partnership.

In a practical sense, protective services workers may find that less-than ideal conditions prevail. Because of funding deficiencies and other problems, some of the services which clients need may not exist. If services are available, clients may not qualify, or they may be placed on waiting lists. The roles which are carried out by area agencies on aging tend to vary from one part of the country to another. A national survey by Blakely and Dolon (1991) found that over 30 percent of the area agencies on aging who responded do not receive referrals of elder abuse from protective services workers or provide case management services to victims. Consequently, protective services workers in the geographic locations which are served by these area agencies on aging must look elsewhere for solutions to problems which are associated with elder mistreatment.

CONCLUSION

In earlier sections of the chapter, information was presented to show that detection and assessment of elder mistreatment were dependent upon support from the community and coordinated efforts by teams of professionals. The same prerequisites are needed to design and execute responsive interventions. However, it cannot be assumed that protective services workers will be able to construct effective interventions when they are denied the financial resources which are necessary to fulfill the protective services role. So long as policy makers fail to provide adequate funding for programs to assist the elderly, victims of mistreatment are likely to remain isolated, untreated, and forgotten. Now is an appropriate time for governmental and public action to reduce the incidence of elder mistreatment (U.S. House of Representatives, 1990). If protective services workers could be freed from the constraints which are imposed by excessive caseloads, and "bare-bones" budgets, they could focus more of their attention on the prevention of elder mistreatment. Interventions are, after all, most effective when they are initiated before the elderly are irrevocably harmed by abuse, neglect, and exploitation.

CHAPTER QUESTIONS

1. What steps have been taken by the federal government to assist in the prevention, detection, and treatment of elder mistreatment? What steps would you recommend?
2. How do characteristics of perpetrators and victims, other than age, affect decisions as to whether elder mistreatment has taken place, who conducts investigations, and what treatments will be utilized?
3. In what ways do culture and society contribute to victimization of the elderly?
4. What situational factors can place stress upon an adult child who provides care for an elderly parent? (You should be able to identify at least six situational stressors.)
5. What factors are likely to contribute to acts of elder mistreatment by the spouses of victims?
6. According to a social exchange model, how would you expect a caregiver to react when dependent elders exhibit maladaptive behaviors?
7. Use the social-exchange and environmental-press models to explain why dependent elders might become frustrated, depressed, or rebellious when they are treated well by caregivers.
8. Why don't protective services workers pay closer attention to theoretical models which can be applied to elder mistreatment?
9. How much support should a protective services worker expect from the public, physicians, community-health nurses, and the police? (Use the results of research to support your answer.)
10. During initial visits to the homes of elderly clients, protective services workers can conduct environmental surveys. What indicators of mistreatment or other problems should workers try to observe?
11. Identify seven ideal characteristics of assessments.
12. What is an assessment protocol? How might it be applied?
13. What are the advantages and disadvantages of using an assessment protocol?
14. What are the stages which are described in the staircase model of intervention?
15. Provide an example of a least-restrictive intervention.
16. How might crisis intervention and protective services be distinguished? How are they similar? Different?

SIMULATED EXERCISES

Simulated Exercise 1

Divide the class into pairs of students. In each pair; one student should play the role of an elderly client and erect barriers to communication. The other student should play the role of a protective services worker and try to overcome the barriers to communication. After a few minutes of interaction, the students can reverse the roles they are playing.

Simulated Exercise 2

Let student volunteers simulate methods which protective services workers might use to gain entry into the homes of clients.

Simulated Exercise 3

Let student volunteers simulate methods which protective services workers might use to overcome resistance which is offered by an elderly perpetrator of mistreatment.

Simulated Exercise 4

Have students find out what methods are used in the local community to convey information to the public and to professional workers about how and where to report elder mistreatment.

Simulated Exercise 5

Have students check with the local postal service and the public utilities to see if a "gatekeeper" program is in operation. A gatekeeper program provides instruction to people who regularly visit the homes of the elderly so they can detect and report cases of mistreatment to protective services.

Simulated Exercise 6

Have students check with local agencies and protective services workers to see what forms of assistance are available for victims and perpetrators of elder mistreatment.

Simulated Exercise 7

Have each student in the class develop three hypotheses which include factors which might cause or contribute to a specific form of elder mistreatment. Use these hypotheses as focal points for class discussion.

APPENDIX A

Additional Internet Resources

The following list provides information in regards to elder mistreatment. Furthermore, these websites present the reader with information specifically on types of elder mistreatment, elder mistreatment situational factors, elder mistreatment preventions, and elder mistreatment responses.

National Center on Elder Abuse (NCEA):
   http://www.elderabusecenter.org/default.cfm
U.S. Administration on Aging:
   http://www.aoa.gov/
Medline Plus, Elder Abuse:
   http://www.nlm.nih.gov/medlineplus/elderabuse.html
American Society on Aging:
   http://www.asaging.org/am/cia2/abuse.html
   http://www.asaging.org/elderabuse/documents/APSethics.pdf
National Center for Victims of Crime:
   http://www.ncvc.org/ncvc/main.aspx?dbName=DocumentViewer&Document
   ID=32350
National Committee for the Prevention of Elder Abuse:
   http://www.preventelderabuse.org/
U.S. Department of Health and Human Services, National Elder Abuse Incidence
Study:
   http://www.aoa.gov/eldfam/Elder_Rights/Elder_Abuse/
   ABuseReport_Full.pdf
American Academy of Family Physicians:
   http://www.aafp.org/afp/990515ap/2804.html
Clearinghouse on Abuse and Neglect of the Elderly (CANE):
   http://db.rdms.udel.edu:8080/CANE/index.jsp
Bureau of Justice Statistics, Report:
   http://www.ojp.usdoj.gov/bjs/pub/pdf/cpa6597.pdf
Geocities- Elder Abuse:
   http://www.geocities.com/~elderly-place/abuse.html
Elder Abuse Prevention:
   http://www.elderabuseprevention-eastbay.org/

Elder Abuse and Neglect, by Linda M. Woolf, Ph.D.:
  http://www.webster.edu/~woolflm/abuse.html
Nursing Home Abuse and Neglect Information Center:
  http://www.nursinghomeabuse.com/
National Clearinghouse on Abuse Later in Life:
  http://www.ncall.us/
The World Heath Organization:
  http://www.who.int/hpr/ageing/elderabuse.htm
Elder abuse and neglect: What physicians can and should do, by Mahnaz Ahmad,
MD, MS and Mark Lachs, MD, MPH:
  http://www.ccjm.org/pdffiles/Ahmad1002.pdf
The Merck Manual of Health and Aging:
  http://www.merck.com/pubs/mmanual_ha/sec4/ch64/ch64a.html
Center on Aging Study:
  http://cas.umkc.edu/casww/causesof.htm
SeniorCitizens.com:
  http://www.seniorcitizens.com/elderabuse/

REFERENCES

American Medical Association Council on Scientific Affairs. (1987). Elder abuse and neglect. *Journal of the American Medical Association, 257,* 966–971.

Anetzberger, G.J., Korbin, J.E., & Tomita, S.K. (2000). Defining elder mistreatment in four ethnic groups across two generations. In R. Tewksbury & P. Gagne (Eds.), *From deviance and deviants: An anthology* (pp. 174–184). Los Angeles: Roxbury Publishing.

Ansello, E.F., King, N.R. & Taler, G. (1986). The environmental press model: A theoretical framework for intervention in elder abuse. In K.A. Pillemer & R.S. Wolf (Eds.), *Elder abuse: Conflict in the family.* Dover, MA: Auburn House.

Atchley, R.C. (1988). *Social forces and aging: An introduction to social gerontology* (5th Edition). Belmont, CA: Wadsworth.

Bergman, J.A. (1989). Responding to abuse and neglect cases: Protective services versus crisis intervention. In R. Filinson & S.R. Ingman (Eds.), Elder abuse: *Practice and policy* (pp. 94–103). New York: Human Sciences Press.

Blakely, B. & Dolon, R. (1991). Area agencies on aging and the prevention of elder abuse: The results of a national study. *Journal of Elder Abuse & Neglect, 3,* 2,21–40.

Block, MR. & Sinnott, J.D. (1979). Methodology and results. In M.R. Block & J.D. Sinnott (Eds.), *The battered elder syndrome: An exploratory study.* Center on Aging, University of Maryland.

Breckman, R.S. & Adelman, R.D. (1988). *Strategies/or helping victims of elder mistreatment.* Beverly Hills, CA: Sage.

Butler, R.N (1969). Ageism: Another form of bigotry. *The Gerontologist, 9,* 243–246.

Byers, B. (1993). Qualitative and Quantitative Profiles of Elder Self-Neglect: Micro-Macro Connections. *Free Inquiry and Creative Sociology, 21,* 149–159.

Byers, B. & Hendricks, J.E. (1993). *Adult protective services: Research and practice.* Springfield, IL: Charles C Thomas, Publisher, Ltd.

Byers, B. & Hendricks, J.E. (1990). Elder financial self-neglect and exploitation: An adult protective services response. *Journal of Free Inquiry and Creative Sociology, 18,* 205–211.

Byers, B. & Lamanna, R.A. (1993). Adult protective services and elder self-endangering behavior. In B. Byers and J.E. Hendricks (Eds.), *Adult protective services: Research and practice* (pp. 61–85). Springfield, IL: Charles C Thomas, Publisher, Ltd.

Clark-Daniels, C.L., Daniels, R.S. & Baumhover, L.A. (1990). Physicians' and nurses' responses to abuse of the elderly: A comparative study of two surveys in Alabama. *Journal of Elder Abuse & Neglect, 1,* 4, 57–72.

Crouse, J.S., Cobb, D., Harris, B., Kopecky, F. & Poertner, J. (1981). *Abuse and neglect of the elderly in Illinois: Incidence and characteristics, legislation, and policy recommendations.* Springfield, IL: Illinois Department of Aging.

Crystal, S. (1987). Elder abuse: The latest crisis. The Public Interest, 87, 56–66.

Daniels, R.S., Baumhover, L.A. & Clark-Daniels, C.L. (1989). Physicians' mandatory reporting of elder abuse. *The Gerontologist, 29,* 3, 321–327.

Davidson, J.L., Hennessey, S. & Sedge, S. (1979). Additional factors related to elder abuse. In M.R. Block & J.D. Sinnott (Eds.), *The battered elder syndrome: An exploratory study.* Center on Aging, University of Maryland.

Dolon, R. & Blakely, B. (1987, March). Elder abuse and neglect: A national study. Presented at the 33rd Annual Meeting of American Society of Aging, Salt Lake City, UT.

Dolon, R. & Blakely, B. (1989a). Elder abuse and neglect: A study of adult protective services workers in the United States. *Journal of Elder Abuse & Neglect, 3,* 31–50.

Dolon, R. & Blakely, B. (1989b, October). The use of physician home visits in elder abuse and neglect cases. Presented at the 6th Annual Adult Protective Services Conference, San Antonio, TX.

Douglass, R.L. (1983). Domestic neglect and abuse of the elderly: Implications for research and service. *Family Relations, 32,* 395–402.

Douglass, R.L., Hickey, T. & Noel, C. (1980). *A study of maltreatment of the elderly and other vulnerable adults.* Final report to the United States Administration on Aging and the Michigan Department of Social Services, The Institute of Gerontology, The University of Michigan.

Dozier, C. (1984). *Report of the elder abuse and neglect assessment field instrument.* Atlanta, GA: Atlanta Regional Commission.

Elder Abuse Project, American Public Welfare Association (1986). *A comprehensive analysis of state policy and practice related to elder abuse.* Washington, DC: American Public Welfare Association, National Association of State Units on Aging.

Fallcreek, S. & Gilbert, N. (1981). Aging network in transition: Problems and prospects. *Social Work,* May, 210–216.

Ferguson, D. & Beck, C. (1983). Half: A tool to assess elder abuse within the family. *Geriatric Nursing, 4,* 5, 301–304.

Filinson, R. & Ingman, S.R. (Eds.) (1989). *Elder abuse: Practice and policy.* New York:

Human Sciences Press.

Finkelhor, D. (1983). Common features of family abuse. In D. Finkelhor, R. Gelles, G. Hotaling & M. Straus (Eds.), *The dark side of families.* Beverly Hills, CA: Sage.

Folstein, M.F., Folstein, S.E. & McHugh, P.R. (1975). Mini-mental state. *Journal of Psychiatric Research, 12,* 3,189–198.

Fulmer, T.T. & Cahill, V. (1984). Assessing elder abuse: A study. *Journal of Gerontological Nursing; 10,* 12, 16–20.

Fulmer, T.T. & O'Malley, T.A. (1987). *Inadequate care of the elderly: A health-care perspective on abuse and neglect.* New York: Springer.

Galbraith, M.W. (1986). Elder abuse: An overview. *Convergence in Aging, 3,* 5–27.

George, L.K. (1986). Caregiver burden: Conflict between norms of reciprocity and solidarity. In K.A. Pillemer & R.S. Wolf (Eds.), *Elder abuse: Conflict in the family.* Dover, MA: Auburn House.

Giordano, N.H. & Giordano, J.J. (1984). Elder abuse: A review of the literature. *Social Work,* 232–236.

Hendricks, J. & Hendricks, C.D. (1986). *Aging in mass society: Myths and realities* (3rd Edition). Boston, MA: Little, Brown.

Hepworth, D.H. & Larsen, J.A. (1986). *Direct social work practice: Theory and skills.* Belmont, CA: Wadsworth.

Hudson, M.F. (1989). Analyses of the concepts of elder mistreatment: Abuse and neglect. *Journal of Elder Abuse & Neglect, 1,* 1, 5–25.

Hudson, M.F. (1986). Elder mistreatment: Current research. In K.A. Pillemer & R.S. Wolf (Eds.), *Elder abuse: Conflict in the family.* Dover, MA: Auburn House.

Hwalek, M.A. & Sengstock, M.C. (1986). Assessing the probability of abuse of the elderly: Toward development of a clinical screening instrument. *Journal of Applied Gerontology, 5,* 153–173.

Janoff-Bulman, R. & Frieze, I. H. (1983). A theoretical perspective for understanding reactions to victimization. *Journal of Social Issues, 39,* 2, 1–17.

Johnson, T. (1986). *Critical issues in the definition of elder mistreatment.* In K.A. Pillemer & R.S. Wolf (Eds.), Elder abuse: Conflict in the family. Dover, MA: Auburn House.

Kahn, R.L., Goldfarb, A.I., Pollack, M. & Peck, A. (1960). Objective measures for the determination of mental status in the aged. *American Journal of Psychiatry, 117,* 4, 326–328.

Kinney, MB., Wendt, R. & Hurst, J. (1986). Elder abuse: Techniques for effective resolution. *Convergence in Aging, 3,* 110–124.

Kosberg, H. (1988). Preventing elder abuse: Identification of high risk factors prior to placement decisions. *The Gerontologist, 28,* 1, 43–50.

Longino, C.F., Soldo, B.J. & Manton, K.G. (1990). Demography of aging in the United States. In K.F. Ferraro (Ed.), *Gerontology: Perspectives and issues.* New York: Springer.

Losee, N., Parham, I,A., Auerbach, S. & Teitelman, J.L. (1988). *Crisis intervention with the elderly.* Springfield, IL: Charles C Thomas, Publisher, Ltd.

McCuan, E.R. & Jenkins, M.B. (1992). A general framework for elder self-neglect. In E.R. McCuan and D.R. Fabian (Eds.), *Self-neglecting elders: A clinical dilemma.*

Westport, CT: Auburn House.

McKean, J.B. & Wilson, D.L. (1993). Adult protective services and the social service system. In B. Byers & J.E. Hendricks (Eds.), *Adult protective services: Research and practice* (pp. 137–167). Springfield, IL: Charles C Thomas, Publisher, Ltd.

McTavish, D.G. (1971). Perceptions of old people: A review of research methodologies and findings. *The Gerontologist, 11,* 90–108.

Miller, T.W. & Veltkamp, L.J. (Eds). (1998). *Clinical handbook of adult exploitation and abuse.* Madison, Conn.: International Universities Press.

Miller, D.T. & Porter, CA. (1983). Self-blame in victims of violence. *Journal of Social Issues, 89,* 2,139–152.

Montoya, V. (1997). Understanding and combating elder abuse in Hispanic communities. *Journal of Elder Abuse & Neglect, 9,* 2, 5–17.

Morris, D. & Blakely, B. (1990, September). Public awareness, concern, and response to mistreatment of older adults. Presented at the Seventh National Forum on Research in Aging. Lincoln, NE.

NEAIS. (1998). *National Elder Abuse Incidence Study.* United States Department of Health and Human Services, Administration on Aging. Washington, DC: U.S. Government Printing Office.

O'Malley, H., Sears, H., Perez, R., Mitchell, V. & Knuepfel, C. (1979). *Elder abuse in Massachusetts: A survey of professionals and paraprofessionals.* Boston, MA: Legal Research and Services for the Elderly.

Perloff, L.S. (1983). Perceptions of vulnerability to victimization. *Journal of Social Issues, 89,* 2, 41–6l.

Peterson, C. & Seligmann, M.E. (1983). Learned helplessness and victimization. *Journal of Social Issues, 39,* 2, 103–116.

Phillips, L.R. (1986). Theoretical explanations of elder abuse: Competing hypotheses and unresolved issues. In K.A. Pillemer & R.S. Wolf (Eds.), *Elder abuse: Conflict in the family.* Dover, MA: Auburn House.

Pillemer, K.A. (1986). Risk factors in elder abuse: Results from a case-control study. In K.A. Pillemer & R.S. Wolf (Eds.), *Elder abuse: Conflict in the family.* Dover, MA: Auburn House.

Pillemer, K.A. & Finkelhor, D. (1989). Causes of elder abuse: Caregiver stress versus problem relatives. *American Journal of Orthopsvchiatry, 59,* 2, 179–187.

Pillemer, K.A. & Suitor, J.J. (1998). Violence and violent feelings: What causes them among family caregivers? In R.K. Bergen (Ed.), *Issues in Intimate Violence.* Thousand Oaks, CA: Sage.

Plotkin, M.R. (1988). *A time for dignity: Police and domestic abuse of the elderly.* Washington, DC: American Association of Retired Persons, Police Executive Research Forum.

Quinn, M.J. (1989). Probate conservatorships and guardianships: Assessment and curative aspects. *Journal of Elder Abuse & Neglect, 1,* 1, 91–101.

Quinn, M.J. & Tomita, S.K. (1986). *Elder abuse and neglect: Causes, diagnosis, and intervention strategies.* New York: Springer.

Regan, J.J. (1978). Intervention through adult protective services programs. *The Gerontologist, 18,* 3, 250–254.

Sager, A. (1986). Mobilizing adequate home-care resources: A mutual aid response to stress within the family. In K.A. Pillemer & R.S. Wolf (Eds.), *Elder abuse: Conflict in the Family*. Dover, MA: Auburn House.

Salem, S.R. & Favre, B.C. (1993). Providing protective services to special populations. In B. Byers & J.E. Hendricks (Eds.), *Adult protective services: Research and practice* (pp. 169–189). Springfield, IL: Charles C Thomas, Publisher, Ltd.

Salend, E., Kane, R.R., Satz, M. & Pynoos, J. (1984). Elder abuse reporting: Limitations of statutes. *The Gerontologist, 25,* 4, 347–349.

Steinmetz, S.K. (1981). Elder abuse. *Aging,* (January-February), 6–10.

Steinmetz, S.K. (1983). Dependency, stress, and violence between middle-aged caregivers and their elderly parents. In J.I. Kosberg (Ed.), *Abuse and maltreatment of the elderly*. Boston: John Wright-PSG.

Tatara, T. (1999). *Understanding elder abuse in minority populations*. Philadelphia, PA: Brunner/Mazel.

Tatara, T. (1993). Understanding the nature and scope of domestic elder abuse with the use of sate aggregate data: Summaries of the key findings of a national survey of state APS and aging agencies. *Journal of Elder Abuse & Neglect, 5,* 4, 35–57.

Taylor, S.E., Lichtman, R.R. & Wood, J.V. (1984). Attributions, beliefs about control and adjustment to breast cancer. *Journal of Personality and Social Psychology, 46,* 489–502.

Tomita, S.K. (1982). Detection and treatment of elderly abuse and neglect: A protocol for health care professionals. *PT & OT in Geriatrics, 2,* 2, 37–51.

Traxler, A.J. (1986). Elder abuse laws: A survey of state statutes. *Convergence in Aging, 8,* 139–167.

U.S. House of Representatives, Select Committee on Aging (1981). *Elder abuse: The hidden problem*. Washington, DC: United States Government Printing Office.

U.S. House of Representatives, Select Committee on Aging, Subcommittee on Health and Longterm Care (1990). *Elder abuse: A decade of shame and inaction*. Washington, DC: United States Government Printing Office.

Viano, E. (1983). Victimology: An overview. In J.I. Kosberg (Ed.), *Abuse and maltreatment of the elderly: Causes and interventions*. Littleton, MA: John Wright-PSG.

Ward, R.A. (1984). *The aging experience: An introduction to social gerontology*. New York: Harper and Row.

Waxman, H.M. Carner, E.A. & Klein, M. (1984). Underutilization of mental health professionals by community elderly. *The Gerontologist, 24,* 1, 23–30.

Wolf, R.S. & McCarthy, ER. (1991). Elder abuse. In B.B. Hess & E.W. Markson (Eds.), *Growing old in America* (Fourth Edition) (pp. 481–501). New Brunswick: Transaction Books.

Wolf, R.S., Strugnell, C.P. & Godkin, M.A. (1982). *Preliminary findings from three model projects on elderly abuse*. Worcester, MA: University of Massachusetts Medical Center, Center on Aging.

Chapter 8

RAPE: VICTIMS AND SURVIVORS

DIANE M. DAANE

INTRODUCTION

To adequately understand the responses and needs of rape victims/survivors, it is essential that we consider rape as a crime of violence and not a sexual act. Moreover, when considering the crime of rape within criminal justice and social service crisis intervention, it is critical that one considers not only victimization but also survivorship. Therefore, it is no longer adequate to consider the victimization experience without also considering the road victims travel. In addition to these issues, there are also many myths within American culture which emphasize the sexual aspect of rape. These same myths discount the violent nature of the life-threatening crime of rape. An effective rape crisis intervener must know the facts surrounding rape, the victimization experience, and the dynamics of survivorship (Foa and Rothbaum, 1998; Resnick and Schnicke, 1993).

Rape is a violent crime with serious physical and psychological implications for the victim/survivor. The victim's mate, family, and friends are also forced to cope with the trauma of rape. It has been suggested that most rape crisis center personnel agree that support programs for significant others and other secondary victims are necessary for the healing process (Brookings, McEvoy and Reed, 1994). In addition to the role of significant others during intervention and recovery, the intervener must also understand the typical and atypical responses of victims and their families to the rape crisis. The intervener must also know how to provide information and support to help the victim draw upon coping skills for bringing about recovery. It is the intervener's responsibility, in part, to demonstrate to the rape victim that s/he is a rape survivor as well. This important definitional process has the potential

233

to shape the victim's/survivor's lifetime self-perception.

With the aforementioned considerations, the potential intervener must examine his or her own motivation for working with rape victims/survivors. If the intervener gives credence to society's myths and misunderstanding about rape, he or she may impede rather than facilitate the victim's/survivor's recovery. Therefore, it is important that the rape intervener have a grasp of not only the most effective intervention strategies, but also an understanding of societal influences, which might confront the rape victim/survivor and subsequently influence the rape intervention process.

A rape crisis intervener may be anyone, with adequate training and empathy, who has contact with a rape victim/survivor immediately after the rape and is in a position to provide immediate person-to-person emotional first-aid. Interveners aren't merely counselors for rape crisis centers or victim advocate programs. The role of rape crisis intervener is much broader and includes a myriad of potential ancillary occupational roles. For instance, interveners in rape cases may include police officers, hospital emergency room personnel, emergency medical technicians or paramedics, nurses, physicians, hospital chaplains, and social workers.

Rape victims may be either female or male. However, the overwhelming majority of known rape victims/survivors are female; therefore, the victim/survivor in this chapter will sometimes be referred to with female pronouns. This is not intended to either deny the existence of male victims/survivors or to trivialize the trauma experienced by male rape victims/survivors. Rather, given that the majority of known rape is perpetrated against women, the pronoun usage is sometimes used to more accurately reflect the majority of cases.

RAPE MYTHS

Our culture has produced many myths about rape, and no one is immune to these myths. Common myths include the following.

Myth: Rape involves intense sexual desire.

Fact: Rape is not an act based on sexual desire or gratification. Rape is an act of power and violence. The fact that sexual intercourse is the means for expressing power, domination, and violence does not make rape sexual in nature. Rape is a violent crime.

Myth: Women secretly want to be raped.

Fact: Women view rape as an act of violence that is terrifying and life threatening. No woman wants to be forced into a violent, aggressive act that results in physical and emotional trauma. Some women may fantasize about being swept off their feet by a loved one or a handsome stranger, but that does not mean that women want to be subjected to a horrifying act of violence.

Myth: Some women deserve to be raped because they ask for it.

Fact: No person deserves to be the victim of a violent crime. No matter how a woman dresses or behaves, she does not deserve to be raped. Women have as much right as men to walk alone, have a drink, sleep with their windows open, and enter drinking establishments without being subjected to acts of violence.

Myth: Careful women do not get raped.

Fact: No female is immune to a rape experience (Brownmiller, 1975). Rapes occur at all times of the day and night, in the home, in the work environment, in public places, and in secluded areas. Women are raped by strangers and by people they know. There is no absolute protection from being raped.

Myth: It is not possible to rape a female who doesn't want to be raped (i.e., a good woman can't be raped).

Fact: No woman wants to be raped. If women could prevent rape, they would. Victims/survivors react to rape the same way that anyone reacts to a terrorizing, life-threatening experience. Some women become immobilized when faced with the threat of rape. Others try to fight the rapist, but may be impeded by the fact that women are generally smaller and less muscular than males, and that women are encouraged by their culture to be more passive (Hendricks, 1983). To assume that every violent crime victim could successfully defend her/himself against an assailant, especially one with a size advantage or a weapon, is ludicrous.

Myth: If a woman finds that rape is inevitable, she should relax and enjoy it.

Fact: Rape is not a pleasurable sexual experience. Rape is a terrifying act of violence. Sexual intercourse under the threat of injury or death is not an experience that can be enjoyed.

Myth: Women falsely cry rape.

Fact: The crime of rape is under reported. Many victims avoid reporting rape because they don't want to face the ordeal of questioning, medical exams, and trial. There is no evidence that rape is falsely reported any more often than any other crime. If anything has been established concerning the official reporting of rape by victims/survivors, it would be that the crime is largely under reported.

Myth: The rapist is usually a stranger.

Fact: While many rapes are committed by a stranger, many are also committed by acquaintances, dates, spouses, and family members.

Myth: Most rapes are interracial.

Fact: As with most types of crime, most rapes are intra-racial.

The myths about rape must be addressed in order to facilitate effective intervention on behalf of victims/survivors. Rape, as a crime, will not be treated in the same manner as other violent crimes against the person until society learns the facts concerning rape and discards the myths.

LEGAL DEFINITION AND FREQUENCY/CHARACTERISTICS OF RAPE

Legal Definition

Criminal law has traditionally defined rape as sexual intercourse with a female, to whom the assailant was not married, by force and against her will. Sexual intercourse was interpreted strictly as penetration of the vagina by a penis. Force was measured by the amount of resistance offered by the female, not by the acts of the assailant. Resistance was measured by injury to the victim/survivor other than penetration. Thus, if a woman did not receive injuries in addition to the rape, legally there was no force, and therefore no rape. This was true even when the assailant used a weapon to force submission. There is no other crime that measures force by the actions of the victim/survivor. Therefore, traditionally the crime of rape stood alone in terms of the legal standards used to define the offense.

Modern criminal law has made some advances in the legal definition of rape. Rape law reform efforts provide broad variation in rape law among the states. Typical statutory changes include: (1) criminalizing rape of the assailant's spouse, at least under some circumstances, (2) making statutes sex neutral, which criminalizes the rape of a male, (3) expanding the definition of sexual intercourse to include fellatio, cunnilingus, anal intercourse, and rape by instrumentation (penetration by an inanimate object), and (4) reducing the resistance required by the victim/survivor to resistance which is reasonable under the circumstances (Daane, 1988). A small number of states have eliminated the victim resistance requirement. Many states, however, still use traditional rape law elements. Interveners, in order to best serve the victim/survivor, should be familiar with the rape law in their state. The term *forcible rape* is often used to differentiate traditional rape from statutory rape, which is sexual intercourse with a female too young to give legal consent. No force is required for statutory rape. While this chapter deals exclusively with forcible rape, crisis intervention is also needed for the statutory rape victim/survivor as well.

Frequency and Characteristics

While it is nearly impossible to discuss the actual frequency of rape within American society, there are statistics offered by a number of sources which help one to grasp this crime's prevalence and incidence. It is important to note at the onset that the act of rape contains a large hidden figure in crime statistics. The hidden figure pertains to that proportion of a particular crime, which is measured, that is unknown. That is, the hidden figure accounts for the entire proportion of a crime which is not reported to the police or on various victimization surveys.

One source of the frequency of rape is the National Crime Victimization Survey (NCVS). The NCVS has the potential to overcome, in part, the problem of the hidden figure in rape victimization given that this source of crime data measures crimes which are known and unknown to the police, and subsequently the Uniform Crime Reports (UCR). The NCVS uses a social survey format in which households are sampled and individuals are interviewed concerning their recent victimization experiences in terms of violent as well as property and household crimes. This data source has revealed that between the years 1987 and 1991 there were 132,172 rapes reported to the NCVS with 58,614 being completed and 73,558 attempted (Bachman, 1994). In 1998, there were 110,270 rapes reported through the NCVS (BJS, 2000) and 1401,070 occurred in 1999 (BJS, 2001). This represents a 1.3 percent increase from 1998 to 1999. According to the UCR, during 1992 there were 109,060 crimes of rape known to the police (McGuire and Pastore, 1994). There were 93,144 rapes reported in 1998 and 89,107 reported in 1999 (FBI, 1999). This represents a 4.3 percent decrease during the same time period. The differences in the number of rapes, when comparing these two data sources would account for part of the hidden figure. As for various demographic characteristics of rape victims, the highest rate of rape victimization occurs for (1) African-American women, (2) those between the ages of 20–24, (3) women with a family income of less than $9,999 per year, (4) women who are divorced/separated or never married, and (5) women living in a central city (Bachman, 1994). According to this same data source, 55 percent of victims/survivors know their assailants while 44 percent reported having been raped by a stranger (Bachman, 1994).

REPORTING RAPE TO THE POLICE

Statistics from official sources, as well as surveys by social scientists, indicate that rape is vastly under reported (Williams, 1984). There are many reasons why victims/survivors choose not to report their rape to the police.

Common reasons include the fear of disbelief by the authorities, harmful publicity, retribution by the rapist, insensitive treatment by the police and hospital staff, rejection by mate or family, blame for the rape, and social stigma. Factors such as the victim's/survivor's age, race, marital status, level of self-confidence, relationship with the rapist, and circumstances of the rape are also factors in the decision to report a rape to the police.

Studies concerning the effect of the victim's/survivor's age, race, and marital status on reporting have conflicting results (Williams, 1984). A study by Cluss, Boughton, Frank, Stewart, and West (1983) indicates that women who report rape to the police are more likely to have greater self-esteem than victims/survivors who do not report a rape to the police. Feldman-Summers and Ashworth (1981) suggest that the victim's/survivor's perceived social support for reporting the rape is an important determinant of whether or not police will be notified of the rape. For example, victims/survivors who have had a prior relationship with the rapist and did not sustain any physical injury are less likely to report the rape than victims/survivors of stranger rape who are injured (Skelton and Burkhart, 1980). These victims/survivors fear being faced with disbelief or blame for their rape. All of the circumstances of the rape, including the type of force used by the assailant, the resistance offered by the victim/survivor, the location of the rape, and the level of violence are important factors in rape reporting. The more violent the rape, the more likely the victim/survivor is to report the rape (Williams, 1984).

According to Dukes and Mattley (1976), a victim/survivor who is extremely frightened immediately after the rape, and who perceives the police as concerned, efficient, and considerate is likely to report the rape to the police. Authorities may be perceived as a haven for safety. Victims/survivors who do not perceive the police as helpful and sensitive are less likely to report the rape. In many cases the decision to report a rape to the police is not made by the victim/survivor. Sometimes a third person acts at the request of the victim/survivor, but in some instances the third person makes the decision (Burgess and Holmstrom, 1973). In some states, hospitals that treat rape victims/survivors have a legal duty to report the rape to the authorities.

TYPES OF RAPE

There are several types of rape, each of which is classified by the victim's/survivor's relationship with the assailant. Technically, each type of rape is included under one rape law. Therefore, criminal law does not classify rape by the relationship between the rape victim/survivor and the rapist.

The types of rape include stranger rape, acquaintance rape, date rape, and marital rape. Stranger rape pertains to the case where the victim/survivor does not know the identity of the rapist prior to the assault. This is probably the most feared type of rape by women. *Stranger rape* is more likely to produce sympathetic reactions by others than any other type of rape. Additionally, there is often less blame assigned to the victim/survivor for stranger rape than for rape where the victim/survivor knows the assailant.

Date rape is defined as forced sexual intercourse, or any forced sexual behavior included under the state's rape law, that occurs after an individual has already agreed to accompany the assailant to a social occasion. It is too often assumed that if the victim/survivor has agreed to some social activity with the assailant, then she also agreed to a sexual relationship. Consent and force are generally the elements that are given the most attention in a date rape case.

Acquaintance rape involves forced sexual activity by someone the victim knows. It differs from date rape in that the victim may not have agreed to accompany the rapist to a social occasion. Consent is also a critical issue in acquaintance rape.

Marital rape occurs when forced sexual activity occurs between spouses. Traditionally, marital rape was not considered to be a crime, but recent statutory changes recognize it as a crime, at least under some circumstances. It is important to remember that marital rape is also a serious violent crime. Many people believe that marital rape involves a trivial misunderstanding between spouses. A recent study reveals, however, that the types of force used during marital rape, and the resulting injuries to the victim/survivor, indicate that marital rape is, in fact, a very violent crime (Daane, 1989).

If the elements of forcible rape are present, the crime is rape, whether the parties are strangers, acquaintances, casual dates, steady lovers, or a married couple.

VICTIM/SURVIVOR REACTION TO RAPE

How a victim/survivor reacts to a rape experience depends on many different factors. The reaction will be affected by age, life situation, personality, the circumstances of the rape, the response from those with whom the victim/survivor comes into contact immediately after the assault, the response of family, the response of the criminal justice system, the support received from family, friends, and coworkers, and the victim's/survivor's own attitudes about rape. Many victims/survivors have adopted society's traditional belief system concerning rape, including many of the myths. The victim/survivor will have greater difficulty understanding and integrating the rape into life experiences and progressing to survivorship if myths are believed.

Victim/survivor responses also vary during the attack. A majority of rape victims/survivors experience traumatic psychological infantilism during their contact with the rapist (Symonds, 1976). Psychological infantilism is induced by terror and results in helplessness, which gives the impression that the victim/survivor appears friendly and cooperative. The victim/survivor experiencing psychological infantilism, also known as *frozen fright response,* will likely submit in order to avoid being killed by the rapist. Unfortunately, this response may be misinterpreted by the victim's/survivor's family, friends, the police, hospital staff, crisis interveners, and even the victim/survivor. Other psychological reactions might include (Salzman and Summergrad, 1988; p. 48):

- Self-blame
- Fear of being killed
- Feelings of degradation and loss of self-esteem
- Feelings of depersonalization
- Recurrent intrusive thoughts
- Anxiety
- Depression

Victims/survivors who misunderstand their own responses during and after the rape may have a more difficult time adjusting to the experience.

Some victims/survivors feel anger as well as fright, but normally if there is any hope for survival, fright will override anger and the victim/survivor will engage in submitting behavior (Symonds, 1976). Anger is often shown through passive or active resistance. When anger is repressed, passive resistance patterns appear in the form of crying, slowness to obey commands, and the appearance that they are unable to understand exactly what is demanded of them. Passive patterns of resistance also include verbal attempts to make the rapist feel guilty or appeals to the rapist's conscience in an attempt to coerce the rapist to cease the attack.

Active patterns of resistance attempt to produce a fear of being hurt or apprehended in the rapist. Since active, physical aggression has traditionally been socially disapproved for women, the rape victim's/survivor's active patterns of resistance are also generally verbal. The victim's/survivor's response at the time of the rape may have a substantial impact upon the ability to cope with the experience. How crisis interveners can help the victim integrate coping strategies at the time of the rape into the recovery process will be explored in the intervention section of this chapter.

There is a lack of consensus in the literature regarding the precise nature of the victim's/survivor's reaction to a rape experience. However, there is agreement on some issues of victim/survivor response to rape. There is agreement that rape is a highly traumatic crisis causing disruption for the victim/survivor physically, behaviorally, emotionally, and interpersonally. There is also agreement that the victim's/survivor's immediate reaction to rape is indicative of extreme disruption, and that long-term effects of the rape experience are fairly significant (Gilmartin, 1985).

Several theorists have labeled and identified stages or phases of recovery for the rape victim/survivor. These phases were originally identified by Burgess and Holmstrom (1974) and identified under the diagnostic label of *Rape Trauma Syndrome*. Some theories divide recovery into three stages while others divide recovery into six or seven stages. To discuss each theory in detail would be too cumbersome and confusing for a single chapter on rape intervention. Therefore, this chapter will instead discuss the commonalties found within the various theories.

The first stage explained in the literature is the time immediately following the rape. During this initial phase, the victim/survivor of rape generally experiences an overwhelming sense of shock and is unable to believe what has happened. Feelings of helplessness and powerlessness are common. It is not uncommon for a victim to say "I can't believe this has happened to me." No one is ever prepared to experience such a traumatic experience. The victim/survivor also generally experiences gross anxiety, total loss of control, confusion, and a sense of unreality. The victim/survivor will generally feel very vulnerable. Guilt and shame are also fairly universal feelings immediately after a sexual assault. The experience itself will often bring on physical exhaustion.

One of the primary victim/survivor responses during this phase is extreme fear, which sometimes borders on panic. A majority of victims/survivors report that they believed their death was imminent. Their entire sense of safety has been shattered. Anger is not a primary emotion at this stage. Anger typically surfaces at later stages in the recovery process. When victims/survivors do feel anger, it is often inner-directed in the form of self-blame for putting themselves in a position to be raped or for not offering more resistance. Their anger may be repressed and experienced as guilt and shame. Women traditionally have been expected to be passive and express less aggression, which often leads to anger being transformed into culturally supported self-blame (Notman and Nadelson, 1976).

Burgess and Holmstrom (1973) identify two different styles of behavior common among rape victims/survivors during this phase. One style is the *expressed style* where feelings of fear, anger, or anxiety are expressed verbally or shown through such behavior as crying, shaking, smiling, restlessness, and tenseness. Victims/survivors with the *controlled style* mask or hide their feelings and appear calm, composed, and subdued. Both behavior styles are common. It is not unusual for one victim/survivor to have both responses during the course of one interview; therefore, these responses tend not to be mutually exclusive. While both responses are common and are to be expected, Forman (1980) notes that the behavioral style most frequently displayed in metropolitan emergency rooms is the controlled style. The normal emotional style of the victim/survivor influences which behavioral style the victim/survivor of sexual assault will adopt during the initial recovery phase. Other factors such as exhaustion, the attitude of those in attendance, and normal verbal style are also factors influencing the adopted behavioral style.

Immediately after the sexual assault, the victim/survivor is also faced with concerns of venereal disease. Female victims/survivors also face gynecological examinations, and the fear of pregnancy as a result of the rape. If victim/survivor plans to cooperate with prosecution, then participation in the criminal justice process is necessary. The victim/survivor will endure many trying moments even though s/he is already emotionally exhausted.

During the next phase of recovery, the victim/survivor appears to have adjusted to the event. In reality, the victim/survivor rarely has adjusted well at all. Pressure from society to return to the previous lifestyle causes the victim/survivor to return to the normal routine as soon as possible, denying the impact of the violent and personal nature of rape. The rape victim/survivor is generally in psychological denial, with little insight into the situation. Life is approached superficially and mechanically.

The victim/survivor normally continues to feel all of the same emotions felt immediately after the rape; however, these feelings generally will be less intense. In addition, victims often feel alienation, isolation, and depression. Nightmares, sleeplessness, flashbacks, and anxiety caused by some small cue, which is a reminder of the rape, may be experienced. These cues may be such things as being alone, darkness, a person with an appearance similar to the rapist, or the make of a car in which the rape occurred. Many victims/survivors begin to avoid situations that elicit such cues.

The rape victim/survivor may also experience physical symptoms such as headaches, stomach or gastrointestinal problems, dizziness, unintentional weight loss, difficulty in breathing, and sexual dysfunction. Emotional responses include moodiness, decreased concentration, crying spells, tension, sadness, decreased self-confidence and self-esteem, and feelings of being out of control (Gilmartin, 1985).

Posttraumatic Stress Disorder, or PTSD, is a possible consequence of rape and other forms of violent victimization (Creamer, 2000; Foa, 1998). Salzman and Summergrad (1988) provide a description of typical and normal long-term psychiatric effects of rape trauma. Under the rubric of posttraumatic stress disorder, there are several symptoms found within the *Diagnostic and Statistical Manual of Mental Disorders,* Fourth Edition (DSM-IV) (American Psychiatric Association, 1994) which typify the victimization experience, including but not limited to rape, posttraumatically. These are:

- recurrent and intrusive distressing recollections of the event, including images, thoughts, or perceptions
- recurrent distressing dreams of the event
- acting or feeling as if the traumatic event were recurring
- intense psychological distress at exposure to internal or external cues that symbolize or resemble an aspect of the traumatic event
- physiological reactivity on exposure to internal or external cues that symbolize or resemble an aspect of the traumatic event (p. 428)

Salzman and Summergrad (1988) also offer a list of possible *long-term post-traumatic symptoms* characteristic of the rape victim/survivor:

- fear of walking or being alone
- fear of men
- repetitive nightmares recapitulating the assault
- continued self-blame for not preventing the attack which manifests itself in alienation from supportive family and friends (p. 49)

The next phase for the rape victim/survivor includes similar responses, but with some adjustment. It is at this time that the victim/survivor tends to make lifestyle changes such as moving, changing jobs, changing phone numbers, refusing to go out alone or at night, and changing patterns of work, study, or socializing. These are also often referred to as behavioral changes. It is at this time that victims/survivors begin to experience more interpersonal problems. They will often begin to experience difficulty in relationships with significant others, parents, children, employer, and friends.

Eventually, a phase, which is characterized by anger, is reached by the victim/survivor. Generally, blame and anger have shifted from the victim/survivor to the rapist. Anger may also be directed toward the police, a prosecutor, society, a counselor, or persons of the same gender as the rapist. Victims/survivors often want someone to suffer for what has happened to them. However, the anger is rarely expressed in aggressive behavior.

The victim/survivor who can successfully integrate the reality of the rape into life experiences will also experience the *resolution phase*. While never forgetting, the victim/survivor will eventually be able to put the experience behind him/her and will be able to discuss the victimization constructively.

While several phases may be identifiable, it does not necessarily mean that each rape victim/survivor experiences each phase in sequence, or that each phase is experienced only once. It is common for rape victims/survivors to have setbacks when they experience another trauma, and especially when they again become involved in criminal justice processing of the rape case.

It is not unusual for victims/survivors to experience extreme trauma during the trial.

Early theorists believed that most rape victims/survivors were able to accomplish resolution in a fairly short period of time. More recent studies indicate that resolution, in which the victim/survivor returns to pre-rape levels of functioning, may not exist for many rape victims/survivors. For those victims/survivors who can reach resolution, it generally requires a substantial period of time. Research by Kilpatrick, Resick, and Veronen (1981) indicates that victims/survivors continue to suffer from the effects of sexual assault for at least one year after the rape. Many problems experienced post-rape are significant, but the primary problems are rape-related fear and anxiety. Kilpatrick, Resick, and Veronen's (1981) work indicates that the bulk of recovery by rape victims/survivors occurs in the first three months following the rape. They found no significant difference in functioning between the three-month, six-month, and one-year time periods.

It is suggested that one's life-stage is a significant factor in adjustment. According to Notman and Nadelson (1976), those who are younger, single, divorced or separated, or middle-aged experience more serious concern over their independence after a rape than those not possessing these characteristics or traits.

It is important to remember that each rape victim/survivor is an individual not easily pigeonholed into phases of recovery. Victims/survivors respond and adjust at their own pace and in their own unique way. Many victims/ survivors are able to return to pre-rape levels of functioning, but others may never reach this point of recovery. As Sales, Baum, and Shore (1984) note, victim/survivor psychosocial resources and the violence of the assault influence the progression of recovery, but such factors may weigh differentially at various stages of recovery.

CRISIS INTERVENTION WITH THE RAPE VICTIM/SURVIVOR

For a rape victim/survivor, counseling is beneficial through all stages of recovery, but crisis intervention during the initial stages immediately after the rape is crucial to adjustment. Effective crisis intervention not only helps the victim/survivor to work through the crisis, but also may prevent psychological disorders resulting from the rape (Burgess and Holmstrom, 1973) and appropriate considerations when addressing the needs of women in crisis (Hartman, 1997). The goal of crisis intervention with a rape victim/survivor is to assist in returning the victim/survivor to pre-crisis (pre-rape) levels of functioning.

Information Gathering

Prior to arrival at the victim's/survivor's location, the intervener should gather as much information as possible about the crisis and the victim/survivor. Sources of information vary, but they may include police officers, police dispatchers, emergency medical personnel, witnesses, friends and relatives of the victim/survivor, and other interveners. Information collected should include the victim's/survivor's name, address, a brief description of the incident, and the names of any witnesses. If the intervener is meeting the victim/survivor some place other than a rape crisis center or the emergency room of a hospital, directions and a description of the neighborhood where the crime occurred should also be obtained. While the more information the intervener can gather the better s/he can assess the crisis, it should not prevent the intervener from making contact with the victim/survivor as soon as possible. The victim/survivor should not be kept waiting for long periods of time while the intervener gathers information.

Initial Contact Between the Victim/Survivor and Intervener

When approaching the victim/survivor, the intervener should be calm, friendly and supportive. An intervener who is obviously upset or nervous about the situation will not be able to help the victim/survivor to be at ease. The intervener should address the victim/survivor with respect, not using the victim's/survivor's first name until invited to do so. The intervener should immediately introduce him/herself to the victim/survivor and explain her/his purpose for being there. It is important that the victim/survivor understand that the intervener is there to help and to be an advocate.

One of the first responsibilities of the intervener is to assess the needs of the victim/survivor. While the needs of the victim/survivor will vary based on individual circumstances and the stage at which the intervener is notified, the rape victim's/survivor's immediate needs generally include the following (Abarbanel, 1976):

Information–The rape victim/survivor will need information about what to do immediately following the rape: where to go for medical services, how to obtain help for the psychological consequences of rape, what will be expected if the rape is reported to the police, and how to obtain legal services if the victim/survivor chooses to cooperate with prosecution.

Medical Care–The rape victim/survivor will need medical services to diagnose and treat any injuries received during the rape, as well as to prevent venereal disease and unwanted pregnancy. In addition, physical evidence is also collected during the medical examination.

Counseling–Counseling will be needed to help the victim/survivor cope with the immediate situation and anticipate future problems that may be encountered.

Sensitive Treatment–Police officers, nurses, social workers, physicians, interveners, and anyone else having direct contact with the victim/survivor must treat the victim/survivor with sensitivity, remembering that the victim/survivor has just experienced an emotional and physical crisis.

Support–The victim/survivor will need support from family and friends to help resolve the crisis.

Legal Assistance–The victim/survivor will need information about legal rights and legal representation in the criminal justice system.

If the intervener is called before the victim/survivor decides whether or not to report the rape to the police, the intervener must help the victim/survivor understand the issues involved and provide sufficient information to the victim/survivor so that an informed decision can be made. It is imperative that the intervener not make the reporting decision on the victim's/survivor's behalf. The rape victim/survivor typically experiences loss of control over life, emotions, and decision making. Allowing the victim/survivor to make the decision to report the crime or to not report the crime will help the victim/survivor to restore, at least in part, a sense of control. It is important that the victim/survivor feel sense of control return as quickly as possible. The intervener, faced with an emotionally devastated individual, may believe it is easier for the victim/survivor by making this decision, but in reality, this merely prolongs recovery.

Emergency Medical Intervention

Whether or not the victim/survivor decides to report the crime to the police, immediate medical attention will be needed. The victim/survivor has suffered physical trauma and must be examined for physical injury. If the intervener has made contact with the victim/survivor prior to seeking medical treatment, the intervener must let the victim/survivor know how important it is to receive medical treatment, regardless of whether the victim/survivor believes injuries exist. The female victim/survivor must not only consider treatment for injuries received but also prevention of pregnancy and venereal disease. Victims/survivors who seek medical attention tend to recover emotionally more quickly than victims/survivors who do not seek medical treatment (Johnson, 1985). Seeking medical attention creates recognition on the part of the victim/survivor that she has undergone a serious physical trauma. The support received from hospital staff often assists in emotional recovery as well.

If the victim/survivor has obvious injuries that need to be treated immediately, an ambulance should be summoned so that the victim/survivor may receive prompt treatment. If the community has a specialized ambulance team for treating rape victims/survivors, they should be called. If possible, the victim/survivor may also choose a hospital or medical center specializing in rape victim/survivor care. If the victim's/survivor's medical needs do not appear to be an emergency, the victim/survivor can be transported to the emergency room or crisis center by the intervener, a friend, or a family member.

The victim/survivor should be advised not to wash, change clothes, or freshen up in any way before proceeding to the hospital. The victim's/survivor's appearance may provide critical evidence for the assailant's future prosecution. Most victims/survivors feel dirty and want to bathe and change clothes before proceeding to the hospital. It is important for her to understand the necessity of preserving any physical evidence of the attack. Even if the victim/survivor does not wish to have the perpetrator prosecuted at this time, the victim/survivor may have a change of heart at some later date.

The victim/survivor should not be left alone in the emergency room. Priority in treatment should also be given. While physical injuries may not appear to be severe, the victim/survivor has experienced an extreme crisis and should be treated as soon as possible. The nature of the emergency room dictates that persons with life-threatening injuries will be treated first. Rape victims/survivors should be given priority after life-threatening injuries.

Hospitals and their staffs have priorities; some include treatment of rape victims/survivors, some do not. The rape victim/survivor should plan to spend several hours in the emergency room. In addition to waiting, time may be spent answering questions and filling out forms before the examination.

The intervener should prepare the victim/survivor for what to expect from the hospital staff. First, a series of questions for admission will be asked, followed by questions about current health and sexual behavior. The victim/survivor will also be asked to provide a summary of the time, place, and circumstances of the sexual assault. This information is necessary to help diagnose and treat the victim/survivor. The victim/survivor will undergo a brief exam to diagnose general trauma. A record will be made of general appearance, physical and emotional condition, bruises, lacerations, and torn or bloody clothing.

The female victim/survivor will also be required to undergo a gynecological examination to evaluate internal injury and to preserve evidence. Specimens will be collected to test for the presence of sperm, seminal fluid, infection, and venereal disease. It is important that the procedures be explained to the victim/survivor prior to the examination. It is difficult for the rape victim/survivor to undergo a pelvic exam immediately after a rape. Both the rape and the exam are viewed as an unwanted intrusion. Young victims/survivors who have never had a pelvic exam before may be especially fearful of the exam. Their concerns must be treated seriously. Allowing them to indicate when they are ready for the exam will help them establish control. This is especially important for a process that may be viewed as being so similar to the sexual assault.

It is also of utmost importance that the victim/survivor be examined in private. Privacy recognizes the trauma the victim/survivor has experienced, as well as allowing the victim/survivor to try to regain some sense of control over the situation. If the hospital staff does not automatically provide the rape victim/survivor with a private examination room, one should explain the medical process and treat the victim/survivor with respect and understanding. It is at this point that the intervener must be an advocate for the victim/survivor. Traditionally, hospital staff did not view the rape victim/survivor as a legitimate consumer of health services because injuries often did not appear to be significant. Attitudes are changing as society is educated about the seriousness of the crime of rape. Today, many hospitals have a group of staff members trained specifically to handle rape cases professionally and sensitively.

The victim/survivor will also be asked to provide blood and urine samples. These tests are conducted primarily to detect a prior pregnancy, venereal disease, and the contraction of HIV (the virus which causes AIDS). However, in some cases the victim's/survivor's blood alcohol level is also determined from the samples. If the victim/survivor is under the influence of alcohol or drugs, the defense may use this evidence to attack the victim's/survivor's credibility as a witness during a rape prosecution. If the witness had a drink after the sexual assault in an attempt to help handle the situation, the hospital staff should be made aware of it. During the trial, the victim's/ survivor's state of sobriety at the time of the assault may be at issue. Head and pubic combings, and fingernail scrapings will also be conducted to collect possible evidence. The victim's/survivor's clothing may also be retained for use as evidence. Photographs of the victim/survivor will most likely be taken. The victim/survivor may request photographs to be taken by someone of the same gender.

In addition to treatment for immediate injuries and the collection and preservation of evidence, the medical exam for female victims/survivors must also address the issues of unwanted pregnancy and the possibility of venereal disease. These are two of the most critical concerns that a female rape victim/survivor faces immediately after the assault. The physician will discuss the victim's/survivor's present birth control method and menstrual cycle with her, consider her present health, and determine whether or not to administer the "morning after pill." The victim should be advised of the side effects of this drug, including nausea and abdominal pains (Burgess and Holmstrom, 1976).

Routine treatment of female rape victims/survivors usually includes antibiotics for the prevention of venereal disease. Even if the victim/survivor receives this treatment, she should be advised that a follow-up medical exam is advisable to detect and treat venereal disease. Tests for pregnancy and venereal disease should be conducted six weeks after the assault.

The intervener may help make the hospital experience less traumatic for the rape victim/survivor by informing the victim/survivor as to what to expect which allows the victim/survivor to predict events and to regain control. There may also be items that the victim/survivor will need. Small items such as safety pins, a glass of water, cigarettes, and a wash basin with warm water (for after the exam), and fresh clothing may make a tremendous difference in the comfort of the rape victim/survivor. Transportation home from the hospital may also be needed.

Victim/Survivor Coping Process and Aftercare

In addition to helping the victim understand and cope with the medical process, the intervener should also be attending to the emotional needs of the victim during and after immediate crisis intervention. One of the most important aspects of crisis counseling a rape victim/survivor is listening, understanding, and being supportive. "When a person is understood, she is no longer alone and is more in control of her situation" (Burgess & Holmstrom, 1973).

One of the primary emotions felt by rape victims/survivors is fear. No matter what behavior type the victim/survivor exhibits in reaction to the crisis, assurance of safety is important. Fear and anxiety will continue to be the most predominate emotions for the victim/survivor to contend with even months after the attack, so no amount of counseling will completely eliminate the fear during the initial stages. However, some amount of safety can be experienced if the proper emotional support is offered.

While it is important for the intervener to allow the victim/survivor to vent feelings and to offer emotional support, the intervener must not force the victim/survivor to discuss or deal with feelings prematurely. A sense of trust must be developed between the crisis counselor and the victim/survivor before any meaningful communication can begin.

Many times the victim/survivor will express unrealistic or irrational concerns. The intervener can help to alleviate such concerns by discussing them with the victim/survivor and explaining why they may be unrealistic or irrational concerns. However, this must not be done in a condescending manner. Anyone who has undergone a severe emotional and physical crisis like rape can be expected to have many concerns, some of which may be more realistic than others.

As mentioned earlier, many rape victims/survivors blame themselves for the rape and this self-blame may continue long after the immediate rape crisis has past. This response is an oft-cited consequence of victim contact with the criminal justice system (Koss, 2000). Victims believe that if they had done something differently, they would not have experienced the assault and subsequent crisis. Perhaps they shouldn't have been sleeping with the window open, or perhaps if they had fought harder they would not have been raped; maybe they shouldn't have accepted a date with someone they had just met. Part of this self-blame is based on society's attitudes and beliefs as well as the myths about rape. At times, others will blame the victim/survivor for having been victimized. Such blame may come from those expected to be supportive and helpful to the victim/survivor such as the police, the victim's family and friends, and hospital workers. The general public may also blame the victim/survivor of rape if there is publicity concerning the incident. These attitudes contribute to the victimization and compounds feelings of self-blame already experienced by the victim/survivor. It is important to help victims/survivors understand why they may feel the way they do and how to cope with the feelings. Part of the self-blame involves anger. Women often learn that anger expressed as aggressive behavior is inappropriate. Women in American culture have learned that it is more acceptable for women to express anger passively through self-blame than through aggression (Notman and Nadelson, 1976).

Some researchers believe that a victim's/survivor's feelings of guilt and self-blame are in fact defense mechanisms (Evans, 1978). For example, if a female victim/survivor believes that she was at fault for the rape, then she may believe that by changing her own behavior, she can prevent a similar event from ever happening to her again. Naturally, the thought of experiencing a second rape is intolerable for her. In believing that she can prevent a rape from happening again, she is able to restore some sense of control and reduce her feelings of vulnerability.

Other researchers believe that guilt and self-blame by the victim/survivor prevents recognition of the trauma experienced by the victim/survivor and interferes with the ability to cope with the crisis. It is also believed that victim-blaming attitudes held by the public lead to inadequate community resources to investigate and prosecute rape as well as to provide services for the victims/survivors of rape (McCombie, Bassuk, Savitz, and Pell, 1976).

Guilt, shame, and self-blame are universal reactions to rape. Neither the level of violence nor the relationship between the rapist and the victim/survivor has an impact on these reactions. Helping the victim/survivor to understand that rape is a violent crime, which uses sex as a method of violence, power, and control, and that rape is not a sex crime, may alleviate some of the victim's/survivor's feelings of guilt and self-blame.

Another important technique in helping a victim/survivor overcome feelings of guilt and self-blame is to explore the coping behavior used before and during the rape. Victims/survivors may not understand their own coping behaviors. They need to understand that the rapist used terrorism which, with most violent crime, leads to immediate compliance by victims/survivors (Symonds, 1976). As discussed earlier, many rape victims/survivors respond to the rapist with traumatic psychological infantilism, or frozen fright, which appears to be cooperative behavior. However, it is merely a coping response to avoid death (Symonds, 1976).

Victims/survivors may respond to the rape situation with a variety of coping behaviors. Understanding the rape victim's/survivor's coping behavior and strategies when faced with the life-threatening situation of rape is an essential step in crisis intervention and emotional aftercare (Burgess and Holmstrom, 1976). By listening to the rape victim/survivor tell the story of the rape, the intervener can identify coping behavior and may help the victim/survivor in understanding behaviors. "This support tells victims/survivors that their coping behavior was a positive adaptive mechanism used to survive a life-threatening situation" (Burgess and Holmstrom, 1976). Exploring coping behavior helps to alleviate the guilt and self-blame suffered by the victim.

Burgess and Holmstrom (1976) identify basic coping strategies used by rape victims before the attack. They include:

Cognitive Assessment–Victims/survivors cope with sexual assault by assessing the situation and determining possible alternatives. This may mean that victims/survivors are looking for a means of escape, but often means that *they* are planning a way to remain calm so that the rapist doesn't panic and further hurt or kill.

Verbal Tactics–Many victims/survivors try to talk their way out of the situation by stalling for time, reasoning with the assailant to change his mind, trying to gain sympathy from the rapist, using flattery, feigning illness, verbal aggression, joking, sarcasm, and threats that someone will be coming soon. The majority of these tactics are verbal.

Physical Action–Some victims/survivors take physical action to prevent the attack. Physical action includes running away and/or trying to fight the rapist.

Victims/survivors suffering from frozen fright are unable to use any of the coping strategies suggested by Burgess and Holmstrom. However, their appearance of cooperativeness is a coping behavior.

Burgess and Holmstrom (1976) also identify coping strategies used by rape victims/survivors during the attack. These include:

Cognitive Strategies–Victims/survivors often focus on something else during the attack to avoid the reality of the event and to focus on their survival.

They also control themselves mentally to remain calm and to prevent provoking any additional violence. Some victims/survivors also concentrate on memorizing details, such as the assailant's face or general appearance; others concentrate on advice they have been given on how to cope with such an event. Compliance is often used to survive the attack.

Verbal Strategies–Verbal strategies vary. They include screaming for help, talking to the assailant to calm him, and threatening the assailant.

Physical Action–Some victims/survivors struggle and fight with the rapist to avoid penetration. Victims/survivors often struggle to a point, then realize it is hopeless, and stop.

Physiological Response–Not all coping behavior is voluntary and conscious. Victims/survivors report such physiological responses as choking, gagging, nausea, vomiting, pain, urination, hyperventilating, and losing consciousness.

Coping behavior is also important immediately after the attack. Victims/survivors must escape from the rapist or free themselves from where they have been left, and tell others of their situation and need for help.

When a rape victim/survivor understands coping behavior, especially coping behavior before and during the assault, then working through feelings of guilt and self-blame is successful and more probable. This, in turn, enhances the ability to restore the victim/survivor to pre-crisis levels of emotional functioning. This will also help to focus anger on the assailant and not the self. Crisis intervention with a rape victim/survivor is not over when the victim leaves the hospital. It involves a series of contacts with the victim/survivor. It is generally recommended that the intervener contact the victim/survivor 24 to 48 hours after the assault to see how the victim/ survivor is handling the situation and to offer additional assistance. Weekly follow-up calls are also suggested until the victim/survivor is no longer in need of the services the intervener can provide.

Many rape victims/survivors need, and may benefit from, further counseling. We know that the effects of rape last for long periods of time for many victims/survivors. Professional counseling is often advisable to help the victim/survivor recover as fully as possible. The crisis intervener should be prepared to refer the victim/survivor to local agencies and programs that offer counseling and other specialized aftercare services for rape victims/survivors.

The intervener should also talk with family and friends that may accompany the victim/survivor to mobilize their support for the victim/survivor. Family members and significant others will have questions and concerns which need to be addressed. They also need to be advised concerning what to expect from the rape victim/survivor, as well as the possible and potential changes the survivor will likely experience as a result of the attack.

FAMILY AND MATE RESPONSE AND INTERVENTION

Rape is also traumatic for the mate, family, and friends of the victim/survivor. In many instances, persons with close relationships with the victim/survivor experience intense emotional reactions to the rape. These feelings and reactions come in several different forms.

If the victim's/survivor's potential support group believes in the same myths, prejudices, and misunderstandings about rape as the general public, their response will be based on the myths. Moreover, it is not unusual for the mate to react to the sexual aspects of the crime rather than the violence (Silverman, 1978). Husbands, boyfriends, and lovers who believe that "good women don't get raped" may feel resentment and anger toward the victim/survivor. They are also more likely to blame the victim/survivor for the rape. If the victim's/survivor's mate or family reacts by blaming her for the rape, her feelings of guilt and self-blame will be reinforced and thus more difficult to overcome. The male mate's anger may be expressed openly or indirectly. Anger that is expressed indirectly often takes the form of doubting the victim's/survivor's story, criticizing her for not being more careful, and wondering whether she enjoyed the experience (Silverman, 1978). Many times the mate is not consciously aware that he is feeling resentment and anger toward the victim/survivor.

Sometimes husbands, boyfriends, and lovers view their female mate as property (Silverman, 1978). The rape of their mate may help these males to feel that their property interest in the woman has been devalued, because she is now tainted, unclean, and used or damaged merchandise. Men manifesting this reaction are not likely to be highly supportive of the victim/survivor. Some mates respond with feelings of guilt. They believe that their masculinity has been challenged by their failure to protect their partner (Notman and Nadelson, 1976). This often leads to the desire for revenge. Revenge may be used to help the mate regain control. Unfortunately, a male who is seeking revenge often puts the victim/survivor in the position of calming and comforting him at a time when she needs support.

It is important to remember that the victim's/survivor's mate does have legitimate reasons for feeling an emotional response to the rape. Someone for whom they care has been victimized in a very personal, violent, and dehumanizing manner. It is normal for the mate to be upset in this situation. It is also important to remember that some males will react with concern and support for the victim/survivor. Parents and siblings of rape victims/survivors may experience a sense of shock, helplessness, rage, or physical revulsion immediately after the rape (Silverman, 1978). These feelings are similar to what the victim/survivor is feeling. Fathers and brothers of the female victim/survivor often feel a desire for revenge similar to the feelings of the male mate.

Family reaction to the rape crisis often results in patronization and over-protection of the victim/survivor (Silverman, 1978). This reaction may result in the victim/survivor losing a sense of independence and self-confidence. It also makes regaining control more difficult. Other families resort to distraction, trying to keep the victim/survivor busy so that the incident can be forgotten. This may make the rape victim/survivor feel that the family is trivializing the trauma and seriousness of the experience. This may result in denying the victim/survivor the opportunity to progress through the phases of recovery and to have genuine support. Some families react with a feeling of shame and humiliation, and the desire to keep the experience a family secret. This reaction reinforces the victim's/survivor's feelings of shame, guilt, and humiliation. It also denies any meaningful support.

Because a victim's/survivor's mate, family, and friends may react to the rape crisis based on their own beliefs in the myths about rape, the victim/survivor may choose not to tell them about the rape or may choose to tell only certain people. Often a rape victim/survivor tells one person and asks him/her to notify other family members. However, most victims do tell their family about the rape. Those victims/survivors who do not disclose the rape incident to their family generally withhold the information for one of five reasons. According to a study by Burgess and Holmstrom (1979), rape victims/survivors decline to tell family members about their rape because: (1) they want to protect the family from upsetting news; (2) they believe that their family will not understand because of their attitudes about rape, their religious orientation, or their disapproval of the victim's/survivor's lifestyle; (3) they want to maintain their independence from their family; (4) they are not psychologically close to their family; or (5) they live some physical distance from their family. Rape victims/survivors are most likely to tell their significant other about the rape (Feldman-Summers & Ashworth, 1981). This is not surprising, since hiding this information would be difficult in an intimate or close relationship.

As a general rule, crisis intervention theory encourages rape victims/survivors to seek support from their family and friends. However, in some cases family members and friends may react negatively and cause further stress for the rape victim/survivor. In such instances, these family members and friends should not be included in the support network if it can be avoided. It is important for the rape victim/survivor to predict how a potential support group will react before disclosing the rape to them (Burgess and Holmstrom, 1979). The victim/survivor should then carefully choose those with whom information concerning the rape is shared.

Interveners should counsel the victims/survivors to make these predictions. Interveners can help victims/survivors remember how family members reacted to prior stressful news, and weigh the advantages of telling and not telling family members. It is important for the intervener to allow the victim/survivor to make the decision whether to disclose the rape to family members, and to support the decision made. If the victim/survivor chooses to tell family members, the intervener should prepare the victim/survivor to address either a reaction of support or a reaction of nonsupport.

"Growing clinical experience makes clear the absolute necessity of involving important members of the victim's [survivor's] social network in the post-rape counseling intervention" (Silverman, 1978). The victim's/survivor's family and mate can provide an environment that facilitates recovery through support, lack of blame, and openness. The family's needs during intervention are similar to the victim's/survivor's needs. These needs include information, counseling, sensitive treatment, and support.

Information is an essential part of crisis intervention with the victim's/survivor's mate and family. They will need information on the nature of the crime of rape. It is important that they understand that rape is a violent crime, not a sexual experience. Understanding that the victim/survivor has been through a life-threatening experience will help them to understand the experience and reactions. Family members should also be given information about the kind of response to expect from the victim/survivor, and that there may be several phases through which the victim/survivor pass. They also need to understand that this is not a trauma that will go away, no matter what they do. Recovery takes time, and in many instances, years.

Working with mates and family members who share society's myths and misunderstandings about rape is both essential and stressful. Interveners should be non-critical in their response to family members and mates of rape victims/survivors. If family members and mates do become defensive, they will not absorb the information that is important for them to help the victim/survivor cope with the crisis. One method of counseling mates is to discuss their injuries and to let them express their pain and loss as a result of the rape. This allows them to ventilate their feelings and to understand that the victim's/survivor's crisis is a shared crisis. They should be encouraged to talk openly about their feelings without being critical. Rape myths should be worked through gently. The mate is generally a victim's/survivor's prime source of emotional support. The victim/survivor does not need a mate who not only adheres to the myths, but has been made defensive by the intervener. Many families and mates are anxious to understand the facts about rape and to discard the myths. They may never have explored these issues before, and welcome the opportunity to have the facts. It is typical for even the most supportive families and mates to feel helpless. They may want to be supportive, but don't have the slightest idea how to be.

The intervener needs to help the family and mate understand that the victim/survivor needs an environment free from blame where the victim/survivor can discuss the incident. They also need to understand that it is counterproductive to attempt to force a discussion of the rape when the victim/survivor doesn't want to discuss it. The victim/survivor needs encouragement and support from the mate and family. Denying that the rape ever occurred or refusal to talk about it with the victim/survivor tends to make the victim/survivor feel isolated. Families and mates should be prepared for the phases through which the victim/survivor may progress. They need to understand that this is normal. It is also important for the family and mate to understand the criminal justice process that the victim/survivor may be encountering and how participating in the system may involve temporary setbacks in the recovery process.

Families and mates also need to understand their own response to the rape. They should be cautioned against responses involving over protection, absolute distraction, shame, humiliation, or extreme secretiveness. Families and mates often want to "make it all better" for the victim/survivor. They need to understand that there is no magic cure, and that their nonaccusing attitude and support are what the victim/survivor needs to activate coping skills.

THE RAPE VICTIM/SURVIVOR AND THE CRIMINAL JUSTICE SYSTEM

The criminal justice system has been accused repeatedly of victimizing the already traumatized rape victim/survivor. These accusations have helped bring about some changes in the criminal justice processing of rape cases. Such changes have occurred primarily in three areas: (1) the use of specialized teams in law enforcement agencies and prosecutors' offices to address rape cases; (2) the development of victim advocate and victim witness programs; and (3) laws reforming the manner in which rape cases are prosecuted (Byington, 1990).

The crisis intervener working with rape victims/survivors should have a basic understanding of criminal justice system operations, policies, and procedures in order to explain to the victim/survivor what might be expected at each stage in the criminal justice process. This section includes a brief description of major factors affecting a rape victim/survivor who passes through the criminal justice process.

Rape Victims/Survivors and the Police

One of the reasons that rape victims/survivors fail to report rape to the police is a belief that the police who investigate the crime will be insensitive.

Several studies support the belief that some police officers have unsympathetic attitudes toward rape victims/survivors. However, one nationwide study (LeDoux and Hazelwood, 1985) indicates that officers are not typically insensitive to the plight of rape victims/survivors. Whether the police officer realizes it or not, the officer who responds to a call for help from a rape victim/survivor is a crisis intervener. This puts the police officer in a position of being an intervener as well as an investigator. These are not necessarily conflicting roles. If the victim/survivor is treated in a professional manner with kindness, understanding, and patience, the victim/survivor is better able and more inclined to be of assistance to the officer acting in the investigative role (Hendricks, 1983). Many police departments have specially trained officers to handle rape cases. However, it is important for all officers to receive training about the nature of the crime of rape, and the intervention process.

Rape Victims/Survivors and the Courts

The rape victim and the culture of the American courtroom has been given some research attention (Taslitz, 1999). The prosecutor and prosecution staff are not immune to the myths about rape. Decisions about the prosecution of a rape case may be made by someone who adheres to the myths. While this is not true of all prosecutors, some treat a rape victim/survivor differently and with more suspicion than any other victim/survivor of violent crime. There have been cases where the prosecution required rape victims/survivors to pass a polygraph examination before the case would be prosecuted. There is no other crime where the victims/survivors are so regularly required to submit to such measures as a prerequisite to prosecution.

Prosecutors have substantial discretion in determining whether and how to proceed with a case. This is known as prosecutorial discretion. One factor that is generally considered before any case is filed is whether or not the state's case is strong enough to secure a conviction. Even when a prosecutor is aware of the facts and is not swayed by the myths about rape, the attitude of the community is sometimes considered when filing a case that may result in a jury trial.

Many rape victims/survivors are dismayed to discover that after they have experienced several periods of questioning, and are asked about specific details of the rape, the prosecution decides not to file formal charges against the offender. It is helpful to the victim/survivor if the prosecutor explains the reason for the decision. This helps the victim/survivor to understand that the prosecutor is not discounting the experience. The victim/survivor may also see a legitimate reason not to proceed with the prosecution. For example, in a state that requires corroborating evidence of the rape by way of witness testimony, or physical evidence, the prosecutor will choose not to proceed with the case if corroborating evidence is not available, or if it is available but not admissible under the rules of evidence.

Before the trial, there may be several pretrial court proceedings. The victim/survivor generally is not required to be in attendance. The initial hearing is merely to advise the accused of the charges. The arraignment allows the defendant to enter a plea to the charges. The initial hearing and arraignment are combined in many jurisdictions. There normally is no need for the victim/survivor to be present at either of these proceedings. The preliminary hearing is a hearing where some evidence is presented against the defendant so that the judge can determine whether the state has sufficient evidence to continue its prosecution. The victim/survivor is often required to testify at the preliminary hearing. The preliminary hearing is generally shorter than the trial and slightly less formal.

In some cases the accused may choose to plead guilty to a crime after making an agreement with the prosecution concerning either the charges or the punishment. Plea bargaining varies substantially from jurisdiction to jurisdiction. In some cases the defendant may agree to plead guilty to a lesser crime than the crime with which the defendant was originally charged. This is often called "charge bargaining." An example would be in a state that classifies rape as either aggravated rape or simple rape, aggravated rape charges may be reduced to simple rape in exchange for a plea of guilt to the lesser offense. It is also possible for the prosecutor to agree to recommend a particular sentence, or to remain quiet and not ask for stiff penalties in exchange for the defendant's plea of guilt.

Many rape victims/survivors feel betrayed by plea bargains, that is, they believe that the offender is being treated too leniently considering what the victim/survivor has been through. Feminists are in disagreement about the legitimacy of plea bargains in rape cases. Some feminists believe that those accused with rape should stand trial and risk a conviction for the original charge. They also believe that those convicted of rape should receive the maximum penalty allowed by law. Other feminists believe that plea bargains spare the victim/survivor the ordeal of the trial, and insure a conviction of the rapist.

The rape victim/survivor is likely to be confused by the plea bargain. It is important that the plea bargain and the reasons for it are explained. Victims/survivors who are provided information about plea bargains are more likely to appreciate the final resolution of the case without trial, and are less likely to feel bitter about the entire experience with the criminal justice system. Unfortunately, busy prosecutors often do not take the time to tell the victim/survivor that there has been a plea bargain, much less explain it.

By the time of the trial, the victim/survivor has generally made substantial emotional and physical recovery. However, when the trial date arrives, the victim/survivor must again deal with the myths, the tears, and the publicity, as well as facing the assailant in court. During this period of time, the recovery level is likely to regress (Evans, 1978). The victim/survivor is once again in need of crisis intervention. It is important for the intervener to be in contact with the victim/survivor during the trial, even if his/her previous conclusion was that the victim/survivor has progressed sufficiently for termination of the relationship.

One of the most stressful aspects of the rape trial for the victim/survivor is taking the witness stand and testifying about the details of the rape in public. While a rape trial does cover sensitive issues, especially for the victim/survivor, the trials are rarely closed to the public. The defendant has the right to a public trial. One advantage of the public trial for the victim/survivor is that the judge and prosecutor may feel pressure to strictly follow all laws and rules of evidence that protect the rape victim/survivor when there are people present in the court room who support rape victim's/survivor's rights.

Rape Shield Statutes

Rape shield statutes protect the victim/survivor from embarrassing questions about previous sexual behavior. Prior to the establishment of rape shield statutes, victims/survivors could be subjected to questioning about their prior sexual experiences and relationships. Most states now have rape shield statutes. Some are very effective; others are not. Even with the best rape shield statutes, some evidence of the victim's/survivor's sexual past is admissible into evidence. For example, if a female victim/survivor is obviously pregnant during trial, she may be required to name the father of the fetus. This is allowed to settle any questions in the minds of the jurors about whether or not the alleged rape resulted in a pregnancy. The victim/survivor may also be required to testify concerning any consensual sexual activity with the accused before the alleged rape. The victim/survivor may also be required to testify concerning any sexual activity that may have occurred close to the time of the alleged rape incident. This is allowed because it could explain any physical evidence of penetration found during the medical exam.

Rape Victims and the Issue of Impeachment

Another rule of evidence that a victim/survivor should have some knowledge of before trial is the rule concerning impeachment. Impeachment allows any witness's credibility to be questioned by the opposing party. The victim's/survivor's credibility may be questioned by the defense. Impeachment takes place during cross-examination.

Impeachment does not imply open season on witnesses. There are very specific rules that must be followed for impeaching a witness. Briefly, these rules are as follows:

1. Anything that would indicate that the victim/survivor could not have knowledge about information to which the victim/survivor has just testified can be used for impeachment. An example is when a female victim/survivor could not see what she claims to have seen due to darkness, vision impairment, or something obstructing her vision. This technique of impeachment can address all of the senses. It also includes the effect of drugs and alcohol on the witness' ability to perceive.

2. If the victim/survivor has a history of psychiatric or psychological problems, they may be used for impeachment. This includes alcohol and drug dependency and abuse.

3. If the victim/survivor has a poor reputation for telling the truth, it may be used. This includes only a general reputation in the community, riot individual opinions about the victim's/survivor's truthfulness.

4. If the victim/survivor has any prior felony convictions, questions may be asked about them. Jurisdictions may have different rules concerning what types of felonies can be introduced and how much information about the felony may be introduced.

5. If the victim/survivor has ever made a statement that is inconsistent with testimony on direct examination, it may be used to impeach. For example, if a female victim/survivor testifies that she had not been drinking before the alleged rape, but she told her friend that she had been drinking, her previous statement may be used by the jury to determine whether or not the victim/survivor is a credible witness.

6. If the victim/survivor feels hostility or bias against the defendant, it may be addressed during cross examination. This is used to prevent malicious prosecutions. If the hostility stems from the alleged rape, this will not be an effective means of impeaching the witness.

Rape Trauma Syndrome and the Courts

Another evidentiary rule that is important for the intervener to discuss with the victim/survivor generally benefits the prosecution. Some courts allow the prosecution to introduce evidence about Rape Trauma Syndrome and how the victim/survivor has reacted to the rape. This evidence is used to support the testimony that the victim/survivor was raped, because she has suffered from the symptoms of the disorder known as Rape Trauma Syndrome. Unfortunately, not all jurisdictions allow the use of this evidence.

Victim Impact Statements

In some states a victim impact statement will be taken, usually by a probation officer, before a convicted defendant will be sentenced. The victim impact statement allows the victim's feelings to be heard before sentence is imposed. In some states the judge has very little discretion in sentencing, and a victim impact statement may not be necessary. In other jurisdictions, for instance California, victim impact statements may be read by the victim/survivor in open court during the sentencing hearing.

CONCLUSION

This chapter addressed various aspects of crisis intervention, criminal justice and social services pertaining to the rape victim/survivor. Discussion centered on the legal definition of rape, the frequency of this type of offense, and various crisis intervention and criminal justice issues and procedures. Attention was given to specific considerations designed to assist the intervener in addressing the emotional and physical needs of the rape victim/survivor.

Rape is a very serious crime which must be dealt with as such by the criminal justice system and within the context of rape crisis intervention and counseling. The trauma of rape is emotionally and physically devastating. Intervention with the rape victim, whether it be crisis related or criminal justice based, must involve sensitivity and empathy. Such intervener qualities enable the rape victim to become a rape survivor.

The aftermath of rape is a time of crisis for the victim/survivor as well as family and loved ones. One needs to do the best one can to attend to the needs of all individuals affected by the crime of rape. While rape crisis intervention is critical in the stages immediately following the assault, support from family, friends, mates and spouses enable the person to strive toward long-term healing.

CHAPTER QUESTIONS

1. How might police officers, emergency medical personnel, nurses, and physicians perform crisis intervention for rape victims/survivors?
2. Why should crisis interveners understand the rape laws in their jurisdiction?
3. Should rape law vary depending on the relationship of the victim/survivor and the rapist? Why or why not?

4. What can be done to educate society about the facts surrounding rape? Will this effectively dispel the myths?
5. Would rape victims/survivors be as likely to feel self-blame and guilt if society discarded the myths about rape?
6. Should interveners encourage rape victims/survivors to report the rape to the police and to cooperate with prosecution? Why or why not?
7. How should an intervener handle the situation where a police officer or hospital employee is obviously being insensitive to a rape victim/ survivor, causing her even more trauma?
8. How can an intervener help the victim/survivor to feel safe?
9. What agencies accept rape victim/survivor referrals in your area? What services do they provide for the victim/survivor?
10. Can you think of any reasons other than those listed in the literature why a victim's/survivor's mate might seek revenge?
11. What is the impact of under reporting the crime of rape?
12. How can we improve the reporting rate for rape?
13. How can the criminal justice system be improved in processing rape cases?
14. Should the prosecution be allowed to introduce evidence of Rape Trauma Syndrome as it relates to the victim/survivor to help establish the fact of a rape?

SIMULATED EXERCISES

Simulated Exercise 1

You are working with a victim advocate program. You receive a phone call at 1:30A.M. on Saturday asking you to meet with a rape victim/survivor at the county hospital. When you arrive at the hospital and meet the victim/survivor you observe several bruises and scratches on her face and neck. The victim/survivor tells you that she was asleep in her apartment when the assailant entered her bedroom and started attacking her. The victim/survivor begins crying and stops her story at that point. Should you suggest to the police officers that they should get information concerning the scratches and bruises if they haven't done so?

Simulated Exercise 2

You are a police officer with a city police department. You are dispatched to a residence where a woman who is crying tells you that her husband has held a loaded gun to her head and has forced her to have sexual intercourse with him. He told her that unless she cooperated he would kill her. The victim/survivor is obviously very distressed but has no apparent injuries. She tells you that her husband has gone to the bar for a few drinks and that she is afraid to be there when he gets home. You live in a state where a husband cannot be convicted of raping his wife unless they are separated. What should you do?

Simulated Exercise 3

You are an emergency room nurse. A young woman is brought in by a police officer after being raped by her boyfriend. You have attended to the needs of the victim/survivor and are talking with her parents who have just arrived. The emergency room is not busy and another nurse is staying with the victim/survivor. Her father is very upset that his daughter has disgraced the family name. How would you help the survivor and the family?

Simulated Exercise 4

You are a hospital social worker. You are called to the emergency room to assist a rape victim/survivor. The victim/survivor is crying and keeps repeating "I can't believe this has happened. I froze, I couldn't move. If only I had fought him off. I wouldn't be here if I had fought him off." How can you help her with her feelings of guilt and self-blame?

Simulated Exercise 5

You are a police officer. You respond to a call where a college student has been raped. Her lab partner asked her to come over to his apartment to study for a midterm. He rapes her, telling her that she knew what would happen when she came over to his apartment. She would like to see the man prosecuted, but she has heard how the criminal justice system treats victims/survivors of rape, especially acquaintance rape. What should you tell her?

APPENDIX A

Additional Internet Resources

Additional information on rape victims and survivors may be found on the following websites. Moreover, these websites specifically address both male and female victims of rape, rape myths, rape stories, characteristics and common reactions of rape victims, along with types of rapes and how a rape should be reported, and emergency medical intervention when dealing with a rape case.

Rape Victim Advocates:
   http://www.rapevictimadvocates.org/
Bureau of Justice Statistics:
   http://www.ojp.usdoj.gov/bjs/cvict.htm
Silent All These Years, Myths:
   http://www.geocities.com/i_sang_holy_holy/myths_facts.html
Rape Recovery Help and Information Page:
   http://www.geocities.com/HotSprings/2402/myths.html
University of Minnesota Duluth, List of Rape Myths:
   http://www.d.umn.edu/cla/faculty/jhamlin/3925/myths.html
Office on Violence Against Women:
   http://www.ojp.usdoj.gov/vawo/
National Organization for Women:
   http://www.now.org/issues/violence/
The Society for the Scientific Study of Sexuality:
   http://www.sexscience.org/publications/index.php?category_id=440&subcategory_id=335
Rape, Abuse & Incest National Network:
   http://www.rainn.org/
National Archive of Criminal Justice Data:
   http://www.icpsr.umich.edu/NACJD/NCVS/
Center for Disease Control and Prevention:
   http://www.cdc.gov/ncipc/factsheets/svfacts.htm
The National Women's Health Information Center:
   http://www.4woman.gov/faq/sexualassault.htm
Sexual Assault Victims Emergency Services, Inc. (SAVES):
   http://www.mmavs.org/savesmd.htm

North Carolina Rape Crisis Volunteers of Cumberland County:
  http://www.rapecrisisonline.com/articles.htm
An Abuse, Rape, and Domestic Violence Aid and Resource Collection:
  http://www.aardvarc.org/rape/about/men.shtml
Douglas County Rape Victim-Survivor Service, Inc.:
  http://www.rvss.org/friends_family.htm
The Broken Spirits Network:
  http://www.brokenspirits.com/information/the_victim.asp
Sexual Assault Response Services of Southern Maine:
  http://sarsonline.org/PDFhandouts/rapeandsa/rts.pdf
The National Center for Victims of Crime:
  http://www.ncvc.org/ncvc/main.aspx?dbName=DocumentViewer&Document
  ID=32361
Planned Parenthood of the Rochester/Syracuse Region, Inc.:
  http://www.pprsr.org/rapecrisis/ineedhelp.cfm
Sexual Assault and Violence Intervention Program:
  http://www.mssm.edu/SAVI/fall1999.shtml

REFERENCES

Abarbanel, G. (1976). Helping victims of rape. *Social Work, 21,* 6, 478–482.

American Psychiatric Association (1994). *Diagnostic and statistical manual of mental disorders,* Fourth Edition (DSM–IV). Washington, D.C.: Author.

BJS. (2001). *Criminal victimization in the United States, 1999 statistical tables.* U.S. Department of Justice, National Crime Victimization Survey. Washington, DC: U.S. Government Printing Office.

BJS. (2000). *Criminal victimization in the United States, 1998 statistical tables.* U.S. Department of Justice, National Crime Victimization Survey. Washington, DC: U.S. Government Printing Office.

Bachman, R. (1994). *Violence against women: A national crime victimization report.* Washington, DC: U.S. Dept. of Justice. U.S. Government Printing Office.

Brookings, J.B., McEvoy, A.W. & Reed, M. (1994). Sexual assault recovery and male significant others. *Journal of Contemporary Human Services, 75,* 295–298.

Brownmiller, S. (1975). *Against our will: Men, women and rape.* New York: Simon & Schuster.

Burgess, A.W. & Holmstrom, L.L. (1976). Coping behavior of the rape victim. *American Journal of Psychiatry, 133,* 4, 413–418.

Burgess, A.W. & Holmstrom, L. (1979). Rape: Disclosure to parental family members. *Women & Health, 4,* 3, 255–268.

Burgess, A.W. & Holmstrom, L.L. (1973). The rape victim in the emergency ward. *American Journal of Nursing, 73,* 10, 1740–1745.

Burgess, A. & Holmstrom, L.L. (1974). Rape trauma syndrome. *American Journal of Psychiatry, 131,* 981–986.

Byington, D.B. (1990). Rape victims and the criminal justice system: Has the system improved? Presented at the Academy of Criminal Justice Sciences Annual Meeting, March 1990.

Cluss, P., Boughton, J., Frank, E., Stewart, B. & West, D. (1983). The rape victim: Psychological correlates of participation in the legal process. *Criminal Justice and Behavior, 10,* 3, 342–357.

Creamer, M. (2000). Posttraumatic stress disorder following violence and aggression. *Aggression and Violent Behavior, 5,* 5, 431–449.

Daane, D.M. (1989). The nature and frequency of marital rape among battered women in Indiana. Presented at the Academy of Criminal Justice Sciences Annual Meeting, April 1989.

Daane, D.M. (1988). Rape law reform: How far have we come. *The Prison Journal, 68,* 2, 3–10.

Dukes, R. & Mattley, C. (1976). Predicting rape victim reportage. *Sociology and Social Research,* GZ 1, 63–84.

Evans, H.I. (1978). Psychotherapy for the rape victim: Some treatment models. *Hospital & Community Psychotherapy, 29,* 5, 309–312.

FBI. (1999). *Crime in the United States, 1999.* U.S. Department of Justice, Uniform Crime Reports. Washington, DC: U.S. Government Printing Office.

Feldman-Summers, S. & Ashworth, C. (1981). Factors related to intentions to report rape. *Journal of Social Issues, 37,* 4, 53–70.

Foa, E.B. & Rothbaum, B.O. (1998). *Treating the trauma of rape: Cognitive-behavioral therapy for PTSD.* New York: Guilford.

Forman, B. (1980). Psychotherapy with rape victims. *Psychotherapy: Theory, Research, and Practice, 17,* 3, 304–311.

Gilmartin-Zena, P. (1985). Rape impact: Immediately and two months later. *Deviant Behavior, 6,* 4, 347–361.

Grossman, R. (1982). *Surviving sexual assault.* New York: Congdon & Weed.

Hartman, L. (1997). *Solutions: The women's crisis handbook.* Boston: Houghton Mifflin.

Hendricks, J.E. (1983). Criminal justice intervention with the rape victim. *Journal of Police Science and Administration, 11,* 2, 225–232.

Hoff, L. & Williams, T. (1975). Counseling the rape victim and her family. *Crisis Intervention, 6,* 4, 2–13.

Johnson, K. (1985). *If you are raped: What every woman needs to know.* Holmes Beach, FL: Learning Publications.

Kilpatrick, D.G., Resick, P.A. & Veronen, L.J. (1981). Effects of a rape experience: A longitudinal study. *Journal of Social Issues, 37,* 4, 105–122.

Koss, M.P. (2000). Blame, shame, and community: Justice responses to violence against women. *American Psychologist, 55,* 11, 1332–1343.

LeDoux, J. & Hazelwood, R. (1985). Police attitudes and beliefs toward rape. *Journal of Police Science and Administration, 13,* 3, 211–219.

Maguire, K. & Pastore, A.L. (Eds.). (1994). *Sourcebook of criminal justice statistics, 1993.* Washington, D.C.: U.S. Dept. of Justice, Bureau of Justice Statistics.

McCombie, S.L., Bassuk, E., Savitz, R. & Pell, S. (1976). Development of a medical center rape crisis intervention program. *American Journal of Psychiatry, 133,* 4, 418–421.

Notman, M. & Nadelson, C.C. (1976). The rape victim: Psychodynamic considerations. *American Journal of Psychiatry, 133,* 4, 408–413.

Resick, P.A. & Schnicke, M.K. (1993). *Cognitive processing therapy for rape victims: A treatment manual.* Newbury Park, CA: Sage Publications.

Sales, E., Baum, M. & Shore, B. (1984). Victim readjustment following assault. *Journal of Social Issues, 40,* 1,117–136.

Salzman, R.M. & Summergrad, P. (1988). The rape victim. In SE. Hyman (Ed.), *Manual of psychiatric emergencies,* second edition (pp. 48–53). Boston: Little, Brown.

Silverman, D.C. (1978). Sharing the crisis of rape: Counseling the mates and families of victims. *American Journal of Orthopsychiatry, 48,* 1,166–173.

Skelton, C. & Burkhart, B. (1980). Sexual assault: Determinants of victim disclosure. *Criminal Justice and Behavior, 6,* 2, 229–236.

Symonds, M. (1976). The rape victim: Psychological patterns of response. *The American Journal of Psychoanalysis, 36,* 1, 27–34.

Taslitz, A.E. (1999). *Rape and the culture of the courtroom.* New York: New York University Press.

Williams, L. (1984). The classic rape: When do victims report? *Social Problems, 31,* 4, 459–467.

Chapter 9

SUICIDE

RICHARD D. CLARK

INTRODUCTION

The topic of suicide and its prevention have been given considerable research attention (Jamison, 1999; Lester, 2000; Rudd, 1990; Suicide is the eighth leading cause of death in the United States with approximately 30,000 individuals committing suicide each year (U.S. Bureau of Census, 1998). The overall rate of suicide in the United States is 11.3 per 100,000 and is the eighth leading cause of death in America (American Society of Suicidology, 1998). The rate of suicide is even higher among young people; suicide is the third leading cause of death for people aged 15 to 34 (Centers for Disease Control–CDC, 2001). Within the United States, the rate is even higher among the elderly. The elderly, defined as 65 and older, have a rate of 16.9 per 100,000 (American Society of Suicidology, 1998). In addition, evidence suggests that many more people attempt suicide. For example, while the yearly suicide rate is approximately 11 per 100,000, the rate of attempted suicide, based on best estimate, is 15,000 per 100,000 (Mans et al., 1992). The large number of individuals attempting suicide is important, since 30 to 40 percent of individuals who complete suicide have made at least one prior attempt.

Even more pronounced is the rate of suicide ideation. While there are no national estimates of suicide ideation, there have been numerous estimates of the percentage of the population that express suicidal ideation. For example, Rudd (1990) estimated that 44 percent of a college population expressed suicidal ideation at some point in time, while Ramsey and Bagley (1985) estimated the lifetime prevalence of suicide ideation at 13 percent for residents of a Canadian city. Other estimates suggest five percent of the general population had expressed ideation within the previous month (Vandivort & Locke, 1979) to 16 percent the residents of a Florida county expressing ideation (Schwab, et al., 1972).

THEORY OF SUICIDE

The study of suicide and its intervention is a complicated subject. The actual incidence of suicide is rare, and for many of us the motivations behind suicide are complex and confusing. However, as Shneidman (1985) points out, in spite of the multiple reasons individuals use for committing suicide, suicides usually have several commonalties. Through understanding these commonalties, one may gain a better grasp of the reasons for suicide, and what steps can be taken to reduce suicidal intention. While these commonalties may not apply to all suicides, they are the most frequent suicide case characteristics. Therefore, they offer the intervener a sound beginning for suicide intervention. Shneidman's (1985) commonalties of suicide are listed below.

The Common Stimulus in Suicide Is Unendurable Psychological Pain. Shneidman (1985) notes that pain is what suicidal people are trying to escape. If one can reduce this pain, then, the individual will be more likely to choose to live. The key, therefore, is the reduction of psychological pain.

The Common Stressor in Suicide Is Frustrated Psychological Needs. Individuals do not commit suicides because of accomplishments. Rather, suicides are committed because of unfilled or blocked needs. As an example, imagine a woman whose marriage or relationship has deteriorated and has the "psychological need" to return the relationship to where it was before it disintegrated. She wants a happy relationship where all the memories, feelings, and emotions existed as they were before the relationship became troubled. As an additional example, imagine a situation where a student who has a "need" to do well in school, but failed a course and is now distressed. Consider a third example from criminal justice. Imagine a suicidal person confronted by the police. Her reason for wanting to commit suicide is to alleviate the psychological pain of chronic mental illness. Unfortunately, she has not received adequate treatment for her condition. According to Shneidman (1985), "The clinical rule (is): address the frustrated needs and the suicide will not occur." However, Shneidman points out that most suicides represent various needs so that focusing on one need may not be enough. Our individual whose relationship is troubled may be upset because she herself was the product of an extremely troubled marriage and she may be concerned that she is mirroring her parent's behavior. Our suicidal student may be distressed not only because he failed a class, but he may also be feeling that he let his parents down and doesn't know how to face them. Therefore, in the third example, the frustration experienced from psychological torment and social isolation, lead our client to a suicidal state. Suicide may be one way the client believes s/he can alleviate these multiple concerns.

The Common Purpose of Suicide Is to Seek a Solution. Suicide is a reaction to a dilemma. The intent of the suicidal person is to solve a perceived problem. The suicidal person is in a situation where s/he feels tremendous psychological pain, and one way to relieve this pain is to commit suicide. The key for intervention is to try and determine what problem(s) the suicide is attempting to solve. Once this question is answered, one can then attempt to help the individual solve the problem.

The Common Goal of Suicide Is Cessation of Consciousness. Suicide is an attempt to end psychological pain. By rendering one unconscious, one achieves this objective. The crisis intervener should understand that the suicidal person is seeking an end to psychological pain.

The Common Emotion in Suicide Is Hopelessness-Helplessness. Suicidal persons have overwhelming feelings that events are beyond their control. Combined with this is a feeling of loneliness. Thus, the suicidal person tends to feel that there is nothing s/he can do and there is no one to help him/her. As noted by Shneidman (1985), the feeling that one is alone can be "totally unnerving." During the course of intervention it is important that the intervener assist the client in realizing that hopelessness and helplessness are often momentary.

The Common Internal Attitude Toward Suicide Is Ambivalence. Even when they are committing the act of suicide, suicidal people are hoping for intervention. Suicidologists often see the act itself as a cry for help. Therefore, the intervener is not necessarily intruding in the person's life. Rather, the intervener is responding to a request for help.

The Common Cognitive State in Suicide Is Constriction. Suicidal individuals have what has been referred to as "tunnel vision." The individual does not see any options other than suicide. This lack of vision is perhaps one of the more dangerous aspects of suicide. For our individual who was upset by the failed relationship, the main choice, to establish the relationship again, is gone. For our student, his option of not failing his class is also gone. For our mentally ill client encountered by the police, her preferred option of not suffering from mental illness is not obtainable given the chronic nature of the condition. While a cure is elusive, treatment may alleviate some of the symptoms. If the individual is considering suicide as the sole option to his/her problem, the risk of suicide is greatly increased. For example, our student who failed his class is facing in his own mind the choices of dishonor or death. In his case, we would need to try to expand those choices by discussing other options with him. As Shneidman (1985) notes, none of these other options may be pain free, but they may at least open the constricted perspective of the client to other possibilities. Faced with these preferred options which are unobtainable, such individuals may choose suicide since they see no other alternative since the preferred option is unrealistic. The key for the intervener is to attempt to expand or reduce the constriction so that the individual is able to see other, available options. The intervener, therefore, needs to guide the individual away from the fixation that suicide is the only choice.

The Common Interpersonal Act in Suicide Is Communication of Intent. In the vast majority of suicides the individual leaves clear cues that something is amiss. Examples of such cues are signals of distress, indications of helplessness, and pleas for help directed toward others. Suicidal persons have also been known to give away meaningful possessions, to put their affairs in order, and to talk only in the past tense as opposed to what will happen in the future. For the intervener, as well as others who may interact with the suicidal individual, these are clear signs that something is wrong and that action needs to be taken.

Lay individuals also need to know that sometimes calmness overcomes the suicidal person shortly before the suicide. Many observers may feel that the crisis has passed since the individual is no longer disturbed. However, the reality of the situation is that the person is calm, because the decision is made to end life, and therefore, mental anguish is no longer omnipresent. Faced with this type of situation, one needs to inquire of the individual whether s/he is still contemplating suicide.

The Common Action in Suicide Is Aggression. A Suicidal person's wish is to leave or exit. Suicide is a way of exiting from one's pain. Unfortunately for the individual and his/her family and friends, suicide is a permanent departure. The intervener may be effective in communicating to the client how aggressive the act of suicide is, and to indicate to the client the finality of the act.

The Common Consistency in Suicide Is with Life-Long Coping Patterns. Shneidman (1985) contends that if we look at how individuals respond to earlier crises, we can get an idea of how they will respond to a present crisis. Those who develop tunnel vision as a response to previous crises, or who do not respond to psychological stress effectively, are at an increased risk for suicide. The key for a police officer, therapist, counselor, teacher, or co-worker is to look at previous behavior and to determine if prior behaviors are consistent with how the individual is now behaving.

MODELS OF SUICIDE

This latter commonalty has been supported by Pulakos (1993) who reviewed two different models of suicide. The first model is a crisis intervention model, which contends that suicide is a one-time behavior and that by dealing with the short-term crisis, the suicidal individual can be kept alive. The second model focuses on continued therapy and is premised on the belief that suicide is part of one's total personality. Treatment, therefore, must be viewed as part of an ongoing process which takes into account both chronic feelings and an individual's coping skills. This latter model also places more responsibility on the client, since it requires that s/he make changes in worldview as well as coping skills. The second model, which is gaining increased acceptance among suicidologists, is clearly in tune with Shneidman's (1985) tenth commonality.

Another approach to the theory of suicide, and its prevention, is centered on the two concepts of "perturbation" and "lethality" (Kral and Sakinofsky, 1994; Shneidman, 1985). Perturbation deals with the amount of distress the individual is feeling. It focuses on such factors as anguish, discomfort, hopelessness, and addresses the issue of psychological pain. Lethality refers to a person's plan for suicide and includes factors such as how, when, and where the suicide may be committed. According to Kral and Sakinofsky (1994), lethality is the "steadfastness of the plan, its accessibility and degree of interest." Perturbation and lethality interact in that an increase in one leads to an increase in the other.

Neither perturbation nor lethality is static. These factors are constantly shifting as the situation changes. The degree of psychological pain one is suffering, as well as how much pain one can manage, may change from day to day. These changes can also affect how far along the individual is in suicide planning. Thus, in assessing the risk of suicide, one must be careful that support isn't withdrawn simply because the immediate crisis appears to be over. Tomorrow's trauma may return the levels of perturbation and lethality to dangerous levels. This is why an understanding of how an individual has handled previous crises is important. People who have had difficulty addressing and managing previous crises are more likely to experience problems with a present crisis.

The key to suicide reduction is to reduce either the level of perturbation or lethality. If one can address the reason that one is upset, then the perturbation that leads to suicidal ideation will be diminished. This reduction will accompany a decrease in lethality. Similarly, if one can disrupt one's plans for suicide (e.g., removal of guns from the house, reducing the amount of prescription drugs that are available for a suicide attempt, have the client sign a "suicide contract" that he/she will not commit suicide for the next 48 hours), the chances of an attempted suicide will also be diminished.

In summation, Shneidman (1985) states that suicide is best treated as a group effort. The focus on intervention need not be on why the individual chooses suicide, but rather on what the underlying problem is and how can it be addressed. The response to suicidal intent is to address the "satisfaction of unmet needs." This may require not only addressing the immediate issue (my marriage is over; I flunked the class), but also any underlying issues that have an impact on the individual's psychological pain.

CORRELATES OF SUICIDE AND SUICIDAL IDEATION

This section will review the correlates of suicide and suicide ideation. It will focus on both sociological and psychological factors that influence the propensity towards suicide. It must be remembered that these variables are risk factors for suicide and not necessarily causes. While risk factors themselves are not enough for a suicide to occur, they do increase the chances of suicide for those who are psychologically distressed.

Social and Demographic Variables

Sex/Gender. Sex or gender is perhaps the most important sociological variable. Rates for men are at least four times higher than those for women (CDC, 2001; Linden and Breed, 1976; Rich et al., 1988). As noted by Garrison (1992), this pattern has been consistent even though the rate of suicide has increased over the last thirty years. Rich et al. (1988) attributes part of the difference between men and women's suicide rates to increased levels of substance abuse and economic stressors among men combined with a greater intent and lethality among men to commit suicide. While men are more likely to die from suicide than women are, females are more likely to attempt suicide (CDC, 2001).

Age. In general, rates of suicide have been higher for those over 45 years of age compared to those younger than 45 (Garrison, 1992). However, while rates for older age groups have been declining, those for younger age groups have been increasing with the suicide rate for those under 30 nearly tripling over the last several decades (CDC, 2001; Rich, et al., 1986). This increase has been attributable to a large increase in suicide for males, both white and black (Garrison, 1992). When comparing age groups, however, the rate for the elderly, especially elderly males, is markedly higher than the rate for younger cohorts.

Race. Historically, suicide rates are higher for whites than for blacks (CDC, 2001; Linden and Breed, 1976; Swanson and Breed, 1976). During

1998, white males accounted for 73 percent of all suicides (CDC, 2001). When one combines white males and white females, we can account for 90 percent of all suicides in the United States (CDC, 2001). Nonwhite males and nonwhite females have suicide rates of 10.5 and 1.8 per 100,000, respectively (American Association of Suicidology, 2001).

Additional Factors. Additional factors that have been identified as being associated with a higher risk of suicide are urbanization, marital status, housing density, household size, religious affiliation, economic conditions, and physical health. Traditionally, suicide rates were believed to be higher in urban areas (Jarvis et al., 1982) although some have questioned this assumption (Garrison, 1992; Linden and Breed, 1976). Other factors that have been linked to an increased risk of suicide are poor physical health (Goldberg, 1981); residing in a single person household (Jarvis, et al., 1982, Moscicki, 1989); economic distress (Buda and Tsuang, 1990); religious affiliation with suicide rates highest among Protestants and lowest among Catholics and Jews (Buda and Tsuang, 1990); and marital status with married individuals having the lowest suicide rate with divorced individuals having the highest rates of suicide (Linden and Breed, 1976; Stack, 1990).

Psychological Factors

In addition to sociological factors, there are also psychological factors that influence one's propensity towards suicide. Some of these factors are:

Depression. Being depressed and/or having Bipolar Disorder is perhaps the major psychological factor associated with an increased risk of suicide (Jamison, 2000). Petronis et al. (1990), reports that depression is one of the best predictors of suicide attempts, with depressed patients having a significantly higher rate of suicide attempts when compared to non depressed patients. Buda and Tsuang (1990) report that 15 percent of depressed patients kill themselves, while Maltsberger (1992) notes that approximately 70 percent of patients who commit suicide have a "significant depressive illness or alcoholism or both."

Substance Abuse. A definitive link has been established between the consumption of alcohol and/or illicit drugs and suicide. Individuals who abuse alcohol or who use illicit drugs are at a higher risk for suicide (Tanskanen et al., 2000; Trezza and Popp, 2000; Lester, 1992; Petronis et al., 1990; Rich et al., 1986; Stack and Wasserman, 1993) and the use of nicotine and caffeine (Tanskanen et al., 2000). For example, Lester reports on two studies that show that approximately 18 percent of all alcoholics commit suicide, while 24 percent of alcoholics have attempted suicide. While some have argued that cocaine use is particularly related to an increased risk of suicide (Petronis et al., 1990), Lester contends that the evidence suggests that no one drug is associated with a higher risk of suicide.

Other Psychological and Social Factors. Factors such as schizophrenia, personality disorders, hopelessness, life stress, and social support have also been associated with suicide. Individuals who have increased mental illness, increased life stress, feel hopeless, or who lack social support are at an increased risk of suicide (Bennet and Turner, 1987; Moscicki, 1989; Rudd, 1990; Tanney, 1992; Yufit and Bongar, 1992). However, research has suggested that social connections and feelings of responsibility toward significant others may work to thwart suicide (Malone et al., 2000).

SUICIDE PREVENTION

General Settings

The movement toward suicide prevention began in the 1950s and 1960s in Great Britain, and moved to the United States shortly thereafter. By 1973, nearly every major metropolitan center in the United States had a suicide intervention/prevention program (Neimeyer and Pfeiffer, 1994).

Prevention of suicide has traditionally followed three general approaches per the classic work of Gerald Caplan and Henry Grunebaum (1967). These approaches are:

(1) *Primary Prevention*–This method focuses on individuals who have not yet contemplated suicide. This approach involves the prevention of suicidal tendencies in individuals. It attempts to improve mental health and mental hygiene in general by developing self-esteem, coping skills, and the ability to communicate.

(2) *Secondary Prevention*–Secondary prevention focuses on interventions with individuals who are expressing suicidal ideation. The focus is on immediate intervention and this approach attempts to reduce the perturbation and/or lethality of those contemplating suicide.

(3) *Tertiary Prevention*–Tertiary prevention attempts to prevent the reoccurrence of suicide attempts for those individuals who have already attempted suicide. This approach is best left to trained professionals since it involves skills such as psychiatric treatment, crisis counseling, and investigations of the additional factors causing psychological distress.

Focusing mainly on tertiary prevention, Kiev (1976) notes that, in comparison to others, the overall prognosis for those who have attempted suicide and entered into treatment is not good. While individuals who have attempted suicide in the presence of others, or who have called for assistance have a better prospect of recovery, those who attempt, and who are also in treatment, have the highest suicide rate of any particular patient group.

The crucial need in crisis intervention is for the counselor to intervene in the critical areas of the patient's life. Kiev (1976) argues that if this can be successfully accomplished, the problems that led to suicidal thoughts can be diminished and the ability to cope should be strengthened. It is also important in counseling to attempt to bring significant others into the suicidal person's life. As noted above, social isolation and the belief that no one cares are factors that increase the risk of suicide. However, one must be careful before introducing significant others in tertiary prevention. If social conflict exist between the client and significant others, or if the significant others are not likely to be supportive of the client, the chance of a successful outcome is diminished. It must be remembered that most of the outward symptoms of suicide ideation create friction within relationships, and this friction often leads to further isolation.

It is also not a good idea for the counselor or others to criticize the client by insisting that he "snap out of it," "grow up," "stop being depressed," etc. Such statements may enhance the suicidal person's feelings of worthlessness, and therefore further push him towards suicide. Any statements or comments that increase negative feelings within the individual will be largely counterproductive.

There is also a need for the counselor to "re-educate" the client. It is generally assumed that we continue to grow as we age. Therefore, change is also possible for suicidal individuals. The role of the counselor is to help the individual improve daily functioning. This can be accomplished by helping them increase awareness of their positive and negative behaviors and attributes. Once this is accomplished, attempts can be made to strengthen one's good points and reduce one's bad points. The counselor must also focus on working with the client to improve his current life situation. The client is discouraged from concentrating on past failures and instead is encouraged to look at why he failed so that previous mistakes will not be repeated. Finally, the client can be helped to reassess his or her goals, and if the old goals are found to be unrealistic, new goals can be substituted.

Broader societal approaches to social problems can also have a positive influence on suicide prevention. For example, job training for the unemployed or economically displaced, drug and alcohol prevention and treatment programs, family interventions with dysfunctional families, counseling for victims of rape or incest as well as survivors of those who suffered a violent death, and attempts to create more social interaction among individuals can all have positive effects on the rate of suicide. This is true even though these programs are geared toward larger societal concerns.

School Settings

There are a variety of suicide programs and approaches for adolescents and younger individuals that can be utilized in school settings (Kirchner et al., 2000). One approach that has been used for students as young as elementary school age is described by Satten (1994). Realizing that younger students are sometimes reluctant to discuss their concerns with adults, Satten (1994) described an outreach program for elementary students that uses puppets to encourage children to open up and discuss their feelings and fears. The program revolves around a series of skits which focus on the topics of feelings; how to deal with a death loss whether it be a family member, friend, or even a pet; and the exploration of other losses and how talking and listening can be beneficial when one is feeling bad.

The children are informed that a puppet show is about to be given, and they may leave if they wish. The puppeteers then come in, introduce their characters, and perform the various skits. Afterwards the puppeteers lead a discussion of the issues involved and the feelings each student has about the topic. The program ends with the puppeteers individually talking to each student in attendance while still holding their puppets.

After the program concludes the puppeteers provide immediate feedback to both the teacher and any counselors who are required to be present. The consultation includes a discussion of any children who may have responded or acted in a mannerism that was disturbing to the puppeteers. Reviews of the program generally agree that children are more likely to discuss their concerns with a puppet than with an adult.

A second and more general approach to suicide prevention in the schools is offered by Tierney et al. (1990). These authors argue that in a school context, a suicide prevention program must be system-wide, needs to be supported by all of the major players in the system, and must focus on all aspects of suicide (i.e., prevention, intervention, and post-vention). Prevention refers to educating students by giving them coping and problem solving skills. Since suicide is often a cry for help, prevention has taken on a more important role over time. Intervention deals with early recognition of suicidal behaviors and focuses on assessment, direct contact, and, if needed, referral. Post-vention involves dealing with the aftermath of a suicide and focuses on giving students and faculty the opportunity to discuss thoughts, feelings, and emotions.

In order for intervention programs to work effectively, schools must establish crisis intervention teams that focus on suicides. The members of these teams must receive training in suicide intervention. In addition, the school must also have a suicide intervention policy in place which allows each member of the team to understand his or her role, what is expected of them and the most appropriate interact with other team members. The policy should also establish links for appropriate referrals to outside agencies and have a follow-up plan to reintegrate the student into school, if appropriate.

Tierney et al. (1990) note that suicide is not just a school-related problem but rather is a community-based concern. However, the schools, being the first institution an individual faces outside of the family, offer a unique opportunity to assist students in dealing with difficult issues such as suicide. The denials of the possibility of a suicide and the fear (myth) of placing the thought of suicide into a child's head are major stumbling blocks for instituting programs in schools. Most suicidologists insist that discussing the subject of suicide is the best way to prevent suicide from occurring.

While not focusing on schools per se, Berman and Jobes (1994) note further difficulties in dealing with adolescent suicide. Suicide is a call for help. However, adolescents are generally very reluctant to seek help, particularly from adults. The reasons for this are a fear of others finding out, and the belief that adults will not understand them. In addition, the parents, while realizing their child is not doing well, may be reluctant to allow outsiders to enter their home for purposes of intervention. This may be particularly true for those families who are most in need of assistance. The result is that counseling and crisis intervention sessions involving an adolescent are often combative and operate in an arena of suspicion and conflict.

However, due to the impact of family dysfunction on an adolescent's risk of suicide, any treatment plan for an adolescent must include the family. As with any other treatment plan for suicide, the counselor must start with the individual's lethality. Once the immediate risk of suicide is diminished, attention can turn to what Berman and Jobes (1994) refer to as "intentionality" or the psychological purpose behind the suicide ideation/attempt. Once one understands whether the suicide attempt was a call for help or a true desire to die, a treatment plan that addresses the adolescent's needs can be implemented. Due to the ever-changing situation with suicide, the treatment plan/intervention approach will need to be continually revised, as client needs change.

Finally, Ryerson (1990) notes that in addition to the school itself, the input of both the parents and teachers is necessary for any program to be effective. Ryerson (1990) maintains that factors such as knowledge and interpretation of warning signs, causes of self-destructive behaviors, and how to access community resources are the types of information that should be disseminated to parents and teachers. In addition, she contends that each school and school district is different. Therefore, in order for an intervention program to work, one must tailor the program to meet the individual needs of each school and its corresponding community.

In an effort to assess the level of suicide intervention programs in schools,

Wass et al. (1990) conducted a study with a stratified sample of 1,000 schools in the United States, pre-kindergarten through twelfth grade. They found that 11 percent of the schools dealt with death education, 17 percent included grief education, and 25 percent dealt with suicide prevention/intervention. Death education was usually taught as part of another class, and the curriculum was usually two weeks or less in duration. The topics that were covered included funeral customs, coping with grief, individual's attitudes and fears, and suicide and other destructive behaviors.

The majority of the grief programs were designed for intervention and dealt with students' feelings, emotional distress, and the grieving process. These programs are usually conducted by counselors and are designed to allow students to discuss their feelings and to ask questions. The suicide prevention/intervention programs are usually activated when a student has committed suicide or is at risk of committing suicide. Students are informed of the dynamics of suicide, and prevention mechanisms such as self-esteem, coping skills, and learning how to communicate are taught.

Wass et al. (1990) note that suicide programs are rarely taught at the elementary level and are usually offered on an "as needed basis" rather than as part of the general curriculum. In spite of the fact that 40 percent of high school girls and 25 percent of high school boys have "seriously thought" of suicide, they found that well over half of the high schools that responded did not have a suicide prevention/intervention program. The survey clearly indicated that the number of suicide prevention/intervention programs in our schools needed to be expanded. Wass et al. (1990) conclude that most school professionals have had little training in either suicide interventions or bereavement counseling.

The prevention of suicide is generally considered to be the most cost effective and constructive approach to the problem of suicide. However, like all prevention programs it requires a long-term commitment in order for it to be effective. In addition to this long-term commitment, school-based prevention programs can be problematic for several reasons (Leenaars and Wenckstern, 1990). First, many people believe that the discussion of suicide has no place in the schools. Second, there is a belief that talking about suicide will cause people to consider committing suicide. Third, when one considers that suicide is still a rare event, a suicide prevention program for most schools will not be cost-effective. And fourth, the presence of a suicide prevention program can be the basis of a lawsuit if the program fails to prevent a suicide.

In response to these allegations, Leenaars and Wenckstern (1990) note that failure to have a suicide prevention program, particularly when it was obvious that the risk of a suicide was high can also lead to litigation. In addition, while the cost-effectiveness of suicide programs may be high, there are ancillary benefits from such intervention programs such as an improvement in the student body's overall mental health. Thus, the benefits derived from suicide programs in schools should not be measured simply by their impact upon suicides or suicidal ideation. And finally, Leenaars and Wenckstern (1990) argue that it is a myth that discussions of suicide lead to an increased risk of suicide. In fact, based upon the argument that suicide is often a byproduct of depression, helplessness, and loneliness, the discussion of the issues involved can only help to overcome the psychological pain felt by those who have ideation.

SUICIDE INTERVENTION

While numerous authors have discussed effective suicide intervention programs and strategies (Foxman, 1990), the present discussion has centered on two types of intervention. First, while presented under the guise of suicide prevention, one might contend that any type of prevention, before an intense crisis situation, is also intervention. Second, and no less important, is the critical role that on-site intervention maintains (Hendricks and McKean, 1995). Therefore, one might argue that intervention can be broadly defined.

Leenaars (1994) has developed a *five-step model* for crisis intervention, which is relevant to the suicidal crisis client.

1) ***Establish Rapport***–Essentially the patient/client talks while the counselor/intervener listens. The intervener/counselor must demonstrate genuineness in his/her caring and be nonjudgmental in his/her response. The intervener/counselor is both attempting to find out what the problem is and allowing the patient to vent.

2) ***Explore***–We define our crises by our perceptions. The rule for the intervener/counselor is to attempt to change the client's perception (see the related discussion of the "definition of the situation" in the chapter on Death Notification). In particular, since suicidal persons often believe that their choices are limited, the role of the intervener/counselor is to change that perception so that the client perceives that more choices are available. As an example, Leenaars (1994) notes a patient who stated "I can't live with this." The answer for the intervener/counselor is to find out what "this" is and then try and redefine "this" into something else that can be dealt with. In so doing, the intervener/counselor must remember that the focus of control is always within the client. The client alone is responsible for his behavior.

3) ***Focus***–The client is usually too upset to focus on what s/he needs to do. Therefore, it is the role of the intervener/counselor to help him/her focus on the issues so that other options will become clearer. Leenaars (1994) cautions that moral reasoning or judgmental behavior will not be helpful. Rather, the intervener/counselor should try statements such as "What is the problem?

What would be most helpful? We've talked a lot, what do you want to discuss?" As noted above, the rule is to reduce the level of perturbation. This, in turn, will reduce the level of lethality and decrease the chance of a suicide.

4) ***Develop Options and a Plan of Action***–Leenaars (1994) notes that suicidal persons tend to view the world as black and white. The task of the intervener/counselor is to point out the "gray." By pointing to other options, even if the client is not favorably disposed to any of them, the intervener/counselor has introduced ambiguity into the client's decision making process. If successful, suicide becomes a less viable option. In the course of rendering the world less black and white, the intervener/counselor must also convey to the client that there is emotional support for the client to make other decisions.

5) ***Terminate***–Termination includes making referrals, contacting other resources as needed and establishing follow-up procedures. This is a critical step in the intervention process in that it involves (a) leaving the physical proximity of the client, and (b) is an important step for establishing client aftercare.

Finally, various treatment programs exist for adolescent runaways. These individuals are at a high risk for suicide. As reported by Borus and Bradley (1991), one study of runaways found that 33 percent of runaway and homeless girls and 16 percent of runaway boys had attempted suicide. Even larger numbers had expressed ideation toward suicide. Clearly, there is also a need for risk assessment and treatment at runaway shelters.

According to Borus and Bradley (1991), shelter programs must include the following crisis intervention components:

1) ***Screening***–This includes risk assessment at admittance.

2) ***Training in Suicide Behavior***–The staff must assess both the warning signs and risks of suicide. The staff needs to be aware that suicidal runaways will often have multiple problems that may impact on one's ideation toward suicide (i.e., family, legal, drug/alcohol abuse, and for females possible sexual abuse or prostitution).

3) ***Protocols for Referrals***–The staff must refer the client to outside helping sources when needed.

4) ***Agreements with Community Agencies for Assistance When Needed***– Shelter programs must have agreements for assistance from outside agencies when such assistance is necessary.

An evaluation of three shelters where this plan was implemented noted a drop in suicide attempts among shelter residents. However, and due to the small base rate for suicide, the findings should be interpreted with caution.

SUICIDE IN JAILS AND PRISONS:
CORRELATES, PREVENTION, AND INTERVENTION

Suicides that occur in jails and prisons are also of particular concern to criminal justice and social service personnel. In 1995, 160 individuals committed suicide in state and federal prisons (Maguire and Pastore, 1997). In addition, a survey of county jails and police lockups noted that 419 jail suicides occur annually (Hayes and Kajdin, 1981). Suicide is the leading cause of death in jails and the suicide rate in both prisons and jails is several times higher than in the general population.

Historically, a suicide in a jail or prison has not been sufficient grounds to establish liability for administrators and/or staff. However, in cases where suicide is foreseeable officials may be liable. Courts have ruled that institutions have been liable where they have failed to establish a suicide policy, failed to identify high-risk inmates, failed to provide adequate supervision for high risk inmates, failed to take steps to prevent suicides such as removing an inmate's belt, failed to train their staff in suicide prevention, exhibited indifference in situations where suicide risk was high, or had known overcrowding or under staffing conditions that would impinge upon medical care involving suicide prevention (Olivero and Roberts, 1990; and Bonner, 1992). Therefore, there are sound reasons for correctional and criminal justice personnel to be concerned over various dimensions of suicides and suicide attempts.

Correlates of Correctional Suicides

Research has identified who is most likely to commit suicide while in jail. According to Hayes and Kajdin (1981), the majority of inmates who commit suicide are white (67%), under the age of 32 (75%), and almost always male (97%). These demographic characteristics may be a by-product of the typical jail and prison population. Almost three-quarters had been incarcerated for a nonviolent offense, while over half of the suicide victims were under the influence of drugs or alcohol at the time of their arrest. Over 50 percent of inmates who commit suicide do so within the first 24 hours of incarceration, and over two-thirds do so when they were held in isolation or seclusion. These general findings have been confirmed elsewhere (Bonner, 1992).

In addition to prisons having a higher suicide rate than the general population, there are also differences between the characteristics of suicide victims in prisons versus jails. As was the case with jails, suicide victims in prisons were almost exclusively male. In contrast to jails, suicide victims in prisons tended to be serving longer sentences, and tended to be violent offenders. Moreover, prison inmates who commit suicide tend to be over the age of 25.

Prison inmates tend to commit suicide when they encounter interpersonal problems within the institution. Case histories of inmates who have committed suicide reveal that almost half of the inmates had documented histories of mental illness and/or had a previous history of suicide attempts.

Based upon the high rates of suicide in jails/prisons, it is clear that incarceration is a highly stressful event that may overwhelm those who are vulnerable. In addition to the stressors already present in the suicidal, the stigma of arrest combined with the fear of the unknown may be insurmountable. Compounding this problem is the isolation and loss of social support that comes from being incarcerated. As Bonner (1992) notes, humans are social beings who experience intense emotional distress when they are lonely and/or isolated. Incarceration, particularly in isolation, exacerbates the suicidal intent among those already in distress. Risk assessment, along with screening for suicidal intent at intake, is essential in preventing suicide, particularly for a short-term institution such as a jail where the stigma and trauma of an arrest is greatest.

Suicide Prevention and Intervention in Prison and Jail

Correctional suicide experts have concluded that human interaction is the most important element in suicide prevention (Bonner, 1992). Creating the means for social interaction and support can counter the loneliness and despair that inmates often feel. Thus housing inmates in dormitories or providing a "buddy system" for inmates who are at risk of self-destructive behavior can reduce the level of suicide in the institution. The federal system, for example, has created a system in which fellow inmates are trained to monitor at-risk inmates and provide them with support.

Much of the suicide prevention training that exists for correctional settings, however, is designed for the professional custodial staff of correctional institutions (Pearson, 2001). As Wicks (1972) maintains in an article featured in *Federal Probation,* there are several factors which correctional personnel must be cognizant of in preventing suicide attempts. In particular, there are unique factors contributing to suicide, according to Wicks, which may be found within the jail or prison setting. As Wicks notes, there are several organic and functional causes of suicide unique to the prison or jail:

- Bad news/letter from home (e.g., divorce request, learning that spouse has been with another partner, death notification);
- Homosexual rape;
- No news from home or loved ones;
- Sudden confinement (this creates a particularly acute crisis for the first time offender);

- An unexpected sentence of an unusually long duration given by the Court;
- Latent victim-specific guilt arising from the crime (e.g., child molestation, murder of a family member);
- Receiving a beating from inmates or severe restraint by staff;
- Confinement for a long period in an unsentenced status (awaiting trial).

While these factors will not, in and of themselves, always produce a crisis that elicits suicidal ideation and an attempt, they are important characteristics for the criminal justice practitioner to keep in mind in suicide prevention.

Many scholars and practitioners would agree that prevention is critically important in addressing the issue of suicide in correctional settings. In particular, the first 24-hour period is critical in assessing suicide risk. According to training materials provided by the Criminal Justice Coordinating Council (CJCC) of Northwest Ohio (1986), there are several (6) key factors which help in assessing inmate suicide risk. These are:

1. Anyone obviously under the influence of either drugs or alcohol;
2. Anyone returning to the jail who has demonstrated suicidal tendencies during previous periods of incarceration;
3. Anyone who seems to be extremely withdrawn or distant;
4. Anyone who seems very depressed;
5. Anyone who makes comments such as: "What is the use of living anymore?" or "Nobody cares about me anyway."
6. Anyone who seems overly anxious. (CJCC, 1986, p. 519)

In confronting the suicidal jail or prison inmate, it is important for the intervener to demonstrate a genuine interest in listening to the inmate and his/her concerns. Moreover, there are certain guidelines which assist personnel in addressing these crisis situations:

- The officer/staff/intervener should be honest in his/her responses;
- The officer/staff/intervener should not be judgmental;
- The officer/staff/intervener should try to understand the suicidal inmate's point of view;
- The officer/staff/intervener should not belittle or make fun of the inmate;
- The officer/staff/intervener should try to talk naturally with the inmate. (CJCC, 1986, p. 523)

These suggestions are intended merely to serve as guidelines for intervention in correctional and other relevant criminal justice settings and may be adapted to various intervention settings involving correctional clientele.

THE POLICE AND SUICIDE

Historically, there has been a link between being a police officer and a propensity for suicidal behavior (Heiman, 1977; Quinnett, 1998; Violanti, 1996). This phenomenon has received increased attention in this last year as the number of suicides in the New York City Police Department has reached record levels (Gibbs, 1994). In addition, other data suggest that not only are police officers twice as likely to commit suicide as the general population, but more officers die at their own hands each year than are killed in the line of duty (Seligmann, 1994).

Similar to the general public, police officers commit suicide for a variety of reasons. Alcohol use and marital problems, for example, are often cited as factors in police suicides. The risk of police suicides is also increased by access to weapons, which increases lethality, and by the presence of occupational stress, public scrutiny, and corruption scandals within the department, which increase perturbation. In addition, officers who face disciplinary problems such as suspensions are also at a higher risk for suicide (Janik and Kravitz, 1994; Gibbs, 1994).

Stress and Officer Suicide

The stress of being a police officer is an important factor in police suicides. It has been established that policing is a stressful vocation. In the course of their duties, the police must deal with people who are angry, upset, and possibly grieving. Regardless of one's psychological fortitude, the experience of dealing with the impact of crime on a daily basis cannot be healthy. Moreover, police officers are trained to be suspicious and hypervigilant. These characteristics which can make one a good officer, unfortunately can be detriments to a healthy life.

This stress has been compounded in recent years as budget cuts and the reluctance of governments to raise taxes have left officers feeling that they are understaffed, underfinanced, outgunned, and unappreciated by the general public. In addition, many street officers report that they feel abandoned by supervisors who, officers claim, fail to give them the support they deserve. Finally, due to the nature of their work, police officers tend to feel most comfortable around other officers. Thus, the broader community support that may be available from others is missing for an officer in psychological distress. As noted by Schneidman (1985), alienation and feelings of loneliness are related to an increased risk of suicide.

One method police departments have used to address the effects of stress and its relationship to suicide is to develop a proactive approach to stress related topics (Mashburn, 1993). This can be accomplished by in-service training that emphasizes the benefits of psychological services. In addition, the officers must feel that the department supports them when they face stressful situations. Officers who face difficult situations respond best to those who are willing to listen to them without offering glib comments or judgments.

Some departments have found that this is most effective when internal peer support teams are used to help officers respond to the aftermath of difficult situations. Due to the nature of police work, individuals who can relate to the officers, who have been in similar situations, may be best able to listen and understand. If a department is going to utilize support teams involving fellow officers, these individuals should receive additional training on stress management and counseling. They should also be encouraged to refer officers to others when they realize that the situation is beyond their expertise. However, officers will only use these services if they feel that seeking assistance for a psychological will not jeopardize their careers or stress related problem.

Police Confrontations with Suicidal Offenders

Law enforcement officials may also face situations involving suicide that are unique to policing. For example, the police may encounter situations where an individual has barricaded him/herself and may be threatening suicide. In addition to being concerned about both neighborhood safety and the safety of the officers, the police also need to be concerned about the possibility of a suspect committing suicide. Negotiators, therefore, have to ascertain this possibility usually by directly asking the subject about his intentions (DiVasto et al., 1992).

Risk factors have been identified with hostage situations and suicide. These include the victims not being true hostages (the subject is not using them as bargaining chips); the subject has recently experienced major life changes or multiple stressors; the subject has a history of male dominance; and the subject has a history of similar problems with the hostage (Fuselier et al., 1991). Other factors that indicate an increased risk of suicide are the subject's propensity to hostility, threats by the subject to injure or kill the hostage, attempts by the subject to try and force a confrontation with the police, the lack of a social support network for the subject, and any alcohol or substance abuse by the subject. As the number of risk factors increase, the chances of a successful outcome decrease.

In an attempt to reduce the chance of a suicide, the police should try to give the subject an avenue to constructively vent anger, express emotions, and discuss feelings. The police can also reduce the chances of suicide if they can determine the subject's preferred method of suicide and then take steps to try and reduce this from happening. For example, if the suspect appears to want to try and kill himself with a firearm, the negotiator may try and get the subject to dismantle the firearm or at least remove the bullets. This will help prevent a compulsive act by the subject which may result in a suicide.

In situations where it appears that suicide may be a factor, the police must ask about suicide so that the topic may be brought out in the open for discussion. This not only allows the subject to discuss the issues involved, but it also allows the police negotiator to offer suggestions and hope to the subject (Divasto et al., 1992). Again, this requires that the police ascertain the intent of the subject considering suicide, as well as the absence or presence of any correlates of suicide (Fuselier et al., 1991).

In addition, police may face situations where a homicide is followed by a suicide. While research suggests that homicide/suicide incidents are rare in the United States, they occur in one to five percent of all homicides, and may also be present in hostage situations. Once again, the police must ascertain or assess the suicidal ideation of the individual to determine the likelihood of a suicide occurring (DiVasto et al., 1992).

Finally, police may face situations where a suspect is suicidal and wishes for the officer to take his/her life via homicide. Such instances have been coined "Suicide by Cop." This phenomenon has just recently been recognized and has received research attention (Homant and Kennedy, 2000; Lord, 2000). Suicide by cop is defined as a homicide by a police officer of a suicidal citizen who wanted the police officer to assist in his/her death. Essentially, the suicidal person engages in intentionally threatening behavior toward a police officer in order to elicit or unleash deadly force. In a study conducted in Los Angeles, it was determined that 11 percent of all officer involved shootings between 1987 and 1997 were "suicide by cop" (Paynter, 2000).

SUICIDE RISK ASSESSMENT

For several reasons, assessing the risk of suicide is a difficult task. First, suicide is a rare event. It has been estimated that for those who enter the "suicide zone," the suicide rate does not exceed more than two percent (Mans et al., 1992). This is good news for a crisis counselor because it means he/she will most likely "overpredict" the risk of suicide. Second, as noted above, suicide risk is a moving target. Changes in "perturbation" and "lethality" influence the chance of suicide and these factors are, in turn, influenced by fatigue, alcohol/drug use, job loss, school failure, the end of a relationship, or the death of a loved one. Thus, it is better to view ones assessment of suicide risk as a short-term prediction, lasting no more than a few hours or days.

Third, each individual is different. Factors that may not seem relevant to one individual may be extremely important to another. Risk assessment, therefore, needs to be tailored to the individual's situation and not to a broad category of clients. For these reasons, it is advisable to assess risk as a scale of one to 100 rather than as a yes or no proposition.

Motto (1992) suggests that risk assessment is best accomplished through two approaches, clinical and empirical. In its purest form, the clinical approach is an interview. This approach enables one to make an assessment of an individual's risk for suicide. The empirical approach is more of a deductive social science approach in which all of the risk factors involved are examined and an informed decision regarding risk is made. While it may be best to use both approaches, it should be noted that the final assessment is a subjective one performed by the clinician or intervener.

What are some factors to look for in assessing risk? The key factor in assessment is the individual's level of psychological pain, both present and anticipated, as well as the individual's level of tolerance for such pain. Other factors include how hopeless/helpless the individual views the situation, and whether he/she suffers from "tunnel vision," and therefore, only sees one available option. Finally, the role of chronicity is important. If it is determined that an individual is chronically suicidal, the risk of suicide increases.

Another factor to consider in assessing risk is the fact that suicide is a multidimensional behavior (Mans et al., 1992). Suicide risk actually encompasses behaviors ranging from suicide ideation, to nonfatal attempts, to suicide itself. These three "behaviors" all reflect differences in the actual risk of suicide and cloud the ability of the intervener to assess actual risk. Risk assessment, therefore, also deals with an assessment of which type of behavior an individual will be prone; although, while the populations of these three groups are somewhat different, they also tend to overlap. Nonfatal attempts, for example, while viewed by some as a call for help, obviously contain an inherent danger. There are also differences in those who make one attempt, and those who are "repeaters." Individuals who have made more than one attempt at suicide show more chronicity of symptoms, higher levels of substance abuse, higher levels of depression, and poorer coping histories than those who make only one suicide attempt.

Mans et al. (1992) and his colleagues propose a model for assessing suicide risk that consist of four components. Whether one is a police officer, correctional officer, probation officer, or other criminal justice/social service personnel, these factors should prove beneficial. These components are:

1) *Psychiatric Diagnosis.* Within this component one looks for psychiatric diagnoses that are consistent with suicide (depression, personality disorders, mental illnesses, etc.)

2) *Biological and Family History.* Here one looks for family factors such as

a history of drug abuse or mental illness. To the extent possible, one also examines variables such as low brain serotonin, which has been linked to suicidal behavior.

3) ***Psychological and Personality Factors.*** Feelings such as hopelessness and/or unrealistic expectations are assessed. The more these feelings are present in the individual, the greater the chance for suicide.

4) ***Sociological, Economical, and Cultural Factors.*** This component of the model focuses on factors such as the presence of a gun, whether the individual is currently unemployed, whether the individual has just experienced a major life event (see Chapter 1 for a discussion of various life events and corresponding crises) which has negative consequences. Again, these are factors that may increase the risk for suicide.

In using these models Mans et al. (1992) caution that some factors will weigh more than others in particular cases. In talking with the individual, the intervener needs to determine which factors are more salient, and then develop a means to address the most pertinent issues.

Felner et al. (1992) focused on suicide risk assessment in youth with a particular emphasis on school-related variables. Youth suicide is not an impulsive act. Most youth who commit suicide will have communicated their intent to others. Therefore, risk assessment takes on added importance when youth are involved. Moreover, and in addition to the risk factors already discussed, youth face other factors that may increase the risk of suicide. These additional factors include being raised in a dysfunctional family, being abused as a child, belonging to a family where there is parental substance abuse, being angry, having a recent argument, ending a relationship, and for adolescent girls, recent criminal assaults or the discovery of pregnancy (Kral & Sakinofsky, 1994).

By virtue of their status as students, youth also face additional risk. For example, a youth who fails in a class, who is transferred from a higher "track" to a lower "track" in school, or has been labeled a juvenile delinquent may not only face embarrassment but may also question their chances for success upon leaving school. Students who attend larger schools, or who transfer from other schools, may also feel lost or lonely. In addition, schools that are undergoing transitions, schools that reside in neighborhoods characterized by social disorder, and/or schools where teachers fail to take an active interest in their students may enhance a vulnerable student's feelings of alienation and loneliness.

Felner (1992) and his colleagues propose three different methods that schools and others in contact with juveniles (e.g., juvenile correctional facilities, and juvenile probation offices) can use to reduce the risk of suicide among youth. First, they note that early childhood education programs that enhance one's self-esteem, coping abilities, social competence, and self-image likely will have a positive effect on suicidal tendencies. These programs may also alleviate other childhood problems such as delinquency, school failure and school dropout.

Second, they contend that there is personal variation in the amount of vulnerability one has. Certain individuals are more vulnerable to suicide ideation than others. The key in risk assessment is not only to identify the risk factors that lead to increased vulnerability, but to also try to identify those that are more vulnerable. Once this is accomplished, one can then alleviate the concerns these individuals have. Assessing vulnerability and its related factors is the key to risk assessment.

Finally, along with assessment, a quality suicide program must also have an *intervention component.* According to Felner et al. (1992), an assessment and intervention program must have five steps. These steps are:

1) Articulate Assumptions About Processes of Suicide Ideation,
2) Assessment Should Focus on Presence and Levels of Predisposing Factors;
3) Prevention Should be Designed to Reduce Vulnerability and Increase Levels of Acceptable Functioning;
4) Evaluation Should Focus on the Goals of the Program;
5) Evaluation Should Examine Issues of Whether or not the Program Reduced Suicide or Suicide Attempts.

In essence, a successful program would understand the processes surrounding an increased risk of suicide, and it would have, in place, a program designed to affect this process by either reducing the risk factors or strengthening individual resolve to life stress. In addition, the program would also have in place a mechanism to measure the level of risk in an individual and a mechanism designed to measure outcomes (i.e., reductions in suicides or suicide risk).

TREATMENT OF SUICIDE

At the basic level, suicide treatment must include an *assessment* of both sociological and psychological risk factors. However, as Frankish (1994) documents, suicide counseling must include more than risk assessment. A good treatment program must consider the seriousness of suicide gestures, diffuse the risk of suicide (by decreasing both perturbation and lethality), encourage and develop social interaction, use an empathic communication style, where appropriate seek consultative support and/or make appropriate referrals, and if possible, make follow-up calls with past clients.

In addition, a successful program also needs to attend to its volunteers and staff. Suicide intervention can be a stressful occupation. If job-related stress is not addressed, staff burnout and turnover can occur, thus diminishing the effectiveness of any program. In an effort to reduce stress, appropriate training must be given to new staff so that they can know both what to expect from clients and how they should respond to various situations. In addition, staff will need time to "blow off steam" and discuss situations that they find upsetting or discomforting. For instance, in work that this author participated in that dealt with interviewing spouses of violent and natural death victims, we found it helpful for our interviewers to meet in a group every six to eight weeks to discuss issues that were troublesome. This gave the interviewers a chance to not only complain about how their jobs were going, but to also discuss interviews that they found difficult, or situations that left them emotionally upset. Similar debriefing sessions may also prove beneficial to the staff of suicide prevention/treatment programs.

Frankish (1994) also noted other features of successful treatment programs. Such programs are characterized by being focused on their role and mission, knowledgeable of the risk and problems of their clientele, able to provide clients with the skills needed to change their situation and develop new opportunities, able to provide the support their clients need in making transitions, able to enable their clients to tap into and utilize the natural support systems available in the community, and having the integrity to rigorously collect data on their effectiveness. Others have also developed models for successful programs.

EFFECTIVENESS OF SUICIDE INTERVENTION AND PREVENTION PROGRAMS

The debate on the effectiveness of suicide prevention centers is still not settled. For example, Lester (1993) utilizing data from 1970 and 1980 concluded that in states where suicide centers were present there was a decrease in the suicide rate from 1970 to 1980. This decrease, measured by Pearson correlation, held even when socioeconomic factors such as divorce rates, the percentage of blacks, the female labor force participation rate, and the gross state product per capita were included. Lester (1993) concluded that a weak but consistent negative relationship existed between the presence of suicide centers and the rate of suicide.

Neimeyer and Pfeiffer (1994) who utilized citywide data to assess the relationship between suicide centers and the suicide rate have reached an opposite conclusion. They found that there was no difference in the rate of suicide between cities with centers compared to those without. This finding of no significant difference held when the data was examined at the county level. However, Neimeyer and Pfeiffer (1994) concluded that certain demographic groups were more likely to be helped by suicide centers. For example, the suicide rate for white females under the age of 25 showed a significant decrease in communities with centers when compared to those without. Neimeyer and Pfeiffer (1994) noted, however, that young white females are also the demographic group most likely to call a crisis hotline looking for help.

Another approach to measure the effectiveness of suicide centers has focused on the needs of callers to suicide hotlines and the callers' perceptions with how satisfied they were with the services received. A study by de Anda and Smith (1993) concluded that the primary reason that most people called two Los Angeles County hotlines was suicide ideation. In addition, they noted that the "causes" behind the ideation differed depending upon one's age and sex. The primary reason for adolescents to call was listed as marital/love problems, while both young adults and adults listed depression. For males, depression was the key factor, while for females, marital/love problems were the number one reason for their calls.

The researchers concluded that the interaction with the crisis volunteer was the sole intervention for the majority of callers. The lack of referral was seen as a problem. They noted that the crisis line appeared to provide services for those experiencing suicide ideation, but was of little help for those who were at high risk for suicide. In addition, they speculated that high-risk individuals do not call hotlines. The mere fact that one is high risk for suicide suggests that one has given up hope and therefore a call to a suicide hotline would not be perceived as beneficial.

Neimeyer and Pfeiffer (1994) offer a somewhat better assessment of the effectiveness of suicide hotlines. They noted that callbacks to clients suggested that most were satisfied with the help they received. The level of caller satisfaction is somewhat surprising since studies of calls to suicide hotlines suggest that such calls are too short in duration to be beneficial. In addition, assessments of the staff of these hotlines suggest that they often lack the training or expertise to be effective. For example, individuals who answer suicide hotline calls often lack the empathy, warmth, or genuineness considered necessary. Neimeyer and Pfeiffer (1994) conclude that suicide crisis counselors lack the specific training necessary to manage suicide hotlines. Not only is more training needed, but also, in particular, training on the specific aspects of suicide and its prevention would be helpful.

SUICIDE BEREAVEMENT

While coping with the loss of a family member or friend is always difficult, the loss from suicide may be particularly traumatic due to the nature of the death. Unfortunately, studies that have dealt with bereavement from suicide are based upon small samples and often deal with different aspects of coping, thus making generalizations difficult.

Suicide is an abnormal death since taking one's life is a behavior that lacks general social acceptance and often calls for official state intervention by police (crisis intervention) or the courts (emergency detention orders). While adjustment to any death may be difficult for the survivor, adjustment to suicide may be problematic due to the atypical nature of the death and the surrounding social stigma. In addition, due to its nature, suicide requires unpleasant interactions with the police and insurance agents, and may also result in unwanted questions from other family members, friends, and neighbors.

Survivors often withdraw into the immediate family, and social support for the bereaved may be diminished (Cain and Fast, 1972; Wallace, 1977). This can result in an individualistic grieving process with poorer overall adjustment. Demi (1984), for example, found that suicide survivors exhibited greater guilt and resentment, while Farberow et al. (1987) found that suicide survivors showed greater anxiety when compared to survivors of natural death. Kitson (1991), in a community-based assessment of reactions to death for a sample of spouses of homicide, suicide, accidental death and natural death widows, found that at three months after the death, survivors of suicides did significantly worse on five measures of psychological symptoms derived from the Behavioral Symptom Inventory. The measures were anxiety, somatization, paranoid ideation, hostility and the total BSI scale. The group that was significantly different from the suicide group varied depending upon the measure of distress used. Interestingly, suicide survivors also did "worse" on the remaining five subscales of the BSI as well as the level of depression measured by the Zung Depression Inventory. These latter differences, however, were not significant.

While the above research has suggested that suicidal bereavement is difficult, other research is more promising. For example, McNeil and Reubin (1988) noted that when compared to survivors of accidental deaths, families of suicide victims showed no differences in family functioning, life stress, and psychiatric symptoms. Barret (1990) in a comparison of suicide survivors to both natural and accidental death survivors noted that while suicide survivors differed in the frequency of grief reactions, the course of recovery was the same for each group suggesting no difference in recovery over time.

Range and Niss (1990) who compared homicide, suicide, accidental death, and natural death survivors in the long-term bereavement process supported this latter finding. Using undergraduate women who had suffered a loss at least two years prior to the study, these researchers concluded that the bereavement process for suicide survivors mirrored that of other deaths. They noted that as time passed, the social support received by suicide survivors increased to the point where it was similar to support received in other types of deaths.

CONCLUSION

Suicide is an escape for individuals who are experiencing too much psychological pain. Risk assessment, which is a measure of how much "pain" the individual is in, is based upon two major factors–perturbation and lethality. The key to the prevention of suicide is the reduction of these factors. However, these factors are constantly shifting making risk assessment a difficult task.

Prevention and treatment of suicide is also a complex task. For many individuals prevention/treatment is a long-term goal that not only involves an understanding of the processes that lead to suicidal thoughts but a strengthening of the mechanisms that can overcome or disrupt the wish to die. It is only through addressing these issues that an individual may overcome chronic suicidal thoughts.

Finally, many crisis counselors, criminal justice personnel, and school officials lack adequate training in suicidal prevention/treatment. Suicidologists are in agreement that increased training in both risk assessment and treatment would be beneficial in reducing the rate of suicide.

DISCUSSION QUESTIONS

1. What is suicide, and how is an understanding of this type of behavior important to the crisis intervener?
2. What is the frequency/incidence of suicide by various demographic groups?
3. List and discuss Shneidman's commonalties of suicide.
4. Discuss the concepts of "perturbation" and "lethality" as these pertain to suicidal behavior.
5. What are some special features to suicides and suicide attempts in correctional settings?

6. List at least three important factors to keep in mind when assessing a person for suicide risk.

7. Discuss the key characteristics of Leenaars' *five-step model* for crisis intervention with the suicidal crisis client.

SIMULATED EXERCISES

Simulated Exercise 1

You have just started to work as a radio dispatcher for the local county police department. You receive a call from a person who is lonely and distraught. The caller indicates that it may be time to "leave this world" and to "throw it all away." Indicate the steps you would employ in assisting this person in refraining from self-destructive behavior until you are able to dispatch a patrol officer.

Simulated Exercise 2

You are a youth worker in a state juvenile correctional facility. You have been observing the behavior of one youth in particular who has withdrawn and is depressed. Prior to ending your shift for the evening, you learn that he had just received a bad letter from home indicating that his mother and father are divorcing. The child is obviously distraught. Based on the material in this chapter, outline what advice and/or recommendations you would give the next team of workers in addressing this emergent crisis situation.

Simulated Exercise 3

Having graduated with a B.S. (major in criminal justice and a minor in counseling psychology), you have just taken a position with a crisis center in a major metropolitan area which specializes in intervention and prevention programs for at-risk street youth. Your position is Youth Suicide Prevention and Intervention Specialist. You have been asked by a local school to conduct an in-service program for teachers and other school officials. Outline the major points of your presentation to the group.

APPENDIX A

Additional Internet Resources

The following websites contain a wealth of information regarding suicide and the role of crisis intervention pertaining to suicide.

Suicide Awareness Voices of Education:
http://www.save.org/
Suicide and Suicide Prevention:
http://www.psycom.net/depression.central.suicide.html
American Association of Suicidology:
http://www.suicidology.org/
American Foundation for Suicide Prevention:
http://www.afsp.org/index-1.htm
Centre for Suicide Prevention:
http://www.suicideinfo.ca/
TeensHealth, Suicide:
http://kidshealth.org/teen/your_mind/mental_health/suicide.html
Suicide Lodge:
http://www.a1b2c3.com/suilodge/
Suicide and the School, by Carol Watkins, MD:
http://www.ncpamd.com/Suicide.htm
American Academy of Pediatrics:
http://www.aap.org/advocacy/childhealthmonth/prevteensuicide.htm
Focus Adolescent Services:
http://www.focusas.com/Suicide.html
National Institute of Mental Health:
http://www.nlm.nih.gov/medlineplus/suicide.html
Stanford Encyclopedia of Philosophy, Definition:
http://plato.stanford.edu/entries/suicide/
Suicide Prevention Resource Center:
http://www.sprc.org/
Center for Disease Control and Prevention:
http://www.cdc.gov/ncipc/factsheets/suifacts.htm
http://www.cdc.gov/mmwr/preview/mmwrhtml/00001755.htm
University of Oxford Centre for Suicide Research:

296

http://cebmh.warne.ox.ac.uk/csr/
DMOZ Open Directory Project, Suicide:
  http://dmoz.org/Health/Mental_Health/Disorders/Suicide/
From Around the World:
  http://www.med.uio.no/iasp/jan2002/4.html
Colorado State, University of Cooperative Extension:
  http://www.ext.colostate.edu/pubs/consumer/10252.html
Suicide and Mental Health Association International (SMHAI):
  http://suicideandmentalhealthassociationinternational.org/SMHAIhome.html

REFERENCES

American Society of Suicidology. (1998). 1998 Official Final Statistics, prepared by John L. McIntosh, for the American Society of Suicidology. http://www.iusb.edu/~jmcintos/SuicideStats.html.

Barret, T.W. (1990). Suicide bereavement and recovery patterns compared with non-suicide bereavement patterns. *Suicide and Life-Threatening Behavior, 20,* 1–15.

Bennet, R.C. & Turner, R.E. (1987). Predictors of accidental death and suicide. *Transnational Association of Life Insurance Annual Meeting, 70,* 36–45.

Berman, A.L., & Jobes, D.A. (1994). Treatment of the suicidal adolescent. *Death Studies, 18,* 375–389.

Bonner, R.L. (1992). Isolation, seclusion, and psychosocial vulnerability as risk factors for suicide behind bars. In R.W. Mans, A.L. Berman, J.T. Maltsberger, & R.I. Yufit (Eds.), *Assessment and prediction of suicide.* New York: The Guilford Press.

Borus, M.J. & Bradley, J. (1991). Triage model for suicidal runaways. *American Journal of Orthopsychiatry, 61,* 122–127.

Buda, M. & Tsuang, M.T. (1990). The epidemiology of suicide: Implications for clinical practice. In S.J. Blumenthal & D.J. Kufer (Eds.), *Suicide over the life cycle.* Washington, DC: American Psychiatric Press.

Cain, A.C. & Fast, I. (1972). The legacy of suicide: Observations on the pathogenic impact of suicide upon marital partners. In A.C. Cain (Ed.), *Survivors of suicide.* Springfield, IL: Charles C Thomas, Publisher, Ltd.

Caplan, G. & Grunebaurn, H. (1967). Perspectives on primary prevention. *Archives of General Psychiatry, 17,* 331–346.

CDC. (2001). Unpublished mortality data from the National Center for Health Statistics (NCHS) Mortality Data Tapes.

CJCC. (1986). *Suicide prevention.* Toledo, OH: Criminal Justice Coordinating Council.

de Anda, D. & Smith, M.A. (1993). Differences among adolescent, young adult, and adult callers of suicide help lines. *Social Work, 38,* 421–428.

Demi, A.S. (1984). Social adjustment of widows after a sudden death: Suicide and nonsuicide survivors compared. *Death Education, 8,* 91–111.

DiVasto, P., Lanceley, F.J., & Gruys, A. (1992). Critical issues in suicide intervention. *FBI Law Enforcement Bulletin, 61,* 13–16.

Farberow, N.L., Gallagher, D.E., Gilewski, M.J., & Thompson, L.W. (1987). An examination of the early impact of bereavement on psychological distress in survivors of suicide. *The Gerontologist, 27,* 592–598.

Felner, R.D., Adan, A.M. & Silverman, M.M. (1992). Risk assessment and prevention of youth suicide in schools and educational contexts. In R.W. Mans, A.L. Berman, F.T. Maltsberger, & RI. Yufit (Eds.), *Assessment and prediction of suicide.* New York: The Guilford Press.

Foxman, J. (1990). *A practical guide to emergency and protective crisis intervention: Dealing with the violent and self-destructive person.* Springfield, IL: Charles C Thomas, Publisher, Ltd.

Frankish, C.J. (1994). Crisis centers and their role in treatment. *Death Studies, 18,* 327–339.

Fuselier, G.D., Van Zandt, C.R., & Lanceley, F.J. (1991). Hostage/barricade incidents. *FBI Law Enforcement Bulletin, 60,* 6–13.

Garrison, C.Z. (1992). Demographic predictors of suicide. In R.W. Mans, A.L. Berman, J.T. Maltsbergen & R.I. Yufit (Eds.), *Assessment and prediction of suicide.* New York: The Guilford Press.

Gibbs, N. (1994). Officers on the edge. Time, Sept. 26, 62–63.

Goldberg, E.L. (1981). Depression and suicide ideation in the young adult. *American Journal of Psychiatry, 138,* 35–40.

Hayes, L.M. & Kajdin, B. (1981). *And darkness closes in . . . national study of jail suicides.* Washington DC: National Center for Institutions and Alternatives.

Heiman, M.F. (1977). Suicide among police. *American Journal of Psychiatry, 134,* 1286–1290.

Hendricks, J.E. & McKean, J.B. (1995). *Crisis intervention: Contemporary issue for on-site intervenors* (2nd edition). Springfield, IL: Charles C Thomas, Publisher, Ltd.

Homant, R.J. & Kennedy, D.B. (2000). Suicide by police: A proposed typology of law enforcement officer-assisted suicide. *Policing, 23,* 3, 339–355.

Jamison, K.R. (2000). Suicide and bipolar disorder. *Journal of Clinical Psychiatry, 61,* 47–51.

Jamison, K.R. (1999). Night falls fast: Understanding suicide. New York: Knopf.

Janik, J. & Kravitz, H.M. (1994). Linking work and domestic problems with police suicide. *Suicide and the Threatening Behavior; 24,* 267–274.

Jarvis, G.K., Ferrence, R.G., Whitehead, P.C. & Johnson, G.F. (1982). The ecology of self-injury: A multivariate analysis. *Suicide and Life-Threatening Behavior, 12,* 90–102.

Kiev, A. (1976). Crisis intervention and suicide prevention. In ES. Shneidman (Ed.), *Suicidology: Contemporary developments.* New York: Grune and Stratton.

Kirchner, J.E., Yoder, M.C., Kramer, T.L. Lindsey, M.S. & Thrush, C.R. (2000). Development of an educational program to increase school personnel's awareness about child and adolescent depression. *Education, 121,* 2, 235–246.

Kitson, G.C. (1991). Initial distress after violent and natural death: The experience of widows. Paper presented at the Third International Conference on Grief and Bereavement in Contemporary Society, Sydney Australia.

Kral, M.J. & Sakinofsky, J. (1994). Clinical model for suicide risk assessment. *Death*

Studies, 18, 311–326.

Leenaars, A.A. (1994). Crisis intervention with highly lethal suicidal People. *Death Studies, 18,* 311–326.

Leenaars. A.A. & Wenckstern, S. (1990). Suicide prevention in schools: An introduction. *Death Studies, 14,* 297–302.

Lester, D. (2000). *Why people kill themselves: A 2000 summary of research on suicide.* Springfield, IL: Charles C Thomas, Publisher, Ltd.

Lester, D. (Ed.). (2000). *Suicide prevention: Resources for the millennium.* Philadelphia: Brunner/Routledge.

Lester, D. (1993). The effectiveness of suicide prevention centers. *Suicide and Life-Threatening Behavior, 23,* 263–267.

Lester, D. (1992). Alcoholism and drug abuse. In R.W. Mans, A.L. Berman, J.T. Maltsberger, & RI. Yufit (Eds.), *Assessment and prediction of suicide.* New York: The Guilford Press.

Linden, L. & Breed, W. (1976). The demographic epidemiology of suicide. In Edwin S. Shneidman (Ed.), *Suicidology: Contemporary developments.* New York: Grune and Stratton.

Lord, V.B. (2000). Law enforcement-assisted suicide. *Criminal Justice and Behavior, 27,* 3, 401–419.

Maguire, K. & Pastore, A.L. (Eds.) (1997). *Sourcebook of criminal justice statistics.* Washington, DC: U.S. Government Printing Office.

Malone, K.M., Oquendo, M.A., Haas, G.L., Ellis, S.P., Li, S. & Mann, J.J. (2000). Protective factors against suicidal acts in major depression: Reasons for living. *American Journal of Psychiatry, 157,* 1084–1088.

Maltsberger, J.T. (1992). The psychodynamic formulation: An aid in assessing suicide risk. In R.W. Mans, A.L. Berman, J.T. Maltsberger & R.I. Yufit (Eds.), *Assessment and prediction of suicide.* New York: The Guilford Press.

Maris, R.W. (1992). The relationship of nonfatal suicide attempts to completed suicides. In R.W. Mans, A.L. Berman, J.T. Maltsberger & RI. Yufit (Eds.), *Assessment and prediction of suicide.* New York: The Guilford Press.

Mans, R.W., Berman, A.L. & Maltsberger, J.T. (1992). Summary and conclusions: What have we learned about suicide assessment and prediction? In R.W. Mans, A.L. Berman, J.T. Maltsberger, & R.I. Yufit (Eds.), *Assessment and prediction of suicide.* New York: The Guilford Press.

Mashburn, M.D. (1993). Critical incident counseling. *FBI Law Enforcement Bulletin, 62,* 5–8.

McNeil, D.E. & Reubin, R. (1988). Family survivors of suicide and accidental death: Consequences for widows. *Suicide and Life-Threatening Behavior, 18,* 137–148.

Moscicki, E.K. (1989). Epidemiologic surveys as tools for studying suicide behavior: A review. *Suicide and Life-Threatening Behavior, 19,* 131–146.

Motto, J.A. (1992). An integrated approach to estimating suicide risk. In R.W. Mans, A.L. Berman, J.T. Maltsberger, & RI. Yufit (Eds.), *Assessment and prediction of suicide.* New York: The Guilford Press.

Neimeyer, R.A. & Pfeiffer; A.M. (1994). Evaluation of suicide intervention effectiveness. *Death Studies, 18,* 131–166.

Olivero, J.M. & Roberts, J.B. (1990). Jail suicide and legal redness. Suicide and Life-Threatening Behavior, 20, 138–147.

Paynter, R.L. (2000). Suicide by cop. *Law Enforcement Technology, 27,* 6, 40–44.

Pearson, C. (2001). Inmate suicide prevention. *Corrections Technology and Management, 5,* 1, 52–54.

Petronis, K.R., Samuels, J.F., Moscicki, E.K. & Anthony, J.C. (1990). An epidemiological investigation of potential risk factors for suicide attempts. *Social Psychiatry and Psychiatric Epidemiology, 25,* 193–199.

Pulakos, J. (1993). Two models of suicide treatment: Evaluations and recommendations. *American Journal of Psychotherapy, 47,* 603–612.

Quinnett, P. (1998). QPR: Police suicide prevention. *FBI Law Enforcement Bulletin, 67,* 7, 19–24.

Ramsey, R. & Bagley, C. (1985). The prevalence of suicide behaviors, attitudes and associated social experiences in an urban population. *Suicide and Life-Threatening Behavior, 15,* 151–167.

Range, L.M. & Niss, N.M. (1990). Long-term bereavement from suicide, homicide, accidents, and natural death. *Death Studies, 14,* 423–434.

Rich, C., Ricketts, J.E., Fowler, R.C. & Young, D. (1988). Some differences between men and women who commit suicide. *American Journal of Psychiatry, 145,* 718–722.

Rich, C., Young, D. & Fowler, R. (1986). San Diego suicide study: Young versus old subjects. *Archives of General Psychiatry, 43,* 577–582.

Rudd, M.D. (1990). An integrative model of suicide ideation. *Suicide and Life-Threatening Behavior, 20,* 16–30.

Rudd, M.D., Joiner, T. & Rajab, M.H. (2001). *Treating suicidal behavior: An effective, time-limited approach.* New York: Guilford Press.

Ryerson, D. (1990). Suicide awareness education in schools. *Death Studies, 14,* 371–390.

Satten, L. (1990). Suicide prevention in elementary schools. *Death Studies, 14,* 327–346.

Schwab, J.J., Warheit, G.J. & Holzer, C.E. (1972). Suicide ideation and behavior in a general population. *Diseases of the Nervous System, 38,* 745–748.

Seligmann, J. (1994). Cops who kill–themselves. *Newsweek,* Sept. 26, 58.

Shneidman, E.W. (1985). *Definition of suicide.* New York: John Wiley & Sons.

Stack, S. (1990). New micro-level data on the impact of divorce on suicide, 1959–1980: A test of two theories. *Journal of Marriage and the Family, 52,* 119–127.

Stack, S. & Wasserman, I. (1993). Marital status, alcohol consumption, and suicide: An analysis of national data. *Journal of Marriage and Family, 55,* 1018–1024.

Swanson, W.C. & Breed, W. (1976). Black suicide in New Orleans. In E.S. Shneidman (Ed.), *Suicidology: Contemporary developments.* New York: Gnune and Stratton.

Tanney, B.L. (1992). Mental disorders, psychiatric patients, and suicide. In R.W. Mans, A.L. Berman, J.T. Maltsberger, & R.I. Yufit (Eds.), *Assessment and prediction of suicide.* New York: The Guilford Press.

Tanskanen, A., Tuomilehto, J., Viinamaki, H. & Vartiainen, E. (2000). Joint heavy use of alcohol, cigarettes, and coffee and the risk of suicide. *Addiction, 95,* 11,

1699–1704.

Tierney, R., Ramsey, R., Tanney, B. & Lang, W. (1990). Comprehensive school suicide prevention programs. *Death Studies, 14,* 347–370.

Trezza, G.R. & Popp, S.M. (2000). The substance user at risk of harm to self or others: Assessment and treatment issues. *Journal of Clinical Psychology, 56,* 9, 1193–1205.

U.S. Bureau of the Census. (1998). *Statistical abstracts of the United States, 1998.* Washington, DC: U.S. Department of Commence.

Vandivort, D.S. & Locke, B.Z. (1979). Suicide ideation: Its relation to depression, suicide and suicide attempt. *Suicide and Life-Threatening Behavior, 9,* 205–218.

Violanti, J. (1996). *Epidemic in blue.* Springfield, IL: Charles C Thomas, Publisher, Ltd.

Wallace, S.E. (1977). On the atypicality of suicide bereavement. In B.L. Danto & A.H. Kutscher (Eds.), *Suicide and bereavement.* New York: Arno Press.

Wass, H., Miller, M.D. & Thronton, G. (1990). Death education and grief/suicide intervention in the public schools. *Death Studies, 14,* 253–268.

Wicks, R.J. (1972). Suicide prevention: A brief for corrections officers. *Federal Probation, 36,* 3, 29–31.

Yufit, R.I. & Bongar, B. (1992). Suicide, stress, and coping with life cycle events. In R.W. Mans, AL. Berman, J.T. Maltsberger, & R.I. Yufit (Eds.), *Assessment and prediction of suicide.* New York: The Guilford Press.

Chapter 10

TERRORISM AND CRISIS INTERVENTION

JENNIFER R. ARNOLD, DANIEL E. ASHMENT
and VERONICA L. ST. CYR

INTRODUCTION

Acts of terrorism, while frequent in other countries, are a relatively new phenomenon within the United States. The World Trade Center car bombing of 1993 was America's first taste of international terrorism on the home front. For years, terrorism against Americans had been a geographically distant fear; the act occurring in a foreign land and the victims often military personnel. The 1993 bombing was devastating to the United States: frightening in terms of the ability of a foreign terrorist group to execute a terrorist plot on American soil. This would be the tip of the iceberg for things to come: the Oklahoma City bombing in 1995, while a case of domestic terrorism committed by Timothy McVeigh, was initially thought to have been performed by Islamic extremists due to the similarities in methods between the 1993 and 1995 bombings. The 1996 Olympics in Atlanta, Georgia, brought another act of domestic terrorism; one in a string of bombings which included the devastation of abortion clinics and gay night clubs, performed by Eric Rudolph. In the late 1990s, America saw school shootings which included the one at Columbine High School. On September 11, 2001, targets within the United States were attacked by the Islamic extremist group, Al-Qaeda. Four planes were hijacked and three flown into American landmarks, causing death and destruction in their wake. The emergency response to the events occurring at the Pentagon and the Twin Towers of the World Trade Center was of unprecedented scale. Many first responders lost their lives attempting to do their jobs assisting others and providing care.

The tragedy on 9-11, as well as the Oklahoma City bombing and the

Columbine school shooting will be discussed in further detail as case studies; however, they are used here to exemplify the variety of events which will be discussed in this chapter to define acts of terrorism. The U.S. State Department, as well as the Federal Bureau of Investigation, use a definition of terrorism which implies the use of force or threatened force on civilians or nonactive military to influence political thinking or activities. While this definition accounts for the players and activities involved, it does little to include the psychological impact of the event. As stated by Everly (2000b), "the explicit goal of any true act of terrorism is to create a condition of fear, uncertainty, demoralization, and helplessness, i.e., 'terror'" (p. 53). The psychological impact is not specifically intended for those who fall victim to the act, rather those that witness the atrocity and are either terrorized by it, or join in support of the actors (Ruby, 2002). For the purposes of this chapter, the focus will be on the crisis intervention response to acts which include the psychological and physical danger found in terrorism; these acts may or may not be based on a desire for political or ideological change.

Hacker (as cited in White, 1998) offered a typology of terrorist actors which applies to the mixed bag of motives found in this chapter. He names them: "the *criminals,* the *crazies* and the *crusaders*" (p. 24). Terrorism perpetrated by the *criminal* subgroup is a very rare occurrence; it normally involves random hostage taking during the act of another crime. There is little or no forethought involved in the action and no ideological or psychological reasoning or motive. Hacker's *crazies* are individuals who are psychologically unstable and turn to violence as a means to achieve an end. As stated by White, "psychological gratification justifies their actions" (p. 24). The two actors in the Columbine school shooting are examples of this subgroup; Klebold and Harris used the terrorist actions of hostage taking and murder to satisfy their psychological misgivings about school and popularity. The final subgroup, the *crusaders,* is exemplary of the most prominent type of terrorist to date; they would include the actors in the 9-11 attack, as well as Eric Rudolph and Ted Kaczynski, a.k.a. the Uni-bomber. These terrorists use acts of terrorism as a means for desired change; whether via religious or secular political ideology, "violence is accepted and justified in the name of the cause" (White, 1998, p. 24).

With that in mind, it is necessary to turn the focus toward the victims of terrorist events; the intervention provided by first responders at the scene is the necessary first step toward the eventual healing and movement of the victim into survivorship. This chapter is formulated to first give the reader a theoretical overview of crisis intervention responses to mass traumatic events. The theory related to the topic will lay the ground work for better understanding of the methods prescribed in the Best Practices section. Both sections are divided into three groups of study: individuals (adults and children), large groups and emergency workers, as well as a study of the conditions of bereavement unique to mass traumatic events. Commonalities exist within the treatment of individuals, groups and service professionals; however each presents a unique challenge which merits its own examination.

THEORETICAL OVERVIEW AND LITERATURE REVIEW

Throughout the course of this book, Dr. Erich Lindemann's essay entitled "Symptomatology and Management of Acute Grief" has been discussed as a seminal work in crisis intervention. Lindemann's insightful essay was brought to fruition in large part through his work with patients who had survived the infamous "Coconut Grove Fire." Dr. Lindemann's work with victims of such a large scale disaster underscored the fact that "the experience of sudden shift from well-being and gaiety to painful and serious injury, and for many the death of some loved ones, created deeply disturbing complications that needed special psychiatric attention" (Lindemann, 1979, pp. 47–48).

According to Lindemann (1979), the Coconut Grove Fire was a horrific tragedy that occurred the evening of a Harvard-Yale football game, in the Coconut Grove nightclub, where approximately 1,000 individuals had gathered to celebrate. The Boston Public Health Commission (BPHC) estimates this number exceeded the club's legal occupancy limit by 400 individuals. BPHC concluded that the most likely cause of the fire was a lit match used by a busboy to change a light bulb in the basement. In all, nearly half the individuals in the club, or 491 club-goers lost their lives in the fire.

The Coconut Grove fire was not a terrorist event; however, survivors' reactions to it were very similar to those who have survived terrorist actions given both are traumatic. Terrorist events often involve a "shift from well-being" to serious injury and the death of loved ones. Individuals involved in mass traumatic events, such as the Coconut Grove fire need, immediate crisis care. The research of Dr. Lindemann and his colleagues regarding the Coconut Grove fire became the foundation for subsequent theorizing of large-scale emergencies such as terrorist events and the role of crisis intervention in these situations as we know them today. If handled appropriately, service professionals performing crisis intervention after a terrorist attack "may prevent prolonged and serious alterations in the patient's social adjustment, as well as potential medical disease" (Lindemann, 1979, p. 74). Crisis intervention performed by properly trained service professionals may assist an individual in crisis to restore a sense of equilibrium (Aguilera, 1994).

The Individual

Terrorist attacks are aimed at inspiring fear and trauma among a large group of people. It is important to note that the group targeted by terrorists is, in fact, a collection of individuals. These individuals differ in several distinct areas. Some of the individuals are adults and others are children. The group will most likely be composed of individuals with varying nationalities and ethnicities. These differences may affect the way in which service professionals are perceived, and subsequently the quality of service they are able to render.

Each of the aforementioned features is important for service professionals to consider when assisting in a traumatic event. While primary needs such as first aid, water, food, shelter and safety must be met quickly and unconditionally; secondary and tertiary needs should evaluate factors unique to the event and attempt to tailor assistance in a personal and caring manner. Aguilera states "the minimum therapeutic goal of crisis intervention is psychological resolution of the individual's immediate crisis and restoration to at least the level of functioning that existed before the crisis period. A maximum goal is improvement in functioning above the precrisis level" (Aguilera, 1994, pp. 17–18). In order to restore and eventually improve functioning, individual characteristics should be considered in treatment and follow-up.

Like adults, children experience a myriad of reactions that require immediate professional attention. Children are vulnerable to crisis events yet "adults tend to underestimate the impact of disasters on children" (Schonfeld, 2004, p. 1400). As a result, only 27 percent of children who experienced severe Posttraumatic Stress Disorder (PTSD) after 9-11 received counseling. The first step in dealing with children is to assure them that the service professional is qualified and prepared to deal with their situation. Preparation and planning should be implemented immediately to ensure an effective response. Prepared and qualified professionals and volunteers must approach children with the same care and concern as they would with adults; it is important that rescue workers do not treat adolescents similar to younger children. An approach which is aimed at normality of a social, interpersonal nature will help children feel safer and more secure.

The Large Group

Terrorism is a unique phenomenon in that terrorist events have the ability to create large-scale trauma and psychological distress. As stated in the introduction, Everly (2000b) proposed, "the explicit goal of any true act of terrorism is to create a condition of fear, uncertainty, demoralization, and helplessness, i.e., 'terror'." Schreiber's study (as cited in Everly, 2000b, p. 53) posits that in many instances of terrorism the victims of the attack are not the true target. The true target is the population as a whole. When an act of terrorism occurs, "the 'psychological casualties' will virtually always outnumber the 'physical casualties'" (Everly, 2000b, p. 53).

To mitigate the psychological effects of terrorist events on large groups of people and the public in general, service professionals have developed a group crisis intervention program entitled Critical Incident Stress Management (CISM) crisis intervention system (Everly, 2000b). CISM can be divided into seven core components.

According to Everly (2000b), these components are:

1. Pre-crisis preparation. This includes stress management education, stress resistance, and crisis mitigation training for both individuals and organizations.
2. Disaster, terrorist, or other large scale incident interventions, including but not limited to: a) demobilization for emergency response personnel, b) crisis management briefings (CMB) for school, corporate, and general civilian populations, c) "town meetings," and d) incident command staff advisement.
3. Defusing. This is a 3-phase, structured small group discussion provided within hours of a crisis for purposes of assessment, triaging, and acute symptom mitigation.
4. Critical Incident Stress Debriefing (CISD) refers to the "ICISF model" (Mitchell & Everly, 1996) 7-phase, structured group discussion, usually provided 1 to 10 days post crisis (3 to 4 weeks post-disaster), and designed to mitigate acute symptoms, assess the need for follow-up, and if possible provide a sense of post-crisis psychological closure.
5. One-on-one crisis intervention/counseling or psychological support throughout the full range of the crisis spectrum (Everly & Mitchell, 1999).
6. a) Family crisis intervention, as well as, b) organizational consultation.
7. Follow-up and referral mechanisms for assessment and treatment, if necessary (p. 54).

A key component of CISM is Crisis Management Briefing (CMB). This element of the CISM model is intended to assist groups of survivors of terrorist attacks ranging from 10 to 300 (Everly, 2000b). CMB is intended to be used as part of a comprehensive CISM system "and should not be used as a 'stand-alone' intervention" (Everly, 2000b, p. 54).

The first step in CMB is to gather survivors of the terrorist attack. This gathering could be done in assembly areas or other large group meeting quarters. To ensure optimum attendance at these gatherings, Everly suggests that public announcements should be offered through the internet, radio, and television. Everly (2000b) posits that this first step of Crisis Management

Briefing is crucial in bringing together a community that has been torn apart by a terrorist attack.

The second step of CMB is to have a credible individual divulge any facts that are available concerning the incident "without breaching issues of confidentiality" (Everly, 2000b, p. 56). When a credible and trustworthy source delivers the information to a group, the message is received with greater confidence. There are three main objectives which step two seeks to accomplish: "(1) control destructive rumors, (2) reduce anticipatory anxiety, and (3) return a sense of control to victims" (p. 56).

After the group has been gathered and given accurate information regarding what took place during the terrorist attack, it is important to allow health-care professionals to disseminate information concerning "the most common *reactions* (signs, symptoms, and psychological themes) that are relevant to a particular crisis event" (Everly, 2000b, p. 56). Some of the reactions that should be discussed in regards to a terrorist attack are "grief, anger, stress, survivor guilt, and even responsibility guilt among survivors, friends and others" (p. 56).

According to Everly, the fourth and final step of CMB is to advise the group of coping strategies they can use in order to alleviate painful reactions to the attack. Stress management should be discussed during this phase of CMB. Questions from the group should also be discussed during this phase. It is important for survivors to know how they can best handle the signs and symptoms discussed in step three. In addition, information should be circulated that indicates where survivors may obtain professional help if required (Everly, 2000b). This stage will assist the victims in moving past the present fears and dangers to the optimal goal of achieving survivorship.

Emergency Workers

Many articles concerning the weeks, months, and years following the 9-11 attacks demonstrated the need for crisis intervention for service professionals. Although the need is clear, there seems to be a debate over when and how a service professional should be counseled. In general, debriefing has had a positive effect on crisis intervention; yet while some critics propose that debriefing should not be performed, many service professionals speak highly of it. Even those who have misgivings about debriefing still believe it should be completed, just at a separate time and location from the critical incident.

Dionne (2002), details the problems experienced by Emergency Medical Services (EMS) workers in the days and months after the events of 9-11. She contends that the Fire Department of New York City (FDNY), as well as other EMS organizations did not provide their emergency workers with adequate support in the days following the attacks which resulted in Posttraumatic Stress Disorder (PTSD) and other anxiety disorders. Of the EMS personnel interviewed for her study (all first responders to the 9-11 attack), many noted having nightmares, sleep disturbances, and various behavioral changes.

The EMS personnel detailed several problems that they believed could have remedied many of the emotional problems they experienced. First, the EMS workers were not debriefed correctly or quickly following the event, as proper CISM would have done. Dionne (2002) contends that debriefing should be completed as soon as possible and on-scene. This was especially noted with EMS working for the FDNY. Every EMS worker interviewed wanted a formal debriefing meeting, regardless of whether they received one during the 9-11 attacks. Second, the EMS staff noted the apparent lack of number and adequacy of counseling services. Third, EMS workers noted that many were reprimanded, and then referred to counseling when they displayed behavior that was a result of experiencing the trauma of 9-11; instead of being sent to counseling. The workers noted frustration because they were aware of these behavioral symptoms, but were unable to receive the time off needed to recuperate or deal with underlying issues. EMS personnel believed that their contribution to that day was overlooked, as well as the losses that they suffered; this perceived lack of appreciation naturally contributed to low morale.

Vogel, Cohen, Habib and Massey (2004) delineate the development and implementation of a support team for both EMS personnel and their families. The program detailed within Vogel, et al. began by using basic CISM techniques within the first few weeks of the event; it later expanded to a multiyear collaboration between EMS and the providing health care system. After the initial program came to the aid of the workers themselves, the providers found that additional counseling was necessary for the families of the EMS workers so that they may all receive services to facilitate recovery from the trauma of the event. The last two years of the program were used for additional development of the EMS crisis team which included a 24-hour hotline and an Employee Assistance Program.

Programs, like the one implemented for EMS workers, are also of great benefit to other medical professionals. Lane (1993–1994) examines the importance of CISM for doctors and nurses. While Lane (1993–1994) does not expressly use individuals involved in trauma caused by terrorism, the benefits of CISM remain the same and the sample users are service providers. Lane (1993–1994) focused her studies on medical personnel within a pediatrics unit and their use of CISM to combat long-term stress and anxiety after a patient's death. The CISM method facilitates a discourse in which members of the team vent and process the event; this aids in the emotional recovery of the workers and gives them the control needed to functionally re-enter their work. Debriefing has three program goals:

> to lessen the impact of distressing critical incidents on the personnel exposed to them, to accelerate recovery from those events before harmful stress reactions have a chance to damage the performance, careers, health, and families of personnel, and finally to facilitate the return of personnel to their functions in the system (Lane, 1993–1994, p. 304).

Lane (1993–1994) detailed a specific CISM debriefing which she observed on the unit and provided a sample information sheet, which in an actual debriefing would be given to the participants. The information sheet illustrates the specific responses in the demeanor of physical, cognitive, emotional, and behavioral reactions. For example, physical responses may appear as, but are not limited to: fatigue, chest pain, thirst, and rapid heart rate. Common cognitive responses include confusion, blaming others and nightmares. Anxiety, guilt, grief, denial and fear are common emotional reactions. Lastly, frequent behavioral reactions to a critical incident consist of changes in activity, changes in speech patterns, withdrawal and loss or increase of appetite. Lane (1993–1994) states that certain elements are essential to the CISM experience: the "opportunity to express feelings, nonjudgmental environment, and sense of shared loss and talking through" (p. 306). The benefits of debriefing are summarized as follows:

> Tension level lowers, participants return to a cognitive orientation, individuals achieve relative emotional control, participants receive help in self observation, opportunity for emotional venting, and opportunity for closure on the incident. (Lane, 1993–1994, p. 308)

The aforementioned principles pertain to the care given to service professionals who respond to critical incidents. These responses are helpful in assisting service professionals throughout the recovery process. In a sense by rendering their services to victims of a traumatic incident these service professionals also experience a traumatic event.

Bereavement

The bereavement process is a difficult period for friends and family of the deceased; however, death, as a result of terrorism or mass disaster, poses specific difficulties in mourning due to the extreme nature of the act and oftentimes the mutilation or lack of remains. These factors lead to a condition known as *ambiguous loss* (Boss, 2002). Typically, viewing the physical body of the deceased "provides cognitive certainty of death" and allows the grieving process to begin (p. 15). Viewing the body allows the survivor to change the way he/she perceives his/her loved one and allows him/her to begin letting go. In terrorist events or those of mass destruction, there is a lack of cues which would normally add to the concrete realization of death, primarily a body, but also including ambiguity of motive and large-scale destruction. Ambiguous loss may present a barrier to the survivors as they travel through the grief process. As stated by Boss (2002), "if the environment remains ambiguous, uncertain, and incomprehensible, cognition is blocked, emotions are frozen, and continued individual and family functioning are severely hampered" (p. 15).

Ambiguous loss can cause depression and anxiety in family and friends due to a variety of factors: confusion about the loss, the adjustment in daily life due to ambiguity, inability to perform typical death rituals, and the loss as a constant reminder of the irrationality and cruelty of life (Boss, 1999). Boss (2002) found that the formulation of personal rituals to memorialize the deceased is productive for those who can move past the ambiguity of the lack of physical remains, for example: the burial of a beloved belonging of the deceased, the urn of ashes given by the City of New York after the September 11 tragedy, or "certificates of presumed death" (pp. 15–16). These rituals present a surrogate as a representation of the deceased, allowing the survivors to undergo the change in perception mentioned; thus allowing them to go forward in the mourning process.

The rituals used by those affected by the disaster range from the small and very personal, as previously mentioned; or they may be large scale, involving members that may not have been directly affected by the tragedy, but have an emotional/psychological bond with the situation or its victims. An example of these rituals is leaving objects, flowers or letters at the scene of the event or at a location related to its victims. This sort of memorialization of the event or the deceased is termed *spontaneous memorialization* (Haney, Leimer and Lowery, 1997). These acts allow members of the general public, persons who would not normally be involved in the mourning process to be active and alleviate any anxiety they have toward the situation. In situations such as the Columbine school shooting, it also allows a community to highlight the cause or problem which resulted in the event. Similar to, but differing slightly from spontaneous memorialization, are community rituals of candle-light vigils or large gatherings to memorialize the deceased. Following large-scale traumatic events, or for events which garner large amounts of media attention, these community rituals are vital in the emotional healing of the community and is a show of support for those directly involved in the tragedy. It is widely noted that death rituals, whether traditional or otherwise are primarily, if not completely for the psychological benefit of the survivors.

VICTIM NEEDS

Introduction

Before delving into Best Practices, it is important that crisis interveners realize and understand basic needs of victims during and after the time of crisis: this is established by the Victims' Needs portion of the chapter. Not all victim needs are directly addressed by first responders; however, it is important to have an understanding of the continuum of care involved.

In responding to mass critical incidents, it is imperative for all responders to understand the primary, secondary, and tertiary needs of victims. Service professionals should also know the most common reactions to crisis events. First, everyone responding on scene must be prepared. As Dr. George S. Everly, co-developer of the International Critical Incident Stress Foundation states, "Get training. . . , When human lives are at stake, it is important to continue your training no matter how well trained you think you are" (Volpe, 1999, ¶58). Dr. Everly implies that training and practice are essential in preparing to respond to traumatic events.

In response to crisis events certain details should be determined in advance. The National Association of Crime Victim Compensation Board (2000) suggests to, "identify the lead agency coordinating the disaster-response effort and establish communication" and "identify and establish communication with the local victim-assistance professional in the area affected by the incident" (p. 5). Following these guidelines allows responders to utilize the benefits of a command center. This center serves as an area in which service professionals can have standards and procedures reiterated to them as needed. Often an outsider may be able to provide essential information that a responder may not think of because of the quick pace or the traumatic environment in which they are working. In addition, off-scene support personnel can easily activate additional help as needed (Morrow, 2001).

It is necessary to realize that crisis interveners may not have immediate access to the crime scene. Law enforcement regulations and procedures such as processing the crime scene take time and often delay other service professionals (Morrow, 2001). When service professionals expect this delay, it engenders patience, knowing that once they arrive they still may not be able to provide immediate assistance. An intervener should not arrive on-scene alone; the general consensus is that at least three members should arrive together.

Executive Director, Dan Eddy of the National Association of Crime Victim Compensation Boards, has stated, "The increasing frequency of bombings and shootings in recent years has dramatically demonstrated how crucial a quick response can be when these terrible incidents occur"

(NACVCB, 2000, p. 8). In addition, there are specific victim needs which must be accounted for. Primary victim needs should be addressed first, followed by secondary needs. Tertiary needs involve following through with additional help such as group or individual therapy.

Primary Needs

Primary needs are the most obvious needs. After a terrorist event or a mass critical incident there are needs that must be met immediately. These basic human needs include water, food, and first aid along with securing the scene and providing protection to the victims. It is crucial for interveners to identify themselves before attempting to provide any services. Service professionals should be extremely sensitive to the needs of the victims, without causing unnecessary hardship.

While meeting the primary needs of individuals, it is important that crisis interveners also attempt to protect lives and property (Volpe, 1999). The moment a service professional arrives, implications and perceptions are developed, and relationships are formed. When possible, those intervening should help victims who have characteristics in common. For instance, police officers are more likely to listen to other police officers; the same exists for firefighters, nurses, clergy, or mental health professionals (Volpe, 1999). In a sense, victims associate and relate to interveners who display characteristics similar to theirs. Peers have a way to explain incidents and occurrences in a manner which their fellow peers will understand. This fact implies that the victim is more comfortable working with individuals that they can identify with on personal level. As the victims realize the empathic approach of service professionals, it allows them to understand that the intervener not only knows what he/she is doing, but the service professional also understands what they are experiencing.

When a crisis event occurs, some very common reactions are lack of trust, anger, betrayal, and insecurities (NACVCB, 2000). A service professional's response must facilitate these needs and attempt to neutralize them. One way of doing this is to remove the stressors or risk-factors of a critical incident and help the victim feel "out of danger's way," all while utilizing the resources available in the most appropriate manner (Volpe, 1999). While providing the most basic needs, a service professional must also attempt to "stabilize and cut down on the amount of stimuli in the environment" (Volpe, p. 52). A stimulus appears in different forms and is decoded through the five senses. Giving information about the incident and understanding what a victim perceives to be his/her own initial needs are two effective ways in calming a victim (Volpe, 1999). Helping a victim regain control and overcome the incident through perseverance is another way to effectively assist a victim in need;

allowing a child to help in the process of bandaging a wound is a simple way to help him/her regain control (Miller, 2002). Although simple, this example illustrates the type of thought process that a victim goes through but also what type of thought process to which a service professional should adhere.

Secondary Needs

Once a service professional has identified the primary needs and cared for the most urgent needs, the secondary needs should be met. Here the crisis intervener would ask such a question as, "What can I do now that will assist in reducing the victim's distress?" (Everly, 2000a, p. 2). While this question is also asked in response to the primary needs, it overlaps into the secondary needs. Without prying or making the situation worse, a service professional should try to gain as much information as possible from the victim. One must remember to always assist and help the victim with the needs at hand rather than looking too far into the future. This process of information gathering is sometimes called debriefing.

Although debriefing is used frequently, Everly and Mitchell (2002) propose that "most crisis intervention is done individually, one-on-one" (p. 43). In that this is an obvious factor in intervening on scene, it is imperative that the service professional is able to relate on an individual basis while considering ones ideologies, behaviors, and attitudes. While questioning the victim, service professionals should attempt to correct any misnomers while trying to return the victim to their original state of mind (Everly and Mitchell, 2002). During this stage a victim should "recount the event in detail" (Flannery, 1999, p. 78). Listening to the facts and being compassionate are very important when dealing with jarred and distraught victims, which is often the case in critical incident events.

In accordance with secondary needs is the ability for a crisis intervener to be able to shepard a victim back to normality. The goal should be to make the transition back to everyday life (Flannery, 1999). Mitchell (n.d.), identifies key principles involved with secondary needs of victims. These principles are: simplicity, immediacy, and pragmatism. Simplicity refers to the idea that in the midst of a crisis event a victim will respond better to simple rather than complex interventions. Immediacy simply means that intervention should be rapid and effective. Pragmatism refers to the practicality of a response. It would be useless to ask a victim what they had for lunch before the incident occurred because this is not a practical response. After a victim is cared for, relieved, and regains control, tertiary needs should be considered.

Tertiary Needs

Tertiary needs are those needs which involve individual and group therapy along with follow-up procedures. These needs will be provided off scene although information will be handed out after emotional stability is recaptured. Information should be in the form of business cards, pamphlets, and/or any other written form. These referrals should include assessment and treatment mechanisms when necessary (Everly, 2000a).

Psychological needs must be met; there seems to be an overall consensus in that there are many different reaction methods; different people perceive events in different ways and therefore react individually (Everly and Mitchell, 2002). In fact, in some cases, as Miller (2002) indicates, "some time must pass" before victims will be receptive to this type of therapy.

When dealing with tertiary needs, Myers (2001) believes service professionals should consider the victim's long-term reactions such as:

> Grief and bereavement; psychosomatic symptoms; stress-induced physical illness; posttraumatic stress disorder; anxiety disorders; phobias; panic disorders; obsessive-compulsive disorder; substance abuse; domestic violence; divorce; work disability and workers' Compensation cases; major depression; suicide. (p. 5)

Once these reactions are identified the service professional will then be able to move on. Helping the victim not only overcome these thoughts, but also they will help the victim live with the crisis rather than be held back from it. Life continues despite lingering memories.

Although it is essential to facilitate primary, secondary and tertiary needs in order; it is not to say that one need is more important than the other; the trio must occur together. It is necessary to stabilize the victim, just as it is very important to debrief the victim in hopes of obtaining as much information as possible. The tertiary needs must not be forgotten; often it is in response to these needs that the victim learns to live with the traumatic event. The needs should be met in a specific order. Although not everyone will need to continue with therapy, the opportunity must be present. With a chance of over 80 percent of Americans being exposed to a traumatic event, being prepared is essential (Everly and Mitchell, 2002). As the old saying goes "practice makes perfect." Mock disasters and other practice circumstances should be performed. It is one thing to know how to do something; it is another to be able to perform. In this line of work, service professionals must have knowledge *and* be able to perform under high amounts of stress.

BEST PRACTICES

Individuals

Adults

Adults are a distinct group of individuals affected by terrorist events. After primary needs have been met, Miller (2002) posits that the first step in crisis intervention regarding adults is for the service professional to identify him or herself as such. An introduction may need to be repeated multiple times even if the respondent is wearing a name tag. The next step involves the ability of the responder to gather as much information as possible from the victim without coming across as overbearing or intimidating; the service professional is there to aid, not interrogate. As Miller suggests, responders of different fields must act as a team; this is an opportunity for them to obtain and share information derived in different styles.

Miller (2002) suggests that respondents should "avoid even unintentional accusatory or incriminatory statements. . . . Avoid platitudes . . ." (p. 7). To "ease the victim's distress" (Miller, p. 7) is the ultimate goal of the intervener. Medical treatment personnel have the obligation to share with the victim the services they are performing. When performing first aid one should adhere to the fact that the victim is in an unstable and emotional state. It is essential for service professionals involved with terrorist events to remember that "what disaster victims often need first is down-to-earth, practical provision of basic services" (Miller, p. 7).

In these situations one must also "re-establish communication networks" (p. 8). Miller states that it is important to "listen to the victim" (p. 7). If the victim is incoherent with no meaning it is still important to listen. This allows the victim a chance to perceive the respondent as a true and genuine person, whose main goal is to aid on a personal level. As Miller (2002) states, "Even the most hardboiled investigator should understand that a sympathetic, supportive, and nonjudgmental approach can do much to restore the terrorist victim's trust and confidence and thereby facilitate all aspects of the case" (p. 7).

Children

Service professionals need to ask the children as many questions as possible without seeming demanding or pushy. At this point the service professional would be debriefing the child. Once the child begins to regain a sense of security and safeness, the service professional should be prepared to give advice not only verbally but also through visual aids. As with adults, follow-ups should be made with the child and their family. It is crucial that a parent is notified immediately of the situation, and that they are informed of available services on both an individual and community level. Services should be preplanned and ready for immediate implementation. For these plans to succeed, they require school officials and service professionals to work together in forming a plan, method and approach in effectively helping children deal with crisis and traumatic events.

Emergency Workers

First responders, who witness and deal with the aftermath of a critical incident or traumatic event, such as 9-11 benefit greatly from Critical Incident Stress Debriefing. Although there is some disagreement as to whether debriefing should occur on-scene, or the following day, those that did not receive any sort of debriefing, or were improperly debriefed, were found to have a variety of anxiety-related behaviors, from sleep disturbances to PTSD (Dionne, 2002). CISM within high stress hospital environments, such as the Pediatric Intensive Care Unit found in Lane (1993–1994), was found to stabilize morale and aid in the productive reintroduction to work after a crisis. Two years after the Oklahoma City bombing, all of the body handlers surveyed noted few, if any, lingering PTSD related problems. Crisis management and debriefing were administered on-scene and healthy coping techniques were used after the event (Tucker, Pfefferbaum, Doughty, Jones, Jordan and Nixon, 2002). This demonstrates, albeit in one case, the utility and results of such practices.

Vogel et al. (2004), examine a short-term care program which developed into a long-term program after experiencing successful results with service providers and their families. The project involved two segments; the first was "to provide psychological support to EMS workers and their families around the individual and family challenges that frequently exist as by-products of this work and are heightened at times of disaster" (p. 36). The second involved providing support for the EMS personnel while working with them as colleagues. The support in need was that "in dealing with emotional issues they confront daily in the populations to which they are providing assistance, support that indirectly may help enhance coping and communication skills with their own children and families" (p. 36).

This process began immediately after the collapse of the World Trade Center. Mental health teams provided support and began discussion sessions. Workers were divided into sections depending upon the degree and exposure to the event. Crisis intervention continued on to the next day in which the issues of the impact on children and families began to surface. As the scheduled meetings were coming to a close the mental health workers were approached by the CEMS staff which had an interest in collaborating-programs; developing and instituting focus groups and family workshops open to all EMS workers. This plan shows the importance of implementing a support unit and in forming collaborations for the betterment of the situation at hand.

The crisis care given within the first week of the 9-11 disaster is an excellent example of the type of care that service professionals require to efficiently perform their job at their highest potential. The development and implementation of crisis emotional/psychological care of service providers is essential to maintaining the health and effectiveness of our most valuable asset during the event.

Bereavement

In the aftermath of terrorist events, it is necessary to recognize the differences and problems associated with the grieving process of family and friends that are specific to terrorism and large-scale disasters. It is necessary for crisis interveners to be aware of ambiguous loss and its short, as well as long-term effects. For friends and family members, rituals memorializing the deceased may be effective in alleviating these effects: they can vary in type, from burying possessions of the deceased to having a gathering of family and friends. Regardless of the form they take, these rituals are a vital step in the process which allows those close to the deceased to let go, and begin to move past the crisis event. It is important that these factors are widely understood by crisis interveners so that they may, first, not interfere in the process and second, so that they may assist in providing the family means by which to work through their loss.

When working with families or others who are dealing with a traumatic loss, such as those encountered after an act of terrorism, consideration given to those individuals should be similar to those outlined by Spungen (1997) in regards to victims of homicide. Spungen details four basic considerations which should be afforded to family members. First, family should be given the choice to view the body—even if severely mutilated, burned, or disintegrated. This offer should be extended with extreme caution and preparation of the survivors. Some time should have elapsed between the notification and the viewing, as well as providing the family with a careful explanation of the body's condition. As mentioned earlier, the physical evidence of death is extremely important in the grieving process. Second, explanations should be given to the family of the reasoning or regulations which may hold back the turning over of the remains for burial or services. This is especially important in cases of terrorism or other crimes which may necessitate further examination or testing of the body for criminal prosecution. Third, if no body is found, this should be clearly stated to the family. Alternatives to traditional death rituals of burial or cremation can then be examined and may incorporate items from the fourth and final consideration; relaying to the family the process by which they may acquire any belongings of the deceased. This could also include explanation of how they may be able to acquire a "certificate of presumed death" or a consolidated memorialization such as the urn of ashes from Ground Zero which was offered by the city of New York after September 11, 2001.

CASE STUDIES

Oklahoma City Bombing

On April 19, 1995, Timothy McVeigh parked a rental truck beside the Alfred P. Murrah Federal Building. The moving truck concealed a bomb composed of approximately 5,000 pounds of ammonium nitrate, found in agricultural fertilizer, and fuel oil. It is reported that McVeigh lit the fuse to the bomb, and then fled the area. At 9:02 A.M., the explosion from the bomb ripped through the north side of the Alfred P. Murrah Federal Building. The blast instantly killed 164 people; 19 of them children, many of whom were playing at the day care center housed within the facility. One rescue worker was killed in the resulting search and rescue effort. In total, 168 individuals were killed in the event; 700 treated for injury; 16,000 individuals were in the downtown area and experienced the blast and 12,000 individuals were involved in the rescue effort (Tucker, et al., 2002). The bomb was so destructive that, of the bodies pulled from the site, only three had not died instantly; fewer than 20 individuals were pulled alive from the wreckage after 10:30 A.M.

Timothy McVeigh was arrested 90 minutes later during a routine traffic stop on unrelated charges. His identity and involvement in the bombing was discovered before he could be released. McVeigh believed that the bombing in Oklahoma City would act as a "call to arms" for individuals with similar political ideologies; primarily that the government was overintrusive and infringing on the right of Americans to bear arms found in the Second Amendment of the U.S. Constitution (Handlin, n.d.). The incidents in Waco, Texas and Ruby Ridge, Montana were in the mind of McVeigh, catalysts to begin an offensive against the federal government; resulting in the devastating Oklahoma City bombing attack.

At present, three individuals have been found guilty in the plot and execution of the bombing in Oklahoma City: Michael Fortier, Terry Nichols and Timothy McVeigh. The three met while serving in the United States Army.

Michael Fortier was found not to be directly involved in the bombing; however, he knew of the plan and failed to alert authorities. For his testimony in the trials of Nichols and McVeigh, Fortier was allowed to plead guilty to four lesser charges of transporting stolen firearms, conspiracy to transport stolen firearms, lying to federal officials and failure to report. Fortier was sentenced to 12 years in federal prison with 34 months of time served and ordered to pay a $200,000 fine. Terry Nichols was sentenced to life in prison without parole for his role in the planning of the bombing, along with 48 years for eight counts of involuntary manslaughter and fined $14 million for building damages. Timothy McVeigh was sentenced to death by lethal injection after being convicted of conspiracy and murder. McVeigh was executed on June 11, 2001.

Response

Immediately following the blast, the Oklahoma City Fire Department (OKCFD) began search and rescue efforts, along with the Oklahoma City Police Department (OKCPD) who assisted and secured the perimeter. The local Sheriff's office and the Oklahoma National Guard assisted the OKCPD with security of the scene. According to Oklahoma City's Incident Command System, the fire department assumes top command of a disaster situation; however, within days a "looser unified command" was created by the OKCDF, the OKCPD and the Federal Bureau of Investigation (FBI) who handled the criminal investigation (Manzi, Powers, and Zetterland, 2002, p. 29).

The Emergency Medical Services Authority (EMSA) was a main supplier of emergency medical care and transport to several local hospitals including: St Anthony's Hospital, Presbyterian Hospital, University Hospital, Children's Hospital, and the Veteran's Administration Medical Center. Other agencies assisting on-scene included the Oklahoma State Bureau of Investigation, the Department of Civil Emergency Management, the Oklahoma State Highway Patrol, and Tinker Air Force Base. After being officially declared a disaster by the federal government, federal monies and resources could be further used on-scene. The Federal Emergency Management Agency (FEMA) contributed funds for local distribution, as well as 11 urban search and rescue squads (Manzi, Powers, and Zetterlund, 2002). Nonprofit organizations, the American Red Cross, the Salvation Army, and Feed the Children, assisted with support to the victims and families, along with providing support and food to the workers.

While search and rescue continued, the needs created by the situation invoked the use of new or dormant programs within the process. To better organize the coordination of communication and distribution of resources between federal, state and local entities, the OKCFD and FEMA created the Multi-Agency Coordination Center (MACC). The MACC opened on April 21, 1995, and was the "principle organizational structure coordinating communication among response entities" (Manzi et al., p. 31). The flow of information through the MACC allowed for a reduction in duplications of requests for supplies which occurred frequently in the first days of the search and rescue operation. MACC also received and distributed the action plans of the Incident Support Team to the various organizations involved. The Joint Information Center was located at the MACC and provided the source for public information on the disaster and rescue efforts.

Shortly after the bombing occurred, the State Medical Examiner's Office requested that the Mortuary Disaster Coordination Plan be implemented. The plan, created by the State Funeral Director's Association, assisted in the collection and dissemination of information concerning victims of large scale disaster. On April 20, 1995, the operation was officially given the title of Family Assistance Center. Along with collecting information about the victims, the center served as a support and counseling center for the families of the missing and deceased. The Center was the only site where official death notification was administered. The American Red Cross assisted the Center by staffing areas in which the families could wait pending notification; they also collected contact information from families who wished to remain in their homes rather than wait at the Family Assistance Center.

To assist with the psychological stress produced by the event, as well as the rescue and clean-up efforts, several agencies were mobilized. These agencies included: the Oklahoma Department of Health (ODH), the Oklahoma Department of Mental Health and Substance Abuse Services (DMHSAS), the Department of Psychiatry and Behavioral Sciences (DPBS), the University of Oklahoma Health Services Center (OUHSC) and the Oklahoma City Public Schools (OCPS) (Tucker et al., 2002). These agencies, along with the American Red Cross, provided counseling and support to all victims of the event, including the many volunteers and rescue workers. Within the first 72 hours of the event, crisis hotlines were established and mobile outreach teams were in place. Staff from the Veteran's Administration Hospital and the Department of Family Medicine at the Health Services Center provided on-scene Critical Incident Stress Management and Debriefing (CISM, CID) to rescue workers after each shift.

In an effort to cover all needed aspects of care, and reduce duplication of services, Project Heartland was created in May of 1995. The project, headed by the DMHSAS, was funded by FEMA through monies provided by the United States Department of Justice, Office for Victims of Crime. A statewide forum was held to incorporate the needs and concerns of project stakeholders; the result was 15 recommendations which dealt with ensuring quality of care, accessibility, and education of the media. The forum also request-ed that special attention be paid to the psychological needs of children in Oklahoma City. Six of the areas schools are located within five miles of the site; one had to be evacuated due to damage from the blast (Pfefferbaum, Sconzo, Flynn, Kearns, Doughty, and Gurwitch et al. 2003).

In turn, Project Heartland provided crisis intervention, individual coun-seling, evaluation and referral, support groups, outreach and educational programs. These services were available to all individuals directly and indi-rectly affected by the bombing including service professionals. To address the needs of area school children, approximately 20 percent of middle and high school children were evaluated to determine possible need of services. A psychologist was provided for the Project Heartland staff to ensure the maintenance of the staff's psychological health and assist in morale issues. This provided the staff with a necessary outlet for dealing with the emotion-al fallout of such a large-scale disaster (Call and Pfefferbaum, 1999).

Lessons Learned

Looking back upon the response to the Oklahoma City bombing, there are several lessons to be learned. First, while the city had a disaster plan, the plan was not designed for a disaster on the scale and psychological magni-tude of the bombing. Upon implementation, government officials quickly found holes in the plan where effective entities would have been helpful; an example being the formation of the Multi-Agency Coordination Center (MACC). One official stated "the MACC is something, that in retrospect, we should have set up immediately" (Manzi, Powers and Zetterlund, 2002, p. 31). Another problem resulted from the Incident Command team neglecting to incorporate local hospitals into the command structure. As a result, the hospitals had little idea of the on-site situation and would often receive redundant requests for supplies from several agencies involved in the rescue.

Second, agencies involved in the mental health response to the disaster did encounter some rivalry during transitional periods (Call and Pfefferbaum, 1999). In "Lesson from the First Two Years of Project Heartland," Call and Pfefferbaum report that the local chapter of the Red Cross was hesitant to relinquish their authority to the project and were reluc-tant to train the project staff; despite the fact that Project Heartland was sanc-tioned by the state as the lead authority in the psychological recovery of the community. Call and Pfefferbaum believe that to resolve issues of authority and rivalry, the government should clearly declare authority and that staff should be trained by the state agency "responsible for developing and main-taining the post-disaster plan" (p. 954). The project staff should become familiar with actors in other post-disaster plan agencies; working with the other agencies before the plan needs to be implemented aids in cohesiveness and ease of use when disaster strikes.

Lastly, the rescue effort encountered problems with various methods of communication during the first few days of the search and rescue process. Phone lines to dispatch and the Emergency Medical Services Authority (EMSA) were quickly overloaded after the bombing occurred. Not only was this a problem for individuals wishing to report damage or injury, but it also created a huge problem of communication between the two agencies. Cellular phones lines were also quickly tied. Authorities found that the most effective and reliable mode of communication was the two-way radio. A study of information flows after the Oklahoma City bombing, by Manzi et al. (2002), states that although loaded with traffic, the two-way radios remained functional throughout the ordeal; they were critical in the early response stages when the other modes of communication were overwhelmed. The rescue effort also employed the use of runners to transfer information. While this mode is dependable, it becomes less feasible as the site size expands.

In summary, the lessons to be learned center around the need for detailed pre-disaster planning; then it is necessary to practice the plan to eliminate possible problems and strengthen weaknesses. By making sure that the agencies involved have a thorough understanding of the plan and that all staff is trained accordingly, the difficult process of disaster relief will run more smoothly, possibly saving lives in the process.

Columbine School Shooting

On April 20, 1999, Eric Harris and Dylan Klebold both seniors at Columbine High School in Littleton, Colorado, arrived at school heavily armed with shotguns, nine millimeter's, and many homemade bombs and went on a rampage before killing themselves (Fast, 2003). A total of 12 classmates and one teacher were killed before the two committed suicide (Aronson, 2004). The event was aired on television and has been considered the "most dramatic and most devastating school shooting" (Aronson, 2004, p. 355) of the 15 that took place in a four-year span.

Consequences of this mass critical incident will never be overcome. Although the tangible evidence can be cleared, Columbine will never be the same. A complete internal makeover was performed immediately after the attack (Hurst, 2004). Rooms were moved; the ceilings and floors were made over. The ceilings were covered with murals, and a security system was installed. The heightened use of school security systems has made Columbine the norm in modern society yet, just five years ago in Columbine High School this was an innovative idea. This security system not only hosts

18 security cameras but it also has an automated gate system (that can seal off sections of the school if an intruder enters) and a computerized identification card which limits access to the school (Hurst, 2004).

Physical changes were not the only ones that took place; unwanted changes naturally occurred. For instance, enrollment dropped, raw feelings derived, and emotional wounds were ripped open (Hurst, 2004). Even though most of the staff have moved on to different schools and the students present at the time have graduated, there is still the reputation: a reputation that will never be reversed. Only time can heal, and after many years, some are still waiting.

Columbine was a wake-up call for the nation. It brought widespread attention because of the high profile of the case, and raised questions as to what constitutes an appropriate response to such incidents. Today we know that being prepared is key and prevention is optimal. We can look at the response teams of Columbine, learn from them, and upgrade our techniques to rise above the idea that they are simply adequate. They should be the best and in the following paragraphs the techniques used in response to the Columbine shooting on the dreaded day of April 20, 1999 will be discussed.

Response

Information for the following section was obtained from the Columbine Report from the CNN/Jefferson County Sheriff's department website: http://denver.rockymountainnews.com/shooting/report/columbinereport/pages/toc.htm.

According to CNN, the first call regarding the situation at Columbine High School was logged by 911 dispatchers at 11:19 A.M., one minute later the second call came in. These two calls were in reference to an explosion that had occurred off of the school premises. It was later determined that this explosion was set up by Harris and Klebold as a diversion tactic. Minutes later, another call was received, which reported a "girl down at Columbine High School." At 11:26, the first officer arrived on-scene.

Deputy Sheriff Neil Gardner was assigned to Columbine High School as the uniformed community resource officer. Mr. Gardner first responded to a custodian's call that he was needed in the "back lot." As soon as he arrived, students were running from the building in all directions. At the same time he heard over the Sheriff's radio "female down." It was 11:23 a.m., and by this time multiple patrol units and emergency vehicles were already on their way. So many personnel were attempting to communicate that the radios were flooded with traffic, which made communication difficult.

"As the first deputies arrived on campus, they were met by chaos and hysteria. Terrified students and teachers were fleeing in all directions from the high school in the suburban neighborhood" (Columbine Report, Deputies on Scene, n.d., p. 15). Many provided the deputies with accounts of what was happening and who the shooters were, or at least what they looked like. Often the stories were vague, inconsistent, and jumbled; leaving the officers without any concrete evidence or information.

During the crisis, it seemed as though the deputies' orders were to stay put, not to enter the building until the SWAT team arrived. Students and teachers sought any type of coverage; many found protection hiding behind patrol cars. Others found structures such as the equipment storage box located on campus. While continuing to provide coverage for students and teachers, officers radioed for backup. Gardner was assisted by two Littleton Fire Rescue units, both of whom arrived on an active scene, which is generally not allowed until the crime scene is secured. The officers told them, "Get the students and go!" The paramedics were able to take groups of students to medical stations while the officers provided cover for them.

The first priority of the deputy sheriffs on scene was to get the students and faculty to a safer location. This was accomplished through teamwork; with officers often transporting the victims from one patrol car to another, and finally to the medical assistance stations. First priority was given to the injured. The deputy sheriffs managed to secure the perimeter of the school, including all possible exits. Officers continued to provide coverage for victims, and to cover other personnel including the SWAT teams entering the school. As victims approached officers, they were checked for weapons and injuries before being transported to a safer location. Students in need of medical assistance were taken to on-site medical stations; others were reunited with anxious and worried family members. At the end of the day, the deputies first to arrive on scene were still working. Not only did they provide the aforementioned services, they were also involved in conducting sweeps with the SWAT teams, setting up outer perimeters, and controlling traffic.

Around 12:06 p.m. the first SWAT team, composed of twelve members from three agencies, prepared to enter the school. SWAT Lt. Manwaring split the twelve officers into two groups. Using a Littleton Fire Truck as protection, the first makeshift SWAT team began making its way toward the school. The second team followed the truck and entered through the west side of the school. The SWAT team members had an outdated floor plan, and inconsistent information about the shooters and their whereabouts. In addition, the team experienced several logistical difficulties, including lack of proper tactical gear and equipment, and a report of a possible sniper on the roof of the school. Their situation was further complicated by the fact that many of the members of this team had never met or worked with each other.

Upon entering the school, the teams were met with mass confusion, loud noises (from the fire alarms), flashing lights, and smoke. As the two teams continued to search, more officers arrived and were added to the search and rescue effort. When students were found, they were immediately evacuated and offered protection. The officers dressed in black (as were Harris and Klebold) found that many students were hesitant to believe that it was safe and that they could have faith, confidence, and trust in them. Throughout the ordeal, bomb squads and technicians were also at work inside the school. Numerous other sweeps were performed; SWAT team members were relieved of their duties, and other agencies joined forces to ensure all bombs were located and victims were reported. For a listing of agencies that provided backup and support on April 20, 1999, see Appendix A.

Victim services responded immediately to the scene with at least 150 counselors from law enforcement agencies taking part (Columbine Report, n.d.). Other service professionals joined victims, parents, and additional family members who had gathered on location. Usually members of the Sheriff's Victim Services staff check in first with a deputy or investigator on scene, and then, if requested by the investigator, talk to a victim one-on-one. The service professional's first goal is to ensure that the victim feels safe and secure. This is accomplished by encouraging the victim to talk about the incident. The magnitude of the crisis at Columbine necessitated an initial response of joining family members, followed by further counseling. Many students and their parents were separated; parents arrived panicked with hopes that their child was not physically injured during the shooting spree (Columbine Report, n.d.).

Advocates not only assisted in reuniting families, but they also sat in on interviews, posted listings of who was located and their condition (Columbine Report, n.d.). Advocates also provided as much information as possible to worried parents, and helped those in need of transportation to area hospitals. Two advocates were assigned to families with a missing child and were also instructed to assist parents who were rushed to the hospital. Mental health professionals insisted that students first needed to reunite with their family, and then they needed to be with fellow students. Once advocates were assigned to a family they normally assisted them throughout the grieving process until funeral services were held. Some of the advocates were volunteers and were required to return to their original job post to continue with their duties.

After the crisis, additional service professionals were hired to attend solely to the Columbine shooting victims. An effort was made to contact every student and staff member of Columbine High School. A Mental Health Unified Management group was established which was referred to as the Columbine Connection (Columbine Report, n.d.). The goal of the Columbine Connection was to provide students, staff members, and family members with local facility in which they could receive education on the events and provide a space for counseling and victim services. The group was established as part of a combined effort which included: the sheriff's office, the Jefferson Center for Mental Health, the First Judicial District Attorney's Office, Foothills Park and Recreation Department, and Parents and Communities Coming Together. Once the facility was opened, the sheriff's department of Victim Services acquired full responsibility for the victims of the Columbine shooting. The department's central objective was preliminary crisis intervention to help the victim through his/her initial response to the critical event. If necessary, the victim was then referred to a mental health professional for long-term counseling.

When the Columbine shooting was over, a total of 188 shots had been fired by Klebold and Harris which left 12 students and one teacher dead, in addition to 21 wounded. The two gunmen ended their shooting spree by committing suicide (Anthony, n.d.). Law enforcement officials found notes from the gunmen which claimed that no other people were responsible for their actions except themselves (Columbine Report, n.d.). The gunmen were quick to note that they had been planning this massacre for at least two years, long before any other school shootings had occurred. In excess of 2000 law enforcement and emergency personnel responded to the Columbine school shooting; a list of all responding law enforcement and fire/EMS personnel can be found in Appendix B. Charges were later filed against the parents of both gunmen. One man was convicted for selling the guns to Klebold and Harris (Columbine Report, n.d.).

Lessons Learned

It is evident that the main concern during the ordeal was communication. With more than 46 agencies dispatched to Columbine High School, the radios were flooded with calls (Columbine Report, n.d.). In addition, many agencies used different frequencies which inhibited their ability to speak directly to one another. Each agency had to go through dispatch to get information from one radio frequency to another. To some, this inability to use a uniform frequency, can be considered a positive circumstance. Officials have speculated that perhaps if all agencies were on one frequency more communication problems would have arisen. Information relayed by one agency might possibly have been confused with information intended for another agency. The central concern by several officials regarding different radio frequencies was the inability to set up a common command channel. This channel is used as a central station that all agencies may turn in order to communicate with the agency in charge of the operation.

In addition, lessons were learned involving members of the SWAT team. Some were deployed to the high school while others were deployed to headquarters. Many who arrived on site were unprepared. They missed briefing sessions (which would have been done at headquarters) and many did not have their tactical gear (Columbine Report, n.d.). This lack of preparedness posed harmful threats to the officers arriving on scene. The situation required an immediate response, which left many officers to enter the school not fully protected.

Many of the problems encountered during the Columbine crisis could not be avoided, such as the varying and often conflicting stories of how many shooters there were and where they were located. Other problems involved the unknown number of bombs and their whereabouts inside and outside the school, reports of potential hostage situations and snipers, arriving parents, evacuations, fleeing students, traffic control, and alarms going off inside the school (Columbine Report, n.d.). In addition, containment of the scene was an obstacle in itself. Organizing agencies into groups in which all tasks could be completed and medical assistance stations that were quickly overwhelmed were also concerns for the responders.

It is apparent from the aforementioned analysis that communication is crucial for an effective response to mass critical incidents. It is of vital importance that agencies and organizations come to an agreement and have a planned response for incidents of this nature. Both intra and interagency cooperation cannot be overstated. By analyzing the Columbine situation, it is evident that first responders set up a perimeter and attended those who needed immediate medical attention (Columbine Report, n.d.). Once fleeing and evacuated students and staff members were out of harm's way, they first were treated for injuries, and then sent to a location set up specifically for them. At this location, they were given food and water and received care by trained service professionals. Students talked to investigators and counselors, and were met by concerned parents.

A lesson shared by all involved in this tragedy is that through teamwork, obstacles can be overcome, and interventions and investigations can succeed. When agencies put aside any differences, this allows all personnel involved to manage the situation in a fully effective manner without bias. Actions are not performed for the good of a single agency, but for the good of all involved. When efforts are concentrated on the task at hand, lives can be saved and tragic situations mitigated.

September 11, 2001

September 11, 2001, is a day that the citizens of America will never forget. On this day, America was attacked by a group of terrorists in an unprecedented manner both in the loss of life and the means by which the loss was inflicted. After the attack, a bipartisan commission was formed by the

President and Congress with the express mandate of investigating the facts surrounding this tragedy. The findings generated by this commission are published and can be found in their report which is entitled: *The 9-11 Commission Report.* The bulk of the following narrative is taken from this report. It is not our intention to be critical of the responses or acts discussed throughout the case study of 9-11; although, since the 9-11 Commission's job was to analyze, investigate, and critique the situation, the information may come across as such.

The 9-11 Commission reported that on September 11, 2001, terrorists hijacked United Airlines flights 93 and 175, as well as American Airlines flights 11 and 77. The accounts given of the hijackings are taken from phone calls delivered by passengers aboard each of the respective flights, as well as evidence collected by various law enforcement agencies. According to accounts given by passengers, the terrorists, armed with knives and or box cutters, stormed the cockpits shortly after takeoff and killed or incapacitated the pilot and first officer of each aircraft, as well as several flight attendants.

The Commission went further to explain that the terrorists then forced the passengers to the rear of the aircrafts and informed them that there was a bomb on board the plane and they should remain calm. After a short amount of time, American Airlines flight 11 crashed into the first World Trade Center tower in New York City. About 17 minutes later, United Airlines flight 175 crashed into the second Tower of the World Trade Center. Shortly thereafter, American Airlines flight 77 struck the Pentagon. United Airlines flight 93 was the final aircraft the terrorists targeted. Due to heavy traffic at the Newark (New Jersey) Liberty International Airport the flight was delayed (9-11 Commission Report).

When the terrorists hijacked flight 93, passengers were able to discover via phone calls the fate of the other aircrafts. The passengers then decided to storm the cockpit and take on the terrorists rather than face a similar fate. After only a few minutes of struggle, the flight went down in an empty Pennsylvania field, killing all aboard. While only 20 minutes away from their presumed target in Washington D.C., the terrorists' plans were foiled, and many lives saved by a group of courageous passengers.

The 9-11 terrorist attacks resulted in a tragic death toll. In all there were nearly 3,000 people killed in the Trade Centers, the Pentagon, and United Flight 93. The attacks resulted in a greater amount of casualties than even the Japanese attack on Pearl Harbor. Throughout the course of 9-11, it became painfully clear that the U.S. was not prepared for terrorist attacks of this nature and magnitude. While service professionals did all that they were trained for, the fact is that terrorism of this nature was not adequately anticipated.

Response

According to the 9-11 Commission Report, "No one at the FAA or the airlines that day had ever dealt with multiple hijackings. Such a plot had not been carried out anywhere in the world in more than 30 years, and never in the United States" (p. 10). This lack of preparation led to miscommunication and lost time with the airlines, the FAA and the U.S. Air Force.

The 9/11 Commission Report concludes that:

> . . . the emergency response to the attacks on 9/11 was necessarily improvised. In New York, the FDNY, NYPD, the Port Authority, WTC employees, and the building occupants themselves did their best to cope with the effects of an unimaginable catastrophe—unfolding furiously over a mere 102 minutes—for which they were unprepared in terms of both training and mindset. As a result of the efforts of first responders, assistance from each other, and their own good instincts and goodwill, the vast majority of civilians below the impact zone were able to evacuate the towers. (p. 315–316)

The Report also states that between 16,400 and 18,800 were working in the World Trade Center at the time of the first attack. Over 2100 of these individuals working in the Towers were killed during the attacks. The Commission also concludes that over 94 percent of these casualties worked or were at meetings at or above the impact site at each Tower. Therefore, the 9-11 Commission's report proposes that "the" data strongly suggest that the evacuation was a success for civilians below the impact zone" (p. 316). Simultaneously after the planes crashed into the Towers, civilians inside the World Trade Center began to call 911; as a result, New York City's emergency lines were flooded all while four primary first responders were dispatched immediately on scene (9-11 Commission Report); these agencies encompassed the Fire Department of New York (FDNY), the New York Police Department (NYPD), the Port Authority Police Department (PAPD), and the Mayor's Office of Emergency Management (OEM). All four agencies combined deployed over a thousand first responders in a 17-minute period (9-11 Commission Report).

"Many senior FDNY leaders, including seven of the 11 most highly ranked chiefs in the department, as well as the Commissioner and any of his deputies and assistants, had begun responding from headquarters in Brooklyn" (p. 289). On their way to the scene, both the Chief of Department and the Chief of Operations had a good idea of the situation at hand. Considering the "fire's magnitude and location near the top of the building, their mission would be primarily one of rescue" (p. 289). From the FDNY, 235 firefighters had been dispatched, multiple engine and ladder companies were included along with the department's elite rescue teams, the department's single Hazmat team, and two of the city's elite squad companies, not to mention the support staff (9-11 Commission Report).

Taking the mission as a rescue mission rather than a firefighting mission, firefighters entered the building through the lobby and began climbing the stairwells, immediately they witnessed several civilians with severe burns. Firefighters continued to line up in the lobby awaiting their orders. The chief in charge, who had already conferred with the former fire safety director, building personnel, Port Authority police personnel and an OEM representative faced a great deal of confusion as they did not know specifics of the mission, very little information was being retrieved—"no one anticipated the possibility of a total collapse" (p. 291). Firefighters continued to climb stairs, stopping on floors, and searching for civilians all while maintaining contact with the command station in hopes that information recovered would be of importance.

As the FDNY was hard at work so was the NYPD. Even though NYPD officers were present the Commission Report implies that their main goal was to land a helicopter on the roof, considering the conditions this was impossible. In addition officers were in charge of setting up the perimeter while they directed fleeing civilians; continuing to assist, officers helped injured civilians and urged others to evacuate the area. They worked with the PAPD in clearing major thoroughfares for emergency vehicles and coordinating the closing of bridges and tunnels.

The Port Authority and OEM initial responses were to activate the Emergency Operations Center. PAPD officials without "standard operating procedures for personnel responding from outside commands to the WTC during a major incident" immediately began search, rescue, and evacuation operations (p. 292). An OEM senior representative and other officials soon joined in on the rescue mission.

All four primary responders were hard at work, putting their lives on the line to save others. True heroes rose to the occasion; many lost their lives; others sought support with peers and loved ones. In the end, these officers were also victims; afterward, those who survived the attack were learning to be strong and live again.

Lessons Learned

In response to the 1993 WTC bombing, the Port Authority had made several changes in emergency protocol. Many of these changes directly involved the World Trade Center and evacuation procedures. Due to these changes and the orchestrated efforts of first responders, the time it took to evacuate the trade centers was reduced from four hours in 1993 to under an hour for most of the civilians in the tower. These changes were directly or indirectly involved in saving many lives.

Service professionals were responsible for saving many lives on 9-11. These lives were saved at a high price, however, due to the numerous first responders who perished during the collapse of the Towers. Several challenges have been noted about the emergency response since the attacks. By addressing these challenges, it is hoped that future civilian and service professional lives will be saved. The following is a list of challenges that the 9-11 Commission found which hampered the emergency response:

1. Lack of protocol for rooftop rescues
2. Lack of comprehensive evacuation of South Tower immediately after the North Tower Impact
3. Impact of fire safety plan and fire drills on evacuation
4. Impact of 911 calls on evacuation
5. Preparedness of individual civilians
6. The challenge of incident command
7. Command and control within first responder agencies
8. Lack of coordination among first responder agencies
9. Radio communication challenges: The effectiveness and urgency of evacuation instructions. (9-11 Commission Report, pp. 317–323)

The World Trade Center did not have any evacuation plans for individuals who were on the upper floors during an event in which they could not descend the stairwells. This type of evacuation would be difficult in that it would require a sustained air rescue, which was complicated by several factors involving the magnitude of attacks experienced on 9-11. After the North Tower was struck, individuals in the South Tower of the WTC were told initially not to evacuate, and remain in their offices. Within 12 minutes of the attack, the Port Authority Police Department (PAPD) and Fire Department of New York City (FDNY) ordered the South Tower evacuated. The 9-11 Commission concludes that this evacuation would have most likely progressed if not for the second aircraft striking the building.

Several individuals wasted valuable time by attempting to reach the rooftops rather than heading directly for the lower levels. In the future, individuals should be informed of any obstacles they might face while evacuating, as well as potential blocked areas, such as the doors leading to the roof. Dispatchers and 911 operators were not adequately prepared for an attack of this size.

In addition, they were not informed of up-to-date information regarding the situation at the Towers. FDNY dispatchers and 911 operators were not made aware of the order given to fully evacuate both of the Towers. This led to some operators telling individuals in the building to stay where they were. Operators were also not informed of the inability to perform rooftop rescues, which would have enabled them to inform callers the only chance of escape was to head down the stairs rather than up. In the future it is important for service responders on the scene of terrorist incidents to provide accurate and timely information to 911 dispatchers and others receiving emergency calls. Furthermore, individuals should be informed of any obstacles they might face while evacuating, as well as potential blocked areas, such as the doors leading to the roof. Ultimately it comes down to the fact that dispatchers and 911 operators were not adequately prepared for an attack of this size.

It is crucial that individual citizens are prepared for emergency situations; it should be noted, however, that these preparations should not overtake the everyday lives of those involved. Individuals should be informed of disaster protocol, and participate in fire drills and other simulations. It is also important for individuals to be aware of the locations of all stairwells and emergency exits. According to the 9-11 Commission Report, some individuals stored flashlights which they felt helped them tremendously in their evacuation of the buildings.

Prior to 9-11, Mayor Giuliani updated an emergency response directive for the city of New York. This directive was formed to designate an agency to be "Incident Commander" (9-11 Commission Report, p. 319) would be in charge of separate large scale emergencies in New York City. The directive recognized that some emergencies involve such a high degree of complexity that it would be unclear what department should take the lead. It therefore provided for the Office of Emergency Management (OEM) to designate an agency to take charge of the situation (9-11 Commission Report). On 9-11, it was clear to emergency responders that the FDNY was responsible for clearing the building of citizens. The New York Police Department (NYPD) assisted in evacuating them once they were out of the building. Communication between agencies was somewhat disjointed, and could be improved for future emergency situations.

One problem which occurred repeatedly during the terrorist attacks on 9-11 was a lack of internal communication and unified control of agency personnel. This is understandable given the huge area of the Twin Towers. The FDNY had difficulties in coordinating each of its units; therefore many firefighters were in places that they did not need to be, and there was a shortage in other areas. In addition, radios were incapable of reaching upper levels of the towers and frequencies were confused.

The 9-11 Commission Report also concludes that because of the high concentration of firefighters at one scene in one place, any additional attacks throughout the city would have "severely compromised" the FDNY's response. The Port Authority experienced several of the same problems as the Fire Department. The Commission found that the NYPD was able to coordinate effectively its response to the incident. Part of this effectiveness could be explained by the fact that the agency was not in the Towers, but handled ground evacuation and traffic control. Another part of the agencies effectiveness may be attributed to the department's previous experience with large crowd control and dispersal.

The agencies that responded to 9-11 were not able to coordinate with each other effectively. Each agency had at its disposal several resources which could have been used in a more efficient manner. The 9-11 Commission writes that in the future, a combined intelligence entity could be used to receive communication from each of the agencies responding to an emergency, including 911 operators. This information could then be relayed on uniform communication frequencies to assist service professionals. According to the Commission, it is also imperative for agencies to invest in more powerful radios and other forms of communication, which have the capability to reach all areas in the event of a large-scale attack.

CONCLUSION

Terrorism within the United States, while infrequent in the past, is a current reality that must be faced with planning and preparation. First responders on the scene of a mass traumatic event have the unique responsibility of assessing the situation, as well as the individuals involved. Responders must first attend to the medical and safety needs of the victims, establishing a sound and secure environment. Then they should go on to address the on-scene crisis as perceived by the victim using prescribed best practices. Emergency responses, in general, are individualized and handled on a case-to-case basis; however comprehensive and detailed theories, models, and best practices can be formed and used in the implementation and preparation for critical incidents. The understanding of best practice techniques and repetition of their implementation is an asset to first responders when faced with a crisis event.

The research completed and techniques formed from the studies of the unfortunate events that took place in Oklahoma City, Columbine, and on September 11, 2001 act as a platform for future disaster planning. Severe emotional trauma, loss of loved ones and other reactions to critical incidents are examined to develop overall best practices in regards to adults, children and services professionals, either as a group or individually. As time passes, they also gain the opportunity of exploring the long-term effects of trauma, along with a detailed evaluation of the crisis intervention employed on-scene. The fact that terrorism is in essence psychological warfare cannot be changed; however, by readying an effective response to these acts we may in turn combat its emotionally destructive nature.

CHAPTER QUESTIONS

1. Discuss the purpose of devising a crisis response plan.
2. How does the work of Dr. Erich Lindemann relate to the treatment of terror victims?
3. Discuss the immediate (primary), secondary and tertiary needs of the victims in the Oklahoma City bombing, the Columbine High School shooting, and 9-11.
4. What are the best practices for crisis response to individuals? Groups? Emergency workers?
5. How does the treatment of children differ from adults? How are they similar?
6. What is *ambiguous loss* and how does it relate to cases of terrorism?
7. How can first responders and other crisis personnel assist those experiencing the loss of a loved one due to a terrorist event?

SIMULATED EXERCISES

Simulated Exercise 1

After critically examining the Columbine shooting responses, develop a crisis response plan for high school officials in regards to an incident similar to that of Columbine High School. Include responses to both the initial event and the aftermath.

a. What could have better facilitated the needs of the victims?

b. What preparations could the responding agencies done in order to prevent such an occurrence?

Simulated Exercise 2

Contact local agencies and determine what type of crisis intervention approach would be implemented if a terrorist or mass critical incident arose.

Simulated Exercise 3

Create a crisis intervention response plan for the criminal justice/social service organization of your choosing.

a. What steps would you take to aid employees during the time of crisis?

b. How is the plan unique to the services provided by your organization?

c. What are the steps for implementation and practice of the plan?

APPENDIX A

Agencies Providing Assistance in the Columbine School Shooting Response

Jefferson County Sheriff's Office, Jefferson County District Attorney's Office, Adams County District Attorney's Office, Adams County Sheriff's Office, Arapahoe County Sheriff's Office, Arvada Police Department, Attorney General's Office, Boulder County Sheriff's Office, Boulder Police Department, Brighton Police Department, Castle Rock Police Department, Clear Creek County Sheriff's Office, Colorado State Patrol, Commerce City Police Department, Denver District Attorney's Office, Denver Police Department, Division of Criminal Justice, Douglas County Sheriff's Office, Englewood Department of Safety Services, Federal Heights Police Department, Gilpin County Sheriff's Office, Greeley Police Department, Greenwood Village Police Department, Lakewood Police Department, Littleton Police Department, Longmont Police Department, Sheridan Police Department, State Court Administrators Office, Thornton Police Department, Westminster Police Department, Boulder County Crisis Intervention Team, Victim Outreach Information, Wings Foundation, The staff of Leawood Elementary, Children's Advocacy Center, Colorado organization for Victim's Assistance, Women in Crisis, the staff of Columbine Public Library, and numerous professionals from private practice.

APPENDIX B

Law Enforcement and Fire/EMS Personnel that Responded to the Columbine School Shooting

Jefferson County Sheriff's Office, Adams County Sheriff's Department, Arapahoe County Sheriff's Office, Arvada Police Department, Aurora Police Department Blackhawk Police Department, Boulder Police Department, Boulder County Sheriff's Department, Bureau of Alcohol, Tobacco and Firearms, Central City Police Department, Colorado Bureau of Investigation, Colorado Attorney General's Office, Colorado National Guard, Colorado State Patrol, Columbine Valley Police Department, Commerce City Police Department, Denver Police Department, Douglas County Sheriff's Office, Drug Enforcement Administration, Edgewater Police Department, Englewood Department of Safety Services, Police Division, Erie Police Department, Federal Bureau of Investigation, First Judicial District Attorney's Office, Gilpin County Sheriff's Department, Golden Police Department, Greenwood Village Police Department, Lafayette Police Department, Lakewood Police Department, Littleton Police Department, Northglenn Police Department, Sheridan Police Department, Thornton Police Department, West Metro Fire Protection District, Westminster police Department, and Wheat Ridge Police Department. Littleton Fire Department, American Medical Response, Columbine Ambulance, Denver Health, Denver Fire, Englewood Fire, Pridemark Paramedic Service, Rural Metro, Sheridan Fire, South Metro Fire, and West Metro Fire Protection District.

APPENDIX C

Additional Internet Resources

The following websites provide the reader with additional information on terrorism, including informative websites on all three case studies presented in the chapter (Oklahoma City bombing, Columbine High School, and 9/11), theories and best practices, along with victim needs, and responses to mass critical incidents.

Rocky Mountain News, Columbine:
   http://www.rockymountainnews.com/drmn/columbine/
National Victim Assistance Academy:
   http://www.nvaa.org/
Substance Abuse and Mental Health Services Administration's National Mental Heath Information Center:
   http://www.mentalhealth.samhsa.gov/
The American Red Cross:
   http://www.redcross.org
Office for Victims of Crime:
   http://www.ojp.usdoj.gov/ovc
American Society of Victimology:
   http://www.american-society-victimology.us/
National Crime Victims Research and Treatment Center:
   http://www.musc.edu/cvc/
Emotional First Aid:
   http://www.emotionalfirstaid.com/intro.php
Oklahoma City National Memorial:
   http://www.oklahomacitynationalmemorial.org/
International Critical Incident Stress Foundation, Inc.:
   http://www.icisf.org/articles/
Federal Emergency Management Agency:
   http://www.fema.gov/
Center for Disease Control and Prevention:
   http://www.cdc.gov

Department of Homeland Security:
  http://www.dhs.gov/dhspublic/
Federal Bureau of Investigation:
  http://www.fbi.gov
GPO Access, 9/11 Commission Report:
  http://www.gpoaccess.gov/911/
Critical Incident Stress Management (CISM):
  http://www.vaonline.org/cism.html
Critical Incident Stress Management Peer Support Training Seminars:
  http://www.cisresponse.com/
Terrorism and Social Work Practice: Memories of Terrorism in Israel, by
Patricia Levy:
  http://bpdupdateonline.bizland.com/bpdupdateonlinespring2002/id1.html
House Committee on Science:
  http://www.house.gov/science/hearings/full04/feb11/mcqueary_supple
  ment_2-11.htm
National Memorial Institute for the Prevention of Terrorism:
  http://www.mipt.org/
Counter-terrorism, Training and Resources for Law Enforcement
  http://www.counterterrorismtraining.gov/

REFERENCES

Aguilera, D. (1994). *Crisis intervention theory and methodology.* St. Louis, Missouri: Mosby.
Anthony, T. (n.d.). *Reconstructing the Columbine horror.* Retrieved May 1, 2005 from Associated Press, The Daily Camera Website: www.boulderdailycamera.com/shooting/reconstruction.html
Aronson, E. (2004). How the Columbine high school tragedy could have been prevented. *Journal of Individual Psychology, 60*(4), 355–360.
Boss, P. (1999). *Ambiguous loss, learning to live with unresolved grief.* Cambridge, MA: Harvard University Press.
Boss, P. (2002 Spring). Ambiguous loss: Working with families of the missing. *Family Process, 41,* 14–17.
Boston Public Health Commission (n.d.). *Chronology of a local disaster.* Retrieved March 5, 2005. from http://www.bphc.org/director/bda_medresponse3.asp
Call, J. & Pfefferbaum, B. (1999, July). Lessons from the first two years of Project Heartland, Oklahoma's mental health response to the 1995 bombing. *Psychiatric Services, 50*(7), 953–955.
Columbine Report (n.d.). *Columbine high school.* Retrieved March 28, 2005 from CNN, Jefferson County Sheriff's department Web site: http://denver.rocky mountainnews.com/shooting/report/columbinereport/pages/toc.htm

Dionne, L. (2002 September). After the fall. Journal of Emergency Medical Services, Retrieved on February 24, 2005 from http://www.icisf.org

Everly & Mitchell (2002.). *A new era and standard care in crisis intervention.* Retrieved April 11, 2005 from International training and response center: Mass casualties, International Critical Incident Stress Foundation. Web site: http://www.public-health.uiowa.edu/icphp/ed_training/ttt/archive/2003/2003_course_materials/0618_Teahan_CISM_Handouts.pdf

Everly, G. S. (2000a). Five principles of crisis intervention: Reducing the risk of premature crisis intervention. *International Journal of Emergency Mental Health, 2*(1), 1–4.

Everly, G. (2000b). Crisis Management Briefings (CMB): Large group crisis intervention in response to terrorism, disasters, and violence. *International Journal of Emergency Mental Health, 2*(1), 53–57.

Fast, J. D. (2003). After Columbine: How people mourn sudden death. *Social Work, 48*(4), 484–491.

Flannery, R. B., Jr. (1999). Critical incident stress management and the assaulted staff action program. *International Journal of Emergency Mental Health, 2,* 103–108.

Haney, C.A., Leimer, C., & Lowery, J. (1997). Spontaneous memorialization: Violent death and emerging mourning ritual. *Omega, 35,* 159–171.

Hurst, M.D. (2004). Columbine High: Five years later. *Education Week, 23*(31), 1–3.

Lane, P. (1993–4). Critical incident stress debriefing for health care workers. *OMEGA-Journal of Death and Dying, 28*(4), 301–315.

Lindemann, E. (1979). *Beyond grief.* New York: Jason Aronson Inc.

Manzi, C., Powers, M. & Zetterlund, K. (2002). Critical information flows in the Alfred P. Murrah building bombing: A case study. Chemical and Biological Arms Control Institute, Special Report #3.

Miller, L. (2002). Psychological interventions for terroristic trauma: Symptoms, syndromes, and treatment strategies. *Psychotherapy: Theory, Research, Practice and Training, 39*(4), 283–296.

Mitchell, J.T. (n.d.). *Crisis intervention and critical incident stress management: A defense of the field.* Retrieved April 3, 2005 from International Critical Incident Stress Foundation, Inc. Web site: http://www.icisf.org/articles/Acrobat%\20Documents/CISM_Defense_of_Field.pdf

Morrow, H. E. (2001). Coordinating a multiple casualty critical incident stress management (CISM) response within a medical/surgical hospital setting. *International Journal of Emergency Mental Health, 3*(1), 27–34.

Myers, D. (2001, August 15–17). *Weapons of mass destruction and terrorism: Mental health consequences and implications for planning and training.* Retrieved February 24, 2005 from ICISF, Orientation Pilot Program Clara Barton Center for Domestic Preparedness Web site: www.icisf.org

National Association of Crime Victim Compensation Boards (NACVCB) (2000). Compensation protocol: A guide to responding to mass-casualty incidents [Electronic version]. *NACVCB website,* 1–9.

National Commission on Terrorist Attacks Upon the United States (9–11 Commission). 2004. The 9/11 Commission Report: Final Report of the National

Commission on Terrorist Attacks Upon the United States (Official Government Edition). Washington, DC: U.S. Government Printing Office.

Pfefferbaum, B., Sconzo, G., Flynn, B., Kearns, L., Doughty, D., Gurwitch, et al. (2003). Case finding and mental health services for children in the aftermath of the Oklahoma City bombing. *Journal of Behavioral Health Services and Research, 30*(2), 215–227.

Ruby, C. (2002). The definition of terrorism. *Analysis of Social Issues and Public Policy, 2*(1), 9–14.

Schonfeld, D. J. (2004). Are we ready and willing to address the mental health needs of Children? Implications from September 11th. *Pediatrics, 113,* 1400–1401.

Spungen, D. (1997). *Homicide: The hidden victims. A guide for professionals.* Thousand Oaks, California: Sage.

Tucker, P., Pfefferbaum, B., Doughty, D., Jones, D., Jordan, F., & Nixon, S. (2002). Body handlers after terrorism in Oklahoma City: Predictors of posttraumatic stress and other symptoms. *American Journal of Orthopsychiatry, 72*(4), 469–475.

Vogel, J. M., Cohen, A. J., Habib, M. S., & Massey, B. D. (2004). In the wake of terrorism: Collaboration between a psychiatry department and a center for emergency medical services (EMS) to support EMS workers and their families. *Families, Systems & Health: The Journal of Collaborative Family HealthCare, 22*(1), 35–46.

Volpe, J. S. (1999). *Trauma response profile: George S. Everly, Jr. Ph. D. and Jeffrey T. Mitchell, Ph. D.* Retrieved April 15, 2005 from The American Academy of Experts in Traumatic Stress. Web site: http://www.aaets.org/article76.htm

White, J. (1998). *Terrorism, an introduction.* (2nd ed.). Albany, NY: West/Wadsworth Publishing Company.

Chapter 11

DEATH NOTIFICATION: THE THEORY AND PRACTICE OF DELIVERING BAD NEWS

BRYAN D. BYERS

INTRODUCTION

This chapter addresses a necessary and important task in the theory and practice of crisis intervention: death notification. However, little attention is given to this activity. Stewart, Lord, and Mercer (2000) note in their survey results of death notifers that 70 percent had performed at least one notification, only 40 percent had not received classroom or experiential learning on how to conduct a delivery. The delivery of "death news" is a task that can befall police officers, police chaplains, coroners/medical examiners, physicians, nurses, and various social service personnel. This is often a challenging and difficult task due to the manner in which society views death. Many issues within society have been designated "taboo" and, as a result, generate anxiety. One of these topics has been mortality. Death is sometimes expected (e.g., a terminal illness), or it may be very unexpected (e.g., traffic accident, homicide, etc.). In either circumstance the survivor; in many instances, has been taught through socialization not to be prepared for death. This is quite natural since few dwell on their demise or that of others. Unfortunately, no amount of forethought can prepare someone for the social and psychological trauma elicited from the news of a loved one's death. The death notification is a crisis situation for the *receiver* (i.e., the person receiving the death notification) and an important crisis intervention task for the *notifier* (i.e., the person delivering the death news). The death notification is a rare crisis intervention encounter, because it is perhaps the only crisis situation where the intervener is bringing the crisis producing precipitating

341

event–the news of death.

It is appropriate at this time to provide the reader with important definitions, which will be used throughout this chapter. First, the term "death notification" denotes the broader task and process of delivering a death notice or telling someone of a death. The term "death notice" describes the moment a person receives the news of someone's death. There are also important definitions concerning the roles involved in this process. The "notifier" is the person who delivers the death notice through the notification process. The notifier may be a police officer/peace officer, police chaplain/clergy, coroner or deputy, social service worker, or someone in the medical profession, such as a physician or a medical social worker. The "receiver" is the designated person receiving the information about the deceased; the label "survivor" may be used synonymously. The receiver will normally be a relative or friend of the one who has died.

There are also important concepts related to crisis intervention. A formal definition for "crisis" is offered below since space does not suffice here; however, the term "intervention" describes any constructive step(s) taken by the notifier in delivering the notice and/or to assist the receiver through a very difficult time. A crisis is normally produced with the onset of a "hazardous event" or "precipitating event" (Smith, 1978; Burgess and Baldwin, 1981). These concepts are used to describe crisis-producing situations, which elicit a crisis reaction; the death of a loved one may be one such event. Within the context of this chapter, "intervener" and "notifier" may be used interchangeably since it is our hope that the person giving the notice will engage in helping behavior, in the form of crisis intervention, directed toward the receiver during the notification process. Other pertinent definitions and concepts not featured above will be fully described below. Now that the essential definitions have been given, we turn to the chapter objective.

The objective of this chapter is to provide the reader with essential background information in the area of crisis intervention and death notification. The first half of the chapter is devoted to the theoretical foundation necessary for understanding a personal crisis and to conduct a professional notification. This is accomplished in two ways. First, the reader is given a theoretical overview of literature pertinent to crisis intervention. Second, specific death notification literature is presented. This provides a foundation of prior literature in this topical area. Third, the attention turns to translating theory into practice through a discussion centered on crisis intervention phase/stage models, model strengths, and limitations.

The second half of the chapter is devoted to the criminal justice aspects of death notification. This is also done in sections. First, pertinent issues related to death notification for criminal justice practitioners are addressed. Aspects of this section include reactions to the death notification task, responsibility for the notification, networking, and special circumstances one might encounter; secondly, a death notification procedure is offered to the reader with the intent of providing a clear delivery strategy. This section also includes a discussion of the death notification situation, roles of both notifier and receiver, the crisis intervention/notification process, and issues related to these elements. Finally, the chapter concludes with summary remarks and simulated exercises.

THEORETICAL OVERVIEW & LITERATURE REVIEW

Classical Crisis Intervention

Classical statements in the area of crisis intervention come from various authors and theorists (Lindemann, 1944; Rapoport, 1962; Caplan, 1964). These theorists outline specific dimensions of the crisis experience and the necessary and appropriate steps for suitable intervention. Most crisis theory is based, at least in part, on the seminal work of Erich Lindemann entitled, "Symptomatology and Management of Acute Grief" (1944). In this benchmark work, the author discusses observations of acute grief in response to death and disaster. In addition, attention is given to normal grieving reactions and the management of both normal and abnormal reactions. Within this classic work, Lindemann introduces such concepts as "grief work," which is the act of emancipating oneself from the image of the deceased, and "anticipatory grief," which involves the symbolic preparation for the loss of a loved one (e.g., such as the soldier going off to war). Lindemann maintains that grief work is essential to the management of acute crisis while there is no assurance that anticipatory grief will prepare someone for ". . . a sudden death notice. . . ." (p. 148), an issue pertinent to this chapter. This point strengthens the need for an effective delivery process in order to minimize the trauma this precipitating event often produces, and to effectively attend to the person in crisis. Following this objective, the author concludes that "prolonged and serious" problems in "social adjustment" may best be curtailed through effective grief management. Such management may be achieved through offers of comfort, relationship review, and verbalization of feelings. All of these strategies focus on assisting the person through the crisis.

Rapoport (1962) also discusses the traumatic nature of personal crisis and practice implications. According to this author, drawing from the classic work of W.I. Thomas, a "crisis" is a call for action and an opportunity to develop new coping mechanisms. Through the crisis experience, a person may learn new and more effective methods of dealing with stress-related crisis events and raise one's level of mental health. The author's use of

Thomasonian theory is quite useful in understanding crisis situations. Straus (1984) also relates the importance of this work in counseling and intervention. Byers (1987) further illustrates the use of such theory in the practice of crisis intervention. In this work, he discusses how the "definition of the situation" can provide valuable insight into the crisis situation for assessment, interpretation, redefinition, and resolution (Byers, 1987). More is offered below concerning the utility of this theory as it applies to death notification.

Gerald Caplan (1964), one of the first prominent crisis theorists, focuses on the idea that a crisis is produced by some stressful stimulus, normally referred to as a "hazardous" event or "precipitating event," and this event creates a state of disequilibrium or emotional imbalance. The imbalance involves the mental status of the person experiencing the crisis to the extent that the person is incapable of "normal" (based on societal standards) functioning. The crisis experience prohibits the person from achieving the normal day-to-day functioning level characteristic of most individuals not in crisis. An imbalance exists in cognition (thought) and affect (feeling); anxiety may exist and normal judgment may be clouded. The disequilibrium, therefore, incapacitates the individual in terms of balance in feeling and thought. Most crisis theorists, including Caplan, maintain that the crisis experience is short in duration, usually lasting not more than ten weeks. The crisis induced by the hazardous event, such as the death of a loved one, may have a short duration; however, one must remember that the normal grief process begins after the crisis and could extend for several months. For Caplan, the goal of crisis intervention is to bring the person to their pre-crisis level of functioning; this is also the goal of many other crisis intervention theories (Smith, 1978).

The onset of a hazardous or precipitating event producing a personal crisis creates intense trauma. One's normally balanced world, involving affect/feeling, cognition/thought, social roles, and coping mechanisms, seemingly disappears. The extent of a personal crisis, and intensity, depends on the individual. No two people experience the same type of hazardous event the very same way. For this reason, one must be cognizant of the variable, and unique, nature of the crisis experience.

Contemporary Crisis Intervention

Contemporary crisis intervention theory and practice owes its origins to the efforts of classical practitioners and theorists. Crisis theory, and crisis intervention, is found in various disciplines such as psychology, counseling, medicine, criminal justice, social welfare and sociology. As Ewing (1978) points out, the crisis theory model is quite different than the traditional medical model (p. 81). Although the classical statements primarily come from the medical and psychiatric traditions, crisis theory and intervention lacks complete unity. This is likely an inevitable by-product of the multidisciplinary nature of crisis theory, but it may also be its strength. However, some authors have suggested attempts to unify the discipline by providing clear conceptual definitions and easily applicable crisis models (Smith, 1978) while others have offered integrated crisis intervention approaches (Baldwin, 1979; Hendricks, 1985; Byers, 1987) and strategies for special populations (Hendricks and Byers, 1983; Byers and Hendricks, 1986).

Baldwin (1979) offers a useful presentation of crisis stages, corollaries of crisis theory, crisis types, and an intervention process. This is a general approach that has broad application to various crisis situations. Hendricks (1985), Romano (1990), Hendricks and Byers (1992), and Hendricks and McKean (1995) provide an approach to crisis intervention with a special emphasis on the criminal justice practitioner. This work gives the reader useful knowledge in the principles of crisis assessment and intervention as applied to specific settings and situations. Earlier, Hendricks and Byers (1983) developed a training approach for death notification as applied to county coroners, and Byers and Hendricks (1986) applied intervention strategies to another specific population. In 1986, they discussed the utility of crisis theory and intervention for the suicidal elder. In the latter work, they presented an applied approach to the elderly again by demonstrating the use of intervention in cases of elder abuse and neglect. Byers' (1987) discussion centers on the utility of an integrated approach of crisis intervention theory and practice and clinical sociology. The use of social psychology and clinical sociology are illustrated in the areas of crisis definition, assessment, and intervention. These authors offer more contemporary presentations building on previous work, and they offer useful applications of crisis intervention theory and practice.

An important element of each classical and contemporary presentation is how a crisis is defined by the individual, and how such an event is perceived by the intervener (Morrice, 1976). According to Lazarus (1966), a crisis is ". . . a limited period in which an individual or group is exposed to threats and demands which are at or near the limits of their resources to cope . . ."(p. 407) and includes important *subjective aspects* in response to situations. Although each crisis experience has its own unique qualities, crises do have common characteristics. As Ewing (1978) notes, crises are ". . . emotional reactions to situations . . ." (p. 81). This point illustrates the importance of the situational definition of a crisis produced from an interpretation of a precipitating or hazardous event.

For clarification, then, the following crisis definition utilizes various crisis themes from Rapoport (1962), Smith (1978), Hendricks (1985), and describes a crisis as (Byers, 1987; p. 105):

The unpleasant psychological and social feelings/sensations, which result from the onset of a perceived insurmountable stressful life event, disrupting stability, and accompanied by an inability to adjust or cope.

Although this definition offers the reader the basic characteristics of a crisis experience, one must be cognizant of the fact that the individual will always have unique perceptions and emotional sensations. This idea of unique experience, and how a crisis manifests itself, is closely linked to the work of W.I. Thomas (1923, 1928). Lydia Rapoport (1962), a prominent crisis theorist, recognizes the value of this social theorist's work. Due to its relevance to death notification, attention is now given to the theory of W.I. Thomas, the "definition of the situation," and applications to crisis intervention.

DEFINITION OF THE SITUATION

The definition of the situation is the unique interpretation of an event, through social perception, involving beliefs concerning the nature of an interpersonal interaction (Thomas, 1923, 1928). Crises involve a definition of the situation. Since a crisis is a situational experience which is defined from a unique individual social and psychological perspective, the notifier and the receiver will have unique situational definitions occurring simultaneously. The receiver will likely have a definition of the situation that is consumed with pain, suffering, and shock. In contrast, the notifier may have a definition of the situation characterized by anxiety, lack of surety, and hopes of conducting the notification effectively thereby minimizing receiver trauma. It is important to always be cognizant of the ever-present reality of dual situational definitions. One is held by the receiver and one by the notifier.

The crisis experience is not only something which may lead to better coping mechanisms, but it is also something which may best be understood situationally. As stated above, Rapoport (1962) introduced the field of crisis intervention to the work of W.I. Thomas. According to Rapoport, drawing from Thomas, a crisis experience may be viewed as an opportunity for a different, and often better, state of mental well being. The crisis is a challenge that may be confronted and dealt with effectively, thereby, eliciting new coping mechanisms for dealing with future crises. Even if this outcome is not achievable, the notifier's understanding of the receiver's situational definition will be useful in interpreting the entire crisis situation.

In order for this understanding to occur, one must empathize with the receiver and attempt to understand their definition of the situation. Each personal crisis experience will be defined differently. This "definition of the situation" (Thomas, 1928) depends on the coping mechanisms the person has at hand and their own unique crisis event interpretation (Byers, 1987). The definition of the situation means that people respond to the *objective features* of a situation *and* the *social meaning* that the situation has for them (Thomas, 1928; Coser, 1977). In other words, the objective feature of a crisis may be the death of a loved one. However, this only provides the notifier with "objective" information; it does not indicate anything about the "experience" the loss will produce for the receiver. The social meaning of the situation is applied to the objective feature of the situation, and the crisis is produced. The social meaning of the situation provides a foundation for the normal and abnormal reactions the receiver may experience depending on his/her own unique situational definition. The following statement summarizes the aforementioned idea and has been referred to as the "Thomas Theorem" (Coser; 1977). "If men [people] define situations as real, they are real in their consequences" (Thomas, 1928). While excusing the obvious masculine pronoun, and noting the emphasis on *people* added, one should readily see how this statement, and the related ideas of situational definitions, applies to crisis theory and intervention. In a word, if a crisis is defined as real in terms of the social meaning, it (the crisis) will be real in its consequences. Once the precipitating/hazardous event is defined as stressful and unpleasant, the person will experience the feelings and thoughts associated with that event (i.e., personal crisis).

There are several elements to the definitional process as this theory relates to crisis intervention and death notification. First, the hazardous event must be interpreted as a crisis before the event becomes a "crisis." The interpretation of the event involves a definitional process that the person experiences from unique life events. Therefore, a crisis cannot manifest itself until the hazardous event (sometimes referred to as the precipitator or precipitating event) has taken place and the definition of the situation has been made. For our present purposes, we may apply this notion to the death notification. For example, the death of a close friend or loved one, ". . . may not be a crisis event until (1) the death notification has been made, and (2) the information has been situationally defined" (Byers, 1987, p. 106).

Once the hazardous event has taken place, and the definition of the situation made, the significance of the event is internalized. This is referred to as the "internalization of the definition of the situation" (Byers, 1987). In this aspect of the process, the person makes the new definition part of the social self. Through this internalization, the definition of the event becomes an immediate and significant part of one's cognitive and behavioral repertoire. As for our present discussion of death notification, the receiver of the death notice internalizes the new definition of the situation of loss when they realize the loss is part of the experience. Further, the person may experience the secondary loss characteristics beyond the initial shock (i.e., pining, denial, bargaining, reminiscence, etc.). At this point also, the person will likely review the personal and social nature, and the consequences of the loss (Byers, 1987).

The crisis event delivered through the death notification elicits a definition of the situation involving the hazardous event, the interpretation, and the internalization process. Through this definitional process, the crisis experience and the corresponding behavioral, social, and psychological consequences emerge. As an assessment tool, the definition of the situation is quite useful. Some even suggest its utility in "redefining" a crisis situation (Straus, 1984; Byers, 1987), or finding a ". . . different definition of the problem" (Morrice, 1976, p. 22) during the final adjustment/adaptation phase of the crisis intervention process. More is offered below concerning these ideas and their application. Suffice it to say at this point, however, that the definition of the situation is a very important interactional element for the receiver *and* the notifier within the context of death notification. Understanding this dynamic will enable the deliverer to provide the necessary level of situational support and empathy and better understand one's own definitions as well.

DEATH NOTIFICATION LITERATURE

Several authors present information on the multifaceted nature of death notification, including its situational nature (Byers, 1996; Hendricks, 1984; Leash, 1994). How people define situations, including that of the death notification is essential to understanding this complex dynamic. The following brief literature review offers an overview of works specifically conducted in the area of death notification. Discussion is given, where appropriate, on how these works relate to the previously mentioned ideas of crisis intervention and the definition of the situation.

One author in this tradition suggests that much more formal education needs to occur in order to provide notifiers with the necessary tools for an effective notification (Hall, 1982). Some authors offer basic recommendations for this procedure (Looney and Winsor, 1982; Wentick, 1991; Sly, 1992), while others provide death notification process coupled with crisis intervention helping strategies (Hendricks, 1984; Byers, 1991). Taking different approaches, others offer analytic presentations of notification strategies employed in various ways (Brewin, 1991) and by various professionals (Charmaz, 1975; McClenahen and Lofland, 1976; Clark and LaBeff, 1982).

Charmaz (1975), one of the first to research death notification, qualitatively analyzes notification strategies through observations within three coroner jurisdictions. Others also employ the qualitative observational methodology for analyzing death notification procedures (Clark and LaBeff, 1982) and the bearing of other forms of bad news by Deputy U.S. Marshals (McClenahen and Lofland, 1976). In one way or another, all of these authors discuss how situations are defined by receivers (Hall, 1982; Looney and Winsor, 1982; Hendricks, 1984) or are defined and "created" by notifiers (Charmaz, 1975; McClenahen and Lofland, 1976; Clark and LaBeff, 1982).

Hall (1982) sets forth a plea for relevant education for death notifiers. She maintains that expert training not only improves the professionalism of police, but it also works positively in the area of police-community relations. This is also suggested by Clark (1981) and Stillman (1987). In fact, Clark maintains that criminal justice personnel have the potential to become effective "psychological paraprofessionals" in crisis situations involving death. This, of course, requires sensitivity on the part of the helper. The police, according to Hall, must sometimes shed the "law enforcer" and "crime preventer roles" for one that is more conducive to the death notification process. A role, or police personality, which fits Hall's discussion, is that of the "social agent" in which the primary focus is on mending the social fabric of a community or solving problems. This approach not only assists the notifier, but it assists the receiver of bad news as well. One very interesting point made by Clark (1981) is the social nature of the death event and attempts at externalization. Due to fear and anxiety concerning mortality, some notifiers create for themselves a definition of the situation that distances themselves from the death scene. This is accomplished by referring to the objective nature of the situation in technical, rather than personal, terms (i.e., making reference to the body as an "investigation" rather than a "person"). Taking a social agent position, without discounting the important criminal justice aspects of the death scene, better enables the notifier to attend to the person needing social support.

Other authors offer practical recommendations (Looney and Winsor, 1982) and crisis intervention strategy (Hendricks, 1984; Hendricks and Byers, 1992). The former offers the reader rather basic suggestions to keep in mind before, during, and after the death notification with little attention given to the process of delivery. The chapter appendix offers a summary of suggestions derived from this source and others. Hendricks (1984) offers a much more detailed approach. His work provides a discussion of survivor reactions, grief and crisis reactions, notifier reactions, and crisis intervention steps (i.e., information gathering, control/direction, assessment and referral) focusing on death notification delivery. Hendricks (1984) maintains that the key to a successful death notification is a combination of ". . . theoretical knowledge, interpersonal skills, and well-developed procedures . . ." (p. 113). This chapter accomplishes this also by utilizing aspects of this procedure, as well as those presented later (Hendricks, 1985; Byers and Hendricks, 1986; Byers, 1987; Hendricks and McKean, 1995), in an attempt to apply crisis intervention strategy to situationally defined death notifications.

While the aforementioned authors focus on the helping role of the notifier in defined situations of death notification, some research addresses the manner in which notifiers and receivers define situations uniquely. Charmaz (1975), for instance, examines the "strategies" coroners employ in the death announcement process in an attempt to shed light on interactional issues, which are coupled with routine bureaucratic activities. She examines three coroner jurisdictions; two encompassing somewhat large metropolitan areas, while the third primarily being rural in nature. In the final analysis, various ideologies and organizational practices seem to be reflected in the different strategies used. Although there are quite divergent views concerning death, the role of the coroner, and views of the receiver, certain "self-protection strategies" are sometimes employed. One method, as mentioned earlier from the works of Clark (1981) and Hall (1982), is to "externalize" the death event. The coroner (or notifier), by distancing and referring to the deceased with inanimate terminology, creates a definition of the situation which prevents the death event from penetrating the notifier's subjective reality (Charmaz, 1975). On a more practical level, key strategic steps often include making sure the correct person is being notified, creating a perception that the coroner's identity is real and legitimate (sometimes referred to as "impression management"), and involving the receiver in the notification process with a desired end of helping the person realize what has happened. All of these strategies fall under the rubric of managing one's impression and the definition of the situation (Charmaz, 1975).

McClenahen and Lofland (1976) offer another situational analysis of the management of bad news. Rather than examining the role of the coroner, however, they analyze tactics of Deputy U.S. Marshals. Marshals deal with crisis situations and the delivery of bad news in the form of arrests and warrants. Concerns of the Marshal in delivering bad news include that the receiver not hold the messenger responsible for the news, that the receiver may not remain calm, and the deputies may have some difficulty in controlling emotions (McClenahen and Lofland, 1976). There are, according to the authors, three main stages of managing bad news: preparing, delivering, and shoring. Preparing involves "distancing" and "presaging." The distancing tactic is closely aligned with that of Charmaz (1975) in terms of "self-protection." Presaging is also related to a Charmaz technique in which the coroner may hope that the receiver ascertains what the bad news is, before it is even delivered, through social interaction and nonverbal cues. Just giving out the information within the delivery context "bit by bit," or presaging, often leads to this same end.

During the delivery phase, the deputy attempts to create a definition of the situation, which promotes the routine nature, or "image" of bad news delivery (McClenahen and Lofland, 1976). It is assumed that the shock of bad news will lose its sharp edge when the notifier treats the information as routine. This particular point, however, is likely to be more applicable in practice for the person delivering news involving warrants and court dates rather than death. A notifier openly treating a death notification, as routine will likely be viewed as cold and callous. However, as Charmaz (1975) notes, this does not diminish the possibility that such instances will be treated as routine. The difference lies in the overt gesture or lack thereof, which could signal to a receiver that the notifier is engaged in a routine occupational act. The final phase, called "shoring," focuses on the need to control the recipient's behavior. The two main strategies for this are "manipulating the news" and "mitigating emotions in interaction" (McClenahen and Lofland, 1976).

Another analytic work in the area of death notification is by Clark and LaBeff (1982). Like the works of Charmaz (1975) and McClenahen and Lofland (1976), this work analyzes the situational nature of the death notification. These researchers use a qualitative research methodology (in-depth unstructured interviews) and examine the strategies of physicians, nurses, law enforcement personnel, and clergy members (n=40). One of the more important situational qualities for the notifier is to have "control" of the situation. This could mean making the notification in a place of privacy. It is noteworthy that a preference was not stated by the respondents for telephone notifications due to the lack of situational control. The setting seems to be very important, because this allows the notifier to stage the situation effectively and reduce the potential trauma the receiver experiences; some preferred areas for notifications include hospital chapels and quiet offices. Interestingly, such settings are often recommended for notifications (Wentick, 1991; Sly, 1992). The setting is very important to the notifier.

Clark and LaBeff (1982) mention, moreover, that the death notifier with the least setting and situational latitude in the delivery of death news is the police officer. The law enforcement officer does not usually have the luxury of conducting the notification under well-staged circumstances. It often occurs in the home, and there is little preparation time available. It is suggested that this reality reflects the law enforcement officers preferred strategy for delivery; that is, the *direct approach* (Clark and LaBeff, 1982). This method involves simply stating that the survivor has experienced a loss. This approach has the potential, however, of creating an image of the notifier as cold and uncaring. In fact, some of the officers interviewed reported feeling heartless or cold when using this strategy. However, this is contrasted with the finding that none of the notifiers wanted to be completely objective concerning the death. Most felt it was important to show some emotion in the interaction as long as the notifier did not lose control of the situation. As the research suggests, the direct approach without sensitivity or emotion has definite limitations, and we do not recommend it here.

Other approaches include elaborate delivery, nonverbal delivery, and conditional delivery. There are useful characteristics in each of these approaches, and elements from each may be utilized effectively. When conducted with sensitivity, using aspects of elaborate delivery may be very effective, because it capitalizes on concrete information and a logical reconstruction of events (there is little need to be morbidly specific, however), but some suggest that using terms such as "dead" and "killed" may be appropriate given these imply seriousness and finality (Wentick, 1991). Aspects of nonverbal delivery may also be useful because of the vital information to be gained from interpersonal cues one may observe through body language and facial expression. This is also the strength of the conditional delivery. Clark and LaBeff (1982) maintain the lack of well-defined death notification methods leads the notifier to construct strategies influenced by ". . . situational and structural factors . . ." of the encounter (p. 379). In other words, notifiers create strategies based on their definitions of these situations and their expectations. In this way, the notifier conducts the death telling based on a definition of the situation and how that definition may fit one of the Clark and LaBeff approaches. While strategies constructed out of the situation can be useful, and sometimes unavoidable, it is much more effective to have flexible strategies available to the notifier before the notification.

In summary, the death notification literature described above illustrates the various approaches others have taken to this topic in terms of intervention strategies, and the analytic discussion of various practice methods. Clark's (1981) suggestion for death education as applied to law enforcement and Hall's (1982) plea for relevant death notification education are well taken. Hendricks (1984) followed with an effective and comprehensive response to this need. This work, and others (Charmaz, 1975; McClenahen and Lofland, 1976; Clark and LaBeff, 1982), provides us with most useful insight into the realities of mortality and the situational nature of death notification and crisis intervention. The prior research illustrates the need for additional attention with the objective of providing the practitioner with flexible delivery strategies designed to best assist the receiver of unpleasant news. Attention will now turn to various crisis intervention models and strategies.

THEORY INTO PRACTICE: INTERVENTION MODELS

Crisis and Traumatic Stress

The characteristic notification conducted by criminal justice personnel normally involves a sudden or unexpected death; such events can complicate the notification process (Stewart, 1999). For this reason, the death notification, and the crisis it often produces, presents a challenging situation for the intervener. Crises come in a variety of forms. The unexpected death of a loved one will be a different crisis situation in contrast to those in which death might be anticipated (e.g., death from a terminal illness), or even one which may be part of a developmental life phase (e.g., leaving home, getting married, etc.) (Morrice, 1976; Baldwin, 1979). Dealing with an unexpected death will present a unique set of crisis characteristics and situational definitions. Morrice (1976) provides a useful dichotomy for understanding different crisis forms. Crises which are termed "accidental" refer to those . . . hazards of life which are less expected" (p. 21). Conversely, the term "developmental" crisis is used to describe temporary upsets in one's social and psychological life, which are expected, yet difficult and painful. Transitional life events fit in this category such as retirement, getting married, graduating from school, and career changes. However, our focus remains on the former, which characterizes sudden, unexpected traumatic stress.

Baldwin (1979) suggests a unique helping approach to accompany the unique crisis produced through sudden traumatic stress. The basic strategy is to "provide or mobilize support" between the crisis onset through to the time that the person can develop independent coping behaviors. Assistance is given so that the person can emotionally acknowledge the new, and often previously unexperienced, situation. Open catharsis of negative feelings should be encouraged and guidance should be provided to assist the individual in adjusting to the crisis producing changes one will experience. This form of crisis (accidental or due to sudden traumatic stress) may involve a longer period of emotional instability than some other crisis forms.

Stage/Phase Models

Most crisis intervention modeling is of the stage, or phase, type. It is important to note that the "stages of crisis" that some theorists describe (Jacobson et al., 1968; Jones and Polak, 1968; Aguilera et al., 1970; McGee, 1974; Rosenbaum and Beebe, 1975; Morrice, 1976; Smith, 1978; Baldwin, 1980) are different than the "stages of intervention" (often referred to as the "crisis intervention process"). The stages of crisis denote the phases through which a person may pass during a crisis experience. These are individually centered, and situationally based. In contrast, the stages of intervention are intervener/client interactions and involve specific strategies developed by crisis interveners to address crisis situations. Crisis stages and intervention stages may run concurrently; however, these are mutually exclusive concepts. One might summarize here by saying that *crisis stages* are normal phases people pass through based on the definition of the crisis experience; whereas, *crisis intervention stages* are phases through which the intervener guides the person in crisis on the way to crisis management and resolution.

Crisis intervention stages emphasize the organized approach of taking the individual through various steps of crisis intervention designed to assist the client in reaching a more effective state of emotional coping. One of the primary strengths of such an approach is the organized nature to the intervention. It provides the intervener with an effective point of reference based on individual behavior and situational circumstances. In other words, it can provide the intervener with a "map" to follow in providing intervention. A serious limitation may exist when the intervention strategy is followed too rigidly when the actual intervention requires flexibility. In such instances, flexibility is necessary and useful. At any rate, one should merely remain cognizant of the distinct possibility that interventions may not always fit into discrete crisis intervention stages. The stage/phase approach is very useful and is advocated here; however, one must always remain flexible and be willing to change, during the process, depending on the unique situation encountered.

Lindemann (1944), one of the earliest crisis theorists, does not opt for a strict intervention strategy. Instead, he advocates a more flexible approach that utilizes support, open catharsis, and relationship review. This type of approach does have a degree of utility depending on the crisis situation. At any rate, these characteristics and practices are effective for any intervener to possess regardless of the approach. Since Lindemann's early work, however, the dominant approach has been the phase/stage method. Therefore, it will be the phase/stage intervention paradigm from which we will operate when describing the death notification process. Specifically, the works of Hendricks (1984, 1985), Byers and Hendricks (1986), and Byers (1987) are utilized most frequently with additional criminal justice applications.

CRIMINAL JUSTICE AND DEATH NOTIFICATION

There are many opportunities to practice crisis intervention within the criminal justice system. An individual who is well-versed in crisis theory and intervention steps is a valuable asset to any department or agency. The benefits the public might reap from such an individual are immeasurable. Effective and efficient crisis intervention is a valuable tool that has the dual benefit to the public and the justice system. In addition to the death notifier role, the knowledgeable crisis intervener will be useful in coroner's offices, corrections, jail and detention work, policing, police-community relations, probation and parole, and dual law enforcement-social welfare functions (such as child and adult protective services). All of these criminal justice roles require some type of crisis intervention. In addition, the death notification may become a new role for the criminal justice practitioner.

CRIMINAL JUSTICE ASPECTS

The Death Notification Task

The task of death notification is one naturally defined by many as undesirable (Scott, 1999). It involves delivering bad news to someone with the potential of causing a serious incapacitating crisis. The receiver of the death notice may experience normal reactions to the news such as shock and disbelief, coupled with feelings of helplessness and despair. Confusion and disorientation may also be present once the receiver has incorporated the information into the definition of the situation. The notifier can experience a wide range of emotions as well including, but not limited to, anxiety and fear. Research by Stewart, Lord, and Mercer (2000) suggests that notifier distress is most prevalent when the notification involves deaths by violent crime, drunk driving, suicide, and also the death of children.

The risk always exists that the receiver of the notification may hold the notifier partially responsible for the incident and react negatively (anger, acting out, etc.). This may occur because the deliverer is the person bearing the bad news and is a convenient outlet for hostility elicited by traumatic stress. In law enforcement, especially, this possibility may only exacerbate an already difficult task of public service. The notifier must always be attuned to such possibilities. Notifiers report that dealing with attempts to harm the self or others, physical acting out, and a survivor's feelings of intense anxiety are the most difficult to manage (Stewart, Lord, and Mercer, 2000). If this unfortunate situation were to arise, the deliverer should avoid perpetuating the hostility. It is quite normal to feel personally hurt and offended if blamed for something that is outside one's domain of control. The key, however, is to avoid incorporating negative or hostile reactions into one's own definition of the situation and realize that the survivor is reacting to the events.

The realization that such behavior is sometimes a normal part of the receiver's reaction in a situation of traumatic stress should enable the notifier to accept this without considering it a personal verbal attack. Each individual responds to this form of trauma uniquely; one must accept whatever definition of the situation the receiver produces and respond appropriately. The most important consideration for the death notifier in this situation, and in all others, is to not perpetuate an already negative situation. If the notifier remains calm and professional, yet caring and empathic, the death notification will proceed much smoother. Presenting a strong nonjudgmental role model to the receiver is an important death notifier objective.

Delegation of Responsibility

Each agency responsible for notifications is able to better serve the public by having a designated person or team trained in crisis intervention and death notification ready to respond. The importance of crisis intervention, law enforcement, and criminal justice is well-documented (Cesnick, Pierce and Puls, 1977; Hendricks, 1984, 1985; Romano, 1990; Sly, 1992; Hendricks and McKean, 1995).

Often, the delegation of responsibility for such a task falls with superiors or to the person handling a particular case. Within the police role, it may fall on a homicide or a violent/special crimes officer or detective. This may be the case for larger departments and jurisdictions. In smaller departments, various criminal justice personnel may share the responsibility. It is also often the case in such instances that a coroner or medical examiner will deliver the death notification (Hendricks and Byers, 1983; Hendricks, 1984; Byers, 1992; Hendricks and Byers, 1992). In short, responsibility varies considerably from jurisdiction to jurisdiction (Stillman, 1987; Wentick, 1991; Sly, 1992).

In some areas, the coroner occupies a comprehensive death investigation role. In these instances the coroner is involved in every aspect of a death investigation including the notification and follow-up. In other areas, the police or other criminal justice-related personnel in cooperation may carry out the notification with the coroner or medical examiner. There are also jurisdictions in which the coroner or medical examiner has little involvement in criminal justice aspects of death other than to render a formal ruling or verdict. In these instances, the death notification almost always falls on other criminal justice staff, clergy, a counselor, or a social worker.

Notifying a Police Survivor

Regardless of the delegation of responsibility, one of the more difficult notifications for a law enforcement officer to make may be to a police survivor. Research attention has been given to the impact of sudden, traumatic death on widows (Constantino, 1981) and the impact of death notifications on police widows in particular (Pastorella, 1991). As Wentick (1991) points out, "A death notification is compounded when it's a police officer that has been killed. This is because the person making the notification, often another officer knows the family. It's much more emotional and difficult to do in cases like that . . ." (p. 375). Police survivors are those individuals, often a widow, who has lost a loved one in the line of duty. Although death is a daily reality for all police, the death of a police officer is a painful experience for the survivors and criminal justice personnel. The delivery of the death notification may be particularly difficult and traumatic for the receiver and notifier alike, if it involves a fellow officer.

Such instances are not only personally painful for the spouse, family and colleagues, but these situations also force police officers to deal with the realities of police work and their own mortality. Perhaps no one is better suited to notify a police survivor than a fellow officer. However, this is contingent upon the ability to not only empathize with the survivor but also to be "in touch" with one's own feelings involving mortality and loss. Feelings of loss and pain are normal. Even if one is a law enforcement officer, such recognition of normal feelings is acceptable. The death notifier, who is a police officer, giving a notice to a police survivor may be better able to serve the survivor, and oneself, with the aforementioned recommendations.

Social support is extremely important for all survivors. In addition to the most valuable support from friends and relatives, there are organized groups designed to provide social support and self-help for specific problems. There are various bereavement support groups available operated by social service and counseling agencies. In addition, police survivors may be referred to a local chapter of Concerns for Police Survivors (COPS) which may be able to provide assistance and support. The notifier may make such a referral. The social support function of crisis intervention and death notification is very important both during the intervention and after. This is also demonstrated in the following section dealing with notification procedures.

A study by Concerns of Police Survivors (COPS) published by the National Institute of Justice (Stillman, 1987) outlines several important points pertaining to line-of-duty deaths, notifications and survivor reactions. First, the study outlines that a survivor's level of stress and emotional distress in response to a line-of-duty death will be influenced by at least three factors. These are:

- The way survivors are notified of the death;
- The emotional support provided by the department;
- The information the department gives concerning insurance and benefits. (Stillman, 1987; p. 2)

Also found in the study, based on interviews with 126 survivors, were common police survivor reactions to the loss. These include:

- Having difficulty concentrating and making decisions, feeling confused, having one's mind go blank;
- Feeling hostile;
- Feeling different from others, feeling alone, being uncomfortable in social situations;

- Fearing people, places, and things, and being anxious of one's ability to survive;
- Re-experiencing the traumatic incident through flashbacks, dreams, or thoughts;
- Feeling emotionally numb, having less interest in previously enjoyed activities, or being unable to return to prior employment;
- Having less ability to express positive and negative emotions;
- Having difficulty falling asleep or remaining asleep;
- Feeling guilty about the way one acted toward the deceased or as if one could have prevented the death. (Stillman, 1987; pp. 2–3)

These reactions, as demonstrated earlier (Lindemann, 1944; Hendricks & Byers, 1983; Hendricks, 1984) are normal acute grief reactions found among survivors.

From these findings and other related assessments of police policy concerning line-of-duty deaths, Stillman (1987) outlines several recommendations for police departments that may assist and facilitate the bereavement healing process among police survivors. Undoubtedly, however, these same recommendations would assist other survivors as well. In particular, Stillman (1987) recommends . . . clear-cut policies concerning notification procedures, psychological services, emotional support, and benefits and compensation for survivors . . ." (pp. 4–5) in order to better serve the family survivors and officers of sudden, traumatic death. We now turn to one key recommendation, notification procedure.

DEATH NOTIFICATION PROCEDURE

The death notifier is placed in a very unique crisis situation. Unlike many other crisis situations where the notifier enters the situation to render assistance after the onset of traumatic stress, the death notifier presents the information, or news, which serves as the precipitating event for the crisis situation. Immediately, then, the notifier is expected to offer guidance, support, empathy, understanding, and control/direction to the situation. In the death notification situation, therefore, one will need to utilize effective death notification-crisis intervention procedures while the person is simultaneously traversing the normal stages of crisis and grief. This duality of the death notification presents the notifier with a challenging situation in which to offer assistance and support. Above all, the notifier needs to provide *the necessary and appropriate response* to the crisis situation. This will involve a demonstrated level of support and empathy given to the receiver, while utilizing effective notification procedures, and exercising flexibility within the interaction depending on the unique nature of the emergent definition of the situation.

Death Notification Process

The death notification process has been presented (Hendricks and Byers, 1983; Hendricks, 1984; Byers, 1991; Hendricks and Byers, 1992) as an effective means by which to deliver a notification. Particular attention is given here to the utility of this approach, as well as other similar efforts using the same and related intervention strategies or steps (Hendricks, 1985; Byers and Hendricks, 1986; Byers, 1987). The primary steps include Information Gathering, Control/Direction, Progress Assessment, and Referral. These are discussed in detail below with particular attention given to the necessary and appropriate response, the definition of the situation, and practical considerations. Before describing the specific stages, however, the issue of crisis assessment is addressed.

Crisis Assessment

As previous crisis intervention authors note, crisis assessment is not necessarily a discrete stage in the crisis intervention process (Smith, 1978; Byers and Hendricks, 1986; Byers, 1987; Hendricks and McKean, 1995). Rather, it tends to be an activity that takes place before, and during, the crisis intervention process. One of the primary concerns of crisis assessment is to "get a handle" on the crisis at hand (Byers, 1987). Naturally, the crisis victim's definition of the situation is very important. In a word, crisis assessment involves taking a complete look at the crisis situation, as objectively and as holistically as possible, with an emphasis on looking at the total situation. This often involves determining the nature of the problem, ascertaining the extent of assistance the crisis victim needs, and defining with the client the objective and subjective nature of the problem. Further, one needs to assess the strengths and weaknesses of the receiver, potential dangers such as self- or other-destructive behaviors, and to visualize potential intervention outcomes. Realizing the totality in the crisis assessment may only be reached through an intentional effort to recognize the sum of the parts of a crisis situation and the receiver's emergent needs. Without an all-encompassing viewpoint in crisis assessment, one may overlook essential information and subjective meaning pertinent to crisis intervention and client crisis resolution.

Step One–Information Gathering

This intervention step has been well established and documented (Rosenbaum and Beebe, 1975; Hendricks, 1984, 1985; Byers and Hendricks, 1986; Byers, 1987). Information gathering involves the primary activity of collecting as much vital and useful information concerning the crisis situation as possible. Since the death notification is a unique crisis situation–one that does not involve "responding" to a crisis situation in the same manner as one would respond to a domestic violence or suicide call–the intervener has the unusual luxury of taking time to prepare before delivering the notice. Rarely does the crisis intervener have time to "prepare" for a crisis situation; therefore, the notifier should use this opportunity to its fullest.

To begin the information gathering stage, Hendricks (1984) notes that one must collect accurate information in this stage of the death notification process. This includes, but is not limited to, the name of the deceased, the names of family and involved parties, the circumstances of the death, the survivor's address, and anything else pertinent to the situation. The accuracy of information is vital for the effective notification. The survivor will likely experience traumatic stress when first informed. If inaccurate information is conveyed, this may only add to the situational trauma. If a notifier acts in good faith during the information gathering stage by collecting as accurate and up-to-date information as possible, this will influence the encounter greatly. Accurate information could mean the difference between an effective notification in which the survivor is assisted well or one in which the survivor is further traumatized and possesses lingering resentment toward the notifier and an agency. To avoid this, one should use the following rule of thumb for crisis intervention information gathering. The following questions from Hendricks (1985) should serve the notifier well, "What has happened? Where did it happen? How did it happen? To whom did it happen?" These will enable the intervener in gathering the minimum of information needed; although, one need not stop with the answers to these questions for information gathering. Moreover, the notifier should continue to ask such questions (e.g., who, what, when, where, how) on a continual basis in order to fully ascertain the circumstances surrounding the death.

The information gathering stage can serve as an ongoing process within the death notification procedure (Hendricks, 1984) and crisis intervention process (Hendricks, 1985; Byers, 1987) by coupling it with crisis assessment. When the initial contact is made with the survivor, the notifier will need to use interactional skills to interpret verbal and nonverbal behavioral cues. Through attentiveness to the important verbal and nonverbal symbols given to the notifier, one is able to form a definition of the situation from the receiver's behavior and verbal statements. The importance of considering this step as an ongoing activity within the notification encounter cannot be overemphasized. It is through a continual awareness of the survivor's experience, demonstrated through overt behavior, that the notifier can use information gathered to assess the situation and assist the survivor.

Although much of the information gathering takes place before the notifier actually meets the survivor face-to-face, and the gathering stage is an ongoing part of the process, normally the first opportunity to utilize the ongoing nature of information gathering is at the survivor's home. Notifications are best conducted at the home in familiar surroundings; however, this is not always possible in the event that the survivor is at a hospital or at a friend's place of residence. Every effort should be made to conduct the notification in the home without delaying the delivery. One of the most important environmental factors in the death notification is that the survivor be in a place of comfort. Notifications in public places or on the street are not recommended. Following this recommendation is not only in the best interests of the survivor, but also the notifier. The place of residence allows the survivor to be at ease without the concern of putting on a "front" of strength and control. Therefore, an important step to information gathering is finding out where the survivor is located. It is recommended that the notifier first go to the survivor's home; if the person is not there, steps need to be taken to locate that person. However, the notification is best done in person at the home, not by telephone, or at some other private location.

Upon reaching the residence, the notifier should verify the address especially if there is any doubt concerning accuracy. Verification is a good general practice of information gathering in all situations. When meeting the person, who answers the door, it is again important to verify the address and the appropriate party (e.g., "Are you Mr. Smith, and is this 3334 Jackson St.?). This is often the first instance of using information gathering as a continual activity. In addition, the mere presence of a stranger (often the notifier and survivor do not know one another), or a person in uniform (in the case of a uniformed officer), might alarm the receiver of something amiss. This is another instance where assessment-oriented information gathering is useful (i.e., interpreting the nonverbal and verbal cues). Sometimes it is useful, if the notifier is a police officer, to put the person at ease by indicating that the visit does not involve a criminal matter in which the survivor or the house occupants are being sought for questioning or apprehension. In the case of a criminal homicide, however, the notification does involve a criminal element. If the survivor is considered a suspect, one's role may change from a crisis intervener to a criminal investigator. Regardless of the circumstances surrounding the death, however, the notification must still be delivered. In most notifications, however, it will not be the case where the receiver is considered a murder suspect.

The most important objectives of information gathering are: obtaining full, accurate and complete information; finding the survivor(s); verifying the parties; interpreting initial cues; and assessing the preliminary definition of the situation. Attention now turns to the second step: Control and Direction.

Step Two—Control and Direction

The initial task in the control step is to gain accepted entrance to the home (Hendricks, 1984; Hendricks and Byers, 1992). A death notification on the doorstep is inappropriate since the survivor may shut the notifier out of the home easily when additional crisis intervention and support is needed. If the death has occurred in the home, it is useful to avoid the area where the body is located. The body will likely provide a diversion to the survivor and notifier and detract from the intervention assistance given. If the survivor would like to leave the scene and go elsewhere for a while, this request should be honored providing there is an appropriate escort.

An important aspect to control is providing a strong role model to the survivor. Confidence exhibited from the notifier will provide the receiver with much needed support during a confusing, traumatic and emotionally disorganized time. The term "control" is not meant to imply that the notifier "take charge" of the situation in an oppressive sense. Rather, it refers to the confident demeanor of the notifier and the creation of an appropriate encounter within which to deliver the notification.

It is also within this step that the "crisis is addressed" (Byers, 1987; p. 112). In other words, it is during this stage that the survivor is told of the death. This is the most likely point in which the notifier will witness traumatic stress in the receiver. This opening phase of the crisis experience has been aptly referred to as "impact" (Morrice, 1976). At the point that a person receives the news of an unexpected death, that individual will likely experience a sense of bewilderment and confusion. The person may become psychologically disorganized and routine day-to-day living may no longer be mastered confidently. In a word, the person becomes psychologically and socially incapacitated. Of course, the nature and extent of this reaction will vary from person to person based on the nature of their situational definition.

Hendricks (1985) notes that control involves ". . . the initial face-to-face contact with the victims (survivors) . . ." and that ". . . the interveners should introduce themselves and make a calm, clear, and concise statement as to why they are there" (p. 42). This is particularly vital to the death notification since the nature of the crisis is so potentially devastating and may produce additional affective disequilibrium. An essential part of the control step is framing the crisis information in a suitable fashion. From the information-gathering step, the notifier has data pertinent, and vital, to the situation at hand.

With the information the notifier has gathered, one is able to provide the survivor with information leading to the definition of the situation. In other words, the crisis information is defined and is conveyed to the receiver (Byers, 1987; p. 112). In this sense, the initial crisis definition is provided for the survivor and the person creates a situational definition from that information. The notifier is in a unique set of circumstances since there is an ability to control the initial delivery. The notifier ideally has the necessary information concerning the situation, which may be used to the survivor's benefit. Furthermore, the ability exists for the notifier to provide the best possible delivery without sacrificing information or accuracy. In a sense, the notifier provides the survivor with an "operational definition of the situation" (Straus, 1984; p. 32) with the notification. Within the death notification process, this definition is formed based on the information conveyed to the receiver and the strategies used in delivery. This enables the notifier to control the situation, to minimize survivor trauma, and to optimize situational safety. The ability to provide to the receiver the best information, in a supportive fashion, better enables the survivor along the road to emotional recovery. Therefore, the deliverer is in a unique helping role based solely on the information held and the manner in which it is delivered. However, one must always remember that this preliminary definition of the situation provided to the survivor will be interpreted and incorporated into a behavior and thought repertoire. In this way, then, the definition of the situation provided by the intervener will be altered once it becomes part of the receiver's thought processes.

With the necessary information in hand, the notifier needs to begin the actual death notification delivery. This involves offering the information slowly and in "doses" (Hendricks, 1984; Hendricks and Byers, 1992). Providing the survivor information that leads to a definition of the situation (i.e., "My husband is dead.") too quickly will likely increase the possibility of additional traumatic stress. Giving the death notification in "doses," or in small segments, allows the notifier to provide controlled information to the survivor which enables the receiver to emotionally prepare and react to the news (Hendricks and Byers, 1983; Hendricks, 1984). For example, after the survivor identity has been established, one could say, "I need to speak with you concerning your son, John." The dialogue could continue with, "John has been in an accident." At this point, the survivor's definition of the situation may prompt the question, "Is he dead?" If this question is asked directly, answer it professionally and calmly. One might say, "Yes, John has died. I am very sorry." If the direct question has not been asked, the survivor will be waiting for more information to incorporate into the definition of the situation. The notifier might continue, in the absence of a direct question with, "Your son John was in a very serious accident. I am sorry, but he is dead." Some may feel that using euphemisms is appropriate in the death notification (e.g., "passed on," "no longer with us," "gone to a better place"). However, there is no way to tell how the survivor might respond to such statements. It is better to avoid these and use some form of the noun "death" in order to avoid confusion or misinterpretation. In addition, one will want to avoid a callous and cold delivery (e.g., "Your wife is dead"). Merely giving the notification bluntly does not allow the survivor to incorporate the information in a unique way, thereby enabling the formation of the definition of the situation. The individual's coping mechanisms will be contained within the definition. Most people have already developed coping mechanisms to respond to situations of traumatic stress. The receiver should be allowed to use these. Quick, hurried, or blunt notifications do not allow the survivor to fully operationalize unique coping mechanisms involved in the definition of the situation.

Sometimes, the survivor's definition of the situation includes self-blame for the death. This may involve any interpretation that the survivor could have, in some way, prevented the death. The self-blame need not be "rational" in order to be quite real to the survivor, or receiver of the death notification. As long as the self-blame for the death has been made part of the overall definition, this makes it a reality for the survivor and an issue for the notifier (recall the definition of the situation and the Thomas Theorem above). Therefore, if some aspect of the definition of the situation is defined as real, in this case self-blame for the death, it will be real (in its consequences) for the survivor. Reasoning with the survivor while experiencing impact, and the trauma immediately to follow, will not likely prove fruitful for the receiver. During periods of disorganization brought on by traumatic stress, the survivor may need to engage in some irrational behavior or thought as a defense to the situation. One should avoid telling the survivor that this conduct and cognition is wrong or inappropriate. However, if the affect and cognition evolves into self- or other-destructive behaviors, something should be done. Depending on one's crisis intervention and/or counseling ability, the extent of the situation, and the potential danger to the survivor or others, one may attempt to provide a redefinition of the situation (Straus, 1979, 1984; Byers, 1987). Steps may be taken to assist the person in redefining the situation into one that is less emotionally damaging and more emotionally productive. As for the presence of self-blame, the notifier may examine the situation and assess the presence of any reasonable, or rational, basis for the blame by talking empathically with the survivor. If there is none, the notifier may provide a coherent and logical argument to the survivor that identifies the mislabeling of blame. This can be quite effective; however, one's own limitations as a crisis intervener, and those of the survivor, must be recognized before attempting such steps.

Direction affords the notifier the opportunity to demonstrate strength and stability (Hendricks, 1984, 1985; Byers and Hendricks, 1986). In being a positive role model by demonstrating these qualities, the survivor in crisis may draw on notifier strength (Byers, 1987). One may combine the control and direction stages, or delineate them, depending on the situation and the receiver's needs. Direction may involve the ability to assist the survivor in areas of immediate decision making. One may find that the receiver wishes to physically flee the situation as if to symbolically leave the reality of a loved one's death. One may provide direction to the survivor by exploring this emergent need and the issues of practicality and safety. The notifier needs to be continually aware of the need to provide direction in order to protect the survivor.

As with control, direction may sometimes involve an attempt to assist the survivor in redefining situations (Byers, 1987). The possible situation of self-blame was mentioned above as a potential characteristic of the death notification encounter. Direction may afford the notifier the opportunity to address such reactions, and others, depending on the potential for additional emotional trauma or self-destructive behavior. If such cognitions indicate a problem, through the activity of ongoing information gathering and assessment, one may wish to provide to the survivor alternatives to self-limiting or self-destructive behavior. One must be aware, however, that such reactions are normal and may be therapeutically useful for the receiver. The key element in providing directive alternatives to the survivor in the form of a redefinition of the situation depends on, (1) the danger, or potential danger, such thoughts and feelings present to the receiver, and (2) the notifier's ability to attend to such needs effectively. In short, the decision to provide such direction will depend on the needs of the survivor and the abilities of the notifier.

Step Three–Progress Assessment

Although the notifier will continually be assessing the events occurring during the notification and gathering information in this ongoing process, "progress assessment" may also be useful (Byers and Hendricks, 1986; Byers, 1987; Hendricks and McKean, 1995). This activity need not be considered an additional step. Rather, it may be used at any point during the notification depending on when it may be needed based on notifier judgment.

Progress assessment involves the assessment of progress toward a desired end (Hendricks and Byers, 1986; Byers, 1987; Hendricks and McKean, 1995). In this instance, it would involve the evaluative assessment of the death notification process and where the process happens to be at any given moment. It will be important for the notifier to make mental notes concerning what information has been provided to the survivor and what information remains to be offered. It will also afford the notifier the opportunity to stop for a moment and simply survey the situation as objectively as possible. Perhaps it may also involve a decision to limit or extend the interventive encounter. In any case, however, it involves an examination of the receiver's present definition of the situation and an assessment of one's own abilities. Progress assessment also provides ample opportunity to determine the need of providing the survivor with additional psychiatric or psychological support.

The skills used during progress assessment involve those found in basic counseling (Benjamin, 1974). One must be alert to the fact that verbal and nonverbal communication helps in assessing the present situational definition. Since much of human communication is nonverbal, one must be aware of body posture, verbal pacing, eye contact, and facial expression. In addition, one must always demonstrate empathy, warmth, genuineness, and understanding. Positive regard demonstrated toward the survivor is the only appropriate interpersonal position to have when conducting a death notification.

Step Four–Referral

Since the death notification involves a brief encounter, and the notifier is often a crisis intervener rather than a counselor, the potential need for additional information and psychological assistance must be recognized. This does not mean, however, that the notifier need not ever see the survivor again. On the contrary, if there is information or assistance sought out by the receiver which the notifier may provide, by all means this should be provided. However, to avoid the unnecessary pain involved in seeking the notifier out at some future time, every effort should be made to answer questions the survivor may have during the notification. This may involve questions concerning how to make funeral arrangements, coroner's office procedures, police procedures, prosecutor/district attorney procedures, court procedures/grand jury, how to view the body, support groups, or victim assistance. This is not an exhaustive list, but it should provide the notifier with some indication of what to expect. One might find that the survivor needs to be referred to another agency for counseling, support, or legal assistance.

If the survivor asks a question which cannot be answered immediately, it is appropriate and a good practice to indicate that an answer will be forthcoming as soon as the information is made available. If the notifier does not know the answer to a question, every effort should be made to find the answer and report back to the survivor or make a referral to the appropriate person or agency. Since the survivor will likely be severely traumatized, this will impede normal cognitive thought processes. With this being the case, it is always useful to write answers to questions on departmental stationary or a business card (Hendricks, 1984). This is also a quite useful procedure in making referrals. This not only assures that the survivor has the most accurate information possible, and consequently helps to avoid confusion and misinterpretation, but it also serves as a memory aid, a physical reminder of the visit, and a means through which the survivor may actualize the loss.

CONCLUSION

A complete summary of this chapter will not be offered considering the extensive length and the depth of information contained herein. A few concluding remarks are offered instead. Death notification is a necessary, yet often avoided and unpleasant task in criminal justice practice. Informing someone of a loss produces traumatic stress and crisis based on the way precipitating events are situationally defined. Individuals will define such hazardous events uniquely based on the definition of the situation.

The death notifier represents a needed support system of stability, order, and structure to the survivor's recently disorganized life. Through a demonstrated level of support and empathy, the notifier may offer the survivor needed understanding and compassion. Attending to the survivor with effective listening and an understanding of the crisis victim's/survivor's definition of the situation will not only assist the receiver in crisis management, but it will also enable him/her to preserve emotional integrity.

CHAPTER QUESTIONS

1. What role does classical and contemporary crisis intervention theory and practice play in death notification?
2. How is a crisis defined and how is this information useful to the notifier?
3. What is a "definition of the situation"? How is it applicable to crisis intervention practice within the death notification?
4. What role does the definition of situation occupy in death notification theory and practice?
5. List and describe the steps in the death notification process. What are the key elements? How might these be used in practice?
6. What are some of the more appropriate qualities to possess when making a death notification? Why?

SIMULATED EXERCISES

Simulated Exercise 1

Notifier: You are a deputy coroner in a small rural county. Having been directly responsible for the death investigation involving a traffic fatality, you are asked by the coroner to deliver the death notification to the victim's father. The deceased is a 20-year-old man who has died in a violent one-car fatality. He was not driving, and alcohol was a factor in the accident. The driver, who was drinking, survived.

Receiver/Survivor. You are the middle-aged father of the deceased man. You and the victim's mother have been divorced for several years. You saw very little of your son, and when you did, the meetings would escalate into fights over his drinking. You tried to help him with an apparent problem with alcohol, but you were unsuccessful.

Simulated Exercise 2

Notifier: You are a police officer who has been called to a residence in regard to an apparent hanging. You enter the residence and the landlord of the victim directs you to the room where the victim is located. Upon entering the room you observe the male victim, approximately 25 years old, hanging in a closet. The death is an apparent suicide. You are responsible for notifying his parents.

Receiver/Survivor. You are the mother of the deceased. Your son is a respected member of the community and you and your husband are lifelong area residents. You have much pride in your family, especially your son. You have scheduled a party for him to be held the next week to celebrate his new job.

Simulated Exercise 3

Notifier: You are the police chaplain and have been recently informed of a suicide. The victim is an elderly man aged 82, a widower for five years, with limited contact with friends or family. The information you have indicates that he had been very distraught in recent weeks just before turning a gun on himself. The chief has asked you to deliver the death notification to the son.

Receiver/Survivor. You are the 50-year-old son of the deceased. You had not been in touch with your father in several weeks. You have been very busy with the new business you have just started and in preparing your daughter for college. As a result, you have not had time to see your father.

APPENDIX A

The information below provides a brief outline of activities in which to engage, and some to avoid, while conducting a death notification. This material was obtained from a packet of handouts from Wood County (Ohio) Hospice and was provided to individuals being trained to work with hospice clients and their families. Some of the recommendations have been adapted to be more applicable to death notification.

Helping the Bereaved

Recommended:
1. Let your genuine concern and caring show.
2. Be available to listen or do whatever else is needed and possible within your role.
3. Indicate your sorrow for their loss and pain.
4. Allow the survivor to express as much grief as they are feeling at the moment and are willing to share.
5. Encourage the survivors to be patient with their feelings and not to impose any "shoulds" on themselves.
6. Allow the survivor to talk about the deceased as much and as often as he/she wishes.
7. Discuss the special, endearing qualities of the deceased if the survivor wishes.
8. Give special attention to each of the family members.

Not Recommended:
1. Avoid letting your own sense of helplessness keep you from reaching out to the bereaved.
2. Do not avoid a survivor because you are uncomfortable.
3. Avoid saying that you know how they feel. Too much identification with the survivor may limit your capacity to help.
4. Do not say, "You ought to be feeling better by now," or anything else which implies a judgment about their feelings.
5. Avoid telling them what they should be feeling or doing.
6. Do not change the subject when the survivor refers to the deceased by name.
7. Do not avoid mentioning the name of the deceased out of fear of reminding them of their pain. They have not forgotten him/her.
8. Avoid pointing out that at least they have other loved ones. People are not interchangeable and cannot replace each other.

369

APPENDIX B

The following are practical considerations to keep in mind for a death notification. Some of these are included within the text of the chapter and this section serves as a quick reference to some important points.

Practical Considerations:

1. Gather as much information as possible regarding the death incident. Asking the who, what, when, where and how of a case will provide you much needed in formation.
2. Make sure positive identification of the victim has been made.
3. Try to maintain a low profile when visiting the home and remain calm.
4. Gain accepted entry into the home before delivering the death notification.
5. Often, a friend or relative to the survivor accompanying the notifier can assist in helping the notification proceed smoother and provide additional support.
6. By making an "on the spot" crisis assessment of the survivor(s), the notifier can make an immediate referral if needed.
7. Use a straightforward approach without being blunt or callous.
8. Console and comfort the survivor(s) to the best of your ability. It is normal to feel as though you have not done enough for the survivor, but your mere presence should indicate that you care.
9. It is best not to leave the recently notified individual alone. Try to contact a friend or relative through the survivor.
10. Do not deliver the news and leave right away. Be prepared to stay and demonstrate support, empathy, sincerity, openness, and understanding. Show the survivor that you have a desire to help while recognizing your own limitations, both professionally and personally.

Source: Looney and Winsor, 1982.

APPENDIX C

Additional Internet Resources

For more information concerning death notification and bereavement visit the following websites:

The Road Less Traveled, Grief and the Homicide Survivor:
    http://ohiocops.com/grief/index.html
National Center for PTSD, Causality and Death Notification:
    http://www.ncptsd.va.gov/facts/disasters/fs_death_notification.html
AVP Traumatic Grief Symposium Handbook, Death Notification:
    http://www.avpphila.org/ovcmanual/dnotif.pdf
Concerns of Police Survivors, Forms and Reference Materials:
    http://www.nationalcops.org/forms.htm
Mothers Against Drunk Driving (MADD):
    http://www.madd.org/victims/
National Organization for Victim Assistance (NOVA):
    http://www.trynova.org/
American Red Cross:
    http://www.redcross.org/

REFERENCES

Aguilera, D.C., Messick, J.M. & Farrell, M. (1970). *Crisis intervention: Theory and methodology.* Saint Louis: C.V. Mosby.

Baldwin, BA. (1979). Crisis intervention: An overview of theory and practice. *Counseling Psychologist, 8,* 43–52.

Baldwin, B.A. (1980). Styles of crisis intervention: Toward a convergent model. *Counseling Psychology, 11,* 113–120.

Benjamin, A. (1974). *The helping interview.* Boston: Houghton Mifflin.

Brewin, T.B. (1991). Three ways of giving bad news. *The Lancet, 337,* 1207–1209.

Burgess, W.A., & Baldwin, B.A. (1981). *Crisis intervention theory and practice.* Englewood Cliffs, NJ: Prentice-Hall.

Byers, B. (1996). Death notification: Theory and practice. In J.E. Hendricks and B. Byers (2nd Edition) (Eds.), *Crisis intervention in criminal justice/social service* (pp.

287–319). Springfield, IL: Charles C Thomas, Publisher, Ltd.

Byers, B. (1992, June). *A moment of crisis: Delivering unpleasant news.* Marshall County Indiana Coroner's Office Workshop.

Byers, B. (1991). Death notification. In J.E. Hendricks (Ed.), *Crisis intervention in criminal justice/social service* (pp. 179–211). Springfield, IL: Charles C Thomas, Publisher, Ltd.

Byers, B.D. (1987). Uses of clinical sociology in crisis intervention practice. *Clinical Sociology Review, 5,* 102–118.

Byers, B. & Hendricks, J.E. (1986). Suicide intervention with the elderly: Analytical and interactional aspects. *Emotional First Aid: A Journal of Crisis Intervention, 3,* 9–23.

Caplan, G. (1964). *Principles of preventive psychiatry.* New York: Basic Books.

Cesnick, C.I., Pierce, M.A. & Puls, M. (1977). Law enforcement and crisis intervention services: A critical relationship. *Suicide and Life-Threatening Behavior, 7,* 211–215.

Charmaz, K.C. (1975). The coroner's strategies for announcing death. *Urban Life, 4,* 296–316.

Clark, D.B. (1981). A death in the family: Providing consultation to the police on the psychological aspects of suicide and accidental death. *Death Education, 5,* 143–155.

Clark, R.E. & LaBeff, E.E. (1982). Death telling: Managing the delivery of bad news. *Journal of Health and Social Behavior 23,* 366–380.

Constantino, R.E. (1981). Bereavement crisis intervention for widows in grief and mourning. *Nursing Research, 30,* 6, 351–353.

Coser, L.A. (1977). *Masters of sociological thought.* New York: Harcourt Brace Jovanovich.

Ewing, C.P. (1978). *Crisis intervention as psychotherapy.* New York: Oxford University Press.

Hall, M.N. (1982). Law enforcement officers and death notification: A plea for relevant education. *Journal of Police Science and Administration, 10,* 189–193.

Hendricks, J.E. (1984). Death notification: The theory and practice of informing survivors. *Journal of Police Science and Administration, 12,* 109–116.

Hendricks, J.E. (1985). *Crisis intervention: Contemporary issues for on-site interveners.* Springfield, IL: Charles C Thomas, Publisher, Ltd.

Hendricks, J.E., & Byers, B. (1983, April). *Delivering the death notice: The coroner's role.* Paper presented at the meeting of the Indiana Commission on Forensic Sciences, Indianapolis, IN.

Hendricks, J.E., & Byers, B. (1992). When the time comes. . . . *Police, 16,* 9, 49–5 1.

Hendricks, J.E. & McKean, J.B. (1995). *Crisis intervention: Contemporary issues for on-site interveners* (2nd Edition). Springfield, IL: Charles C Thomas, Publisher, Ltd.

Jacobson, G.F., Strickler, M. & Morley, WE. (1968). Generic and individual approaches to crisis intervention. *American Journal of Public Health, 58,* 338–343.

Jones, M. & Polak, P. (1968). Crisis and confrontation. *British Journal of Psychiatry, 114,* 169–174.

Lazarus, R.S. (1966). *Psychological stress and the coping process.* New York: McGraw-Hill.

Leash, R.M. (1994). *Death notification: A practical guide to the process.* Hinesburg, VT:

Upper Access.

Lindemann, E. (1944). Symptomatology and management of acute grief. *American Journal of Psychiatry, 101,* 141–148.

Looney, H. & Winsor, I.L. (1982). Death notification: Some recommendations. *Police Chief,* March, 30–31.

McClenahen, L. & Lofland, J. (1976). Bearing bad news: Tactics of the Deputy U.S. Marshal. *Sociology of Work and Occupations, 3,* 251–272.

Morrice, J.K.W. (1976). *Crisis intervention: Studies in community care.* Oxford: Pergamon Press.

Pastorella, R. (1991). Impact of the death notification upon a police widow. In J.T. Reece, J.M. Horn, & C. Dunning (Eds.), *Critical incidents in policing* (pp. 261–268). Washington, DC: U.S. Department of Justice, Federal Bureau of Investigation. U.S. Government Printing Office.

Rapoport, L. (1962). The state of crisis: Some theoretical considerations. *Social Service Review, 36,* 211–217.

Romano, A.T. (1990). *Taking charge: Crisis intervention in criminal justice.* New York: Greenwood Press.

Rosenbaum, C.P. & Beebe, J.E. (1975). *Psychiatric treatment: Crisis, clinic, consultation.* New York: McGraw Hill.

Scott, B.J. (1999). Preferred protocol for death notification. *FBI Law Enforcement Bulletin, 68,* 8, 11–15.

Sly, R. (1992). I'm sorry to inform you . . . *Law and Order,* May, 26–28.

Smith, L.L. (1978). A review of crisis intervention theory. *Social Casework, 59,* 396–405.

Stewart, A.E. (1999). Complicated bereavement and posttraumatic stress disorder following fatal car crashes: Recommendations for death notification practice. *Death Studies, 23,* 4, 289–321.

Stewart, A.E., Lord, J.H. & Mercer, D.L. (2000). A survey of professionals' training and experiences in delivering death notifications. *Death Studies, 24,* 7, 611–631.

Stillman, F.A. (1987). Line-of-duty deaths: Survivor and departmental responses. *Research in Brief, National Institute of Justice.* Washington, DC: U.S. Government Printing Office.

Straus, R.A. (1979). Clinical sociology: An idea whose time has come . . . again. *Case Analysis, 1,* 21–43.

Straus, R.A. (1984). Changing the definition of the situation: Toward a theory of sociological intervention. *Clinical Sociology Review, 2,* 51–63.

Thomas, W.I. (1928). *The child in America.* New York: Alfred A. Knopf.

Thomas, W.I. (1923). *The unadjusted girl.* Boston: Little, Brown.

Wentick, W.R. (1991). A devastating experience: Death notification. In J.T. Reece, J.M. Horn & C. Dunning (Eds.), *Critical incidents in policing* (pp. 373–376). Washington, DC: U.S. Department of Justice, Federal Bureau of Investigation. U.S. Government Printing Office.

Wood County Hospice. (1984). Handouts for hospice volunteers. Bowling Green, OH.

NAME INDEX

SUBJECT INDEX

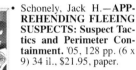
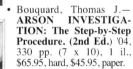
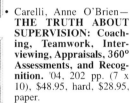
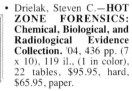